AF575609

On Earth as in Heaven

THEOPOLIS FUNDAMENTALS

On Earth as in Heaven

THEOPOLIS FUNDAMENTALS

Peter J. Leithart

On Earth as in Heaven: Theopolis Fundamentals

Lexham Press, 1313 Commercial St., Bellingham, WA 98225
LexhamPress.com

Print ISBN 9781683596134
Digital ISBN 9781683596141
Library of Congress Control Number 2022933927

Lexham Editorial: Todd Hains, Kelsey Matthews, Mandi Newell
Cover Design: Brittany Schrock
Typesetting: Danielle Thevenaz, Mandi Newell

To the winner of birth race—
Raylan Daniel Leithart

Contents

Acknowledgments

Each of the four parts of *Theopolis Fundamentals* started life as a separate short volume, published during 2019–2020. I have revised transitional sections and some other details to turn those four volumes into a single book, but the substance of this omnibus volume is the same as the earlier books. Like many people of a certain age, I repeat myself. There's overlap and repetition, but I hope not so much as to be annoying to the reader, not so much as to reveal the intensity of my dementia. Those four books remain in print, in case you're looking for something with somewhat less heft to it.

Over the course of the past two years, I've had the help of a number of colleagues and friends. My oldest son, Woelke, used a part of his enforced vacation to proofread an early draft of *The Theopolitan Vision*. Pastor Steve Jeffery, now of All Saints Presbyterian Church in Fort Worth, Texas, gave his wise input on the Vision volume, which I, foolishly, didn't always take. My Theopolis colleagues Alastair Roberts, Jeff Meyers, and John Crawford read through the manuscripts and offered many corrections and suggestions. In the later stages, John Barach and Brian and Ashton Moats copy-edited and proofed the manuscripts, cleaning up a lot of sloppy errors; Chris Kou typeset each volume; all the while, my daughter Emma kept things on schedule. As always, Jim Jordan is present in with and under every sentence of this book. I am grateful to him for decades of friendship and collaboration.

I'm grateful to the original publishers, Athanasius Press, and especially to Jarrod Richey and Zach Parker. And I'm grateful too to Todd Hains and Jesse Myers of Lexham Press for their interest in this combined volume.

On Earth as in Heaven is dedicated to my fifteenth grandchild, Raylan Daniel Leithart, who joined Jordan, Jamie, and

Ava in October 2021. With Raylan's birth, our grandsons edge into a narrow 8–7 lead over the granddaughters. It's only the top of the fourth, so I expect the girls will stage a comeback. In the meantime, Raylan occupies an honored branch of the family tree. As grateful as I am to have another grandson, I'm far more grateful that he is already a junior citizen of the future city of God. May he flourish like an oak in the courts of the Lord and stand as a pillar in his Father's house.

Prayer

IN THE NAME of the Father and of the Son and of the Holy Spirit. Amen.

YET GOD is my King from of old,
Who works salvation in the midst of the land. *Ps 74:12*

My soul faints for Your salvation;
In Your word I put my hope. *Ps 119:81*

You send Your Spirit; They are created.
And You renew the face of the ground. *Ps 104:30*

You crown the year with Your goodness,
And Your cart paths drop with fatness. *Ps 65:11*

The earth has yielded her produce;
God will bless us, our God. *Ps 67:6*

Blessed be Yahweh, God, the God of Israel,
Who alone does wonders.

And blessed be His glorious name everlastingly,
And filled with His glory be all the earth.
Amen! Yes, Amen! *Ps 72:18–19*

GLORY BE to the Father and to the Son and to the Holy Spirit,
as it was in the beginning, is now, and will be forever. Amen.

O GOD, you are the protector of all who trust in you, without whom nothing is strong and nothing is holy. Increase and multiply upon us your mercy, that, with you as our ruler and guide, we may so pass through things temporal, that in the end we do not lose the things eternal. Through Jesus Christ, your Son, our Lord, who lives and reigns with you and the Holy Spirit, one God, now and forever. Amen.

"Blessed City"

—JOHN MASON NEALE

1 Blessed city, heavenly Salem,
vision dear of peace and love,
who of living stones art builded
in the height of heaven above,
and with angel hosts encircled,
as a bride dost earthward move!

2 From celestial realms descending,
bridal glory round thee shed,
meet for him whose love espoused
thee,
to thy Lord shalt thou be led;
all thy streets and all thy bulwarks
of pure gold are fashioned.

3 Bright thy gates of pearl are
shining,
they are open evermore;
and by virtue of his merits
thither faithful souls do soar,
who for Christ's dear name in this
world
pain and tribulation bore.

4 Many a blow and biting sculpture
polished well those stones elect,
in their places now compacted
by the heavenly Architect,
who therewith hath willed for ever
that his palace should be decked.

5 To this temple, where we call thee,
come, O Lord of Hosts, to-day;
with thy wonted loving-kindness
hear thy servants as they pray,
and thy fullest benediction
shed within its walls alway.

6 Here vouchsafe to all thy servants
what they ask of thee to gain,
what they gain from thee for ever
with the blessed to retain,
and hereafter in thy glory
evermore with thee to reign.

7 Laud and honour to the Father,
laud and honour to the Son,
laud and honour to the Spirit,
ever Three, and ever One,
consubstantial, co-eternal,
while unending ages run.

To the Reader

I had a particular kind of reader in mind as I wrote the *Theopolis Fundamentals*. I'm going to assume you're that kind of reader.

My ideal reader is young, or young-ish. You're an Evangelical Christian. I'm Protestant and I mainly write to Protestants, but my ideal reader could be in any denomination. Wherever you are in the church, you're an Evangelical if you're committed to the Bible. You may be a pastor or priest or seminary student. You may be a lay leader in the church, or a member observing from a distance.

You share a desire to follow Jesus and become more like Him, your interest in the Bible, your love for the church. These loves shape everything in your life.

You love the church's tradition, but you aren't a traditionalist. You realize that the church has to address the challenges of the present, but you aren't a progressive.

But there's something else: A restless hunger for something more.

If you're a pastor or teacher, you feel you're skimming the surface of the biblical text but don't know how to dig deeper. You know it's God's word, but you wonder why it's so weird. You may find yourself avoiding some biblical books (Leviticus, parts of Judges, the early chapters of 1 Chronicles) and sticking to the clearer, safer bits, where you at least have some idea of what's going on.

If you're a layman or laywoman, you're edified by your pastor's sermons, but you suspect there's so much more to be said. You ask questions, but they don't get answered. You Google, but you're rightly cautious about what passes for theology on the Internet.

You attend worship at least once a week, but you wonder if there isn't more. If you attend a Bible church, you might have slipped away in the last few months to attend an Anglican Evensong or a Catholic Mass, and that somehow seems much more like worship. You know some churches have weekly Communion. That seems intuitively right, though you're not sure why.

You sense there's something deeply wrong with today's world, and you're anxious for the future. But you don't want to turn the clock back, you don't want to stand with the doomsayers, and you think that the politicization of Christianity does more harm than good. Your skin crawls when other Christians merge Christian faith with patriotism. Your skin also crawls when Christians hitch their faith to the latest fad.

You know Jesus is the answer, and that the church is called to carry on Jesus' ministry of healing, justice, salvation. You want to be part of something big, and Jesus' mission is as big as it gets. But you wonder if the church is up to the challenge.

You don't want to switch churches. If you're not Catholic or Orthodox, you don't want to become Roman Catholic or Orthodox. You have Catholic and Orthodox friends and you know they're Christians. Yet you don't buy the papacy and don't want to venerate icons. Besides, your mother would roll in her grave if you swam the Tiber or moved to Constantinople.

(If you're Catholic or Orthodox, you don't want to become a Protestant; mothers roll in their graves when their children move in that direction too.)

You love your church. You love its vigor and its commitment to the Bible. You love its evangelistic fervor. Yet, whether you're a Protestant, a Catholic, or an Orthodox Christian, you're appalled at the church's divisiveness. You long for the church to be united.

Worst of all, you think you're the only one in the world who feels this way. You have coffee every other week with another pastor who shares your longings, but the two of you seem alone in the wilderness. You have a friend or two at church with whom you carry on whispered conversations about your restlessness.

You don't want to be divisive. You know that your pastor is responsible for you, and you want to honor him. You don't quite know what you want to be different. Only that you want something more. And you have trouble being patient.

Sound familiar? Then this book is for you. It's for pastors and laypeople who are looking for something more. That "more" is what I'm calling the "Theopolitan vision."

What's that? Theopolis Fundamentals will explain it as straightforwardly and simply as I can. But let me give you the gist right here.

The Theopolitan vision is a view of the church and her role in the world. I'm going to show that the church is an outpost of the future city of God. The city of God exists now, in the present, as a real-life society among the societies of men. This real-world, visible community is the family of the Father, the body of the Son, the temple of the Spirit. It exists to transform and renew human societies, inside and out, top to bottom. As God's city, the church's carries out a global mission of urban renewal. That's the theme of Part 1.

Worship is the primary work of God's city. Christian worship should be attuned to the liturgical tradition of the church, the whole church, but it should avoid traditionalism and nostalgia. Our practice and understanding of worship must be shaped by the whole Bible—from Genesis through Leviticus and Chronicles to Revelation. Worship should be saturated with Scripture—Scripture read, Scripture taught, Scripture sung, Scripture turned into a dialogue of love between the Lord and His Bride. Scripture is my focus in Part 2.

Worship is thinly Christian unless it culminates in joyous festivity of the Lord's table. The liturgy is the place where we encounter the Word of God, where our worlds are shattered and rebuilt, where we learn to inhabit the symbolic universe of Scripture. I talk about liturgy in Part 3.

A church that worships biblically, a church whose worship is saturated by Scripture, a church whose members have learned to navigate biblically through life, a church that shares Christ's body and blood each week—that is a church prepared for mission, which is the topic in Part 4.

The garden, the place of worship, is the source of the living water that flows to the world. The sanctuary is the beacon whose light shines out among the nations. Unless we taste the kingdom in worship—and I mean literally taste—we won't have the words of life that the world needs to hear. If we don't encounter the light of Jesus in His word and at His table, we won't be lights in the darkness.

Some of you are pastors or aspiring pastors. If that's you, I commend you. Pastoral ministry isn't what you'd call a "sexy" profession. "A clergyman is nothing," says Mary Crawford in Jane Austen's *Mansfield Park*, and Mary Crawford knows a thing or two about sexiness.

As a pastor, you won't get rich. You won't win prestige. You won't gain attention unless you make a point of being provocative.

You'll grind away, week in and week out, teaching the Bible to more-or-less attentive parishioners, counseling, confronting, comforting. You'll spend an inordinate number of hours sharing the crisis moments of life—sickness, marital breakdown, wayward children, job losses. There's no reliable way to measure success. Your work may seem pointless, the results meager.

Yet you've chosen this vocation, or been chosen for it. I don't commend you for your willingness to accept obscurity. I commend you for believing that this vocation matters.

Because, despite widespread opinion, it does. It matters more than anything. A pastor at the pulpit is at the wheel of the ship of the world. A pastor offering the body and blood of

Jesus at the Lord's table is at the center of the universe. A pastor leads the charge in mission, equipping the troops to fight Jesus' holy war.

I believe that God calls men, not women, to be pastors, and they have to be men, ready to act with courage, ready to fight, ready to lead. The Theopolitan vision aims to give you your marching orders.

But the Theopolitan vision isn't just for pastors. It's a vision for the church, and the church has vastly more non-pastors than pastors. The Spirit equips every man, woman, and child in the church with gifts to build the city and serve its mission.

More than the pastor, you non-pastors straddle the boundary between the heavenly city and the earthly city. It's you, the people—the laos, "laity"—who take the word and bread and glory of worship out into the corners and byways of the cities of men. Filled with the Spirit, you're the agents of God's city who carry out Jesus' urban renewal program.

I should warn you at the beginning: The cities of men won't receive what you have to offer—not peaceably. Jesus warned His disciples they would be beaten, arrested, scourged, crucified (Matt 10), and that is forever the life of the church. The world understands, sometimes better than Christians, how radical the gospel is, how fundamental the repentance it demands, how much things will have to change if the gospel is true. The world doesn't want to repent and it doesn't like people who call for repentance.

Don't think for a moment that throwing yourself into the mission of God's city is a safe decision. Jesus calls you to lay down your life—perhaps in literal ways—to follow Him and build His city.

The world is always hostile to the church, but some worlds are more hostile than others. Our world is more hostile than many, since it's built on an explicit rejection of Christian faith. Our world is also fracturing and decaying. Politically, geopolitically, economically, culturally, the world is crumbling. That only makes it more vicious: A cornered bear is a dangerous bear.

Tragically, many sectors of the church have become so worldly that they too are hostile to the demands of Jesus. If you call the church to repentance, be prepared for the assaults. Don't take up the task unless you're prepared to die.

Death isn't a defeat. Far from it. We share in Christ's dying so that we can share in His abundant life and glory. When we share in Christ's death, when we are like the early martyrs who did not "love life even to death" (Rev 12), we become a world-changing force. Courageous witness shatters old worlds and lays the foundations for new ones. It's through the cross that God's city renews the cities of men.

That is the Theopolitan vision of the city of God: A city founded on the blood of Jesus, sustained by the witness and blood of His disciples, established in the world to uproot and to plant, to tear down and to build up.

Part I

The Theopolitan Vision

1

Blessed City

AND HE CARRIED ME AWAY IN SPIRIT TO A GREAT AND HIGH MOUNTAIN AND SHOWED ME THE HOLY CITY, JERUSALEM, COMING DOWN OUT OF HEAVEN FROM GOD.
—REVELATION 21:10

The book of Revelation has an odd ending. The third in-Spirit vision (cf. Rev 1:9–10; 4:1–2) takes John into the wilderness, where he sees the harlot city Babylon drinking the blood of saints and riding on a scarlet beast (Rev 17:1–6). As he watches, the horns of the beast turn on Babylon, strip, eat, and burn her (17:16). Two chapters later, the beast and the false prophet—introduced as the sea and land beasts in chapter 13—are thrown into the lake of fire (19:19–21). Jesus chains Satan and sets the martyrs on thrones, where they reign for a thousand years (20:1–6).

After the thousand years, the dragon is released, deceives the nations, besieges the saints, but is consumed by fire from heaven and thrown into the lake of fire (20:7–10). A final judgment scene follows (20:11–15), and John sees the new heaven and new earth come from heaven, Jerusalem, the Bride who takes the place of the whore (21:1–8).

John has seen the church's three great enemies: the dragon (Rev 12), the sea and land beast (Rev 13) and the harlot

(Rev 17). Then he sees them eliminated in reverse order: the harlot (Rev 17), the beasts (Rev 19), and the dragon (Rev 20). Finally the city descends, the city we look for, the future city whose builder and maker is God.

Everything's done. It's all neat and tidy. Time for the credits to roll. After all, what's left to see or say after a final judgment that ushers in a new heaven and new earth?

Here's the odd thing: There's *another* vision. One last time, John is caught up in Spirit, this time to a mountain (Rev 21:10). And—oddity on top of oddity—the vision is of "the holy city, Jerusalem, coming down out of heaven from God" (21:10). We'd excuse John if he tapped the angel on the shoulder and said, "Um. I've seen this one already."

What gives? Why does the city descend twice? Are there two cities?

No, there's only one city of God. To understand the final vision of Revelation, we have to remember the Old Testament. John isn't the first prophet to ascend a mountain and see a vision of a building. Moses climbed Sinai to see the pattern of the tabernacle (Exod 25:9, 40), the blueprints that guided Israel as they built God's house. Yahweh showed David the pattern of the temple and its furnishings (1 Chr 28:11–19), which he passed on to Solomon the temple builder. Ezekiel was shown a wondrous new temple, city, and land (Ezek 40–48), a set of plans to inspire the exiles returning from Babylon.

Prophets are sacred architects. The Spirit gives them plans, and then the same Spirit equips others to build according to the pattern.

That's what John is doing on the mountain at the end of Revelation: In Spirit, he sees the plan of heavenly Jerusalem and conveys the plans to his first readers and, centuries later, to us. And that same Spirit makes us wise craftsmen to build that city on earth. It's an ideal city, but it's an ideal that we are called to realize.

Revelation ends, in short, with an implied commission: "Go, build."

New Jerusalem is the people of God. We do long to enter the final city, but already *now* we're citizens of that city. The heavenly city is church in the *present*, not the final city of the future (which is described in Rev 21:1–8). It's you and me; it's us. It's us *right now*. It's the city where we already dwell, the city God wants us to keep building, repairing, beautifying until the end of all things.

That's the Theopolitan vision in a nutshell. The word "theo-polis" comes from two Greek words, *theos* and *polis*, and means "God's city." The Theopolitan vision is John's vision, a vision of the church, what the church is and does as a city among the nations.

Throughout this book, we'll be filling out the picture. I'll explain what this city does and what it looks like. We'll be coming back to Revelation 21 a lot. But for now, I want to do one simple thing: to convince you that the church is in fact a city among the cities of men.

Why do I need to convince you? Because many Christians are confused about the nature of the church.

WHAT IS THE CHURCH?

Let's start with the obvious. When you say, "I'm a member of a church" or, "I'm going to church," what does the word "church" mean? In the first instance, "church" doesn't refer to a building with a steeple. To see the church, you have to open the door to see all the people.

The church is *people*. Every Christian knows that. But it's so easy to forget. We need to follow through, doggedly, on that basic truth.

Because the church is people, it's a real-world community, as visible as any other group of people. Real people with real bodies and souls become members of the church through the rite of baptism, which uses water, the most abundant material substance on the planet. Real men and women and children with real bodies and souls gather regularly to hear a real man with a real tongue and vocal chords read and teach in real words from a book, to vibrate molecules of air with words of prayer and sung words of praise, to chew physical bread and drink physical wine at the Lord's table.

When we're not gathered, we (still real men and women and children with real bodies and souls) are supposed to pray for one another, encourage one another, help one another in times of crisis, weep and laugh and rant together. When we're not gathered, we strive to live lives faithful to Jesus, to take opportunities to be witnesses to Jesus, to cultivate faith in our families, to use our vocations to honor our Lord.

All of these are visible, bodily activities, photographable and video-able.

Local groups of Christians are often part of larger bodies. Anglicans are, in the main, part of the global Anglican Communion. Roman Catholics are part of a billion-plus-member church centered in Rome. Orthodox Christians are members of one or another family of Orthodox churches. Protestants group themselves into various denominations. First, Second, Third and up to Ninth Baptist Church may be all part of the Southern Baptist Convention, while First and Second and Third Presbyterian church come from different streams of Presbyterianism.

We can't see all the Anglicans or Catholics or Lutherans at once. But these wider networks consist of real men and women and children with real bodies and souls. These wider networks consist of local congregations that gather and disperse. They are as visible, as photographable and video-able in principle as the local gathering.

All of these different local communities and larger networks form the complex international reality of the catholic, or universal, church. This catholic church is as visible in principle as any sub-group within the catholic church. It would be theoretically possible, if practically unfeasible, to assemble all Christians from all over the world into one place (a corner of Texas would do), throw up a drone, and take a photo of the whole lot.

For all the specific differences among the subgroups, far-flung as we are, we're all recognizably part of the same real-world community. All these individuals and groups have certain things in common. What makes them all Christians is a common confession of Jesus Christ as Lord, many shared beliefs, a common baptism, a rhythm of liturgical gathering, and missional dispersal.

Things are somewhat more complicated. Some Christians wouldn't be able to show up for the group photo because they'd risk persecution if they openly professed Jesus.

There would be debates among those who show up about who belongs in the group photo and who doesn't. Some Catholics would want to keep their distance from anyone who is not in communion with Roman Pontiff. Some Protestants might want to take their own picture in another corner of Texas. Some Protestants would exclude Roman Catholics and Protestants outside their own denomination. Everyone would have to think about whether to make room for some of the odder African Independent Churches, whose links to historic Christianity are tenuous.

So there would be boundary disputes about who's in and who's out. But that doesn't make the church invisible. It means it's a visible global communion of local communities with fluid boundaries—just like every other real-world group, the Irish or Nigerians or the Masons.

The church is invisible because we can't see it all at once. The church is sometimes invisible because it has to go into hiding to survive. The church extends beyond the living to include the dead, from Adam and Abel on to yesterday's martyr. We commune with the whole church throughout all the ages, with saints who are visible and saints who are invisible. But those dimensions don't mean that invisibility is a defining quality of the church. The church's invisibility is empirical, not theological.

Think of Israel. Israel started with Abraham, a real man with a real body and a real wife named Sarah and (eventually) two sons and a company of servants. When Yahweh told Abraham to circumcise his household (Gen 17), he had only one son—Ishmael. The rest of the men and boys who got circumcised weren't related to Abraham by blood. They were part of his traveling city. This was the first Israel, marked out by the physical sign of circumcision, as visible as any nomadic company of men and women and children.

Throughout her history, Israel remained a visible community, a nation and a people. They escaped Egypt as a people, conquered the land as a people, established a monarchy as a people. Even when they were driven from the land, they retained their identity as a people, so that one day they could return to the land to rebuild the temple. Exile was the death of Israel as a visible people.

This was the people of God. What made them part of the same nation was their common trust in the God of the exodus, their common participation in the rites of worship, their common way of life.

INVISIBLE CHURCH?

Perhaps this surprises you. Perhaps someone taught you that "invisible" is a proper modifier for "church." Perhaps you learned that the *real* church is the invisible church.

The distinction between visible and invisible does capture some important truths. It's a way of saying that not everyone in the church will enjoy eternal life in the new creation and that some who are presently outside the church will one day join with the Bride. The visible/invisible distinction emphasizes that some churches, because of their disbelief and disobedience, negate the word and signs that define the church. There are invisible dimensions to the church—the Spirit's work that unites the members to Christ and to one another as His body.

The Bible says these things, but the Bible doesn't say them by talking about an invisible church. The Spirit's work is invisible, but the Spirit's work in itself isn't a "church." In the Bible, the church is a visible community among other communities of men and women and children—among nations, cities, families, social clubs, political parties, etc.

But you might say Paul tells us that "not all Israel is of Israel," that not everyone who was a member of the visible people of

Israel was committed to the God of Israel. What makes someone a member of Israel in truth isn't circumcision but the condition of his heart.

That's a border dispute and doesn't change the fact that the true Israelite was a real man or woman or child with a real body, a member of a real historical people. There wasn't some invisible people of God lurking behind Israel. There wasn't a pristine history of faithfulness hidden in, with, or under the checkered history of Israel. The history of Israel—with all its triumphs and failures, its heroes and villains, its ups and downs—*that* is the history of the people of God.

But, you object: Sure, Israel was a visible community, but the church is an altogether different thing. Israel was defined by flesh, but there is no fleshly connection between members of the church. Israel was a visible physical people, but the church is an invisible spiritual community.

That's not the vision of the New Testament. Jesus was a real man with a real body, and He spent His earthly life gathering real men and women to be His disciples and to carry on as His little flock after His resurrection and ascension. Once they received the Spirit, they didn't cease being real men and women and children with real bodies and souls. Filled with the Spirit, they bore witness to Jesus, gathered to break bread and pray, testified to Jews and gentiles, used the gifts of the Spirit to build up the community, called the body of Christ.

Christians get confused about this because they make a fundamental theological error. It's been a common theological error throughout the church's history, but that doesn't make it any less erroneous. That error is a dualistic understanding of nature and grace, or the natural and the supernatural.

That's a mouthful, so let me explain. The natural world includes Dalmatians and daisies, galaxies, quarks, and quasars. It also includes the natural activities that all human beings share in to one degree or another—eating and drinking and procreating, growing and preparing food. It includes social, economic, and cultural activities—labor, family and neighborhood organization, sculpture and sonatas, architecture and city planning, politics.

In a dualistic understanding, this natural and cultural world has its own laws and principles. Christians will confess that God created the natural world and providentially guides human history, of course. But the realm of nature doesn't belong to Christians. You don't need to be a Christian to know how to grow peas or write code. Christians don't have any monopoly of artistic skill; it sometimes seems the opposite is true. The Bible doesn't tell you how to run your business or win an election and lead a nation.

What Christianity offers—in this dualistic understanding—is communion with God, spiritual experience, forgiveness of sins, freedom from the curse. These blessings of salvation are added to the natural business of life. In addition to the insight I gain from observation, reason, science, I can gain spiritual insight from the Bible. That phrase "in addition to" is key: Christianity is a supernatural layer on top of the natural cake of life.

Dualism conceives of Christianity vertically: It sits on top of the natural world.

For a strict dualist, the "supernatural" doesn't touch natural life: The fact that I'm a Christian doesn't have *anything* to do with my work, business, family, politics. I read my Bible and listen to sermons to commune with Jesus, not to be told how to vote or spend my money. At its worst, this dualism can imply that Christianity is an escape from the demands of the natural world.

No Christian is a strict dualist in practice. It's hard to be a strict dualist if you've read any of the New Testament. Paul gives pretty explicit instructions about marriage and family (Eph 5–6), encourages us to work to the glory of God, and explains the purpose of civil government (Rom 13).

But many Christians are soft dualists when it comes to church. If you think of the church as an invisible, spiritual community, rather than a real-life visible society with and among other societies, you have a dualistic mindset. You're a dualist if you think that, in addition to the natural meals that keep your body chugging along, you now get to eat a supernatural meal at church, which keeps your soul chugging along. Church adds a supernatural dimension to my life but leaves my natural world more or less intact.

We should renounce nature-supernatural dualism and all its works and all its pomp. Everything comes from God. Creation is as much a gift of God's unmerited grace as redemption. Everything lives, moves, and has its being in God. Redemption transforms and fulfills nature; it's *not* a detached addition to it. Through His Spirit, Jesus is remaking and will remake everything about you and everything about the world.

Keep this in mind, because I'll come back to it several times throughout Part 1 and the rest of this book. For now, remember: The church isn't an invisible entity, a "supernatural" addition on top of natural human societies. The church is a transformed human society.

Instead of thinking vertically, we should think horizontally, which means thinking: The church is the future city that has entered into the present, the city we build that will be perfected in a new heavens and new earth.

PEOPLE OF THE TRIUNE GOD

I have emphasized—perhaps belabored—the visibility of the church, but I have good reason for it. Erroneous beliefs slip into our heads, and dangerous habits slip into our lives, when we don't acknowledge that the church is a real-world community of real men and women and children with real bodies and souls.

If we think the church is an invisible community of true believers, we might be tempted to avoid the mess of membership in a real community. After all, other people are tough to live with. If we pound a wedge between the church-as-she-appears and the church-as-she-truly-is, we mistake the very nature of redemption. We might be tempted to think that being a Christian—being saved—means escaping from the real world with all its trials, temptations, and challenges, to search for a secret back door to God.

The Bible doesn't allow that option. There's only the front door, the west door, which is the entry door to the church. If you want to commune with your Creator, you're going to have to do it together with other real men and women and children with real bodies and souls, who also want to commune with their Creator. Redemption isn't escape from this world or from others. Redemption is becoming a member of a new society of which God's Spirit is the animating breath and of which Jesus Christ is head.

There's only the front door because the church—the visible, empirical communion of men and women and children—is more than a mere human society. It's a human society, but it's an utterly unique human society. As a visible society, with its fluid boundaries, for all its checkered history, the church is the people of the Triune God. It is a communion of real-life human beings joined in communion with the Creator.

The New Testament describes the church in relation to each person of the Trinity.

We are adopted children of our heavenly Father (1 John 3:1), and thus constitute a family of brothers and sisters (Matt 12:48–50). The family of the Father isn't some inaccessible invisible family but the real-world church. If you want to be a child of God, you have to be among the children of God.

We are the body of Christ, each of us a member and organ of Christ as our eyes, ears, hands, and feet are members of our personal body (Rom 12; 1 Cor 12; Eph 4). If you want to be united to Christ, you need to be united to His body.

As the body of Christ, the church is animated by the Spirit of Jesus. The Spirit distributes gifts to each part (1 Cor 12), enables the body to build itself up into maturity (Eph 4), sanctifies us as saints. The Spirit prays in and through our groans (Rom 8). The church is the temple of that Spirit (1 Cor 3:16). You can't be a living stone in that Spiritual temple unless you're part of a structure made of living stones.

All of these descriptions of the church—children of the Father, body of the incarnate Son, temple of the Spirit—are descriptions of the real-world, historical community of real men and women and children with real bodies and souls.

They're all descriptions of the heavenly city that has taken its place among the cities and nations of men.

In His high priestly prayer (John 17), Jesus prays that the disciples would be one as He is one with the Father. That unity is a unity of mutual indwelling: The Son is in the Father, and the Father is in the Son. Jesus prays that His disciples would form a communion so deeply one that it resembles this divine unity of mutual indwelling.

Jesus also prays that the disciples would be incorporated into the mutual indwelling of the Father and Son: "they in Us ... I in them and Thou in Me" (vv. 21, 23). Just as the Father indwells the Son who indwells Him, so the disciples of Jesus are indwelt by the God whom they also simultaneously indwell. God makes the disciples His home, even as He is the disciples' home. Jesus wants His disciples to become part of the society that exists between the Father and Son in the Spirit.

This communion of mutual indwelling among disciples—this *church*—is a *visible* communion of disciples. Jesus doesn't bring His disciples to communion with God by elevating up and out of their bodies to swirl in invisible spiritual bliss. The disciples don't form a communion that is visible only to the eyes of faith. It's a communion visible to the *world*, with a unity visible to the world (17:21). The church's unity of mutual indwelling should be visible enough to convince the unbelieving *world* that the Father sent the Son.

The church has invisible dimensions and depths, deep as the depths of God Himself. But these invisible dimensions are depths of a real-world church. *As* a real-world people, made of up real men and women and children with real bodies and souls, the visible church is called to manifest on earth the eternal communion of Father and Son.

That means you and your fellow church members, in whatever kind of church you are and wherever you live. Together with your brothers and sisters, you are a visible people joined with one another because the Spirit has brought you into communion with the Father and Son. Your home church is a family of the Father, united as the body of the incarnate Son, indwelt by the Spirit. Your mundane, apparently pathetic little church is the greatest mystery in the universe.

GOD'S FUTURE POLIS

You've followed this far. You may be skeptical, suspicious, even angry—at me or at someone who misled you in the past. If you've come this far, I'm going to risk another step: The church isn't simply a real-world, visible and historical society of real-life men, women, and children with real bodies and souls. It's a particular *kind* of human society.

The church is a *city*. It's the heavenly city, the city of the *future*.

This brings up another invisible dimension of the church, another reason to say that the church isn't just another interest group, club, or nation. Remember the beginning of this chapter: John sees the heavenly city descend *twice*. The first descent comes *after* the final judgment. It's the final city, the new heavens and the new earth. The second vision of the city shows the city in history and provides the pattern that guides our building in the present.

The city of God is the present form of a future city. It's the city that will one day be identical with the new heavens and new earth. Rome rose and fell. London was once the center of an empire but has contracted. Washington's dominance of the world won't last forever, nor will Beijing's (if China's the next lord of history).

But the city of God *will* last until the end and beyond the end. The church is the present presence of a perfect city to come. It's the *now* of a city that is not yet. Your mundane, apparently pathetic home church is a people in communion with the Triune God. It's also an outpost of a perfect new creation, future utopia here and now, ahead of time. You should greet one another as if you were in a sci-fi movie: "Hi, I'm from the future. Are you?"

Because the church is the presence of God's city, His theo-polis, the church is inherently *political*. It's inherently like a city, a civic reality. The New Testament makes this clear in the terminology it uses to describe the church, nearly all of which comes from ancient political theory.

Outside the New Testament, the term "church" (Gr. *ekklesia*) refers to an assembly, a calling-together, of the citizens of an ancient Greek city-state. Faced with military threat, political upheaval, or natural disaster, citizens gathered as the *ekklesia* to deliberate about what to do. The good order and future of the city depended on the work of the assembly.

For the early Christians, the church is God's assembly, with its own civic order, its own leaders, its own festivals and rituals, its own way of life. And the early Christians believed their assemblies—their *ekklesiai*—determined the future of the city where they assembled. The flourishing and future of Ephesus didn't depend on the *ekklesia* of Ephesian citizens. It depended on the assembly of Ephesian saints who called on the name of the Lord. No matter how small or weak by the world's standards, the Christian *ekklesiai*, because they were the body of Christ the Lord of all, had their hands on the reins of history.

John describes the church as a *koinonia* (1 John 1:7), a participation in the common good of the Spirit, using a term that Aristotle used to describe the "community" of the city. Ancient thinkers imagined nations as political bodies, like the body of Christ (Rom 12; 1 Cor 12). Paul tells the Philippians that their citizenship is in heaven (Phil 3:20–21). Peter draws from Exodus 19 to describe the church as a holy *nation* (1 Pet 2:9–10).

The formation of God's *polis* is inherent in the gospel. Jesus didn't die and rise again simply to rescue us from the eternal torments of hell. He *did* that, but that was not the limit of His work. He died in order to break down the dividing wall between Jew and gentile and form a new human race, constituted from men and women from every tribe, tongue, people, and nation (Eph 2:11–22). He is the new Abel, who suffered outside the gates, not to found a Cainite Babel but to found new Jerusalem.

The good news is that Jesus has dealt with our sin and given us new life in the Spirit. The good news is *equally* that Jesus has founded a new city on the earth, a city as visible as any other city, full of real-life men and women and children with real bodies and souls, a city with a real history. The gospel calls us to repent and seek the mercy of Christ. It also calls us to leave the world behind to become members of a new society, the body of Christ. The gospel is fundamentally political; the church, God's *polis*, is embedded within it.

Human beings are social creatures. God created us to speak to, work with, love one another. It was not good for Adam to be alone, and so God provided a helper suitable to him. Together they formed a "we," a family. It's not good for families to be alone, so human beings form larger groupings, the larger "we" of a tribe, city, or nation.

If God is to save human beings as we actually are—social and civic creatures—then He has to save us in our social and civic relationships and institutions. If God has acted in history to save the world—if salvation is a reality *now*—then it *must* take the form of a redeemed community, a redeemed city.

The church isn't merely a means for individuals to be saved. The church isn't a channel of salvation. The church is humanity saved. The church *is* communion with God and one another in God; it is the future perfect city in an imperfect present. The church *is* salvation in social form.

CITY ON A MISSION

Salvation is an eschatological reality from top to bottom. Jesus proclaims that the kingdom of God is near. He says that His death is the judgment of this world and the casting out of the prince of this world (John 12). When He dies, He announces, "It is finished." By His resurrection and ascension, Jesus enters fully into the new creation, the Last Adam who has become life-giving Spirit (1 Cor 15).

We're united to Christ by the Spirit and thus receive a share in the new creation. Paul says that wherever anyone is in Christ, new creation has broken through into the old (2 Cor 5:17). We're united to the risen Christ *together* so that the church, filled with the Spirit, is new creation. This message is inherent in the gospel: The future has taken root in the present, the coming kingdom has come, the new Jerusalem has nestled among the nations.

For the present, and until Jesus returns, the city of God remains flawed. Her blemishes are all-too-obvious. Her history will continue to bump up and down. There will be villains as well as heroes. But the church—the real-world visible church, the historical communion of real men and women and children with real bodies and souls—*that* church is the present form of the future city. She is presently the bride who will be unveiled in glory at the last judgment.

We still look for a city whose builder and maker is God. We hope for a bridal city to unite heaven and earth forever. But we also believe that this city already has an earthly address. The world is dotted with outposts of the heavenly city. It is a sign of a future city, but not a mere sign. It's an *effective* sign, a present sign that gives us a taste now of the city to come.

The church's mission is, in the first instance, simply to *be* what the Lord says she is: the family of the Father, the body of Christ, the temple of the Spirit. The church's vocation is to be a communion of disciples, each dwelling in each as they dwell together in the God who dwells in them. The church's vocation is to proclaim the gospel, teach the commandments of Jesus, baptize converts and their children, break bread, encourage and correct.

John has brought the blueprints from the mountain. For two millennia, Christians have been building. We're called to do our share in that cosmic construction project.

The heavenly city isn't static. It's not merely *placed* in the world, among the cities and nations of men. God established His city among the cities of men to *redeem* those human cities. Jesus commissioned the church to disciple nations. He established His city to engage in an urban renewal project.

In cities full of dislocated and disoriented strangers, the church offers communion and the safety of home. In food deserts, the church gives bread. Where men are enslaved to addictive sin, the church proclaims the good news of liberation through the Spirit who breaks chains and raises the dead.

To addicts and prostitutes who hide themselves in shame, the church preaches the blood of Jesus that cleanses sin and the gift of the Spirit who clothes in glory. When politicians prey on the weak, the church steps in to defend the vulnerable and demand justice. In cities of greed and gluttony, the church proclaims the fruits of the Spirit. Where housing collapses, the church opens a homeless shelter.

The church's mission isn't hopeless. The hope the church offers isn't merely a hope for the distant future, a future after death. God has announced His kingdom and established His city to fulfill His promise to Abraham, the promise to bless the nations. The kingdom came as a stone that shattered the empires of the ancient world. But it's God's kingdom, the fifth monarchy, that will grow into a mountain that fills the whole earth (Dan 2). The Son of Man inherits the dominion of the bestial ancient empires so that the saints of the highest one reign in the authority given by the Ancient of Days (Dan 7).

The city of God is a city of light that illumines a dark world (Rev 21:23–24). It's the source of living waters, which brings life to a desert land (22:1–5). Through the Son and Spirit, the Lord has established Zion as the chief of the mountains, Jerusalem as the queen of cities. As the law of Yahweh flows out, the nations are drawn to Zion to learn the Lord's ways. They beat their swords into ploughs and their spears into pruning hooks, transforming weapons of war into tools of peaceful productivity (Isa 2:1–4). Jesus has been raised and enthroned, and He *will* reign until all His enemies, including death itself, are placed beneath His feet.

That is to say, the church *will* fulfill the mission that Jesus has assigned her. The city of God, sent to renew the cities of men, *will* renew the cities of men.

Over the centuries, millions upon millions of individuals will hear the gospel, be awakened by the Spirit, be baptized into the body of Christ, and live in Christian faithfulness. But the church's mission doesn't end with the gathering of a global network of local churches. As she gathers individuals, the church disrupts the patterns of corporate life in the cities of men, dismantles institutions of injustice and structures that promote ungodliness. As the church is the church, as she is the people of the Triune God, as she is the effective sign of the city to come, Jesus' Spirit transforms families, tribes, cities, nations through the ministries of the church.

The church that carries out this mission is the church of Jesus Christ, the crucified and risen Lord. *Crucified* Lord. Jesus didn't go to the cross to save us the trouble of sharing the cross. The opposite is true: Jesus went to the cross to give us a share in His suffering so that, in Him, we can offer ourselves for the life of the world.

The city of man is quite content to be what it has always been. It doesn't like to be disrupted, and the church is a disruption. The church's very existence is a rebuke to the city of man, to the world's pretensions, idolatries, violence, lusts, perversions. The rebuke stings, and the city of man responds violently to the sting.

We will complete the mission Jesus has given us, but we'll complete that mission in the way Jesus did: by suffering, by enduring hatred and unreasonable opposition, through brutal attacks from the world and sometimes from other citizens of the city of God. That opposition doesn't spell defeat. It's the way of victory. When we suffer in Christ, we dynamite the foundations of the city so that a new city can be built from the rubble.

Some cities are friendlier to the church. Some cities and nations profess Christ. That's not a problem. That's the aim of Christian mission, that all nations would acknowledge the Lord as King. Yet the church can *never* be complacent. We are still called to bear the cross. If the church never provokes the city of man, we're probably not being faithful to the crucified Lord of the church, who has called us to take up the cross to follow Him.

THE THEOPOLITAN ALTERNATIVE

Christians today feel that the world is coming apart at the seams. Politically, economically, culturally, morally, everything seems to be in upheaval. Christians have responded by proposing various remedies: political strategies, tactical withdrawals into quasi-monastic communities of virtue, compromise.

Most of these responses miss the heart of the matter.

Central to the Theopolitan vision is the conviction that the church drives history, for good or ill. Political and cultural trends are secondary to happenings and movements in the church.

The needs of the world can only be met by the Triune God, and He has caught the church up in his work of renewing and glorifying creation. The cities of men can be revived and renewed only as the Spirit of Jesus works through the real-world communion of real men and women and children with real bodies and souls that constitutes the church. The cities of men can be renewed only by that community that shares the suffering and glory of Jesus through his Spirit.

When the world is in disarray, we hope for another world. We want to grasp utopia. But utopia is in our midst. The other world—the world of the future—has become present through Jesus and His Spirit, as the church of Jesus Christ. Only the church can bring the powers of the age to come into the present age. Because it is the Spirit-filled Bride and Body of the Son of God, only the city of God gives hope to the cities of men.

2

Tasting the End

AND THE CITY IS LAID OUT AS A SQUARE,
AND ITS LENGTH IS AS GREAT AS THE WIDTH. ...
ITS LENGTH AND WIDTH AND HEIGHT ARE EQUAL.
—REVELATION 21:16

The Theopolitan vision is a vision of the church in her relation to the world. It highlights the political nature and mission of the church and the political character of the gospel that the church proclaims. Jesus founded the city of God among the cities of men to witness and to transform those cities. God will fulfill the commission Jesus gave the church. The nations are being, and will continue to be, discipled. The kingdoms of this world have become and are becoming the kingdom of our Lord and of His Christ.

How does that happen? Is this anything more than wishfulness or nostalgia?

It happens because the church is a city whose length, breadth, and height are the same.

Say what? What do the dimensions of new Jerusalem have to do with the mission of the church? Much in every way.

From a mountain, John, like Moses, sees the pattern of heaven. He writes it and sends it to the church so that we can replicate the heavenly pattern on earth. He gives us the blueprints. We're the builders.

Nearly every phrase and clause of John's description of new Jerusalem comes from an Old Testament text. The city has twelve gates, marked with the names of the tribes of Israel, three gates at each point of the compass (Rev 21:12–13). It's a civilized (i.e., "citified") version of Israel's wilderness camp, when three tribes camped on each of the four sides of the tabernacle.

The city gleams like a jewel, like pure gold (Rev 21:11, 18). Her foundation stones are gemstones, twelve of them (21:19–20). With her gold walls and streets, she resembles the temple with its gold-plated walls and floor. Her twelve gemstones are like the gems on the breastplate of the high priest (Exod 28). Jerusalem is a bridal city, but she's dressed like a priest. The throne of God and of the Lamb is in the city, the source of living water (22:1).

These descriptions aren't grabbed randomly from a thesaurus of biblical imagery. They form a coherent overall picture: The city is Israel, the camp of Israel, the temple, a priestly city.

The dimensions reinforce this in a particular way. The city is a cube, like the Most Holy Place of Israel's tabernacle and temple (Exod 26:31–33; 1 Kgs 6:20). Jerusalem is the inner sanctuary all growed up into a city.

Let's take a moment to pause over that. The Most Holy Place was Yahweh's throne room, inaccessible to any but the high priest (Lev 16:1–2). In new Jerusalem, the citizens live in the throne room, serving the Lord and seeing His face (Rev 22:3–4). The Most Holy Place was the center of Israel's liturgical system. The temple occupied a large portion of ancient Jerusalem, but there was a difference between temple and city. In new Jerusalem, though, the gap between city and temple has been closed. The equal dimensions tell us that the whole city is liturgical space, of the holiest variety.

That gives us a clue about the work of the city of God among the cities of men. The church is the Spirit's instrument for accomplishing God's mission, and the church's participation in mission centers what happens in the sanctuary. We carry out our mission through the proclamation and teaching of the word of God, liturgical gathering around the Lord's word and table, faithful witness to the kingship of Jesus, and careful pastoral guidance.

As the church does her churchy things, she brings the life of the age to come to the nations. We're builders of the city, and the chief labor of building takes place on our day of rest, in the liturgy. We all are builders because the liturgy is the work of the whole people, not merely the work of the pastor. The church fulfills Jesus' mission by being what she is, a liturgical city.

Mission starts with liturgy. Liturgy is the time and place where the church gathers as the city council, the ekklesia of God, an assembly of the heavenly city. As the real men and women and children with real bodies and souls gather for worship and disperse from worship, heavenly life comes to earth. Having tasted the good things of the age to come, the church goes out to share those goods in the marketplace. The sanctuary, the place of worship and communion with God, is the center of the world. It always has been, right from the beginning.

Or, put it this way:

WATCH THE WATER

When God first created the world, He mapped it into several territories. He planted a garden in the east of a land called Eden. Outside Eden were other lands, like the land of Havilah where the Creator buried gold and precious stones. The world wasn't homogenous but differentiated. From the beginning, God organized the world into a garden, a land, and a wider world.

Eden's garden was the original sanctuary, the place of worship and communion with God (Gen 2). At the center of the garden were two trees, a tree that communicated life and a tree that opened eyes to give knowledge of good and evil. Yahweh intended to commune with Adam and Eve in the garden. When He expelled them, He set up cherubim at the gate to keep them out. Later sanctuaries are full of cherubim figures (Exod 25:18–22; 1 Kgs 6:23–28), guardians of the house and throne room of Yahweh.

Adam and Eve had other responsibilities in the other zones of creation. They were commissioned to fill, subdue, and rule the earth. They would trek down to Havilah to mine the gold and precious stones. The garden was planted within the land of Eden, a land that would serve as humanity's first home. Adam and Eve were called to work in the land and to have dominion in the world. In the garden, they were called to worship.

A river sprang up in the land of Eden and flowed through the garden (Gen 2). From there, it split into four rivers that went out to the corners of earth. Water sprang up from the higher ground of the land, where the Lord was enthroned, but flowed through the sanctuary before it spread to the world. Living water from the presence of God was mediated to the world through the place of worship.

Throughout the Bible, sanctuaries are "well-watered places," like the garden of God. In the courtyard of the tabernacle was a laver full of water for cleansing sacrifices and priests (Exod 30:17–21). In Solomon's temple, that laver had expanded into a gigantic bronze sea, carried on the backs of twelve oxen (1 Kgs 7:23–26). The bronze sea depicted the vocation of Israel among the nations. As a cosmic image, it showed that Israel was the "Atlas" nation, bearing the firmament on it shoulders, holding up the heavenly waters above. As an image of international order, it showed that Israel bore the "sea of nations" on their backs. The temple in Jerusalem, not Babylon or Susa or Athens or Rome, was the axis of the ancient world.

Solomon made ten water basins on wheeled structures that resembled chariots (1 Kgs 7:27–37). Heavenly water was available in the house of God, but the chariots hinted that the Lord was sending water out to the world. Solomon's temple had a reservoir, but it was also the source of a river—just like Eden.

After describing the new temple in excruciating detail, Ezekiel spies water flowing from the house (Ezek 47). At first, it's only a little trickle from the throne of God, streaming out into the temple courts. As it crosses the temple threshold, it gets wider and deeper and keeps growing as it flows down from Zion out to the land. First, the water is up to Ezekiel's ankles, then to his knees, and finally so deep he cannot cross it. As it flows, *where* it flows, trees spring up, bearing fruit. Ezekiel's river flows east, all the way to the Dead Sea, where it freshens the salt water and brings dead fish to life. It's a vision of God's transforming work in the world, but the source of the water is crucial to the vision: It brings life as it flows from the sanctuary, out of the place of worship.

In the recesses of the Most Holy Place, Yahweh kept His treasure chest under His cherubim throne. That chest—known as the ark of the covenant—contained three things: the tablets of the law from Sinai, a jar of manna from the wilderness, and Aaron's rod that budded and bore fruit in the presence of the Lord (Heb 9:4). No ancient Israelite was permitted to enter the Most Holy Place to enjoy these treasures. In Ezekiel, that changes. The river that flows from Ezekiel's temple begins from that very throne room. It carries Yahweh's hidden treasures out to the world.

Ezekiel's river is a picture of Israel. The people gather to receive the word of the Lord from the priests and to feast in His presence. When they disperse, they are themselves the living waters, flowing out to the nations.

As we've seen, the Bible ends with a similar vision. John sees the new Jerusalem descend as a Bride from heaven. Nations stream into her, bringing their treasures. And a river flows through her, lined with trees of life that bear fruit every month and whose leaves bring healing to the nations (Rev 22:1–5). It's a vision of the church as sanctuary, a place of worship that serves as the source of life-giving water to the nations. It's a vision of the church as a community whose liturgical life is for the life of the world.

Revelation also provides a contrary example. When the third trumpet sounds, a star falls onto the springs and rivers (Rev 8:10–11). The star is named Wormwood, and it poisons the water sources, which turns the water deadly. Springs and rivers represent the temple in Jerusalem as the source of life, but the temple has become so corrupt that she spreads death rather than life.

The church's liturgy is a source of life or death to the world. It's a spring of living water or a fountain of poison. How can we tell whether the church's worship is spreading life or death? What kind of worship is a source of life-giving water to the world?

At one level, the answer is simple: The church's worship brings life if it conforms to God's requirements for worship. It brings life if it's shaped and saturated by God's word. What might that mean?

BIBLICAL WORSHIP

The church's worship is a source of life when it is conformed to the word of God. The first commandment demands exclusive worship of Yahweh, but the Lord isn't satisfied with telling us whom to worship. He also tells us how to worship. God gave liturgical instructions to Israel, which are far more detailed than the instructions He gave them about, say, private property or environmental justice. And the rules that governed the sanctuary carried stiff penalties. Nadab and Abihu offered "strange fire" and received fire in return, burn for burn (Lev 10).

Christian worship is different from the worship of ancient Israel, radically so. At Jesus' death, the veil of the temple was torn from top to bottom, a sign that there would be free comings and goings into the house of God. The church as a whole is now most sacred space. We now gather before the Lord unveiled, without a screen to separate the people from the presence of the Lord or the Lord from the people. Jesus the heavenly High Priest has entered the heavenly sanctuary, and by His Spirit He brings out the hidden treasures of heaven—the heavenly word and the bread of angels.

Christian worship is radically different from the worship of ancient Israel, but it is no less governed by the word. Christian worship, like the worship of Israel, must be worship by the book. It must be biblical.

When you hear that, you might immediately think of the depictions of early Christian worship in Acts or 1 Corinthians.

You might think that Christian worship must be guided by New Testament teaching about worship.

Christians live in a new covenantal order, but it's a dangerous error to think that the New Testament alone is our guide for worship or for anything.

We can't even know what worship is unless we understand Leviticus, the biblical book about worship. And we can't grasp Leviticus without knowing Eden and the exodus. We can't grasp the biblical teaching about liturgical music without immersing ourselves in Psalms and 1–2 Chronicles. We won't understand the meaning of holy communion unless we glimpse the rich biblical theology of food and festivity, which runs from Genesis 1 to Revelation 22. When we say Christian worship must be biblical, we mean it must be patterned by the whole Bible.

In Part 3 I will spell out details of liturgical theology and practice in more depth, but let me offer some illustrations of how the whole Bible helps us answer liturgical questions.

Is there a right order of worship? In Scripture, worship is covenant renewal, and covenant ceremonies are arranged in a specific sequence of actions. Israel gathers at Sinai, purifies herself for the Lord's appearance, hears the word, and then feasts in the Lord's presence (Exod 19–24). When Israelites offered a series of sacrifices, they began with a sin offering for cleansing, added an ascension offering to enter the presence of God, and ended with a peace offering that involved a meal (Num 6; 2 Chr 29:20–33). Israel's order of worship anticipates the order of historic Christian liturgies: confession and cleansing; consecration in word; communion at the Lord's table. Historic liturgies often divide the service into a liturgy of the word (*synaxis*) and a liturgy of the table (Eucharist). That's an error. Biblically, the liturgy is a united sequence of actions, a single complex act of covenant renewal.

What posture should we adopt at the Lord's table? There is no biblical command, but various considerations indicate that we should sit for communion. Jesus commanded the multitudes sit before He fed them (Matt 14:19; Mark 6:39; John 6:10). Sitting is the posture of kings, and the Lord's table is a table for the king's friends (John 15:13–14; cf. 1 Kgs 4:5). The Supper is celebration, not contrition; we eat and drink as priest-kings, not as penitents.

Should the church observe a church calendar? There's no command to observe a church calendar, but Israel's worship provides a guide (Lev 23; Deut 14–16). Each year, Israel commemorated the great acts of Yahweh in the exodus (Passover), the giving of the law (Pentecost), and the preservation of Israel in the wilderness (Feast of Booths). Israel's weeks were structured by a dance of work and Sabbath, and her year also had a liturgical rhythm. The church does well to follow Israel's example in this regard.

Should a minister wear a robe when he leads the liturgy? There is no command for pastors to wear robes, but Israel again provides a salutary example. The priests wore distinctive clothing that manifested their office (Exod 28). Throughout Scripture, clothing is a mark of authority and glory (cf. Gen 37:37–45; 1 Sam 15:27; 1 Kgs 11:26–40). The church isn't a democracy. There are leaders and rulers in the church, as there are in any city. Liturgical roles aren't interchangeable. The hierarchical character of church order should be manifested in the liturgy.

Should there be any artwork in the place of worship? Israel's sanctuaries were richly adorned with gold, embroidered images of cherubim and plants, carvings of palm trees and flowers (Exod 25–31; 1 Kgs 6–8). The decorations signified that the sanctuaries are reconstituted Edens. The second commandment didn't prohibit making images or even placing images in the sanctuary. It prohibited using images as a means for making contact with God (Exod 20:4–6). It still does. Scripture rejects icon veneration in the strongest terms.

To say that worship must be biblical doesn't only mean that Scripture teaches us what we do and don't do in worship or that Scripture teaches us what worship is and means. Worship must be biblical also in the sense that it includes Bible reading and Bible teaching. God spoke to Israel from Sinai in a context of covenant-making, a liturgical setting. The early Christians gathered to pray and break bread, also to receive the apostles' teaching. Christian liturgy is a liturgy of word and table.

A Christian worship service that minimizes the place of Scripture isn't too liturgical. It's not liturgical enough.

The church's liturgy should be Bible-saturated. There should be readings from Scripture, generous readings, not a few snippets from a lectionary or a few lines as a sermon text. The readings shouldn't skip the difficult or embarrassing parts—the tent pegs through the brains, the details about the impurity of menstruation, the severe things Jesus and Paul have to say about first-century Jews.

In worship, the congregation should listen to the word read, receiving it by ear. We can read with our eyes at home. We should sing the Scriptures in psalms and speak the Scriptures to one another in liturgical dialogue—rolling the word on our tongues. The pastor should teach the Bible—the Bible, not a review of the week's news or an anecdote from his personal life. The sermon isn't an occasion for a theological lecture. But it should be substantial, as solid as the congregation can handle. Pastors should aspire to offer solid food rather than skim milk, oatmeal stout rather than Bud Light.

The liturgy is the primary location for the church's encounter with Scripture. The liturgy does more than communicate things about the Bible. In the liturgy, we are brought into the story of the Bible and begin to inhabit the world the Bible describes. Through the word in the liturgy, our lives are taken up into the great narrative of redemption. They become subplots of the story of the world, the story that is reenacted each week.

Let's make this concrete: Within the liturgy, the hundreds of biblical stories about food become our story as we share the Lord's table. God feeds us too, as He fed Adam, Abraham, Israel, David, the multitudes who followed Jesus. The dozens of water crossings and water rescues are realized in the church in baptism. In the liturgy, we commune with the living God, standing in the place of Adam, Abraham, Moses, Aaron, Israel, David, Jeremiah, Isaiah, and all the rest. Their stories and experiences become ours—not in pretense but in reality.

Through the word in worship, we become more than a people with Bible knowledge. We become a people molded inside and out, in our imaginations and identity, in our minds and hearts, by Scripture. The Bible presses its patterns on us. It seeps into us so that we become a Bible-shaped people whose veins bleed bibline.

FESTIVE WORSHIP

Christian worship is word-centered worship. As real men and women and children with real bodies and souls gather, we hear the word read and taught, sing the word, speak the word. And, crucially, we eat the word.

The Lord's Supper should be part of every Lord's day liturgy. Worship in the Bible always takes place at a table. An altar is a table (cf. Ezek 41:22), and ever since the flood, the people of God have erected altars at places of worship (Gen 8:20; 12:7–8; 33:20; Exod 20:24).

If you could see an ancient Israelite preparing for a feast, you'd see him pick an unblemished animal from his flock or herd, prepare flour or bread, and grab a flagon of wine. If you didn't know better, you might suspect he's preparing for a barbeque. Because he is. At the tabernacle and temple, priests offer the Lord's bread, and worshipers share His food (cf. Lev 21–22). Covenant renewal climaxes with a covenant meal, a sign of restored harmony between the parties to the covenant.

Biblically, worship without a meal isn't worship at all. When we worship without the Supper, it's as if we're disciples on the road to Emmaus, who hear Jesus speak but never recognize Him because we don't stick around for the breaking of bread (Luke 24). A liturgy without the Supper is like a contract without signatures; it is (not just like) a wedding feast without food, a party without hors d'oeuvres and wine, as if the Lord were to open His house to extend hospitality but never offer chips or bring the beer out of the fridge.

Neglect and abuse of the Lord's Supper is one of the disasters of church history. In the medieval church, lay Christians were all but excluded from the meal, which had been re-defined and reserved for the priests. The Reformers demanded bread for ordinary Christians. All the baptized are priests, Luther insisted, by virtue of their baptism; all are holy, and the Supper is holy food for the holy ones. Calvin wanted to have the Supper every week.

After that sound start, much of the Protestant world drifted into the old medieval neglect of the Supper. Of course, Protestants say they're doing the opposite. They say they have the Supper infrequently to keep it special. That doesn't fly. Protestants are supposed to follow the Bible in liturgy and life, but with regard to the Supper, many have adopted a position that is completely at odds with biblical conceptions of worship.

Restoring the Supper to its central place in Christian worship should be one of the church's highest priorities. Without it, we cannot be the source of living water to the world. Without it, we will not be effective as the heavenly city on a mission to transform the cities of men.

Does this sound extreme? To some Protestant ears, this sounds like a demand to reverse the Reformation and return to Rome. It sounds like a call to give up the word-centeredness of worship for dead sacramentalism. You might be thinking, "Who would want to have the Lord's Supper every week anyway? It's dreary and depressing, all that self-examination and anxiety, all that gloom and contrition. It leaves me depressed." Or, you might be thinking, "It extends worship by a good half hour, and I need to get home for the kickoff."

These objections rest on a superficial understanding of the Supper. Let me start with the final more practical objections. It's true that many churches, including many Protestant churches, celebrate the Lord's Supper as if it were a wake. (That's not quite right. Wakes can be raucous affairs. But you get the idea.) Many churches keep the Lord's Supper as if they were gathering at a tomb rather than a table; and that tomb isn't an empty one. Paul's exhortation to self-examination becomes the dominant motif to the whole event (1 Cor 11).

We should take Paul with utter seriousness. We must come to the table worthily, and that means we have to engage in self-examination and repentance. But that self-examination doesn't take place at the table. The table is, well, a table. Bread is food, and wine is a festive drink. Nowhere in the Bible do people gather at a table to mourn their sins. If God wanted us to mourn our sins, He would have commanded a weekly fast, not a weekly feast.

Tables are for eating, drinking, and rejoicing. In Israel, the sanctuary was a place of joy, where Israel could eat, drink, and rejoice (Deut 12). When Israel gathered, they were to eat, drink, and rejoice (Deut 16). If we celebrate the Lord's Supper as it ought to be celebrated, every Lord's Day will be a day of gladness, and every worship service will be a journey into joy.

The Supper commemorates the gruesome death of Jesus on the cross. "Commemorate" is too weak. It's not merely that we remember the death of Jesus. We eat and drink the death of Jesus so that, like our daily food, His sacrifice becomes part of us, so that our flesh is conformed to His flesh, and our veins flow with His blood. To share in the Lord's Supper is to share in the sacrifice of Jesus and so to be called to a life of continuous sacrifice.

As I stressed in chapter 1, we cannot hope for painless renewal in the church or the world. The church is renewed by sharing by the Spirit in the dying and rising of Jesus. The church is made a new body through a painful passage of dismemberment. The world must be shattered to pieces before it can be rebuilt. Every time we receive the body and blood of Jesus, we're called to become, and we are becoming, a community of sacrifice, a people prepared for world-destroying, world-building witness.

Yet I have said that the Supper is an overflowing cup not an empty plate, bright laughter not black morbidity. How can we rejoice when we share the cup of Jesus that calls us to a life of self-emptying love?

We rejoice in the cup of sacrifice because we follow Jesus. He suffered agony in Gethsemane, but He went to the cross for the joy that was set before Him (Heb 12:2), the joy of His vindication and glorification. That joyful fulfillment is in our past, and in the Supper we rejoice now in the joy that is yet to come. We taste heavenly joy so that we can, like Jesus, take up the cross in gladness. Or: We recognize the privilege of suffering with Jesus so that the meal of joy and the meal of self-sacrifice are one meal. Like the disciples, we rejoice that we are worthy to suffer shame for His name (Acts 5:41).

Regular celebration of the Supper keeps the church Christ-centered. Preachers preach on all sorts of things, quite properly so, because the Bible addresses all and everything. But all things cohere in Christ (Col 1:17). Whatever the sermon topic, the incarnation, death, resurrection, ascension and reign of the Son of God is at the heart of the sermon. The Supper keeps the preacher on point, forcing him to connect every topic or text to the central reality of Jesus.

A preacher may preach on the case laws of Exodus or the genealogies of 1 Chronicles, but then he has to stand at the table. Even if he doesn't say anything to connect the sermon to the Supper, the connection is made: The case laws somehow reveal Christ; the genealogies are part of the backstory of Jesus.

During Jesus' conversation with the disciples on the road to Emmaus, He tells them "everything concerning Himself in all the Scripture" (Luke 24). The whole Bible is about Jesus. But Jesus has a body, and so everything in the Bible that is about Jesus—which is everything—is also about His body, the church. And this Jesus, who is the center of Scripture and who has a churchly body, also offers His body and blood to us in bread and wine. Thus: everything in the Bible that is about Jesus—which is everything—also discloses some facet of the Eucharistic meal.

Jesus is the new Adam, and in Him we are a new Adamic humanity, admitted to the garden to eat from the trees of life and knowledge (Gen 2). Jesus is the seed of Abraham, and in Him we gather for a meal with the Triune God (Gen 18). Jesus tabernacles among us (John 1:14); His body is the temple (John 2:21), and so we gather to Him to eat, drink, and rejoice in His presence. Jesus is the new Moses, leading us out of Egypt and giving

Himself as true bread from heaven. Jesus is the Bridegroom, and the Supper is a love feast where the Bride feasts on the body of her Beloved (Rev 19:7).

The Supper isn't some marginal concern in Scripture, with a few cameo roles here and there in the Gospels and Paul. The Supper fulfills the main thread of Scripture and the history it tells. As we commune together in the Supper, that history becomes ours. We are knit into the biblical story as part of its ongoing unfolding.

FOR THE LIFE OF THE WORLD

When we have said all that, we still need to clarify why the Supper is so crucial to the formation of God's city. We need to explain why celebrating the Supper is a critical dimension of the church's response to the varied and ever-shifting crises of world history. We need to grasp that we celebrate the Eucharist for the life of the world.

In one sense, the answer is obvious: Jesus is the solution to the impotence of the church and the darkness of the world. When you communicate Jesus through the word to the people of God, you're offering the solution, the only solution, to this battered, sinful world. A congregation who eats and drinks at the Lord's table participates in the body and blood of Christ. Our union with Jesus is deepened. We are conformed to His death and share in His resurrection. We drink the Spirit and so are equipped to serve Jesus when we disperse.

We who share the loaf and cup become one body with Christ our Bridegroom (1 Cor 10:16–17). We go out as limbs and members and organs of the Lord Jesus. We go out as an extension of Christ in the world.

But we can say more. Many Christians have described the Supper as a Eucharist, thanksgiving, a name derived from Jesus' prayers of thanksgiving for the bread and wine (cf. Matt 26:27; Matt 15:36; Mark 8:6). When we share this Eucharistic meal, we're united with Jesus in His one great thanksgiving to the Father, offered in His cross and resurrection. United to Christ, we're formed by the Spirit to live lives of continuous thanksgiving for all things in all circumstances.

That's the only sane way to live. All that we have is gift, and so the only rational stance in life is one of constant thanks for the gift of every breath, every heartbeat, every good and perfect gift that comes from above. Sharing Eucharist, we become a different sort of people, a grateful people in the midst of a humanity that, like Adam, does not acknowledge God as God or give thanks (Rom 1:18–32). A thankful people is a people attuned to reality, reality as a gift of the Father through the Son and Spirit. By the Eucharist, we become a people that models genuine human life before the world.

The Supper has a horizontal as well as a vertical dimension. In it, the Spirit unites us to the Son of the Father; in it, the Spirit also unites us to one another. We participate in the body and blood of Christ as we eat and drink; we also become one body as we partake of one loaf (1 Cor 10:16–17). Through the Supper, the church becomes who she is—the new humanity united in the Son by the Spirit; the one people constituted from every tribe, tongue, people, and nation; the people of Easter and Pentecost. By common participation in the meal, we become the city that we are called to be.

We might say that the Supper depicts the redeemed human society that is the city of God. "Depict" is too weak. The Supper isn't merely a visible sign of an invisible society. The church gathered at the Supper is the city of God, more and more a living sign of the perfected city to come. At the Supper, the church is a sign that accomplishes what it signifies: Sharing bread, we signify the future city and are that future city in the present.

This cannot but be a rebuke to the Babelic cities of men. Every time we portray the heavenly city in the Supper, we call attention to the injustice, violence, greed, and wickedness of the earthly city. Every time we celebrate the Supper, we are reminded of our own evils and violence and are called to repentance. Through celebration of this meal, we become a city of witness, a witness against the fallen city because we are a witness to the city that is to come.

The cities of men are acquisitive, competing for scarce goods; at the table, the citizens of God's city share bread and wine, resources as infinite as the God who gives them. The cities of men are consumerist, finding their meaning in the abundance of goods; the city of God consumes the body and blood of Jesus and becomes what she eats. The cities of men marginalize the economically useless, the unborn and children, the mad and the handicapped; at the Lord's table, the city of God welcomes all sorts and conditions of men and gives more abundant honor to those without honor.

While they exclude, the cities of men congratulate themselves for their tolerance, endorsing whatever perverse pattern of life the imagination can devise; the city of God calls sinners to repentance so that the penitent can share in the bread of God, feasting in the Lord's presence without shame. The cities of men oscillate between an idolatrous attachment to things and gnostic hostility to matter; at the Supper, the city of God affirms the goodness of created things and the goodness of cultural products like bread and wine, which become means of communion with the living God. (That means, note, that our work itself becomes a means of communion.)

The cities of men are divided by race, culture, language, hatreds of centuries; the city of God doesn't erase differences, but unites people of every nation in the family meal of the Father, since the Spirit makes all of them brothers in the Son. The cities of men operate by power; the citizens of the city of God, gathered at His table, display His power made perfect in the weakness of cruciform witness. In the Lord's presence, kings kneel in penitence; at the Lord's table, kings share a meal with beggars. In the liturgy, the wealthy have no special status over the poor; at the Lord's table, rich and poor, men and women, elite and ordinary share a common meal.

FOR KIDS

Men and women ... and children. The children of the church should be included in the meal of the church.

Under Torah, there were various meals with various rules of access. Priests alone could eat most holy sacrificial food; their families were allowed to eat certain portions that no one else could eat; some food was available to anyone, priests and non-priests, who was in a state of purity (Lev 22).

No meal, however, included adult non-priests and excluded their children. Whenever an Israelite adult feasted before the Lord—at Passover, Pentecost, the Feast of Booths, with a peace offering at non-festival times—he brought his children along so that they could eat and drink and rejoice, "you and your children and your stranger who is within your gates" (Deut 12; 16).

Nothing in the New Testament changes this. If anything, Jesus intensifies the church's reception and love of children, by placing small children in the midst of His disciples as object-lessons, by welcoming the little children to His lap.

Paul's exhortations in 1 Corinthians 11 don't change this. Corinthians didn't become unworthy because they didn't have the right theology of the real presence or because they were too young to answer catechism questions. They were unworthy because of their divisiveness, because they brought their petty factions to the table of unity. Paul exhorts the Corinthians to reconcile with one another before sharing the meal of reconciliation with God. Nothing in 1 Corinthians 11 excludes children from the Lord's table. Small children are as capable of being at peace with their parents, siblings, and friends, as adults are.

Before you eat dinner, you wash your hands. For us, this is a matter of hygiene. For ancient Jews, it was a matter of ceremonial purity. Unclean Israelites were excluded from the courts of the sanctuary and its feasts, but the Lord kindly gave Israel rituals for cleansing. By washing his or her body and clothing, an unclean person is made clean, fit for an appearance in Yahweh's presence and at His table (Lev 12–15; Num 19). To use a Thomistic formula, the rites of purity were ordered to festivity.

In the new covenant, all those washings are concentrated in the single cleansing rite of baptism, which is as once-for-all as the cross of Jesus. Baptism doesn't just cleanse for a moment or for a few weeks. Baptism's power doesn't leak out over time. Because of his one baptism, the sinner is cleansed throughout his life, qualified to enter the presence of God, washed up for the meal.

The Supper isn't a bare sign of communion with Christ in the Spirit. It's the event of communion and a real present of the future city of peace. In the same way, baptism isn't a sign of an incorporation that takes invisibly, somewhere else. Baptism is the event of incorporation, an act of Jesus and His Spirit by which the Father adopts a person as a son or daughter. Baptism grafts the baptized into the body of Christ and makes him a priest in the temple of the Spirit. A baptized person might prove a wayward son, a cancer in the body, an unholy priest. But baptism is a gift of membership, the cleansing and sanctifying rite that makes saints.

We can close the logical circle: If children belong at the table, if we're to rejoice at the feast of the kingdom with our sons and daughters, then they've got to be washed up. If our children belong at the table of the Father, if they participate in the body and blood of the Lord, if they share the holy things as living stones in the temple of the Spirit, then they should also receive the effective sign of baptism.

The role of children in the church divides Baptistic Christians from others. It's not a minor issue. Whether we baptize babies or not, we're making a statement about the boundaries of the city of God. And not just a statement: The way we baptize, whom we baptize, shapes the kind of city we are.

Without children, the church is a club for the religiously mature. Without children, the feasts of the church are more restrictive than the feast of old Israel, as if God's hospitality had, unthinkably, contracted after the coming of the Son and Spirit. Without children, the church cannot be the new humanity that extends as far as the old humanity, from the cradle to the deathbed. Without children, the church is something less than the city of God. Without children, it may be a city under judgment, a city without children laughing in the streets and playing in the squares.

Liturgy: It's, you know, for kids.

SPIRITUAL WEAPONS

So far, we've been talking about the indirect effects of the liturgy on the world. So far, the target of the liturgy has been the church. Through the word, the Lord forms a people that lives within the biblical story, teaches His promises and commands, convicts and encourages. At the table, we're formed into one body by the Spirit as we eat one loaf and receive one cup. The liturgy gathers the heavenly city on earth, and through the liturgy we become more and more the city we're called to be. The Spirit employs word and table to form us into the city of God that renews the cities of men.

Without this—without a ministry of word and bread—the church is hungry and blind, stumbling in darkness. And a church in the darkness cannot be a light to the world. Through liturgical practice, we acquire new skills—skills of praise, prayer, thanksgiving, the skill of reading our world in biblical terms. These skills give us new powers of perception: We see what others cannot see, like the just hand of God in the collapse of a city, the shattering power of children singing, the glory of God in a crucified man.

Yet the liturgy also has a direct effect on the world because the citizens of God's city are also citizens and actors in earthly cities. If the liturgy changes us, it changes the way we live outside the liturgy. Or, to put it otherwise: For Christians, the whole city is a sanctuary, and all of life is liturgy. Monday through Saturday is an outflow and extension of Sunday, and the liturgy of the Lord's day imprints itself on week and work days.

Let's be concrete. A politician hears a sermon about justice for the poor, and he begins drafting legislation to assist them. A prominent businessman has succeeded by cutting corners, but after a sermon on Zaccheus, he repents and begins making restitution to the people he cheated. Hearing a sermon on loving one's neighbor, a manager in an auto plant changes the way he deals with his employees; an assembly line worker in the same plant is convicted of his ingratitude and laziness and strives to be a productive worker.

A politician shares the Lord's table with a homeless family and is inspired to seek remedies for homelessness in his city. Recognizing that the Eucharist calls him to a life of generosity, a Scrooge sets up a charitable foundation. That plant manager realizes that he should stop abusing the Lord's table companions, and that assembly line worker realizes that thanksgiving should extend to his daily work.

In short, the liturgy never simply targets the church. Even when it targets the church, it targets the church for the sake of the world. The liturgy brings us into contact with God, gives us a taste of future and heavenly things, shines on us the light of the future city. But we receive light to give light, to be like Moses, reflecting the glory we have seen to those around us, back into the cities of men. That glory will blind some; the aroma of Christ in us will smell like death to some (2 Cor 2:14–16). Citizens of the cities of men won't welcome us and may respond with hatred. But that's all to the good since it only enhances our communion in the cross of Jesus.

Besides all that, the liturgy includes moments and actions that reach beyond the walls of the church to change the world. I'm talking about prayer and praise, which may be treated together.

The church is the city of God called to carry out a mission of renewing the cities of men. The church is God's urban renewal project. We can't do this from our own resources because we have none. W have only what has been given. God renews the cities of men, and the church is nothing except what she receives from Jesus and His Spirit. She is nothing unless she is the body of the risen Christ and the temple of the Spirit. When we say "the church transforms the world," that always, always means "the Spirit uses the church to transform the world."

This is why prayer is so crucial to the church's role in the world. Prayer draws us near to God. Prayer exercises and increases faith. Prayer is one part of an ongoing conversation with the God who speaks. But in Scripture, prayer is most often a request for God to act. Prayer arises from dissatisfaction with the status quo. It's an appeal to God to change the state of affairs.

In Jesus' model prayer, He instructs us to pray not only for forgiveness and daily bread, but for the world: "Hallowed be Thy name, Thy kingdom come, Thy will be done on earth as it is in heaven." When we pray that prayer (and we should, preferably singing it), we are asking God to change the world so that blasphemous persons and nations begin to sanctify God's name, so that the kingdoms of this world become the kingdoms of the Lord and His Christ, so that God's will is as readily and thoroughly obeyed here on earth as it is by angels in heaven.

Jesus' prayer is like the prayers of the Old Testament, which are frequently prayers for Yahweh to intervene into the disorder to put things in order. Psalm 2 sets the tone for the Psalter, with its vivid image of the nations in uproar and the Lord's king on Zion. Psalms often ask God to judge the earth and praise Him when He answers the prayer. A jarring number of psalms include imprecations, prayers that call on God to curse or destroy His enemies. Psalm 72 lays out a vision of royal justice, and Psalms 50, 82, and 94 warn that God will correct political injustice.

In this respect if in no other, the liturgy has an inescapably political edge to it. We cannot pray as the Bible instructs us without praying for God to change the world, to bring justice and peace to the nations, to cast down unjust rulers and raise up faithful ones.

Importantly, we don't merely pray for amelioration of this or that particular injustice. Injustice can be built into political and cultural systems. Evil can be enacted by decree and become so habitual that it seems normal. Most Americans, for instance, live most days without a thought to the unborn infants being slaughtered a few miles down the road. We enjoy the comforts of home while our military engages in violent adventuring on the other side of the planet.

When we pray for justice, we pray that God will bare His arm to break systems with a rod of iron and shatter them like earthenware. This is part of the church's urban-renewal mission: Unjust systems must be torn down so that just systems can be established. So we ask the living God of perfect justice to do just that.

If we're not praying like that, we're not praying as we ought. If we're not praying like that, we're not praying like the city of God among the cities of men.

SINGING PSALMS

The Psalms should be the model prayers for the church. And the church's song should center on singing Psalms. Until quite recently, it has. Christians in the New Testament sang and prayed the Psalms. From the time of St. Benedict to the present, monks sang through the entire Psalter every week. Protestants paraphrased the Psalms for congregational singing or included Psalm chants in their prayer books or wrote hymns that were based on Psalms.

Many churches today sing virtually no Psalms. If they sing Psalms at all, they sing a few lines, detached from context, lines that express a particular emotion but neglect the political rough-and-tumble, the anguish and desperation, that is so prominent in the Psalter.

Few items on the church's to-do list are more important than this: The Psalms must become the church's primary hymnal.

The Psalms express the full range of human experience and emotion. There are psalms of unutterable joy ("we were like those who dream"), psalms of ungodly anguish ("My God, My God, why have you forsaken Me?"; "darkness is my only friend"; "out of the depths I cried"), and everything in between. Without the Psalms, we're reluctant to speak openly in the presence of God. We are reluctant to be emotionally honest with God, to tell Him to His face how disappointed we are when His promises don't come to pass. Without the Psalms, we typically descend into infantile fantasizing, using worship music to buoy us up with glib happiness rather than to face the evils of the world, rather than face up to our own temptation to despair. Without the Psalms, we have no words to speak our pain, and so we are reduced to silence.

If we neglect the examples of Psalms, we would never think to sing a hymn like Psalm 83, which calls on God to turn His enemies to fertilizer ("dung" in the precious language of most English translations; better rendered as "shit"). Do these violent psalms reek of masculine bravado? Hardly. If you're looking for some really bloodthirsty lyrics, check out the songs of Miriam (Exod 15), Deborah (Judg 5), Hannah (1 Sam 2), and Mary (Luke 1). The Bride of the Lamb rejoices in His victories.

Liturgical music isn't simply a matter of individual or corporate expression. We sing in order to fulfill and mature in our vocation as priests, kings, and prophets in Christ, the high Priest-King and chief Prophet. Music is a sacrifice of praise. Through music, we ascend in our own breath and body (not through the blood and body of an animal) to the presence of God. When we sing, we circle the cities of men with trumpets and voices, shouting until the walls fall flat (Josh 6). Faced with an invasion, Jehoshaphat called out the choir (2 Chr 20), who sang and played until the invaders were destroyed. When we as the priestly city lift up the Lord on our praises, the Lord terrorizes our enemies.

We sing as warriors of the greater David, the sweet royal singer of Israel who defeated evil spirits with a lyre and learned to fight with his fingers (1 Sam 16; Psalm 144). As we sing in the Spirit, the Spirit who gripped and clothed Gideon, Samson, Saul, David, Jesus, Peter, and Paul arms us for spiritual war. Huguenots aroused the hatred of Catholics by marching through the streets singing Psalm 68: "God shall arise and by His might, put all his enemies to flight. In conquest shall He quell them." Like them, as we offer our breath in song, we are being prepared to offer our blood in witness. Our songs ascend so that we might follow, ascending to be enthroned with Christ in heavenly places.

When Yahweh commissioned Jeremiah, He told him that His words would plant and uproot, establish and destroy (Jer 1:10). Jeremiah's prophetic words had divine power, the power to undo and remake worlds, the power to create and destroy. In song, we prophesy (cf. 1 Chr 25:1), shattering worlds and building new ones. If that seems like an exaggeration, think of how opera shaped radical movements in nineteenth-century Europe or of the revolutionary power of rock 'n roll, which pulled out the foundations of 1950s America and created the world that we inhabit.

The music itself must be suitable to the words. Sweet melodies have their place, but they can't carry the weight of words like Psalm 94: "Rise up, O Judge of the earth! Render a reward to the proud!" The church has her own musical tradition, which is the deep source of the tradition of Western music. Too much church music today takes its cues from pop culture, which produces commercialized music. Pop music has its place, but that place isn't in the liturgy.

Church musicians and composers should certainly write new music, updated settings for the Psalms, and hardy new hymns. But they should first immerse themselves in the Christian musical tradition.

TO THE READER

If you're who I think you are, you want to make a difference. You want to be part of the solution to the impotence of the church and the darkness of the world. You might be tempted to think that to do that, you need to find some outside activity, something beyond the mundane ministry of a local church. You may think you need to blog (don't! blogs are old news!), become active on Twitter and Facebook, speak at conferences, or become a political advocate and activist.

Some Christians are called to that kind of ministry. God regularly raised up celebrity leaders in Israel—Gideon, Samson, Samuel, David, Elijah and Elisha, Isaiah and Jeremiah. And every believer should be alert to the many opportunities for witness outside of the local church. But you don't have to do any of those things to make a difference, a big difference, the biggest difference.

If you're a pastor, when you teach the Bible to the gathered people of God, preside at the Lord's table, lead the church in an ascent of praise to the throne of God, pray on behalf of the world, you are at the center of the universe. The very center.

If you're not a pastor, you're still at the center of the world every week, and your work there is as crucial as the pastor's. The liturgy is the work of the whole people. Every time you gather with other real men and women and children with real bodies as the body of Christ, the word of God that brought this world into being remakes you so that you, remade, can go out to renew the human city.

Every week, you are conformed more to the dying and living of Christ as you share His body and blood; every week, you make this dying and living out to the world. Every week, you pray that the Lord of all would bring in His justice and peace. Every week, you praise God with priestly sacrifices of song and are filled with His royal and prophetic Spirit to act and speak with Spiritual power.

Twitter might get you more followers, and an interview on a local newscast may serve the interests of justice. But those activities are far at the margins. The church is a city whose walls are equal in length, breadth, and width. The church is a liturgical city. As the sanctuary, Jerusalem is the center of the world, and those who are called to serve and receive God's word and God's food, those who sing and pray in the presence of the King, perform the most important activity known to man. The Spirit equips us with His power so that we go out from the sanctuary to kill and to heal, to destroy and to make alive.

3

City of Light

AND THE CITY HAS NO NEED OF THE SUN
OR OF THE MOON TO SHINE UPON IT, FOR THE GLORY
OF GOD HAS ILLUMINED IT AND ITS LAMP IS THE LAMB.
AND THE NATIONS SHALL WALK BY ITS LIGHT.
—REVELATION 21:23–24

The Spirit sweeps John to the top of a mountain where he can survey the heavenly city descending to earth. He's like Moses, David, and Ezekiel, prophets who glimpse the heavenly pattern that is to be fulfilled on earth. He relays that vision to the first-century church, to the seven churches of Asia and the believers in Jerusalem and Rome who are beginning to feel the earth quaking beneath their feet.

Like Moses, David, and Ezekiel, he relays that vision in language. To realize the ideal city, the church has to conform to a pattern of *words* (2 Tim 1:13).

This is the essence of what's called "typology." It's not merely a way of reading the Bible, but a theology of history and a claim about the relationship of heaven and earth.

Heaven is the original, the "archetype." God created earth according to the pattern of heaven so that from the very beginning, creation is a copy or "ectype" of heaven. At the beginning, the copy isn't completely conformed to the original. It's like a child's drawing, and it's supposed to become more and more like the archetype. God placed Adam and Eve in the world to glorify it so that it fulfills its destiny as a copy of heaven. Through godly human action, the heavenly archetype presses itself, like a signet on a glob of wax, onto earth.

The world matures through words. It matures as God speaks and His people hear and obey. As we receive and believe the living, creative word of the Creator, we're conformed to Jesus, the heavenly man (1 Cor 15). When we live as doers of Jesus' word, the world itself is conformed to heaven. Our prayer is answered: God's will is done on earth as it is in heaven. God does it, but He does it through us.

John expresses this in his vision through the imagery of light. The word of God created light (Gen 1:3–4) because the word *is* light (Ps 119:105). Ultimately, the Word of God is God, the God who is with God, the Word that is the life and light of men (John 1:1–5). That's the light that illumines the city, the light of the glory of God and the Lamb (Rev 21:23).

Because the Word dwells in the city, because the words of the Word are spoken in the city, the city shines with light. When the citizens of the heavenly city keep the commands of Jesus, we become light that shines before men and brings glory to the Father. Full of obedient citizens, the city is a light on a hill (Matt 5:14–16), and the nations are drawn to the light and walk in the light (Rev 21:24). Isaiah's vision of Zion is behind John's description of the city. In Isaiah, it's the Torah that beams out to draw the nations and turns them peaceable (Isa 2:1–4).

Only as the city of the Word can the city of God serve and transform the cities of men.

New Jerusalem fulfills Jesus' urban renewal project only if we are a city guided by the light. Let's think through this, starting with basics.

THE GOD WHO SPEAKS

God speaks. That's one of the most fundamental teachings of the Bible. God speaks on the first page of Scripture, speaks a world into existence and then commissions creatures, issues commands, pronounces judgments and curses.

When we get to the New Testament, we discover that Word isn't something secondary to the life of God. The God of the Bible wasn't a God of eternal silence before He spoke the *fiat lux*. In the beginning was the Word, and the Word was toward God, and the Word was God (John 1:1–3). The God of the Bible doesn't *happen* to speak. He is Himself, eternally and essentially, *Word* and *Breath* as well as Speaker.

God speaks *human*. He addresses human beings in human language. We don't know what kind of communication occurs in the eternal conversation that is the Father, the Word, and the Breath. But we know God can communicate with human beings. We don't know what language God spoke when He told Adam and Eve to be fruitful and multiply and fill the earth, or when He prohibited Adam from eating the fruit of the tree of knowledge, or when He told Adam that he would eat by the sweat of his brow and Eve that her pain in childbirth would be multiplied. We do know He spoke a language they understood.

The Word became flesh and dwelt among us, living a fully human life from womb to tomb and beyond. Long before, the Word entered into human discourse, speaking to Adam, Cain, Noah, Abraham, Hagar, Isaac, Jacob, Joseph, Moses, Gideon, Samuel, David, Solomon, Jeremiah, Ezekiel, Daniel. He doesn't speak some esoteric perfect language. To humans God speaks human.

God's human speech can be recorded in written form. Yahweh Himself wrote on tablets of stone with the finger of His Spirit (Exod 31:18), and Jesus the incarnate Word wrote in the dust (John 8:6). More often, God's speech takes written form as the Spirit carries saints to record God-breathed words (2 Pet 1:20–21). Some Christians want to distinguish the words of Scripture from the thoughts God wishes to communicate. According to this view, the ideas Scripture communicates are from God, but the words are human words. Paul won't have any of this: The *Scriptures*, he says, are breathed out and so are useful for every good work. The *writings* come from God, and so they are reliable and true, sufficient to equip the man of God for every good work (2 Tim 3:16–17).

The writings come from God, and that means the forms and patterns of Scripture are part of the truth God communicates. We need to pay attention to the structures of Scripture, the recurring narratives, the twists and turns of its poetry, its puns and metaphors. The form of Scripture isn't a human carrier of the divine word. The form is God's word to us.

Some Christians say that the Bible speaks truth in relation to spiritual realities but is an unreliable witness to history, the sciences, or the social sciences. A quick glance at the Bible will show that this is a ruse. It's very, *very* difficult to find anything in Scripture that deals with exclusively spiritual or heavenly realities. On the face of things, the Bible purports to be about history, *this* world, real human beings in real human situations, human beings in relation to God, the Creator and Lord of the covenant. Scripture includes a chronology of the ancient world, one that runs from the creation right through the ministry of Jesus and the apostles. The Bible describes events in the history of Israel, in which Israel often intersects with other ancient peoples. It focuses on a particular piece of land with hills and rivers and seas and cities that can be found on maps.

If the Bible is an unreliable witness to history, then it's unreliable full stop, and we ought to can it.

Some Christians worry that we can't express the ineffable realities of God in human language. In the nature of the case, they say, human talk distorts the infinite God; at best, human language gives us only the slightest glimpses of God as He truly is. We can be far more confident about what God is *not* than about who or what He *is*.

There's a bit of truth here. We don't know all there is to know about God, and never will. But that doesn't imply He can't reveal Himself truly in human language. To doubt that God can speak truly to us is another manifestation of the old nature/

supernatural dichotomy I discussed in chapter 1. It assumes that creation is an obstacle to God's efforts to communicate with us, a veil that screens off God from His creatures. It's as if God's speech gets distorted as soon as it begins to vibrate the air with sound waves, as soon as it takes the form of ink marks on parchment.

That's not the biblical view of God's speech and its relation to created media. God created the world to manifest His glory. That's what the universe *is*, a created radiance of the uncreated glory of God. Creation isn't a veil between God and us; at its deepest essence, it's a *vehicle* of communication. God created the vibrating air; as Lord of air, He can shape it to His purposes, shape it to communicate exactly what He wants to communicate. God the Word created a speaking world, which speaks of him. And God the Word speaks into that speaking world.

SOLA SCRIPTURA

I'll come back to this point about creation, which is an exceedingly important one for understanding both the Bible and creation. For now, let me pursue another point: God's words are the words of the *Lord*. If God speaks and writes, then those spoken and written words carry the authority of the speaker and writer. It won't do to say, "I honor the authority of my parents, my pastor, my government, but I don't have to obey what they *say*."

Authority is *always* exercised through words. Honoring authority means honoring the words that authorities speak. If we bow to the authority of God the Lord, then we bow to the authority of His Word. His Word is the ultimate Word, bearing ultimate authority. If anything contradicts the Lord's Word, it must be false. Every other authority has to submit to the authority of the Word of God.

This conviction is the basis for the Reformation's dispute with Rome. It's the essence of *sola scriptura*. The Reformers didn't reject other authorities. They acknowledged the authority of the church fathers, of the church's creeds and traditions, of the church's liturgical heritage, of the church's pastors, as well as the authority of rulers outside the church—parents, kings, masters. But they insisted that *all* these authorities had to submit to the higher authority of the Word of God. No matter how venerable the tradition, no matter how widely believed or practiced, if it contradicted the Word of God, it had to be changed.

Augustine might have defined justification as "making-just," but if that's not what Paul meant, then even the most august of church fathers has to be corrected. Aquinas defended transubstantiation and the veneration of the consecrated Host, but if those don't measure up to Scripture, they must be revised or discarded.

Sola scriptura isn't naïve about the role of human interpretation. God speaks human, and the human language He speaks and writes has all the possibilities and limits of human language. Biblical Hebrew and Greek aren't magic languages that somehow elude the ambiguities and gnarled knots of normal human languages. We don't come to understand God's written word by a sudden bolt from the sky. We study the text, unearth what we can about the language and historical context of the text, puzzle over the oddities and inescapable ambiguities in the text, listen to and debate with others, including ancient brothers who read the same Scripture we do.

To say that interpretation is necessary, though, isn't to say we can never know what the text means. To say that interpretation is necessary doesn't mean that the interpretive process is a barrier God can't break through. We must interpret, but that obvious fact doesn't undermine the basic reality: When God speaks human to humans, He communicates. His Word gets through. Through our study, prayer, meditation, debate, with all our limits and errors, the Spirit who carried the writers carries the church to understanding.

Sola scriptura is ultimately a statement about Jesus' lordship over His church. The question is this: Can Jesus speak to His Bride to correct and guide her? Or are all the words that the church hears simply the words of the Bride? Are preaching, theology, commentary, teaching no more than different ways in which the Bride talks to herself? Is the church's speech a monologue or a dialogue?

In the midst of history, the Bridegroom's voice is contested. The Bride talks back, and there are plenty of pretenders to the Bridegroom's role, slick serpentine suitors who would seduce the Bride. In the midst of history, the Bride's hearing is partial and self-interested. She tends to hear only the voices she wants to hear.

But the question remains: In the midst of all this, does the Bridegroom have an independent voice? Can the Spirit speak to and in the church? Once the question is put this way, we can again see that this question comes back to the old nature/supernatural problem. To say that human interpretation prevents Jesus from addressing His church is to say that nature is closed to the Word that comes from beyond nature. Or, it's to say that God cannot overcome the Bride's deafness. That's to say that Jesus is not the healer He seems to be. And that's to say that the kingdom has not come, and we are still in our sins.

Sola scriptura is a confession that Jesus is Lord. As Lord, He must be able to correct and renew His church by His Word. He must have an independent voice in the church. That voice is the voice of Scripture, the written word in which we hear what the Spirit of Jesus says to the churches.

SCRIPTURE AND PROTESTANT TRADITIONALISM

Ask the Reformers. They'll tell you that clinging to the authority of the Word isn't always safe. It's dangerous to challenge long-held traditions in the name of God's word. It can get you crucified.

This is one reason why Protestants, while professing *sola scriptura*, don't always practice it. Protestants too can become traditionalists, as locked into our confessions as Catholics are to the papacy and the magisterium. If we're serious about *sola scriptura*, we need to ask questions like: Is it possible that the Reformers didn't grasp everything that the Bible says about justification? Is it possible that we may discover new things in Paul's letters, things that the Reformers missed? Is it possible that we've gained fresh insight into Scripture over the past five centuries?

Even when Protestants get things right, our theology is often guided by extra-biblical categories. Debates about the Eucharist, for instance, often become philosophical debates about the real presence, which explore the nature of symbolism, the relation of matter and Spirit or of heaven and earth, the semantic question of what "is" means in "This is my body."

Those are important questions, and we need to address them. But the Bible doesn't present the Lord's Supper in these categories. Paul never forgets that the Supper is a *meal*, celebrated by the church. He never uses a zoom lens to focus on the bread and the wine, as if they could be isolated from the people who are eating and drinking.

The Bible sets the Lord's Supper in the context of a rich theology of food, one that begins with Adam in the garden, runs through Abraham's meal with God through the Passover and the manna and the feasts of Israel, to the promise of a feast spread on Zion, a promise fulfilled in the movable feast that is the ministry of Jesus. These biblical events, categories, and images provide the categories for our understanding and practice of the Supper. We get closer to the base-line level of the Supper's reality when we say, "We feast like Mephibosheth at David's table" than when we say, "A sacrament is a visible sign of an invisible grace" (something the Bible never asserts).

This is one illustration of a more general point: Theologians often treat the Bible as if it were a collection of raw data to be mined, polished, and organized into a system of theology. Preachers treat the Bible as a book of illustrations and moral principles. We read the Bible as if it were a sacred version of Aesop's fables, full of stories designed to illustrate doctrine or to set an example for Christian living or, these days, to illustrate the single message that God's grace extends to wretches like Noah, Abraham, Isaac, Jacob, Samson, and David. This last reading is a profound *mis*reading: Noah, Abraham, Isaac, and, yes, Jacob, Jephthah, Samson, and David are heroes of *faith*

(Heb 11). If they're examples, they're chiefly examples of how we *ought* to live.

Even if we interpret these stories correctly, though, it's a mistake to treat the Bible as a collection of moralizing tales. If we do that, we miss the main thrust of Scripture. The Bible is a record of public history, from creation and fall to the consummation when the bridal city completes her procession from heaven to earth. That historical, *this*-worldly focus should be reflected in the way theologians go about theology and in the way pastors go about their teaching and preaching. The emphases of Scripture should be the emphases of our teaching and preaching.

I affirm predestination, but the Bible says a great deal more about politics than it does about predestination. I believe believers enter heaven at death, but the Bible teaches a lot more about animals than it does about the heavenly state. If we're going to preach, teach, and write about the Bible as it is, we'll have to say a lot more about land, gardens, sex, bodies, architecture, barrenness and birth, death and impurity, war and geopolitics than we normally do. We'll have to unlearn the habit of spiritualizing the visceral contents of Scripture.

We need to allow ourselves to be confronted and corrected by the Bible. We should submit to the Bible and strive to hear *what* it says to us, *how* it says it. We should strive to make Scripture's emphases our own and to let the Bible speak on its own terms rather than forcing it to speak in the idioms and patterns that we're used to. The Spirit unmakes us, including our speech and thought, so that He can put us back together. Don't resist the un-making. Don't quench the Spirit.

Of course, there are *always* heresies to confront, always false teachings to battle. Historically, much of the church's theology and teaching has focused on contested issues—the Triune nature of God, the relation of divine and human in Jesus, the way of justification, the nature of sacraments and the church. Of course, those are still proper topics for theologians and pastors to teach, for Christians to study. But we shouldn't think that we've mastered the Bible when we've mastered these contested questions. And we shouldn't let our diet of Scripture be restricted to passages that deal with those issues.

In our day, the perversions and confusions surrounding sexuality are one of the major battlegrounds for the church. False teaching about male and female, transgenderism, sodomy and lesbian sin, abortion, and extra-marital sex must be combatted head-on. A theologian or pastor who dodges these issues is unfaithful.

But we need to resist the temptation to fight these battles with a few key texts, while missing the Bible's overall teaching. We need to study to discover what the Bible's actual teaching is on these subjects, working within biblical categories and patterns rather than from cultural assumptions, philosophy, social science data, or pressing culture-war questions.

A huge swathe of the Bible is about sex—from the creation of man as male and female and the invitation to become one flesh, through the laws of the Torah and the escapades of various kings and the allegories of the Song of Songs and the prophets, through the ministry of Jesus to women and His rescue of His Bride, with whom He becomes one flesh, to the consummation in the marriage supper of the Lamb, when the Bride and Bridegroom are joined forever. If we want to cultivate healthy Christian sexuality, we need to grasp as much of that as we can.

THE BIBLE SPEAKS TO EVERYTHING

Scripture carries God's own authority, which is why the psalmist of Psalm 119 virtually worships the Torah (v. 48). *All* of Scripture is God's authoritative word to His people and to the world. We're not allowed to skip what we think of as the boring parts or the parts that we find difficult. We'll miss some essential teaching about worship if we skim lightly over Leviticus. We won't understand how to apply the Ten Commandments without working through the Book of the Covenant, Leviticus, the laws of Numbers, the book of Deuteronomy. We won't grasp what Revelation is talking about unless we have spent a lot of time in the numbingly detailed final chapters of Ezekiel.

The authority of Scripture isn't limited. We can't squeeze what Scripture teaches into some narrow category we think of as "religious" or "spiritual." The Bible is authoritative about everything it touches on, and it touches on everything.

Scripture makes claims about the origins of the universe: God created the heavens and the earth by His Word, over the course of a week. It makes claims about ancient history: Abraham left Ur in Chaldea to follow the call of God. It makes claims about human beings: We are good creatures of God, created as male and female, called to rule other creatures; through one man's transgression, sin entered the world, and death through sin, so that all sinned. We are created lower than the angels, but in Christ have been elevated above angels.

The Bible makes claims about linguistic, cultural, and religious diversity: Babel was a crucial episode in this history. The Bible makes claims about politics: A large chunk of the Old Testament amounts to a political history of Israel, Paul talks about the "powers that be," and John sees the Roman empire revealed as a terrifying beast from the sea.

When we formulate our opinions about political issues, we reason from Torah as well as other portions of Scripture. When a Christian politician puzzles over a policy issue, the Bible speaks authoritatively to it. Our understanding of the purpose of wealth, the nature of property, our responsibility to the poor and immigrants, and the limits and aims of property have to be guided by what the law, prophets, Jesus, and apostles say about wealth (which is a great deal).

The Bible doesn't tell us how to build a widget, but it tells us a lot that informs our widget-building. It tells us *why* we labor, teaches us to devote our widget-building energies to serving our neighbor, commands us to be honest in our widget-building, requires us to love the widget-builders beside or under us. Sometimes the Bible's instruction is very general: Whatever you do, whether you eat or drink, do all to the glory of God (1 Cor 10:31). Sometimes, it's very specific: If someone slaps you on the right cheek, turn the other cheek (Matt 5:39). General or specific or somewhere between, Scripture speaks to all people in every circumstance.

There is nothing in human life outside the authority of Scripture. If Jesus is Lord of all, He governs *all* by His Word. That means there is no space that's safe from a turf war between Jesus and other authorities. Scripture challenges the status quo, calling for repentance, calling us to die and rise. If Jesus is Lord of all, there are no Scripture-free zones.

THINGS CONCERNING JESUS

At the heart of the Theopolitan vision is a way of reading, studying, and teaching the Bible. Scripture has a universal scope. In it, God speaks with authority to all of human life—what we are to believe, how we are to live as individuals and as societies, what we are to expect in the future.

But the Bible has a focal point, a center. It's a record of human history, centered on the history of Israel. That history comes to a climax in the life, death, and resurrection of Jesus. Jesus is the principal character of Scripture. The Bible is *His* story, and His life is the hinge of the ages, the turning point of world history.

Scripture's single, complex history can be disentangled into three strands. It is a story of *redemption*: Adam sinned and was cast from the garden, but God promised a Savior. God called Abraham and chose Israel to be an instrument of redemption, to bring the savior into the world. After a long and uneven history, God fulfilled His promise by sending Jesus, who gave Himself on the cross for the sins of the world and was raised for our justification.

The story of the Bible is also a story of *holy war*. God placed Adam in the garden to guard and tend it. Adam failed when he allowed the serpent to seduce and deceive Eve. Adam's sin was a failure to make war on the serpent. But God promised a Seed who would crush the serpent's head, a son of Adam who would be a faithful holy warrior.

Throughout the Old Testament, the Lord sent many saviors to rescue Israel, His Bride: Moses, Joshua, Gideon, Samson,

David, Hezekiah, Josiah. But these dimly foreshadowed the Holy Warrior who was still to come. Jesus combats Satan directly, in the wilderness and at the cross, when the prince of this world is cast out. Because of Jesus, Satan falls from heaven like lightning, and the dragon falls to the earth. Jesus gathers an army to battle alongside Him, head-crushers and giant-killers, who carry on His holy war until the end of the world, when the dragon, the serpent of old, will finally be thrown into the lake of fire.

The Bible is also a story of *maturation*, the growth of humanity from Adamic infancy to new-Adamic maturity. Adam was a newborn when he was placed in the garden, not yet ready for the solid food of the tree of knowledge. He was created a priest in the garden-sanctuary, but through battle with the serpent was supposed to train as a king. Adam failed as priest and was thrown from the garden, but God's plan to raise humanity from childhood continued. God still intended to raise the children of Adam from priests to kings to prophets.

Paul says that Israel was like a minor who is heir of a great treasure (Gal 4:1–7). So long as the heir is a child, he's treated like a servant, under angelic guardians and managers, under the tutelage of the law. When the Son comes into the world, He brings the children to maturity. Jesus brings many sons to glory (Heb 2:10), to raise us onto thrones, so that we can share in His rule over the creation. Through the Last Adam, we're set on track to complete the first Adam's task of dominion. We're set back on track to grow up to mature humanity.

We can tell the story of the Bible in each of these ways and in many more. However we tell the story of the Bible, we tell it as a story of *Jesus*, of preparation for Jesus, the coming of Jesus, and the church's participation by the Spirit in the work of Jesus.

Jesus isn't just the end of the story. He's unveiled *throughout* the story. As Jesus told His disciples after His resurrection, everything in Moses, the psalms, and the prophets concerns Him (Luke 24). The Old Testament is a complex tapestry of types and shadows of Jesus in His suffering and glory.

Every major protagonist of the Old Testament reveals something of Jesus. Jesus is the Last Adam, the head of a renewed human race. Jesus suffers at the hands of His brothers as Abel died at the hand of Cain. Jesus is the true Seed of Abraham, the true Isaac, who dies and rises. Jesus is the new Joseph, who suffers in patience until He is exalted to rule and give bread to the hungry world. Jesus is Joshua, conquering the land. Jesus is a new warrior king like David, a sage on the throne like Solomon, a child-king rescued from death like Joash. He is the rebuilder of the temple, like Joshua and Zerubbabel, the builder of city walls like Nehemiah.

Every office and institution of the Old Testament foreshadows Jesus. Jesus is a priest of the order of Melchizedek, a priestly order superior to the fleshly priesthood of Aaron (Heb 7). Jesus is great King David's greater Son. Jesus is a miracle-working prophet like Elisha and a weeping prophet of doom like Jeremiah. Jesus tabernacles in human flesh, and His body is the temple. Jesus' death is a sacrifice, fulfilling all the offerings of the Levitical system.

The Old Testament doesn't merely give us momentary snapshots of Jesus, but also records sequences of events that foreshadow the life and ministry of Jesus. Again and again, Old Testament characters experience an exodus. They're exiled from the land, prosper in the midst of oppression, and finally escape slavery with much plunder. Abraham, Jacob, Moses himself, and David all experience exodus. Israel goes through two exoduses, from Egypt and then from Babylon. Luke tells us that Jesus comes to lead an exodus (Luke 9:31), which leads from sin and death but also from the doomed people of Israel. Martyrs above the firmament sing the song of Moses, having experienced an exodus from earth to heaven (Rev 14–15). The disciples of Jesus troop out of Judaism as Israel marched from Egypt, bearing the oracles of God as plunder.

What I've been describing is what is traditionally called "typological" reading of Scripture. It's analogous to the literary technique of "foreshadowing." Early in a novel, an author drops hints of later episodes. God, who writes with events and not merely with words, foreshadows the final act in earlier acts. The New Testament writers read the Old Testament this way, as a foreshadowing of what God has done in Jesus and through the church. We should learn our method of interpretation from the apostles.

Sometimes, though, typology becomes a method for transposing the earthly and historical events of the Old Testament into a heavenly and spiritual key: Old Israel was a polity, but the church is a spiritual reality. The exodus was an earthly rescue, but it foreshadowed the spiritual salvation Christians experience.

That way of reading is another manifestation of the old nature/supernatural dichotomy: The Old Testament is about natural Israel, and the New Testament is about supernatural salvation.

That's not how the Bible works. Jesus is just as material as Moses. His death is as real as any Old Testament sacrifice. The salvation He achieves is as this-worldly as the rescue of Israel from Egypt or Babylon. Jesus rescues from Satan and sin. But sin shapes systematic cultural and political systems, what Paul calls "principalities and powers." Jesus delivers from social malfunctions, political oppression, cultural perversions and incorporates us into the realm of the Spirit who forms the social body of new Jerusalem, God's city.

Nor is typology some effete aesthetic imposed on, and designed to evade, the hard realities of history. To read the Bible that way would again manifest a nature/supernatural dichotomy. Typology isn't a literary device, a flourish on the factual surface of the text. Typology is about the shape of history. Typology isn't just about the *telling* of history. A typological reading unveils the pattern in the tapestry of historical events themselves.

God works in regular patterns. Again and again, history runs through a similar sequence—a pattern of seven, a movement of exile-and-exodus, death-and-resurrection, fall-judgment-decline-final judgment-recreation, separation and reunion. As we read the Bible, we develop a feel for the rhythms of history, which are God's rhythms.

Creation itself is a set of types and shadows of God. God speaks light into existence, light that makes visible the eternal light that He is. He shapes light into sun, moon, and stars so that these physical realties manifest the light and glory of God. God creates rocks because He is the Rock of Israel; some rocks contain light. God created man as His image to more fully reveal His character.

Creation is a manifestation of the glory of God, not in some general way but in the specific ways that Scripture explains and expresses. The Bible forms us into a people who grasp reality as it is. The Bible enables us to hear the tune of the times. The Bible gives us new eyes to see reality as it truly is, as a revelation of the glory of God. The Bible enables us to live in a world of symbols, which is the *real* world.

TO THE READER

Theologians and Bible scholars often think that they're the primary teachers of the church. They're wrong.

Theology and biblical scholarship are ministries of the church, which means that scholars are servants of pastors, preachers, and people. Theology doesn't come to its climax in a plenary lecture at the Society of Biblical Literature or in a paper published in *Modern Theology* or in a widely-reviewed book that wins a *Christianity Today* award. Theology and biblical scholarship come to their climax in the liturgical assembly of the people of God, where a pastor delivers the word of the Lord to the people of God at the Lord's table.

To you theologians and scholars, remember that you serve the church, its pastors and its people. And to those who are pastors, theologians exist for *your* sake, to assist you as you do the really big work of theology. Don't let them belittle you.

And to those in the pews: The whole apparatus of Bible study and teaching is for *you* so that you can be shattered and reborn by the hammer of God's Word. The Word of God is the light of God, and everything that comes into light is light (Eph 5:13). If you receive the light of the Word, you're being made over into a light source. As you obey the word, your good works shine before the nations.

New Jerusalem can be a city of light only if *you* are lights, witnesses through the Spirit in suffering and glory. New Jerusalem draws and guides the nations only if *you* are lit by the Word.

You want to make a difference, a big difference, the biggest difference? Hear the word, believe the word, sing the word, speak the word, obey the word, and the Spirit will ignite you as the city of light shining out in the darkness.

4

Angels at the Gates

IT HAD A GREAT AND HIGH WALL WITH TWELVE GATES, AND AT THE GATES TWELVE ANGELS.

—REVELATION 21:12

God formed Adam from the ground and placed him in a garden east in the land of Eden. Yahweh told him to guard and serve the garden (Gen 2:15). We find out later in the Bible that guard duty and service are Levitical and priestly responsibilities (cf. Num 1:53; 3:10; Deut 10:8). Adam was a priest in the garden, a watchman who protected Eve and the garden itself from intruders.

When Moses built a tent-garden at the foot of Sinai, Aaron, his sons, and the Levites took up Adamic guard duty. Non-priests and unclean people had to be kept away from the house of Yahweh. If the house got polluted, Yahweh would abandon it and leave Israel as prey to vicious gentiles.

In the new covenant, that Adamic-Aaronic task belongs *especially* to pastors. In John's vision of new Jerusalem, there are angels at the gates. They permit kings to bring in their treasures (Rev 21:24) but screen out impurity and abominations (21:27).

Earlier in Revelation, Jesus sends messages to the angels of the churches of Asia (Rev 2–3). These *must* be pastors and overseers rather than spiritual beings: Why would Jesus *write* to spiritual angels? From those messages, we see that Jesus holds the angels responsible for the state of the church. The angels should drive out the Balaamites and followers of Jezebel. They need to deal with the Nicolaitans. They need to keep the churches faithful, to awaken the drowsily complacent Laodiceans who are neither hot nor cold.

In John's final vision, the angels are also human beings, shepherds who guard the flock, watchmen who keep the city, even to the point of laying down their lives.

New Jerusalem is a liturgical city, a city of the Word, a city of light. But she remains so only if there are angels at the gates, only if these angels are equipped and faithful.

HEIRS OF AARON'S ROD

The church is a real-world society of real men and women and children with real bodies and souls. This visible communion of people—the Bride and body of Christ, the family of the Father, the temple of the Spirit—is an outpost, an effective sign and real present, of the future city of God.

The future city is the new creation, a new heavens and a new earth, joined in marriage to the Lamb. As I've emphasized, new creation isn't simply future. Jesus brought salvation into the world, and that salvation takes human form as a communion of forgiven and Spirit-filled men and women and children. Heaven and earth are *already* joined, and the church is the historical form of that union. The church is salvation in historical form.

The church doesn't exist for her own sake, but for the sake of the world. The mission of the church is to be herself, God's city. Because she is God's city, she is whisked up by the Spirit into the mission of Jesus. As new Jerusalem, she exists to bring life to the nations. She is on a mission from God, an urban-renewal mission.

The church's mission includes evangelism in the narrow sense of proclaiming the gospel to individuals, baptizing them into the Eucharistic community, discipling them in the church, equipping them to serve the Lord Jesus. But the mission of the church is bigger and broader than that. As individuals believe the gospel and become citizens of God's city, the cities of men are transformed. As the church lives in the light of the word, the city becomes a beacon to the nations. God's light shines from the city of God into the cities of men, and whatever is in the light is light (Eph 5:13). The cities of men begin to shine, however dimly, with the glory of God and the light of the Lamb.

But that's not all. The church also exists to disciple cities and nations. As the body of Christ animated by the Spirit of Jesus, the church calls the kingdoms of this world to become the kingdoms of the Lord and of His Christ. Political, social and economic structures are to be infused with the gospel. Cultural values are to take on the shading of faith, hope, and love. The words of Scripture are to be translated into musical notes, paint, wood and stone, poetry and story. Kings and civic leaders are to imitate the humility of Jesus and, like Jesus, defend the interests of the least of their subjects.

No city in this age, in this time between the first and final Advent of the Son, will ever perfectly conform to the city to come. No human society perfectly embodies the gospel and conforms perfectly to the word of God. That includes the church, which will always be a people on the way, always beset with enemies within, always a church militant.

However imperfect, the church *is* the body of Christ, the family of the Father, the temple of the Spirit, the reality of salvation as well as a sign of a salvation to come. However partially, the cities of men that come under the influence of the church do begin to resemble the heavenly Jerusalem.

That is a breathtaking vision. I hope that it takes your breath away. But the next step is even more breathtaking: The weapons of the church's warfare, the tools of her construction, are baptism and teaching in the Eucharistic community. Jesus gives the church a bowl of water, His commandments, a loaf of bread and a jug of wine, and then He says, "Go at it! Make disciples of the nations! Build the city of God in the world! Bring the life of the city of God to the cities of men. Renew the city. Light the nations. Suffer with Me, witness to Me, triumph in Me. You've got water, My word, bread, and wine. *What more could you possibly need*?"

This doesn't seem reasonable. If the church is going to fulfill the planetary mission of Jesus, we think, surely she needs something more than *this*. She needs a strategic plan, a lobbying consultant, a PR firm, a web site, Facebook page, a Twitter account. She needs to have some tactics for taking, holding, and wielding *real* power in the world.

Jesus isn't reasonable. He promises to go with us by His Spirit; He is the Captain of the Host, but the armies that follow Him have only spiritual weapons. The church carries out her mission to the world by bringing out the hidden treasures of God's house. The city of God transforms the cities of men by being herself, a community of word and table.

But notice that there's a third item hidden in the inner sanctuary. Along with the tablets of the law and a jar of manna is the rod of Aaron the priest (cf. Num 17). When we get to that third item, we begin to see how human beings fit into the program.

The word doesn't teach itself. Sermons don't preach themselves. The Spirit doesn't directly reveal things to every individual. God has chosen to build up His people through teachers. Jesus has chosen to address His church by equipping *pastors* to speak on His behalf.

Bread doesn't serve itself, and wine doesn't pour itself. The liturgy doesn't happen on its own. It must be *led*. At the Lord's table, someone has to take Jesus' part, blessing and breaking bread, giving thanks for the cup and passing it out.

Teaching happens all the time. Parents teach their children. Sunday school teachers teach. But there are angels in the church, pastors who are ordained to teach. If you're a pastor, you're commissioned by Jesus to teach your church everything that Jesus commanded. Other people can baptize. Sometimes, the church celebrates the Supper without a pastor. But *you're* designated and equipped by the Spirit to do these things.

Do you realize what this means? The book and the bread are the most potent powers in the world. The word of God called the universe into existence, and you get to wield the word of God among the people of God. You get to proclaim the new-creating gospel. The bread is participation in the body of Christ, and the cup is participation in the blood of Christ, and Jesus put that bread in *your* hands so you can serve Christ to the gathered people of God. The book and the bread are the most powerful weapons in the arsenal, and the Commander of the church has entrusted them to *you*.

So much depends on good pastors. Pastors are the sinews and ligaments of the body of Christ. Without pastors, the church is a flabby mess. It has no structure. It has no vision. It flounders. It cannot be God's city or carry out His mission of urban renewal.

"Pastor" means "shepherd," and in the Bible a shepherd is a *king*. Moses the shepherd did what Adam didn't: He fought off enemies and protected the bride (Exod 2:17). David—the David who defeated Goliath, drove out Philistines, was a terror to surrounding nations—David shepherded Israel (Ps 78:70–72). Yahweh is the ultimate Shepherd, who defends and leads His flock with a mighty hand. Jesus is the Good Shepherd who battles false shepherds to the point of laying down His life for the sheep. When the church has no shepherds, or weak and vacillating shepherds, she is prey to wolves, false shepherds, and dragons.

If you're not willing to confront the sins of the church and culture, don't take a step toward the pulpit. If you can't endure the backlash from your congregation or the world outside, don't pretend to preach. If you're not ready to fight, don't become a pastor. If you're a pastor and have given up fighting, repent or resign.

Or, try this picture: Paul calls himself a wise master builder (1 Cor 3:10), equipped by the Spirit, like Bezalel and Oholiab (Exod 36:1), to make God's tent. As pastor, you're a general contractor under the greater Solomon, overseeing the construction of God's city in your own city. Build with the right materials. Hay, straw, wood will be burned up as soon as God stokes a fire in the church. But if you build with gold, silver, and precious stones, the fire will just make them shine brighter.

A church without faithful pastors can't do what Jesus wants the church to do—be the city of God among the cities of men, the light to the world, the discipler of nations. Jesus is the Good Shepherd. He will guide and lead and protect His church even when wolves take over. But that's not normal practice. Normal practice is for Jesus to guide and lead and protect His church through men like you.

Pastor, your calling is gigantic. What do you do?

AT THE TABLE

Every Sunday, you get to lead the people of God into the presence of God so they can hear His word and feast at His table. Every Sunday, you stand at the center of the universe, in the Most Holy Place, to bring out God's treasures. Every Sunday, you lead the church in spiritual war in preaching, prayer, song, and Eucharist. Every Sunday, you edify (= "build") the city of God and equip the saints to carry out the urban renewal movement that is the church's mission.

Leading the liturgy has some theatrical elements to it. You need to learn to speak, move, gesture in a way that is appropriate to the occasion. Tossing off "This is the body of Christ, given for you" in a casual, perfunctory manner suggests you don't believe what you're saying.

But the liturgy isn't theater. You aren't playing at something. You're doing something. At the command of Jesus, you're gathering the church in the presence of God, leading them in confession, teaching them the Scriptures, and breaking bread with them, the one loaf that knits them together as the one body of Christ. You lead the church as she becomes what she is—a present outpost of the future bridal city.

Several moments of the liturgy are critical. By a pleasing serendipity, each can be named with a word beginning with "C": Call, Confession, Consecration, Communion, Commission.

I. THE CALL IS THE LORD'S invitation for people to gather in His presence. It shouldn't be taken for granted. We ought not to sashay into God's presence, sipping a latte and chatting about the football game. In the liturgy, we enter the presence of the living God. He's *actually* there. He is our Father, but He is also Lord and Judge. We appear before Him, in part, to stand for inspection. It's your privilege as pastor to summon people, to extend the Father's invitation to His children, the King's invitation to His courtiers.

II. WE ENTER THE COURTS of the Lord with joy. We also enter His courts with fear. We know we have sinned. We know we're unclean, and need to be washed before we can come to His table. In the Old Testament, Israelites went through repeated washings. We receive only the one baptism for forgiveness of sins. But each week, that one baptismal washing is refreshed. As pastor, you have the duty to remind the congregation that they need forgiveness. As pastor, you have the privilege to call the people of God to *confess* their sins.

That means that you have the privilege of establishing the liturgy as a zone of transparent honesty in a world of spin, scapegoating, and blame. Few things are more crucial for the health of God's city than this. The church should be one place on earth without subterfuge or dodging. It's called to be the city of truth.

It's the city of truth because it's the city of forgiveness, the city of expiations. After leading the people in confession, you have the privilege of assuring them that they *are* forgiven. You pronounce absolution, telling those who have confessed that God has heard their prayers.

Some pastors hedge. Some liturgical traditions turn the declaration of forgiveness into a further prayer. Some are laden with conditionals that undermine assurance ("*if* you repent"—but I thought I just did!). Don't do that. Speak forthrightly. Say "I declare to you that your sins are forgiven" or, more boldly, "I, as a called and ordained servant of the Word, forgive your sins."

It's not pride. You're not forgiving by your own authority. You speak with the authority of Jesus. Speak like Jesus. He breathed His Spirit on His disciples so they could forgive sins in His name (John 20:22–23). Every believer has the same Spirit, and so each has authority to forgive sin. But you as pastor have a particular responsibility and privilege: You get to declare *public* absolution to the people of God in the public liturgy. You get to announce that the city of truth is a city of mercy.

Israel went through a series of purifications at the foot of Sinai. They washed their clothes and bathed their bodies and offered offerings. Only then did Moses ascend to the cloud. Christians still need cleansing before we ascend. That's what confession is for: If we confess our sins, God is faithful and just to forgive our sins and cleanse us from all unrighteousness (1 John 1:9–10).

III. Having been cleansed, we ascend. This is our *consecration*. In the new covenant, the one who ascends the mountain is Jesus, the greater Moses. Unlike Moses, He doesn't leave us at the foot. When He ascends, He takes us, His body, with Him. We haven't come to Sinai but to the heavenly Zion, to the assembly of angels and the hosts of heaven (Heb 12:18–24).

Somewhere in most of the historic liturgies, the pastor and congregation exchange these words: "Lift up your hearts. We lift them up to the Lord." It's a small thing, but its implications are monstrous. It's a little sign that we enter the presence of God in heaven. Like John, we hear the trumpet voice of the call, and the Spirit snatches us up to join the liturgy of the future.

This is *real*. Heaven and earth join in the liturgy. That's what makes the liturgy an effective sign of the kingdom. That's what makes the assembly of God's city a real presence of the future city. That's what makes it possible for new Jerusalem to be a light of new life among the cities of men.

This is mysterious. The liturgy is a mystical experience in the truest sense. But let's keep this concrete. What does this ascension look like? In Levitical worship, an animal was killed and dismembered, then turned to smoke. As smoke, the animal entered the presence of God, bringing a sweet-smelling savor and covering the stench of sin. We don't offer animals. Anointed by the Spirit, we're enveloped in the fragrance of Christ. In Him, *we* ascend as a sweet-smelling savor.

What do we observe as the *church* ascends? No animals, no fire or smoke. We observe the church ascending as a sweet-sounding *song*. Song is the sacrifice of praise (Heb 13:15). Song is the ladder of ascent. Israel sang "Psalms of ascent" as they walked the dusty road up to Jerusalem; so too we sing as we ascend to heavenly Zion. We sing as we process into the Most Holy Place to receive God's gifts.

At the mountaintop, the Lord speaks. That means *you* speak. You speak in the name of the Lord. Jesus authorized you as His spokesman. You'd better stick to the script. This is such an important part of a pastor's work that I've devoted a separate section to it below.

Somewhere in the liturgy, you lead the people in prayer. Every Christian can pray, of course. But the liturgy is the act of the whole church. Pastors are ordained to act on behalf of the church. Prayer, as I've explained in chapter 2, is one of the chief weapons of our warfare, one of our chief tools for urban renewal. God hears and answers and acts on our behalf. We pray in accord with God's promises, and He keeps His promises. We ask that His justice and peace would prevail among nations. We ask that he would break the teeth of bestial men and regimes. We ask that He would avenge the blood of His saints. We pray for the peace of the city. He hears and does what we ask.

IV. YOU'RE NOT DONE WHEN you're done with the sermon. You're not done when you've offered a pastoral prayer. There's still *communion* to come. In fact, the whole service is a Eucharistic service. The whole liturgy is an ascent toward joy, the joy of the wedding feast.

You get to stand in for Jesus, the host of His table. You get to do what Jesus did. And you *should* do what Jesus did. Sometimes that means you shouldn't do what the church's liturgical tradition says you should do. Some liturgies tell you to consecrate the bread and wine. Some tell you to set the elements apart for holy use. Jesus, though, *blessed* the bread and *gave thanks* for the cup. His prayer was Eucharist, thanksgiving (Matt 26:26–27). True, Paul says that we sanctify all of God's gifts through prayer and thanksgiving (1 Tim 4:4). So Jesus did sanctify the bread and the wine by giving thanks. You should consecrate the way Jesus did, by offering thanksgiving.

Jesus prayed *two* prayers, one for the bread and one for the cup (cf. Matt 26:26–27). So should you. Jesus broke the bread, passed it out, and all ate. Jesus blessed the cup, passed it out, and all drank. Two separate prayers, two separate distributions, two separate acts of consuming.

Churches tend to mash all that together. The pastor offers only one Eucharistic prayer or dips the bread into the wine so both are consumed together. Does it matter? It mattered if an Aaronic priest reversed the order of an offering, eating his portion before offering the Lord's portion on the altar. It mattered a lot: That's one of the "great sins" that got Hophni and Phinehas killed (1 Sam 2:12–17). The God who dictated Leviticus from Sinai, the God who killed Hophni and Phinehas, took flesh in Jesus. He's the same God, with the same concern for liturgical precision. Best to be on the safe side: Do what Jesus did. Do *exactly* what Jesus did.

V. THE CITY OF GOD gathers for covenant renewal. The church is called into assembly, openly confesses sin and receives forgiveness, ascends in song to heavenly Zion, where she hears the word and feasts at the Lord's table. That builds the church. In the liturgy, the city of God is most fully herself. And in the liturgy, the city of God is repaired, built, glorified so that she becomes more like the city to come.

Yet the church doesn't gather for her own sake. She prays on behalf of kings and all sorts and conditions of men. She gathers in the presence of the glory to be transformed into the image of glory. The church gathers before God so that she becomes a mirror of His beauty. In the *commission and benediction*, you have the privilege of sending the people of God back out into the world, back down the mountain, to love and serve Jesus the Christ. You send them out with the blessing of God so that the church, dispersed, can carry on the urban renewal project that is our mission.

PREACH THE WORD

If you don't know it now, you'll know it soon enough: The demands on pastors are back-breaking. You're supposed to inspire joy during festive seasons and mourn in repentance during seasons of penitence. You enter every scene of carnage—death, sickness, divorce, bankruptcy, abuse and shame—and every battlefield—husbands *versus* wives, parents *versus* children, employer *versus* employee, member *versus* pastor—and you're supposed to have something challenging or comforting to say.

All these demands can be intimidating, even overwhelming. There is no bottom to the damage your people do to themselves, to one another, to strangers, no limit to the harm they suffer. You're called to labor in the infinite abyss of human misery.

You might have trouble figuring out what you're supposed to do next, how to prioritize your time. That's why you need to keep yourself focused on the main things you are called to do and be. You are a servant of Jesus Christ, a minister of the Word and Sacraments, ordained as a leader of Christ's church to teach, preach, and lead worship. That's the way you carry out the royal office of shepherd, your role as an angel at the gates.

Your work is work in the Word. Don't let that slide. Whatever you do, don't stop reading, praying over, tarrying with, meditating on, and studying the Bible. Don't think you've got it all down because you've been to seminary. Don't think that you can have an effective, godly ministry by cutting corners, by devoting your time to what might seem more effective activities. You have one book to master, the book that is designed to master you.

You are called to teach the Bible. The *Bible*, and not some other authoritative text, not some message that would be deemed relevant by the editorial board of the *New York Times*, not anecdotes about your cuddly kids or your sex life. *The*

Bible. When you teach every Sunday, you should be teaching Scripture, explaining it to the real men and women and children who are listening.

Here's what you want to do, every Sunday: Explain what the text says, what it's about. Teach the people the basic, literal context of Scripture. Show them how the passage reveals Jesus, because everything in Scripture says something about Jesus.

Tell them how the passage affects them. They are in Christ, and so every passage that teaches about Jesus—which is *every* passage—teaches something about their lives as disciples. You don't need to come up with "Dos" or "Don'ts" every Sunday. You don't have to give them a list. But everything you teach them should affect the way they lean into and live in the world. The church's trust in the word and obedience to it constitute the best reading of Scripture. The life of the people is where the Bible comes to be real.

Sometimes you need to give them dos and don'ts. In a world where everything goes, where God's commandments are ignored, even by many Christians, you must say what the Bible says. You need to say what the Bible says even if it's controversial and politically incorrect, even if you'll get attacked.

Try this: Scripture takes for granted the reality of slavery and regulates it so that it conforms to God's justice and mercy. What Jesus said about divorce no doubt applies to slavery: It exists because of the hardness of people's hearts. Over time, the church rightly strove to abolish slavery entirely.

Yet neither Moses nor Paul is an abolitionist. The accent in Torah is on freeing slaves: Having been delivered from the house of bondage in the exodus, Israel was to imitate Yahweh in liberating slaves and the oppressed.

Otherwise, the law regulates slavery to bend it toward social goods. An indebted man works off his debt by becoming a bond-servant. That serves everyone's interests: It restores the creditor's loss. It enhances the dignity to the debtor because he is able to pay his debt. If the creditor is conscientious, he'll use the time of servitude to help his servant learn to live as a free man so that he won't slip back into slavery in the future. In six years, he has to go free, unless he wants to remain in his master's home forever.

Judged by biblical standards, American slavery was evil: Slaves were kidnapped and sold to slave traders; they weren't allowed to go free; and their masters often denied them the training and tools they needed to live as free men and women. Judged by biblical standards, most historical forms of slavery have been wicked.

But that doesn't change the facts on the page: The Bible condemns certain forms of slavery but permits others. That's what the Bible *actually says* about slavery. We should probe these passages to learn how Christians should deal with contemporary slavery (it still exists!) and to gain wisdom about how to address other social evils.

Say any of that in public, and people will stop listening and start shouting. You'll get attacked as a bigot and a racist.

Or try this: Start preaching through Leviticus 18 and 20. Most everyone will accept the rules of incest, though some will blanch when they discover that God imposed the death penalty for certain forms of incest. When you get to sodomy, you'll get everyone's attention. Yahweh calls it an "abomination" when a man lies with a man as with a woman. Paul says that same-sex passion is unnatural, a sign that God has given a culture to its destructive desires (Rom 1:18–32).

Even once-straightforward, once-commonsensical teachings of Scripture have become controversial. "Male and female created He them." "Be fruitful, multiple, fill, subdue, and rule the earth." That sounds like hate speech to many today. But the Bible says these things, and pastors must say what Scripture says. You're angel-messengers at the gates, and you must relay the message of your Master.

Don't provoke controversy for the sake of provoking controversy. Don't exaggerate the harshness of the Bible for effect. Study hard and deeply so that you know what the text actually says. Remember when you're teaching on homosexuality or transgenderism or greed that you may have church members who battle disordered desires. Teach in a way that encourages them to overcome their shame and seek your help.

Yet, having covered all those bases, don't shy away from preaching and teaching the whole Bible, every last puzzling or appalling syllable. Everything in Scripture is about Jesus. Every word is the word of the living Word, who is the life-giving Word. Trust every word. Teach every word.

Often, you should aim your sermon at the imagination more than at the will. You don't merely want the congregation to *act* differently. You want them to see the world through Bible eyes, to recognize the patterns of history that Scripture reveals, so they can discover new and surprising paths of faithfulness.

Finally, you want to remind them of what they have to hope for. If every text reveals something about Jesus, it reveals something about what is yet to come, since Jesus is the once *and coming* King. Encourage them to hope for God's deliverance and aid in this world as well as in the next. Encourage them to expect the kingdom of God to grow into a mountain that fills the earth, to rise to be chief of the mountains, and encourage them to find ways to fit into God's great movement of re-creation. Encourage them to hope that God's city will transform the cities of men.

Whenever you pick up a Bible to teach, teach your listeners what they should believe, what they should do, what they should hope for. Teach them to seek the Spirit's fruits of faith, love, and hope.

THE CATHOLIC PASTOR

Then it's Monday. Now what?

You've got to get another sermon ready. You have administrative commitments. You have Bible studies to prepare and deliver. You have members to counsel. You have coffee scheduled with an unbeliever you met during an evangelistic campaign. You have visits on your calendar. You have meetings and meetings and more meetings—meetings with the treasurer, meetings with the deacons, meetings with the elders, meetings with the pastoral staff, meetings with the pastor for meetings.

Through it all, don't lose sight of the purpose: You're an angel at the gate. You're the head of the local suburb of the heavenly city. You're there to build, repair, and guide God's city, to make it shine with the light of heaven, to make sure that refreshing water flows out. That's what all those meetings and visits are for. Don't be satisfied with preserving enough stability and peace so you can get your next sermon prepared and have evenings off. You're a city builder. You're a specialist in urban renewal. You're not a caretaker. You're called to be a culture-maker, and the first culture you cultivate is your church.

Primarily you do that through your teaching and liturgical leadership. But your teaching has to become particular and personal. You don't merely speak to the congregation on Sunday. You speak to individual men and women and children throughout the week. A lot of that conversation takes the form of encouragement, comfort in sorrow, even small talk.

Unlike lawyers or doctors, you don't have a professional area. You don't specialize in caring for their bodies, or for their legal problems, or their taxes and annuities, or for their parenting and vocation. You don't simply care for their spiritual life or their piety. You watch over their souls, which means you care for their *lives* in all their dimensions.

You especially watch over their souls when they're threatened with death. If you have a specialty at all, it's a specialization in death, big deaths and small deaths, the thousand natural shocks that flesh is heir to. When someone is sick, they call the doctor—and you. When a member is in legal trouble, they call the lawyer—and you. When someone loses a job, they consult with an employment agency—and you.

When a couple is having marital problems, you're the counselor of first resort. When one of the kids is drifting or rushing toward ruin, they expect you to have something to say. When an aging parent is dying, you're there with the hospice nurse. When a young woman is dying too young, you're there to weep with those who weep. In the emergency room, in the troubled home, with the battered wife or the abused child, at the lawyer's office, in court—you're there through it all.

In it all, you speak the Lord's word. You speak for Jesus. You *are* the presence of Jesus. You're called to call them to faithfulness in the midst of their anguish. You're a witness, and you're called to show them how their circumstances, no matter how devastating, present opportunities for witness.

Apart from moments of crisis, you're called to guide the members of your church to Christian maturity. You suggest how they can cultivate the gifts of the Spirit so that each becomes the fullest possible version of himself, making the fullest possible contribution to building God's city. You need to study the members of your congregation to discover their passions, interests, talents. And you should direct them toward work, within the church and without, where they can flourish.

This is one of the key ways the city of God transforms the cities of men, as pastors deploy gifted members to strategic locations in the world and guide those men and women to use their gifts effectively. As pastor, you urge members not only to ask, "How can I make a living?" or "How can I support my family?" You urge members to ask, above all, "How can I use my gifts to do the work of Christ in the world? How can I love God and my neighbor in my vocation? How can my gifts contribute to building the city of God and renewing the cities of men?"

These aren't one-way conversations. I use the word "deploy" to capture the military dimension of the pastor's role. But of course you don't simply give orders: "You, there, you're good with numbers. You're an accountant." There is give-and-take as you help them discover their gifts. Throughout those conversations, you have an agenda—to direct their attention to asking how their gifts are gifts to the church and the world. You must keep re-directing them to this question: "How can I live and work as X in a Christ-like way?"

The members of your congregation are sent into the cities of men to disrupt, to derail the wicked ways of the world. Don't encourage them to go along to get along, to slip easily into dehumanizing and debilitating systems. Encourage them to be faithful witnesses even if they bear financial, vocational, or reputational costs as a result. Teach them to expect opposition and that the suffering they endure is a privilege of disciples. Teach them to count themselves worthy to suffer shame for the sake of Jesus. You are a witness, a martyr, leading a company of martyrs.

That's all part of the catholic vocation of the pastor. You don't do everything, either in the church or in the world. You aren't a one-man congregation, and you aren't a one-man city. But your work has a universal scope. Through the people you serve and teach and train, you send out the light and life of God into every corner of the city of man. Pastoral ministry is intensively catholic.

This isn't a dream. It's not a vague hope. This is God's plan. The Father sent the Son and Spirit to renew individuals, societies, creation, everything. Through Christ, everything is made new. New creation breaks in.

Prophets see this as a restoration of the garden: When the Spirit is poured out, people are given new hearts of obedience, and the desert blossoms like Eden (Ezek 36). When the Spirit is poured out, the broken city rises from the dust. In the last days, the days of Jesus' reign, the mountain of the house of the Lord rises to be chief of the mountains. The law flows out, the nations stream in, and they learn peace. Lambs and lions lie down together. Children play beside snakes' nests (Isa 11). The nations beat their swords to ploughs and stop making war (Isa 2).

When you form a communion of witnesses, you're carrying out the Lord's catholic program of universal redemption.

Your work is catholic in another sense too. Since the eleventh century, the church has been divided east and west. Since the Reformation, the western church has been divided between Roman Catholics and Protestants. Early on, Protestantism split between German and Swiss varieties and has continued to split into ever-smaller subdivisions since.

We must say it bluntly: This is *not* what Jesus wants for His church. Jesus asked His Father to make His disciples one, one like the Son is one with the Father and the Father with the Son. The Father is in the Son and the Son in the Father, and Jesus wants the church to be united in the same fashion. He wants the church to be a visible, human, communal manifestation of the unity of Father and Son. The disciples of Jesus can be one in this way because the Spirit takes us up into the unity of the Father and Son. They are in us, and we are in Them (John 17), and so we may be in each other.

In this prayer, Jesus is simply asking that His Father complete the work He began with Abraham. Even without sin, human beings would have developed in a variety of ways. Some would have settled near the sea and become traders; others would have farmed. Some would have been in cities, some in the country. Cultures and languages would have developed differently. Sinless Eskimos would still have their umpteen words for snow. Yet the human race would have been at peace, the different languages and cultures in harmony. Without sin, different interests and values would not have led to war.

That's not what happened. When he sinned, Adam was estranged from God. He was also estranged from his wife, and in the next generation one of his sons murdered the other. Ten generations later, the world was so filled with violence that God ended it all with the flood. Even after the flood, human beings rebelled. At Babel, they attempted to unite the human race, but in defiance of God. In response, God scattered them, confusing their languages. The linguistic, cultural, and religious diversity of our world is touched by the sin of Adam and Babel. Whatever legitimate diversity there is sours into hatred and bloodshed.

After Babel, God didn't wipe the world clean as He had done in the flood. Instead, He determined to renew the world from within. He called Abraham and promised that in his seed all the nations of the earth would be blessed. They would remain different. They would retain their cultural customs and linguistic habits. But they would all be brought under the blessing of God. And they would live in harmony. This promise to Abraham is the source of the prophetic visions of global peace.

Jesus is the seed of Abraham, the one in whom this promise, like all promises, is fulfilled. Jesus broke down the dividing wall between Jew and gentile. In Him there is no Jew or gentile. At Pentecost, the Spirit provided the antidote to Babel. The Spirit makes it possible for the gospel to be understood in every one of the confused tongues of Babel. The Spirit didn't erase linguistic differences. He harmonized those differences. Gathered by the Spirit, the body of Christ consists of people from every tribe, tongue, nation, and people. The church is the new human race, a diverse yet harmonious city.

Or, she *should* be.

Not all church divisions are wrong. Sometimes, churches become synagogues of Satan, and true believers need to flee. Sometimes, churches switch sides and begin to persecute the faithful. The Harlot who drinks martyr blood is a false church (Rev 17).

Not all church conflicts are wrong. Conflicts are unavoidable, and often good. Sometimes the gospel is under attack, and pastors especially must defend it. Sometimes heretics and unbelievers take charge, and the faithful need to fight. Until the new Jerusalem is consummated as a new heavens and new earth, the church will know war.

This isn't unfortunate. It's one of the fields of Jesus' holy war. It's one of the privileges of being with Jesus: We get to fight alongside Him. Some divisions are the result of our stage in history—the fact that we haven't crossed the finish line yet. The city is still under construction, still descending from heaven.

Yet when we're honest, we realize that many of the church's conflicts are not like this. Many of them are manifestations of pride, lust for power, jockeying for prestige or fame. Often the church divides because she follows the national, cultural, and tribal divisions of the world. American Christians support American wars against European Christians. The Pentecostal church, called to be a city of peace and harmony, mirrors Babel. The Bride stops listening to the Bridegroom and gets seduced by a serpent. For centuries, many Christians have refused to seek or preserve unity. For centuries, the church has betrayed herself and her Lord.

You're called to work in whatever ways you can to overcome these divisions and pursue unity in the church. That means at least this: You should have a catholic understanding of the church. That means you should recognize that the church is universal and all congregations are part of the same global communion.

Practically, it means you should receive all other believers from every church at the Lord's table. The table belongs to Jesus, and the church has no right to exclude someone whom Jesus accepts. Catholics, Orthodox, Protestants, Pentecostals, and every other coloration of Christian should be at the same table as the one Bride of the one Husband.

It also means this: Don't receive anyone as a member of your church who has been disciplined by another church. The other church may be wrong; they may be a cult. But don't take anyone's say-so. Check with the previous church. Honor other pastors as servants of Christ.

But this pursuit of catholicity can take many other forms. Get to know the other pastors in your neighborhood or town. Visit them, talk to them, listen to them, pray for and with them. Ask them for prayer requests, and pray for their needs during public worship. Look for opportunities to worship and serve together. Have an annual communion meal together with as many churches as you can get.

Most towns in the U.S. have pastors' associations where pastors from various churches meet regularly for a meal and fellowship, perhaps for prayer. That's a wonderful thing and a sign of the unity of the church.

But it's only a beginning. Together, the pastors of the churches are the guardians of the city. They are the "angels" at the gates of new Jerusalem (Rev 2–3), messengers and spokesmen for God. And pastors are guardians of the city of man in which they minister. Pray together to discover ways to fulfill this vocation. Invite city leaders to visit the pastors' association. Visit the mayor and ask him what the city needs. Visit the police chief, the fire chief, the city attorney, the city controller. Pray for them, pastor them.

You represent God's city within the city, and you lead the urban renewal project that is the church's mission. Be alert to the city's needs—food deserts, high crime, gang violence, poverty and unemployment. Pray and plan with other pastors about how the churches can help to address these needs.

Jesus wants His church to be united. He also wants His church to be pure. We aren't allowed to choose one over the other. We're called to seek unity in truth, as well as the truth of unity. Fighting heresy and false teaching is part of unifying the church because false teaching and idolatry are the fundamental sources of division.

The pursuit of unity is disruptive in itself. Don't think that you can pursue unity without riling up other Christians. Denominational traditions become so engrained that churches view any deviation as apostasy. It becomes nearly impossible to admit that my tradition might have gotten some things wrong or that I have something to learn from Christians outside my church. If you're a Protestant pastor and you start fraternizing with Catholic or Orthodox priests, expect other Protestants to protest.

Don't let the protests deter you. Fight for the truth. Fight for unity. Fight opponents of unity with as much vigor as you fight enemies of truth.

The rewards are great. As the church expresses her unity, she becomes a real alternative to the fractured, polarized city of man. As the church acts on this unity, she brings out the leaves of the tree of life, which are for the healing of the nations. As you fulfill your role as a catholic pastor, you are an angel at the gate.

TO PASTORS

Pastoral ministry is a demanding job. It's a big job, than which none is bigger. It's not for the lazy or time-servers. It's not a calling for cowards. It requires all the fruits of the Spirit—passionate, relentless love, love that is patient, humble, courageous, cunning.

But it has rewards. These rewards rarely take the form of fame and fortune. Instead, pastoral ministry comes with the reward of sharing in the ministry of Jesus by the Spirit. Sharing Jesus' ministry means the privilege to suffer shame for His name

(Acts 5:41). It comes with the reward of sharing in Jesus' grand construction project, His work of transforming the cities of men into the city of God. In that work, you are a foreman. Get to work.

But there might be a hitch. Perhaps this vision of pastoral ministry inspires you. Maybe you want to have weekly Eucharist, but you can't persuade your elders or the people even to use the word "Eucharist." Perhaps you want to pursue local unity among the churches but fear reprisals from other pastors in your denomination.

Real life can be frustrating to reformers. Don't give in to frustration. Minister to the people in front of you. Serve their needs. Teach, correct, disciple, pray for them. Lead them into the Lord's presence in worship. Plant seeds of renewal in the church, and wait for the Spirit to water and grow them. Even if the church isn't all you hope for, even if the church appears embarrassingly feeble, so long as you are faithful, you're building God's city.

Jesus is the Lord of His church and will guide it as He pleases. Trust Him, and be patient.

5

Treasures of Kings

THE NATIONS SHALL WALK BY ITS LIGHT,
AND THE KINGS OF THE EARTH SHALL BRING
THEIR GLORY INTO IT. ... AND THE LEAVES
OF THE TREE [OF LIFE] WERE FOR
THE HEALING OF THE NATIONS.

—REVELATION 21:24; 22:2

Many of you are pastors. Many more of you are not. With such a stress on the role of the pastor in chapter 4, does the Theopolitan vision have anything left for the non-pastor? Is the Theopolitan vision a latter-day form of clericalism?

Not at all. The church is a visible community of real-life men and women and children with real bodies and souls. It's a city among the cities of men. John's vision makes it clear that new Jerusalem is the whole people of God. The gates are named for people—the twelve tribes of Israel (Rev 21:12). The foundation stones are named for people—the twelve apostles (21:14).From Peter (1 Pet 2:9–10), we know that the church's walls are made from living stones—people, church members.

That's implicit in the materials that make up the foundation stones. The foundations of Jerusalem are precious gems, twelve of them (21:19–20). In the Mosaic system, the priest wore a breastplate with twelve gems, each of which was engraved with a name of a tribe of Israel (Exod 29). New Jerusalem is a Bride dressed like a priest, and her gemstones, like the priest's, represent people.

Throughout Scripture, the houses of God represent the people of God. The tabernacle was modeled after the garden of Eden and Mount Sinai. It was also an architectural representation of the people of God. When Nebuchadnezzar took Judah into exile, the temple, its furnishings, and its liturgical tools went into exile too (cf. 2 Kgs 25). Those furnishings and tools represented the people of Israel devoted to Yahweh's service.

I've assumed throughout this book that new Jerusalem in all its details is a description of people. It's a liturgical city where the people of God gather. It's a city of light because the Word is preached there. The water that flows through and out of the city is the Spirit, who carries men and women from the city into their mission in the world.

So the Theopolitan vision isn't a vision of *pastoral* ministry alone. It's a vision of the church in the world and of the church's mission in and to the world. It's a vision of the church, the *whole* church, as God's heavenly city on earth.

As a city, the church has an order. That order is inherent in the church, not some add-on pasted on the outer wall. The order has a hierarchical aspect: Some are leaders, most are not. That hierarchy is inherent in the church, not some visible accident on an invisibly egalitarian substance. The church is a city, God's city, God's future city in the present, and cities are organized communities with responsibility and authority distributed in unequal measure.

That doesn't exclude lay men and women any more than stressing the need for good political leadership rules out the role of citizens. The two are necessary to one another, mutually defining. Without shepherds, the flock wanders, but without a flock, what's the use of a shepherd?

Besides, the hierarchy of the church is a complex, mobile hierarchy. There are leaders, but the leaders lead a community of the gifted. *Every* member shares the same Spirit that equips the leaders to lead wisely and well. *Every* member receives gifts from the Spirit that are necessary for edifying, building up, the body of Christ. Each member is an organ of the body that serves the needs of the entire body. A member may see, hear, smell, handle, walk, or speak, but he or she does it for the sake of the whole body.

A pastor is a spokesman in the church, the mouth of the body of Christ. With respect to public, liturgical speech, there's a hierarchy with the pastor at the peak of the pyramid. Yet the pastor's speech is hardly the only speech in the church. His speech is priestly speech, speech that establishes foundations; it's angelic speech that guards gates. But within those gates, people speak in prayer, praise, teaching, correction, rebuke, encouragement, sympathy. In many situations, the pastor's speech isn't at the peak. Often, the pastor *listens*.

To speak effectively, the pastor relies on other organs. If the church is going to be more than talk, it needs to be more than a big mouth. It needs hands to serve, feet to go, chests to fight. When we think of the church as a teaching body (which it is), the pastor may be seen as the honcho. When we think of the church as a ministry of mercy (which it is), the women in the soup kitchen take the lead. When we think of the church as a house of prayer (which it is), the old lady in her prayer chair is chief.

This isn't an egalitarian community of interchangeable parts. It's a body of many members, with a complex, oscillating hierarchy that depends on the activity and perspective.

All that is to say that you non-pastors are as essential to the church as your brothers who are pastors. You are essential to the liturgical work of the church. *You* are the body, called by Jesus and equipped by His Spirit, to build yourself up into the full stature of Christ. *You* are the army deployed to bring the kingdoms of the world into the kingdom of Christ, to bring the treasures of Havilah into the Edenic city. *You* are the water flowing from the sanctuary to refresh the land; your works are the light shining out to the nations so that the kings of the earth bring their treasures.

Pretty picture. But how does that actually work?

We can start to answer that question by recalling that the church, like Israel, is a kingdom of priests, a royal priesthood (1 Pet 2:9–10). What might that mean?

PRIESTLY PEOPLE

In the old covenant, priesthood was limited to the descendants of Aaron and later restricted to the clan of Zadok among the descendants of Aaron. Qualification for priesthood was, the writer to the Hebrews says, "fleshly" (Heb 7), which is to say, genealogical.

Jesus is the new High Priest, but of a different order. He's a priest after the order of Melchizedek, a priest greater than Abraham and therefore greater than Aaron, who descended from Abraham. Judged by flesh, Jesus doesn't qualify for priesthood. He's qualified differently. He's priest by the "power of an indestructible life," priest by resurrection (Heb 7:16).

Jesus alters the form of priesthood. When there's a change of priesthood, there's also a change of law (Heb 7:12). Specifically, the law that changes is the law that governs inclusion in the priesthood. Jesus shatters that law by becoming a priest differently.But He doesn't just shatter it only for Himself. He shatters it for the people of God. From Jesus' resurrection onward, priests are no longer qualified by genealogy. A man doesn't become a priest by physical descent from a priest, nor even by a success of ordination. In the new covenant, a priest becomes a priest by resurrection, by baptismal incorporation into the resurrection of Christ.

That's what Luther said: All of the baptized are priests. Men and women and children are ordained into the Christian priesthood by passing through the waters of baptism. They are all, in Thomas Aquinas's terminology, "deputed" (I prefer to translate it as "deputized") to a role in the Christian liturgy. Within the company of the baptized, some men are further designated as pastors to lead the liturgy and guard the gates. Pastors are priests leading a communion of priests. But the pastor is no more a priest than the lowest member.

If we're all priests, then the liturgy—the priestly service—is an act of the entire congregation. In the medieval Catholic Church, the congregation passively watched as the priests performed the Mass in a strange language. That still happens in some traditions today. That isn't how Christian worship is supposed to work. It's not a biblical model of worship. The liturgy is the work of the *people*, the whole people, each in his or her different capacity.

That means: Every member of the church draws near to the courts of the Lord in song and accepts the Lord's invitation to enter His house. Every member confesses sin and believes the pastor's declaration of forgiveness. Every member ascends in song into heavenly places. Every member prays. Every member hears the reading and preaching of the word. Every member shares the bread and cup, and every member receives the good word, as the name of God is pronounced over and placed on them.

This all sounds very formal, perhaps even formalistic. It sounds dead. It isn't. In the liturgy, Christians enter into the most intimate communion with God, together. We hear and eat and drink Jesus, so that we are His and He is ours, so that He is in us as we are in Him. The liturgy is the place and time when heaven and earth meet, when we are caught up to heavenly places to join the angels and saints in their joyful assembly (Heb 12:18–24). It's the time when the Spirit descends to hover over the earth to form it afresh.

In the liturgy, we anticipate the ultimate future of humanity and of the universe. Someday, all creation will be gathered before the throne in praise. Someday, the human race will sing to the Lamb in an eternal city. Someday, we will celebrate the marriage supper of the Lamb, when our Husband will rejoice over us with exultation and speak to us with words of grace.

That someday comes every Sunday. The liturgy isn't just a picture of what will be. It's a *foretaste* of what will be. It's not merely a glimpse of the city to come. It *is* the city to come, present in the present, the coming city come among us. If you're baptized into the Christian priesthood, you have an essential role anticipating new Jerusalem. If you're a member of the body, you *are* the coming city.

New Jerusalem wouldn't exist without you. Without you, there'd be no sanctuary-city whose breadth, length, and height are the same. Without you, there'd be no city where the light of the word is spoken, believed, done. Without you, there'd be no life in the city, only an empty plaza with very, very high walls.

Pastors should organize the service to maximize congregational participation. Liturgy is active, vigorous, a spoken or, better, a sung dialogue between pastor and people, between Christ's representative and the Bride. There's a role for choirs but, as a rule, the congregation shouldn't sit watching and listening, as if the liturgy were a clerical concern. The congregation should confess faith together, pray together, say the "Amen" together. The liturgy should include common prayers—collects spoken by the whole congregation, the Lord's prayer, litanies in which the congregation responds to the minister's calls to prayer.

Some churches try to correct congregational passivity by giving various people in the congregation a leadership role in worship. One member reads the Scripture, another prays, another sings a solo. That's a liturgical mistake, in two ways.

It's a mistake because the pastor is ordained for the specific purpose of leading the liturgy. That's his job and should no more be delegated to others than a quarterback should delegate his role to the left tackle (which he may do—but only for a trick play).

It's a mistake also because it assumes that liturgical leadership is the only form of liturgical participation. Members don't need to take over leadership to participate. In a biblically organized liturgy, the people are never simply watching the minister do the liturgy. They do the liturgy along with the minister, precisely in their role as the people. They are active in worship by being the congregation.

To do the liturgy well, members should prepare. Families can sing hymns and psalms in their homes. The church's leaders might organize evenings of Psalm-singing to teach the congregation to sing better and to teach new psalms and hymns. Parents should teach their children prayers and creeds. Members might want to read the upcoming sermon texts ahead of time and reflect on them afterward.

We're idolaters, and the liturgy doesn't come naturally. We need training, and the family is one place where we can be trained. Family worship isn't the same as congregational worship, but it can be boot camp for congregational worship.

Some of you might be inspired by the Theopolitan vision but find yourselves in churches that are indifferent or hostile. You want the church to sing psalms, but the pastor and congregation prefer sappy but familiar hymns. You want weekly communion, but the pastor is worried it will become rote. You're looking for a church where the congregation is vigorously active in the worship, but every church has a praise band that performs before a passive congregation.

What should you do? If the church is faithful to the gospel, start by giving thanks for the congregation, pastor, and church you already attend. Thank God for their faithfulness, for their ministries and evangelism, for the truth that is communicated.

Thankfulness isn't complacency. You can give thanks and also criticize and offer suggestions. But without thankfulness, even legitimate criticisms and suggestions will arise from an ungodly, embittered spirit. If you can't find anything to give thanks for, you shouldn't be there. If the church has betrayed the gospel, protest. If the protest fails, leave.

When you do criticize, do it directly to the church's leaders. Don't start talking to other members to form a sub-congregation of complaint, what Pastor Douglas Wilson calls a "fellowship of the grievance." Grievance is a powerful force for forming bonds, but the bonds are demonic. Whatever criticisms or suggestions you offer to the pastor or other leaders, remember that they are your shepherds who are charged by Jesus to keep watch for your soul (Heb 13:17).

Remember that you are called to obey them and honor them (Heb 13:17). You don't have to agree with them. But you *must* honor them as Christ's appointed shepherds. Appeal, don't demand. Suggest, don't give orders. And pray that the Lord will lead the leaders into a deeper appreciation of biblical worship. And remember that, however feeble the church seems, it is contributing to the work of building God's city. However pathetic, it *is* the city of the living God, heaven sent to earth.

BUILDING THE BODY

We were talking about being priests. Priestly work is liturgical work. But priests do other things besides worship.

Guarding was one of the chief duties of Levites and priests. They stood armed at the doorways of the tabernacle and temple to prevent unauthorized intruders (Num 1:53; 3:10).

That role was essential to Israel's health and safety. If the Lord's house became defiled, He wouldn't stay. Ezekiel took a tour of Solomon's temple, which had become as filled with idols and images as an Egyptian temple. No wonder that was followed by a vision of Yahweh's glory leaving the temple (Ezekiel 8–11). Yahweh is holy, and He doesn't stay in an unholy house.

The prospect of the Lord's departure was a terror to Israel. Yahweh was their shield, their mighty man, their king. Without Him, they were easy prey for the larger and more militant nations around them. Without Him, they were doomed to lose their king, their temple, their land. Without Yahweh and His Name in the temple, Israel wasn't Israel.

If you're baptized, then you're a priestly guardian of the new house of God, the temple of the Spirit that is the church. Your pastor or pastors have a special responsibility to guard the house, since they're the angels at the gates. But you can't leave it to the pastors to guard the purity of the house alone. *You* are responsible to keep the holy house holy.

If a brother sins against you, confront and correct him, involving other church members if necessary (Matt 18:15–20). If a sister is drifting away, you're equipped with the Spirit to restore her with gentle humility (Gal 6:1). If you know that a member of the church is developing an evil spirit of bitterness and ingratitude, drifting into unbelief, don't wait around for the pastor to notice. *You're* supposed to intervene (Heb 3:12).

In a healthy congregation, most of the pastoral care and correction isn't carried out by the pastor. It's carried out by members, as they "one-another one another," exhorting, encouraging, confronting, correcting, loving. The church has a pastor-police force, but they're chief policemen of a self-policing community.

That's hard work. It's not easy to confront someone else with his or her sin. You'd rather avoid it, and you may even be tempted to excuse your inaction with a pious gloss: "I'm covering it with love," you tell yourself. Sometimes, that's the right thing to do. Often, it's an evasion. Christians need to confront far more than they do. We need to learn what it means to be our brothers' keepers.

You do this for the same reason that the priests and Levites guarded the temple. If idolatry takes root in the church, if the church drifts into lukewarmness and lethargy, if the church begins to follow false teachers or shrinks back from courageous witness—then Jesus will remove the candlestick (cf. Rev 2–3). The Spirit abandoned Saul when he persisted in rebellion (1 Sam 16:14). The Spirit abandoned the temple when Israel worshiped idols (Ezek 8–11). The Spirit will withdraw from a believer or a church that becomes infested with idolatry, unrepented sin, impurities (Eph 4:30; 1 Thess 5:19). We're called to weed the garden and fight off the serpents so that we don't get expelled.

First and foremost, we're responsible for *ourselves*. Each of us is a temple of the Spirit, called to guard the doors of our hearts so that we don't grieve or quench the Spirit. We guard our eyes, ears, hands, feet from whatever might defile us. We're careful about what we see and hear, what our hands do, where our feet take us.

When we do sin and need cleansing, we confess: "If we confess our sins, God who is faithful and just will forgive our sins and cleanse us from all unrighteousness" (1 John 1:9–10). The church shouldn't be a place where sin hides and festers. Like a poisonous fungus, sin grows deadly in the dark. It dies when it's brought to light. We bring our own sins to light in confession. That's one of the main ways we guard the holy city of God.

Take the log out of your eye first, Jesus says. He doesn't say we should ignore the speck in our brother's eye. We remove the log from our own eye so we can see clearly to help our brother with his minor vision problem.

This sounds defensive, negative. That's partly true. A guard has a defensive role. But the new covenant brings something new, something more aggressive and positive.

Under the old covenant, death spread. Touch a woman during her menstrual period, and you're defiled. Sit where she sat, and you're defiled. If she touches you, you're defiled. Same with a man who has a polluting flow from his genitals (Lev 15). To avoid impurity, Jews avoided lepers, menstruants, other impure persons, or washed themselves constantly to get rid of the stain.

Not Jesus. A woman with a flow of blood touches Jesus, and Jesus remains clean and the woman is healed (Mark 5:25–34). Jesus touches dead bodies and remains clean. The dead rise (John 11). Jesus enters a world of spreading death and arrests its spread. Death stops here, with Jesus.

Then Jesus throws death into reverse. The life of the Spirit spreads from Jesus to lepers, to women, to the dead, to us. Then, in Acts, the Spirit equips the apostles to do the same. Like Jesus (and Elijah and Elisha before Him), the apostles raise dead bodies (Acts 9:36–39; 20:7–12). Because the life-Spirit of Jesus dwells in them, they aren't defiled, but overcome defilement.

We must still guard ourselves from the defilement of lies, lust, anger, all the things that come out of our hearts but are encouraged by what goes into our eyes and ears (Matt 15:10–11). But we're filled with the same Spirit that filled Jesus. We're clothed with the Spirit of life, and we're His agents for the conquest of death. We guard, but we don't cower in fear. We guard in hope, confident of our victory. We enter the realm of death and defilement to bring life and health.

Guarding is one of the chief responsibilities of the Christian priesthood. But it's not the only one. Christian priests are also teachers. Not all members of the church have the gifts and training to teach officially. But every member has some teaching role.

If you are a parent, God requires you to teach His word to His children (Deut 6; Prov 1; Eph 6:1–4), to train them to mature as disciples of Jesus. If you're a single adult, you're called to teach your friends and family members as opportunity arises. If you learn that one of your friends is going off the rails, doubting basic biblical teaching, you're called to teach correctively. When another member suffers, you teach by reminding them of the Lord's faithfulness. You teach by your faithful, Christlike co-presence in the heart of their pain.

Every member is a witness, called to teach unbelieving friends, family members, co-workers, as opportunities arise. Even children teach one another. Nearly every Christian parent has heard one of his or her exhortations repeated by one child to another: "You shouldn't do that. Jesus doesn't like that."

Priests alone entered the holy place to offer incense at the golden altar (Lev 24), the incense that represented the ascending prayers of the saints (Ps 141:2). Even in the old covenant, the priestly nation could pray anywhere at any time. After Solomon built the temple, their prayers were directed toward the house (1 Kgs 8), where the Lord promised to put His eyes and ears. The temple was an exchange point between earthly Israel and their heavenly Lord. As they prayed toward the house, the Lord heard and answered from heaven.

We no longer pray toward an architectural temple in a particular location on earth. We have a human temple, the incarnate Name. In the new covenant, the Son of God has taken on human eyes and ears so that He can hear when we pray "in His Name."

Prayer is one of the chief ways we one-another one another. We bring all the little needs and annoyances of life to God in prayer. We cast our anxieties, and the anxieties of our brothers and sisters, on the Lord.

As a former pastor of mine used to say, biblical prayers usually have a "so that" clause, and the "so that" is crucial. "Heal Aunt Agatha," we pray ... but *why*? Why do we want Agatha back on her feet? We need a "so that": "Heal Aunt Agatha so she can get back to teaching Sunday School, or volunteering at the soup kitchen, or serving Christ as an executive of a multi-national corporation." Prayers for the little needs are prayers for the extension of the ministry of the church. Even the smallest prayer is ultimately about building the heavenly city that renews the cities of men.

Our prayers should reach as far as God's promises. He promises to save us from the guilt and penalty of sin, yes. We should pray for that, for ourselves, our families, friends, neighbors. But He also promises to make the kingdoms of this world the kingdom of the Lord and of His Christ (Rev 11:15). He promises that kingdom will grow from a stone into a mountain that fills the earth (Dan 2). He promises that the kingdom that started as small as a mustard seed will become a tree where the birds nest (Matt 13). He promises that the earth will be filled with the knowledge of the Lord as the waters cover the sea (Isa 11:9).

He promises that Jesus will reign until all His enemies are placed beneath His feet (1 Cor 15:25). He promises to break the teeth of oppressors (Ps 58:6), to install His Son as king to quiet the raging nations (Ps 2), to establish justice and peace among nations (Ps 72; Isa 9), to raise up good kings who will be nursing fathers to His church (Isa 60:10–22). To be faithful in prayer, make your prayers political.

Tune your prayers to His promises, and so participate in His work of global redemption.

THE LITURGY AFTER THE LITURGY

In case you haven't noticed, let me alert you to a pattern: What you do in the liturgy is what you do, in a different mode and key, outside the liturgy.

In the liturgy, the pastor comforts and rebukes and shepherds you by word; so you should do the same within the body. In the liturgy, you confess and intercede; and that sets the pattern for a life of prayer. In the liturgy, you receive the Lord's hospitality at His table. And He commands you, "Go and do likewise." The heavenly city is a sanctuary city, its entire civic life a liturgy. The gathered liturgy of the Lord's day sets the pattern for the dispersed liturgy of day-to-day life.

Jesus spends a lot of His ministry at table, and He uses the table as a model of discipleship (Luke 14). How do you behave at the table? Do you jockey for position? Do you want to sit near the coolest and most important people? Or do you take the lowest seat? Whom do you invite to your table? Important people, who will return the invitation and help you climb the social ladder? Or do you invite the lame, blind, outcasts from the highways and byways?

The answer to these questions should be determined by the answer to this question: How does *Jesus* conduct Himself at table? Whom does *He* invite?

God's hospitality forms the one body. Our hospitality to one another builds the body. Our tables extend Eucharist, filling our lives with festive thanksgiving. The Father gives His Son in the Spirit at His table. At our table, we share the good gifts of God with one another, extending the gifts that God has given at His table. At His table, God gives honor to those who lack honor, and we should do the same at our tables. Our tables are opportunities to extend the joy, life, and gratitude of the liturgy into everyday life. The table is the main biblical model of charity—not a self-negating gift but a sharing and exchange and mutual enjoyment of goods.

In all these ways, and more, the liturgy extends into a liturgy of body life, a liturgy that builds the body.

When we recognize this dynamic, debates about ordination take on a different color. Today, churches are deeply divided over the question of women's ordination. I believe that only men should be ordained. But that is *far* from saying that only men have a role in the work of the church. Every member—man, woman, child—is responsible to guard and build the body. Every member has a place in the liturgy, both on the Lord's day and during the week.

The big event of the church's life is the liturgy, but the liturgy is the work of the *whole* people. The minister leads, but he leads the congregation in a corporate act. And apart from the liturgy, *most* of the work of the church *isn't* done by the pastors. Most of it is done by men and women and children who edify the body in myriads of ways.

"All well and good," you might say. "But I could find something similar in other manuals of church life. How does this differ from other agendas for church community? How is this a *Theopolitan* vision?" Good question. It's a question I asked myself, as you can see from the fact that I wrote the question down a couple of sentences back.

Remember chapter 1? There I pointed out that the New Testament describes the church in political terms, as an outpost of the city that is to come, as the *ekklesia*, the assembly of a new city, a new assembly that determines the health and future of the cities of men where it takes root. All the aspects of "body life" that I've been describing are dimensions of the "civic life" of the church. These are some of the ways that the church exists, grows, and matures as the city of God within the cities of men. These are some of the ways the church becomes a counter-city that disrupts, provokes, and challenges the civic pathologies that surround it.

Your church may not look much like a city. You don't all live in the same part of town. You don't have a roads department or a fire department or a police department. You can't tax or issue business licenses. Your church might seem more a parasite on the city than a city. You drive to church using roads that the city maintains. Your church building had to meet local building and zoning codes. Your pastor calls you using a cell phone network that doesn't belong to the church. Your church may look less like a city than like another subgroup within the city.

That's all true. The church doesn't have *all* the features of a city, whether ancient or modern. But the Bible still describes it as a city, and we need to think through what that means. In what ways is the church city-like?

For starters, your church has geographic limits. Even if the members of your church live forty miles apart at opposite ends of a metropolis, you occupy roughly the same space on the planet. You have a common way of life and loyalty to one another. Your church has leaders, budgets, buildings, organization, holidays and celebrations. The church reflects the variety of the human race—old and young, men and women, people from various tribes and tongues and nations—like a cosmopolitan city.

Every city has a distinctive way of life. Every city has an ethos. New Yorkers are bustling, Bostonians are rude, Londoners are cool, and residents of Birmingham, Alabama, have an inferiority complex toward Atlanta. Every city has particular practices, whether it's a port city, a political center, a tourist destination.

The church is a civic community because it has a distinct ethos and a distinct way of life. How? Let me suggest some specific ways.

Every week, Christians assemble to worship. We honor Jesus as Lord and King. These are *public* truths. Jesus isn't my personal Savior and Lord the way my fitness coach (if I had one) is my personal trainer. Jesus is Lord of all. He is King of kings. In every worship service, we acknowledge and rejoice in His kingship. Every worship service, we declare our loyalty to another king and another kingdom, a city that has come and will come. In every worship service, we remind the leaders of the city of man that they are subjects of the High King. We remind the world and ourselves that our final loyalty isn't to the nation, people, or city of our natural birth but the new city of the baptized.

The early church was unique in its sexual ethics. Romans held marriage and family in high esteem, but their conception of family was quite different from Christians'. Roman men had mistresses, visited prostitutes, had free rein to take sexual advantage of male or female slaves. Roman women accepted the men's license and the double standard. Christians condemned all extra-marital sexual activity as unholy, for men as much as for women. And they policed the sexual activity of members. Paul commanded the Corinthians to expel a man who was committing incest (1 Cor 6). Still today, in our "enlightened" age, the church is called to teach and live by a biblical sexual ethic. That alone sets apart the church radically from most of the cities in which she dwells.

Christian priests teach, and Christian parents teach children. If you're called to train them as disciples, then you're going to have to reject alternative training that would deform them as un-disciples. You're called to provide a Christian *paideia*, not the statist *paideia* of liberal democracy. Yes, I'm saying you should get your kids out of public schools. Do it now. Don't let your children—the children of *Jesus*—be discipled as unbelievers. Taking our responsibility to disciple our children seriously will make us a very different sort of people from the cities in which we live. Over generations, those who are discipled under the pedagogy of the church will live in a different moral and intellectual and cultural universe than citizens of the cities of men. This is what is happening in the U.S. as graduates of home school and Christian schools come to adulthood.

These are aspects of the liturgy after the liturgy, the liturgy that is the way of life of the city of God.

As I've stressed throughout, being God's city among the cities of men comes with a cost. The city of man has its own liturgies—liturgies of consumerist commerce, liturgies of sexual freedom, liturgies of messianic politics (can you say "Trump rally"?). The church doesn't play out her liturgy in a liturgy-free environment. She enacts God's liturgy to confront the liturgies of men.

The liturgies of the human city encourage unchecked consumerism, insatiable desire for goods, 24/7 consumption; the liturgy of the city of God is a liturgy of thankfulness and contentment. The liturgies of the human city celebrate nearly infinite sexual freedom and treat Christian sexual ethics as repressive; the liturgy of the city of God is a liturgy of chastity, marital faithfulness, union in sexual difference. The liturgy of the human city places hope in the next Great Leader; the liturgy of the city of God confesses *one* Lord, Jesus the Christ. We enact the Christian liturgy for the sake of the cities of men so that their cultural liturgies are dismantled and transformed, so that their civic habits and values conform to the word of the King whom we worship.

When we really live out the liturgy after the liturgy, we're bound to clash with the city of man. We're bound to have opportunities for some form of martyrdom.

THE CHURCH IS MISSION

Every Christian is a priest with a liturgical vocation. Every Christian participates in the public work of the liturgy. Every Christian is gifted by the Spirit to build up the body of Christ, to extend the truth-telling, word, and table of the liturgy into the everyday life of the church. Every Christian participates in "reasonable service," the liturgy of body life (Rom 12).

Every Christian is also a missionary, a participant in the mission of the church. Among Evangelicals Protestants, this is a truism, but it's understood reductively if mission is reduced to personal evangelism.

We *should* take every opportunity that arises to speak the good news to people who do not know Jesus. Churches need to train members to do declare the gospel, and individual church members should participate in evangelism efforts.

But if the gospel is inherently political, if God's polis is inherent in the gospel, evangelism will look quite different. Gospel presentations like those found in old tracts, or used in older evangelism programs like the Four Spiritual Laws or Evangelism Explosion focus on individual sin, individual conversion, individual faith, individual salvation. The cross of Jesus is a bridge to bring us across the chasm back to God. Jesus is the answer to the question, "Why should I let you into my heaven?"

Those kinds of presentations have their place, but they miss the political and cosmic scope of the gospel. The good news is that Jesus is installed as king. It's not merely a message of individual salvation. It's a message of cosmic salvation. The evangelistic invitation is a call to corporate as well as individual repentance.

We might write an evangelism tract along these lines: "Jesus the Son of God is the world's true King. He's King over *you* too. If you don't honor Him as King, you're a rebel, and He punishes rebels. If you want to live now and forever, you'd better get on His good side. You'd better turn from your sins and be loyal to Him."

The end game of evangelism should be membership in the Eucharistic community. The evangelist doesn't aim to get someone to pray a sinner's prayer (perfectly good in itself) or to confess Christ (necessary in itself). Like the apostles on the day of Pentecost, the evangelist urges penitent sinners to be baptized to receive the Holy Spirit (Acts 2). Evangelism is an invitation to a wedding feast (Matt 21), the wedding feast that is the kingdom coming, the wedding feast that is already now at the center of the life of the city of God.

The evangelist urges unbelievers to leave the world, the city of man, and to become citizens of God's city, with its vocation of worship and edification and mission. Evangelism is recruitment of new evangelists. Missionary work aims to expand the number of workers in the mission. We preach the gospel so that others will be caught up by the Spirit in Jesus' work of blessing the nations.

Such an understanding of the gospel greatly expands opportunities for evangelism. You don't need to steer a conversation, awkwardly and unnaturally, toward spiritual things. Every single conversation has to do with something Jesus claims as His own. As Abraham Kuyper said, "There's not one square inch of creation of which Jesus does not say, 'It is mine.'"

A conversation about the weather is a conversation about the Lord of wind and rain. A conversation about child-rearing or marriage is a conversation about the God who loves His Bride and His children. A conversation about political corruption is a conversation about the God who is Just, the God who intends to establish justice on earth. A conversation about yard work is a conversation about Adam's first calling. A conversation about social media is a conversation about the nature of true community. A conversation about fashion is a conversation about man and woman in the image of God.

If you're filled with awe at the scope of Christ's kingship, if you truly believe that Jesus claims every inch, there's no need to manipulate a conversation toward Jesus. Jesus is always already implicated in everything, for in Him all things cohere.

Even *this* is too narrow a conception of the mission of the church. The church's mission is as broad, as universal, as catholic, as the vocation of humanity. Adam and Eve were created to be fruitful and multiply, to fill the earth, to subdue and rule it (Gen 1:26–28). Men and women exist to carry out this "cultural mandate" to care for the creation and to transform and glorify the creation until the garden becomes a city. God first created earth formless and void, then sculpted it into the ordered and beautiful cosmos we inhabit. As His images, we sculpt the already glorious creation so that it matures from glory to glory.

After Adam sinned, the human race was derailed from that vocation. Human beings continued to fill, subdue, and rule creation, but they filled the earth with violent idolaters, laid waste to the world, abused their brothers and sisters. Jesus comes as Last Adam to put us back on track, to reorient the cultural work of sinners toward the original Adamic mandate, to transform this world into something resembling the city that is yet to come.

The church as an institution doesn't directly carry out this mandate. It's not as if engineers, lawyers, farmers, builders, mayors, homemakers, miners, teachers, doctors, and all the rest are on the church's payroll. The church doesn't carry out the Adamic cultural program in that sense. Yet the church *is* the new Adamic humanity, and in our weekday work as much as in our Sunday liturgical work, we're citizens of the heavenly city. On weekdays as much as on Sundays, we seek the transformation of the city of man so that it comes to image the city of God. Even when we move out of the sanctuary, when we move into the marketplace or courthouse, we enact the liturgy outside the liturgy.

Let's try to be concrete:

God wants His creation beautified. Beautifying creation was a central part of Adam's commission. Every vocation that contributes to the beautification of the city of man is fulfilling the cultural mandate—from city officials who plan parks, to the engineers who design elegant and efficient roads and bridges, to the caretakers who maintain suburban lawns, to the men who pick up garbage. Many who engage in this work don't intend to fulfill the church's mission, but they contribute to the church's mission nonetheless, insofar as they genuinely make the city of man more like the city of God. Christians involved in any of these vocations are *consciously* glorifying God by glorifying creation, consciously infusing the beauty of the city of God into the city of man. Shining with the light of the Lamb, refreshed by the water and fruit of life, believers bring the life of the Spirit into the work of beautification.

The cultural mandate isn't only about the relation of human beings to the creation. It's about human beings in relationship with other human beings. Politics and social work are as much a part of the dominion mandate as engineering. Service industries contribute to the comfort, health, joy, and prosperity of the ones they serve. They build up the human city as the exercise of spiritual gifts builds up the body of Christ. A farmer cultivates land to produce a crop that will, at the other end of the chain, sustain people he never meets. He loves distant neighbors. A taxi driver serves his passengers, loves them by bringing them safely (if a little rattled) to their destination. An ambulance driver may be crucial to the survival of a heart attack victim. The nurses, doctors, and other personnel who care for the patient at the hospital edify the city. Many carry out these vocations without a thought for Jesus or His city; but they are bringing their treasures into the city in spite of themselves. Christians engage in these vocations with a conscious intent to transform the city of man into something more like the coming heavenly city. Having received the love of Christ, they share the love of Christ in the world.

Artists fulfill the creation mandate in a direct way. A musician beautifies the air itself. A painter captures an angle of vision on the world, or imagines another world, which enhances the viewer's vision of reality. These art works adorn the city of man and make it more like the gem-encrusted city of God. Again, Christian artists and musicians do their work for the express purpose of glorifying the city so that it becomes more like the heavenly city of John's vision.

Christians in political office don't cease to be Christians. Christian political leaders should legislate, judge, act in a way that directs the city of man toward the city of God. They are still citizens of another city, still under the command of king Jesus. In their political actions as in their private lives, they are under the authority of the church and may be disciplined for advocating or enacting ungodly policies.

It's easy to misunderstand the Christian notion of vocation. Sometimes, we think that the world has its own pre-set menu of callings and that Christians are called to slip in quietly and do their calling Christianly.

That scenario is far too peaceful. The city of man is structured to inhibit Christian faithfulness. We can see obvious examples around us: Christian teachers can't pray at the beginning of a class in American public schools or universities. Christian business owners are pressured to conform to contemporary sexual codes. The lure of commercial success encourages Christians to organize their businesses to maximize profit rather than to serve God and neighbor. The world, as Paul says, is under the control of principalities and powers, world systems that are being overthrown by the Sprit of Jesus.

In such a system, Christians can't simply continue business as usual. If we are faithful, we *will* be disruptive. If we are deeply Christian in our callings, we will find opportunity for martyrdom.

What lies on the far side of the disruption? What kind of city of man do we hope for? We will devote future volumes in this series to answering that question in detail, but at base the answer is simple.

The church is the city of God on a mission of urban renewal. Our aim is to make the city of man more like the city of God, more conformed to the pattern of the heavenly city that John saw from the mountain. As the city of God infiltrates the city of man, Jesus will be acknowledged as King of kings, as ruler of all cities on earth. As the city of God shines the light of the Lamb, the rulers of the city of man will become more attentive to the weak and vulnerable, use their coercive power to beat down the ruthless, shape economic life to the ends of justice, welcome strangers and seek peace. The city of man will never become the city of God; it will never replace the church, the heavenly city, or make it superfluous. But the earthly city of man *will* be—and *has* been—remade into an image of the heavenly city.

YOU ARE MY WITNESSES

In the end, we come back to witness. A Christian journalist who unmasks the truth about an unjust war, or political corruption, is bearing witness. And he may make the city of man a little more like the coming city of truth. A Christian lawyer devoted to seeking justice and truth is bearing witness. A factory worker who works with cheerfulness and gratitude, who looks for ways to love his fellow-workers, is bearing witness. Only bad artists manipulate their work to evangelistic ends, but artistic work is a form of witness nonetheless.

Illumined by the word and table of the liturgy, every form of life, every vocation, can become light. Every form of life can be shaped Christianly.

A form of life shaped Christianly is a form of life shaped cruciformly. You bear a cross. You're called to follow Jesus no matter what, no matter the cost. Even if a journalist risks being fired if he shines light into a dark corner, he still has to speak. If a Christian lawyer is threatened by powerful people for shattering injustice, he must still pursue justice. If a factory worker discovers that his fellow workers are stealing, he shouldn't stay silent, even if he risks a beating in the parking lot.

Christians often treat their work as a means for achieving a comfortable life. We avoid discomfort. We find ways to cut corners and avert our eyes and assimilate so that we don't risk anything. Whatever Christian living is, it's not riskless. It always involves witness, and witness is always potential martyrdom. If you're a pastor, you're a witness, and a trainer of witnesses. You're a martyr called to form a company of martyrs.

Martyrdom isn't defeat. Martyrdom is victory. When believers witness faithfully in their words and work, we shine the light of God to the world. If we suffer, we end up bearing the bond-marks of Jesus before the world. Whether we succeed or fail, we succeed. Win or lose, we win.

This is the story of Revelation. The martyrs under the altar (Rev 6) are joined by 144,000 additional martyrs (Rev 14), and together they ascend above the firmament to join the heavenly choir (Rev 15). That's good for the martyrs. On earth, their blood shakes down Babylon and shatters the firmament dividing heaven and earth. Eventually, martyrs rule in heaven, seated on thrones (Rev 20), and the heavenly city descends to earth through the hole that martyrs make in the firmament. Witnesses win.

Note that martyrs don't win merely because God commends and exalts them. Martyrs win because their witness in blood shatters the systems and structures of the city of man. Martyrs win because we share in Jesus' triumph over the principalities and powers of this world. As we witness faithfully, God tears down so that He can build up; He uproots so that a new garden can be planted. Martyrdom is a *political* success.

As I said earlier, the mission of the church is *intensively* catholic. Pastors encourage church members to find ways to live out their vocation as witness, in conformity with the commands of Jesus. Christians go about their everyday activities as a way of fulfilling the Lord's mission in the world.

The mission of the church is also *extensively* catholic. The church is called to be one body of mutually indwelling persons and communities. All Christians, not just pastors, are called to seek this unity. All Christians are called to pursue catholicity and unity. Every Christian is a catholic Christian.

Lay Christians are crucial to the church's growth toward unity. By the nature of their vocation, most pastors spend most of their time with church members—caring for their needs, teaching and preparing to teach, leading worship or preparing to lead worship. Pastors should be involved in mission outside the church, but their primary vocation is to lead the church to be the church.

Non-pastors, though, are out in the marketplace and city squares, interacting with Christians from other churches on a daily basis. The woman at the next desk is Antiochene Orthodox. The real estate agent is a Southern Baptist. The man who does your wife's hair is Methodist.

Most Christians aren't called to engage in "high level" ecumenical discussions, but men and women of the church can help break down barriers of prejudice, suspicion, and hatred. For starters, treat other believers as brothers and sisters. If they're baptized in the Triune name and attend a church that confesses the truth of Scripture as summarized in the Apostles' Creed, they should be treated as fellow Christians. Conversation may reveal that they don't in fact believe any of it, or that they're living in sin. Then, respond the way you should to a wayward brother in your home church: Correct, rebuke, teach.

Being a catholic Christian has significant implications for your political views. I can speak with some knowledge only about the United States, but perhaps it will be relevant to readers in other countries.

Currently, the U.S. appears to be deeply polarized. The vocal leaders of the different political parties are at odds. A talking head on Fox News blames everything on unpatriotic liberals. Flip the channel, and you'll find a talking head on CNN or MSNBC who blames everything on fascist, racist conservatives.

Those elite differences seem to be dividing citizens outside the District of Columbia and far from TV studios. We cannot be sure whether these divisions will last or whether they will deepen into something more dangerous. I suspect that our divisions run deep and that the U.S. has a rocky century ahead of us.

How does a Christian respond to this? It's devilishly easy to choose sides, to become an echo chamber for your favorite talk radio celebrity, to subject yourself to the discipleship of Fox or CNN. As a starting point, you must resist that. *Jesus*, not American conservatism or liberalism, is Lord. Jesus' commands, not the Constitution, are absolute.

Of course, there are issues where one or another side of the political spectrum has it *right*. Conservatives are right to protect unborn babies. But then liberals are right to insist on our duties to care for refugees and immigrants. Neither side of the political spectrum speaks with the authority of Scripture or even the authority of the church. Christians have to learn to evaluate *every* political issue by Scripture—not by the latest deliverances from your favorite pundit.

Christians must learn to evaluate political questions from the viewpoint of the city of God rather than from the viewpoint of the nation or the city of man. Immigration provides an excellent test case.

This is an exceedingly complicated question. My colleague Alastair Roberts asks *some* of the difficult questions that need to be answered:

> 80% of Nigerian doctors want to move to the West; should we welcome immigration that strips a country of its skilled population? Should we encourage immigration to the US from the Middle East when displaced persons can be settled in the region? To what extent should we accommodate radically different cultures, religions, and social values, and to what extent should we expect people to assimilate? What about the ways that immigration has been weaponized to break down historic Christian cultural norms in Western societies ... through multiculturalism or used to empower business and elites through offering cheap labor, while pushing indigenous working classes out of their traditional

neighborhoods in many parts of the country? What is a reasonable number to admit? To what extent do we have a responsibility to economic immigrants?

Christians cannot address these and the hundreds of other questions about immigration simply as citizens of a particular country. We can't simply ask, "Is this good for our nation?" We have to think these questions through as citizens of another city, asking what the *church's* responsibility is to strangers who show up on our doorstep.

Looking at these questions from the viewpoint of the church highlights some neglected realities: Many immigrants to the U.S. are Christians. Catholic parishes in the U.S. have been revived by the presence of Latin American immigrants, and African immigrants in New York City are planting churches so fast that they don't have enough pastors. In Europe too, some of the fastest-growing churches consist of African immigrants.

If immigrants are invaders, as some pundits tell us, we need to ask why God is allowing the once-Christian nations of Europe and the U.S. to be invaded. Is this judgment for our cruelty, greed, lust, unbelief, and idolatry?

Working out a politics centered on the church is especially important in international relations. Christians have too often adopted a simple nationalist stance toward other countries: If my country goes to war, I support it, even if my country is killing Christians and bombing churches in another country. When we do that, we're putting the interests and values of the city of man ahead of the interests of the city of God. It's quite literally demonic and must be exorcised.

In international relations as in domestic policy, we should form our opinions as citizens of God's city.

Immigration and international relations are complex issues, and I don't intend to sort through all the questions here. My point is a more general one: Christians must resist being captured by political ideologies and combat the temptation to think through political issues in terms of the politics of the city of man. We must retrain ourselves to think and act as citizens of another city.

This won't win you any friends. Conservatives will think you're a globalist turncoat. Liberals will think you're a nostalgic localist. But the Christian can neither choose sides nor simply split the difference. Our political calculus includes a factor that Left and Right all but ignore, the central factor of world politics: God's heavenly city.

TO THE READER

Whether you're a pastor or not, you're part of the city of God. By the Spirit, you're equipped as a builder. By the Spirit, you're caught up in the mission of Jesus. You're the light that draws the kings of the earth to Jerusalem, leaves of the tree of life that heal the nations, the river of the water of life. It's through your witness that the principalities and powers will be thrown down, the systems of this world broken to pieces, and a new city take shape. It's through you that Jesus carries out His urban renewal mission to transform the kingdoms of this world into the kingdoms of our Lord and His Christ.

Conclusion: On Vision

I love to read. I read everything I can get my mitts on. I'm not so eager to *do*. Doing is hard work. I can't do from my recliner.

I hope you enjoyed reading Part 1. I hope it was inspiring and edifying. I hope that you are inspired by the breadth, height, depth, the universal scope of the church's mission.

But I don't want you to stop with reading. I want you to do something. I want you to take whatever is good and right in the Theopolitan vision, and do it.

Start where you are. Do what you can. But do.

For you who are pastors, re-commit yourself to studying and teaching the word, all of it, in as much depth as you can. Start singing psalms. Nudge your congregation toward weekly communion. Teach your people that they're part of Jesus' mission of urban renewal. Inspire them to see how they're part of the biggest deal there is.

For those of you who aren't pastors, throw yourself into the life of your local church. Pray for your pastors and leaders. Pray that they would conform the church's worship more and more to the Bible. Pray that they would see the breadth and scope of their work and of the church's mission. Sign up to participate in the existing ministries of your home church.

Look for opportunities for witness. Discover how your labors fit into the Spirit's work of re-creation. Serve, pray, study.

Jesus the Son of the Father builds His city by His Spirit. But He has given us the astonishing task of sharing in that work. All of you have a job to do. Get to work.

Part II

Theopolitan Reading

Interlude: On Reading

SOLID FOOD IS FOR THE MATURE, WHO BECAUSE OF PRACTICE HAVE THEIR SENSES TRAINED TO DISCERN GOOD AND EVIL.

—HEBREWS 5:14

Above, in Part 1, I wrote,

> Authority is *always* exercised through words. Honoring authority means honoring the words that authorities speak. If we bow to the authority of God the Lord, then we bow to the authority of His Word. His Word is the ultimate Word, bearing ultimate authority. If anything contradicts the Lord's Word, it must be false. Every other authority has to submit to the authority of the Word of God.

I also wrote,

> There is nothing in human life outside the authority of Scripture. If Jesus is Lord of all, He governs *all* by His Word. That means there is no space that's safe from a turf war between Jesus and other authorities. Scripture challenges the status quo, calling for

repentance, calling us to die and rise. If Jesus is Lord of all, there are no Scripture-free zones.

As apologist Cornelius Van Til liked to say, Scripture is authoritative on everything about which it speaks, and it speaks about everything.

We can't leave it at that, though. We need to ponder how Scripture speaks to everything. We might hope it works something like this:

> Theo has a decision to make.
>
> Theo consults the Bible.
>
> The Bible tells Theo what decision to make.

For some questions, the Bible functions just like that:

> Theo is trying to decide whether or not to start an affair with his secretary.
>
> Theo consults the Bible and finds Exodus 20.
>
> The Bible tells Theo, "*No!*"

Everyone knows the Bible doesn't work like that for everything. It can't.

> Theo is trying to choose between two different job offers.
>
> Theo consults the Bible and finds nothing.
>
> Theo takes the job with the highest salary.

After that, Theo puts his Bible on the shelf and never looks at it again on a weekday.

When people discover the Bible doesn't directly and specifically address every question they ask or every dilemma they face, they might decide to dispense with Scripture or at least relegate it to a secondary status. The Bible gives spiritual direction, but when it comes to real life, we need wisdom or natural law, not the Bible. The Bible isn't detailed enough to be practical, and, besides, it's awfully vague.

That response is just another version of Theo's decision to store his Bible. If Theo is looking for something on the order of, "Thou shalt take the HVAC job," it's not surprising he can't find what he is looking for. But that doesn't mean the Bible has nothing to say. Indulge me while I quote myself again:

> The Bible doesn't tell us how to build a widget, but it tells us a lot that informs our widget-building. It tells us *why* we labor, teaches us to devote our widget-building energies to serving our neighbor, commands us to be honest in our widget-building, requires us to love the widget-builders beside or under us. Sometimes the Bible's instruction is very general: Whatever you do, whether you eat or drink, do all to the glory of God (1 Cor 10:31). Sometimes, it's very specific: If someone slaps you on the right cheek, turn the other cheek (Matt 5:39). General or specific or somewhere between, Scripture speaks to all people in every circumstance.

Scripture is our final and highest authority for everything, in all circumstances. Scripture doesn't give you a shortcut. You can't avoid the tough work of sorting out the issues. You need to give thoughtful consideration to facts. You need to ask advice. You need to pay attention to your desires, the circumstances of your life, the good of your community and church, and on and on. Scripture commands or encourages all of these efforts. God doesn't speak to my life in a way that bypasses me.

Yet, even when we get advice from the wise (which we should) or examine the facts (which we can't avoid), we still run the advice and our interpretation of the facts through the sifter of Scripture. All through the process, we're engaged with Scripture. There's no Bible-free zone. There's no Bible-free moment. All the time, in all circumstances, we answer to the Word of God. We're always saying Yes or No to the Bible.

Theo made a key mistake. Many Christians do. Scripture isn't written mainly to answer my questions or make my decisions.

It's not primarily addressed to my circumstances or dilemmas. It's addressed to me. Through His Word, God transforms me into a living image of the living Word. He remakes us so we can remake the world according to the pattern of Scripture. He trains our senses to know good and evil.

That includes moral formation. Scripture teaches us what is good and evil. It includes intellectual formation. It teaches us what is true and false. We forget that Scripture also forms our imaginations. And we forget that a Scripturally-shaped imagination is essential to moral and intellectual formation and action.

We face a moral choice, which seems to present clear-cut options: X or Y. Join the militant first-century Zealots or just keep your head down and look away? It takes imagination to see another option: "Turn the other cheek. Give your cloak. Go the second mile." Jesus teaches neither revolution nor quietism but martyrdom: resistant witness.

You're faced with an intellectual puzzle: Apples fall. Planets stay in their orbits. Perhaps—Sir Isaac says in a blaze of insight—perhaps these are two manifestations of the same force. Modern physics rests on an imaginative leap that was later demonstrated by mathematics and experimentation.

You're faced with a political dilemma: When a novel virus begins to spread throughout the world, should you shut down schools, businesses, and churches? Or should you control the spread and wait it out? Especially when all the pressure in the world pushes you to move in one direction or another, it takes an extraordinarily imaginative leader to find an alternative route.

We make moral and intellectual breakthroughs when we learn to see the world anew.

That's what the Bible does. It targets our hearts, minds, senses, emotions, and imaginations to form us so we engage the world with a well-stocked, that is, a biblically-stocked imagination. If you submit to what you hear in the Word, it transforms the way you see, the way you take hold of things, your ability to sniff out problems and unexpected solutions, your taste for defeat and delight. Scripture applies to everything because it applies to all of you. It gives you new ears and eyes and hands, a new nose and tongue.

We never leave it behind or move it to the background. We always consult it with specific questions because we never know ahead of time if it will give us a specific answer. But we don't consult it periodically when we have a tough choice. We maintain a steady diet of Scripture because over time the Spirit uses the Word to train our bodies to do justice. Through the Spirit, the Word matures us to become kings and queens, prepared for every good work. If Part 2 awakens your imagination, even for a moment, I will have accomplished my purpose.

But we still can't leave it at that. We need to ask how Scripture speaks, how it rouses our imaginations. We have to ask which "method" of interpretation we should follow. We have to discuss hermeneutics, the theory of interpretation. That's what Part 2 is about.

I've puzzled over what to call the "hermeneutics method" I present here. It doesn't show up on most hermeneutical maps. It doesn't seem to belong anywhere.

I happily stand with Fundamentalists who believe the Bible is true in the everyday sense of "true." The days of creation were normal days, Balaam's donkey spoke, Jesus raised Lazarus and multiplied loaves and fish. I love Fundamentalists so much I called this book *Theopolis Fundamentals*. Unfortunately, Fundamentalists won't have me. Unlike most Fundamentalists, I'm not a literalist. My friends and I get positively giddy about the symbolic dimensions of Scripture.

We admire premodern interpretation, but we're too Protestant to be allegorists. Like allegorists, we're convinced that every detail matters, no matter how minute. The Spirit speaks in all these details, and He doesn't waste His breath. We love unraveling puzzles like: Why is the heifer red (Num 19:2)? Why does Scripture record the number of baskets of leftovers after Jesus fed the multitudes (Matt 14:20; 15:37)? We assume these numbers mean something, but what? Why did John say the disciples caught 153 fish (John 21:11)? Scripture leaves out a lot of details. Biblical writers are reticent. We always need to ask why they include what they do include. There's always a reason, and the details always edify. It's the glory of God to conceal a matter, and He's hidden a lot of treasure in the pages of Scripture. He does that to train us to be kings, whose glory is to uncover secret things (Prov 25:2).

Unlike many allegorists, though, we don't translate the Bible into some moral or philosophical idiom. We don't move from body to soul, from letter to spirit, or from this world to heaven. That shift betrays the nature-supernatural dichotomy I railed against in Part 1. We renounce allegory of that sort, with all its pomp and show. I'm too enamored of the letter to be comfortable among allegorists. I do pretty much the opposite of allegory. I want Scripture to judge and refine every language and system. I want to read the Bible on its own terms and not allow some other ideology to set the terms for Scripture. My friends and I don't translate the Bible into a worldly language. We translate the world into Biblese.

If typology refers to a theology of history, what I do counts as typology. That's not what most people mean by typology. They usually mean the habit of digging through Scripture for snippets and snapshots of Jesus. I agree Scripture is filled with snapshots and shadows, but it's more complex than that. We're alert to internal analogies (e.g., Saul is a new Gideon, Sarah a new Eve, Sinai a new Eden), and we need to be suspicious when someone "jumps to Jesus" before exploring the immediate historical and literary context in depth.

Besides, the Old Testament doesn't just foreshadow Jesus. It foreshadows what Augustine called the "whole Christ," head-and-body, Jesus and the church. Adam is a type of Christ, but Eve is a type of the church (Eph 6:22–33). Moses is a type of Jesus, but Moses is head of Israel. The exodus is a type of salvation—specifically, a type of baptism and Eucharist (1 Cor 10:1–5). When you begin to catch the scent of the body of Christ within types of Christ, you can find yourself within the typologies of the Bible. The whole Bible is about Christ, but He is head of His body, so it's all about the church. The whole Bible is about Christ, but you are a member of His body, so it's all about *you*. The whole Bible is about Christ, but the Eucharist is His body and blood, so the whole Bible is about the bath and the table. Typology expands to encompass the cosmos: The whole Bible is about Christ, but Jesus is the new Adam who reigns over and fills all things. The Bible is about Christ, but all things cohere in Him. The Bible is about Christ, and just for that reason, it's about everything. If that's what you mean by typology, then, sure, I do typology.

I might call it biblical theology or redemptive-historical, but everybody uses those terms. They don't capture the distinctiveness of Theopolitan reading and teaching. I might call it literary reading, and there's something to that. We've learned a lot from literary studies of the Bible, but we get queasy when literary readers rely on categories of modern criticism (like genre). And I'm too concerned with politics—with the import of the text for the real world—to stop at literary analysis. We agree with John Frame: Theology is application. It's gotta preach.

Years ago, Jim Jordan criticized the "interpretive minimalism" of biblical studies, and someone decided he must favor "interpretive maximalism." That's a misleading label. We *do* want to hear everything God speaks, and we think everything He says means something. But reading isn't a game where the reader with the most connections wins.

I might call it symbolic interpretation. That's accurate enough, and important. The loss of the symbolic imagination is one of the diseases of modernity, and it infects the church. But we reject symbolic or mythical readings that deny the Bible's historicity. Besides, we don't treat the Bible as a code where every X (water, fire, tree) stands directly and necessarily for some Y (baptism, sacrifice, the cross). We're too attuned to the immediate context, too enamored of the letter, for that.

The method I present in Part 2 looks a lot like the medieval quadriga, which explored the "fourfold sense" of Scripture. According to this model, every passage of Scripture tells us what happened (literal), what to believe (allegorical), what to do (tropological), and what to hope for (anagogical). Every passage reports on real people and events, points to Christ, guides our lives, projects us toward a glorious future. But "quadriga" is unfamiliar, and it's even weirder when we turn it into an adjective. Trust me, you can't use "Quadrigal Hermeneutics" in a fundraising letter.

At bottom, I'm skeptical of hermeneutical "method" in general. Methods pre-determine what questions get asked and what answers count. Reading is artful. It's not a mechanistic process where inputs chug out predictable outcomes. Hermeneutical method often implies that the ideal reader is a lone scholar in his study, rather than a worshiper in a liturgical assembly. Methods can make us forget the role of mentors and conversation partners. Armed with a method, the reader reads to master the text when he's supposed to be mastered by it.

There's no substitute for soaking in Scripture, reading it again and again and again, until it's in our bones and blood. There's no substitute for mentors and models who train you to read. There's no substitute for being in a church where Scripture is read, sung, chanted, prayed, preached, and taught. There's no substitute for a thorough, weekly liturgical basting in the Bible. Theopolitan reading (Part 2) is inseparable from the dialogue of Theopolitan liturgy (Part 3).

In the end, I'm ready to throw in the towel on this exercise in naming. It looks as if we'll have to take our own place on the map. Let's just call it a "Theopolitan reading," and there an end.

One last introductory comment, and we'll be off. A book will help you become a better reader. Hopefully, this book will help. But Part 2 won't help by giving you rules and procedures. To read well, you don't need a set of rules. What you need are models, mentors, and teachers who follow the reading of Jesus.

In the last analysis, that's all I have to offer: myself as a mentor and model. I ask you, as Paul does, to imitate me insofar as I imitate Jesus, *the* Model Reader. If I am truly reading in the Spirit, following me will keep you in step with the Spirit. And then you will mature, with your senses trained to know good and evil.

6

Spiritual Reading

MY EARS YOU HAVE OPENED.
—PSALM 40:6

Let's review some ground we covered in Part 1. God speaks. He speaks the world into being (Gen 1). His speech sustains the swirling universe in its swirling. He speaks before there is anyone to hear or answer. He speaks to form those who hear and answer. He speaks in the last days in human flesh (John 1:1–4). He will speak again at the last day, sending many to everlasting glory and some to everlasting torment.

God speaks because God is Word—eternally Word. From forever and forever, unto ages of ages, whether or not the world ever is or was, the Father speaks the Word. And the Spirit (Heb. *ruach*; Gr. *pneuma*) is the energetic Breath of God, the Lord and Giver of life, who enlivens Father and Son and gives force to the Father's eternal Word.

God not only speaks but writes. He engraves Ten Words with His finger on the tablets of stone (Exod 31:18; Deut 9:10). He comes as Word to Abraham (Gen 15:4), Samuel (1 Sam 15:10), Nathan (2 Sam 7:4), Isaiah (Isa 38:4), and He comes as Word to inspire prophets to write words (Jer 30:2; Ezek 1:3; 3:4–6; Hos 1:1; 4:1).

Even in the new covenant, when the covenant of the letter has given way to the covenant of Spirit, Paul spends his career writing epistles, and John is repeatedly told to write what he sees and hears (Rev 1:11, 19; 2:1; 3:1; 14:13; 19:9; 21:5). Words on parchment make the Corinthians into a living epistle, Paul's corporate "letter of recommendation" (2 Cor 3:1–7). By Paul's words, they receive the Word of God, solid food to make them mature.

"Jesus never wrote anything," you'll often hear from Christians who want to minimize the centrality of the Bible in the life of the church. Au contraire! As the Word, He's been writing since He met Moses on Mount Sinai.

Like the Word, the Spirit writes. He is God's Finger (compare Matt 2:28 with Luke 11:20), the Finger who does wonders beyond the skill of Egypt's magicians (Exod 8:19) and the Finger who writes on Sinai's stone tablets (Exod 31:18). The Word comes to the prophets, but the Spirit "carries" them to speak from God (2 Pet 1:21). The writings (Gr. *graphai*) are God-breathed, God's breath made text, "Spirited-out" (Gr. *theopneustos*) for our instruction (2 Tim 3:16–17).

That's who God is: Eternal Speaker, Eternal Word, Eternal Breath.

At the climax of the creation week, God forms man, male and female, and declares man is made in the image and likeness of God (Gen 1:26–28). What does that mean? An obvious way to answer that question is to answer these first: What has God been doing? What is God like?

We learn a lot about God from Genesis 1, but one thing stands out: God speaks. If we're made in the image of this God, we must be speaking beings—creatures who communicate in unique ways with the Creator, creatures with ears to hear the Creator's voice, creatures who share the Creator's power to make-by-speaking, creatures who speak and write and feast on the Creator's Word.

Adam becomes a living soul by the "breath" of God (Gen 2:7). The Hebrew word for "soul" (*nephesh*) derives from a verb (*naphash*) that means "to take a breath." Adam is given breath so he can speak back to the speaking God.

Breath gives our spoken words force. Without breath, we couldn't speak at all. Spoken words *are* articulated breath. We control airflow to form meaningful sounds—"o" rather than "a," "p" rather than "c," "pin" rather than "sin." Our breath gives rhetorical force to what we speak. We decrease or increase the volume, speak in staccato or legato, raise or lower the pitch. We are speaking beings because we are "living souls" who live by the Breath of God.

As the Father speaks His eternal Word by the power of His eternal Breath, so we His creatures speak by the power of breath.

Christians are sometimes puzzled by the very existence of the Bible. How can a God who is Spirit communicate through physical means: markings on a page or vibrations in the air? Why would He? Surely God must speak in a more refined, less crassly material fashion.

That's not how the God revealed in Scripture works. He speaks in human language, taking time to speak to us. It takes time to hear and read His Word. Our bodies are involved as we train our eyes and ears. All human learning takes place through language, which means that all language engages our bodies and affirms the goodness of time and space and all created things. The Creator speaks to His creatures through His creation.

The Bible—the physical book made of nothing but ink on paper—is the product of the Father's speaking by Word and Spirit. Scripture is God's words in human words because our God is omnilingual, a Speaker of every human tongue.

To read such a text well, we need to read in step with the Word and Spirit who are the Author of the text. Right reading of a Spirit-inspired book must be Spiritual reading.

MODELS AND MENTORS

How did you learn to speak? Did your parents lock you in isolation for a year or two until you gained linguistic competence? Were you alone as you prepared to unleash yourself on other speakers? If so, congratulations! You're the first of your kind.

We may have a biological or genetic predisposition toward language. But we learn actual languages by being spoken to and by learning to speak back. We learn to speak in communion. Our drive to speak arises from a desire for communion. Speech deepens and sustains communion. Conversation is the ground in which our created capacity for language becomes fruitful. As in God, Word and Breath are the bond of our communion.

How did you learn to read? Were you locked in your first-grade cubicle and sternly warned not to come out until you were ready? Probably not, unless Dickens's Mr. M'Choakumchild was your primary school teacher. You learned to read the way you learned to speak—through parents who read to you and teachers who taught you to recognize letters and to string letters into words and words into sentences, paragraphs, and books.

You learned to read because you had models and mentors—people who showed you how to read by reading, people who peered over your shoulder to guide your reading, to correct misreading, and to commend your right readings.

We learn to read well in the same way. You don't become an intelligent or insightful reader in an isolation chamber. Textbooks and rules can help, but books can't teach everything you need to learn. Sometimes rulebooks are counter-productive since they can seduce you into thinking reading is a mechanical process: Stuff the right ingredients in one end, and sausage will come out the other.

To read well, you need models and mentors. You need to watch or read or hear people reading well and learn to mimic them. You need a mature reader standing beside your shoulder to tell you what you're doing right and what you're doing wrong, until you learn to hear with his ears and see with his eyes.

Spiritual reading is reading guided by the Spirit of God. We discern the Author's full intent by being filled with the Author Himself. When Christ the Word dwells in us, we receive the written word rightly. The Spirit is our Mentor.

Above all, the Spirit teaches us to read by pointing us to the Model Reader, Jesus. Spiritual reading means reading as Jesus read.

As the Word anointed by the Spirit beyond measure, He is the Model Reader of the law. According to Jesus' reading, the Torah is focused on justice, mercy, and truth (Matt 23:23). According to Jesus, keeping the law is identical to following Him (Matt 5–7).

Jesus comes to fulfill the law (Matt 5:17–19) in the first instance by doing justice in His own life. Jesus shows what the First Word requires by loving and obeying His Father above all things, even at the cost of His life. He wars against hypocrites, against the practical idolatry prohibited in the Third Word. By healing on the Sabbath, He gives Sabbath to the weary and heavy-laden. He doesn't merely refrain from killing but offers Himself up to murderers. He doesn't merely refrain from theft but pays debts He doesn't owe—our debts. He is the faithful witness even though His true witness leads to a Roman cross. His entire life is a reading of the Torah.

Jews categorize a large portion of the Hebrew Bible as prophecy. They view the books Christians usually call historical books as "former prophets," while what we call prophecy they consider "latter prophets." By His teaching and life, the Spirit-anointed Jesus is the Model Reader of prophecy just as He's the Model Reader of the law.

Jesus is literally another Joshua, sharing the name of the conqueror of Canaan and carrying Joshua's war against idols at a deeper level. Clothed with the Spirit, Jesus is another Gideon or Samson. He's the "son of David," a King greater than Solomon (Matt 12:42). His body is a temple, ruined like Solomon's but rebuilt as in the days of Joshua and Zerubbabel (John 2:13–20). He fulfills Hosea 11:1 by escaping from a Pharaoh-like king of the Jews (Matt 2:14–15). He's Isaiah's Spirit-filled Servant (Luke 4:16–21), a greater Elijah who feeds outcast widows (Luke 4:25–26), and a greater Elisha who cleanses gentile lepers (Luke 4:27). Jesus is the key to Israel's history and prophecy.

Jesus sums it all up when He appears to the disciples after His resurrection. On the road to Emmaus, He's appalled that the two disciples don't understand that the Christ had to suffer and die and be raised. Beginning with Moses and moving through all the prophets, He tells them "in all the Scriptures the things concerning Himself" (Luke 24:27; cf. 24:44–49).

Even after they walk with Jesus from Jerusalem to Emmaus, even after they feel their hearts burning in them, even after Jesus teaches them about the Christ from all the Scripture, the two disciples still don't recognize Him. Jesus is the Model Reader, but even that isn't enough.

The disciples recognize Jesus is with them only when Jesus gives thanks and breaks bread. Then their eyes are open. Jesus the Model Reader is also Jesus the Host and table companion (Luke 24:30–31). Bible and liturgy can't be separated.[1] Scripture needs to be before our eyes, ringing in our ears, and tasted on our tongues. Within the liturgy, Scripture trains our senses so we can receive the solid food of Scripture so we become ever more mature. We learn to read well when we break bread with the Master.

You might be looking for an out: "OK, Jesus is the Model Reader, but I can learn to read from Jesus without any help from any other human beings. I've got the Spirit and Jesus and the book. What else do I need?"

Protestants are apt to be seduced by this line of thought. We confess the perspicuity of Scripture, its clarity. We stress the priesthood of all believers and believe each believer has access to God. It seems reasonable to conclude that the Spirit gives us insight into the Word He inspired. Each of us can sit in his cell and learn to read. Sure, when we learn the natural process of reading, we need teachers. But when it comes to supernatural, Spiritual reading, we can dispense with models, mentors and teachers.

True, the Spirit is our teacher. He's the Finger by which Jesus bores open our deaf ears so we can hear what He has to say (Mark 7:33). But it's an error to conclude that the Spirit bypasses teachers, our bodies, and time. The Spirit guides us through means. We mature as we become more like our mentors and models.

[1] For more, see "Theopolitan Liturgy," ch. 12.

It's always been so. The ascended Jesus gives gifts to the church, including teachers and pastors (Eph 4:7–16). The Spirit of Jesus equips those who teach with the ability to edify the church in their teaching (Rom 12:3–8; 1 Cor 12:4–11). You can't be in step with the Spirit if you reject the Spirit's gifts. You can't be a Spiritual reader without learning from Spirit-filled teachers (cf. Acts 8:1).

Jesus is the model Reader, but the New Testament is the work of many Spirit-filled model readers. Matthew, Mark, Luke, and John paint the life of Jesus from the palette of the Old Testament. The Gospels teach how the events, characters, and institutions of Scripture come to fulfillment in the Christ.

Paul teaches that Jesus is the new Adam (Rom 5:12–21), the Spiritual son of Abraham (Gal 3:1–14; 4:21–31), the seed of David (Rom 1:1–4). The writer to the Hebrews says Jesus' blood speaks a better word than the blood of Abel (Heb 12:24) and that Jesus is a priest after the order of Melchizedek, surpassing the order of Aaron (Heb 7). Jesus' death, resurrection, and ascent fulfill the sacrifices of the Mosaic order (Heb 9–10). And so on and on and still on. The apostles learned well from the Model Reader and teach the Scriptures just as He taught.

Jesus still models reading by giving us model readers. The Scriptures are clear, written for every follower of Jesus. That doesn't mean they are equally clear to everyone. It doesn't mean the Scriptures are clear in the absence of teachers to clarify. Scripture is clear because the Spirit guides our reading by giving us guides.

Protestants often transpose priesthood of all believers into a democratic tune or an egalitarian etude. Because we're all priests, we think we all have equal skill in reading, teaching, grasping texts.

That's an error. Some men and women are more naturally gifted to understand texts. Some have devoted focused energy and enormous time to learning how to read well. Some have drunk the milk, trained their senses, and learned to eat solid food. Such mature readers are better readers than the rest of us. The best thing you can do is recognize their superiority and put yourself under their tutelage, imitating them as they imitate Christ.

Think about rules for reading as an instruction manual for car repair. If you're a beginner, you need the manual. You may have to follow the instructions quite strictly: Remove this bolt, replace this washer, turn the oil filter that direction, and never NEVER! remove this hose when the engine is hot. As long as you're following the manual, you're not a good mechanic. Good mechanics know engines. They can diagnose by listening to the clicks and clacks coming from under the hood. You become a good mechanic by apprenticeship to a car guy. He embodies the rules, and you infer the rules of the game from watching him work. Or, even better, you imitate the master mechanic until the feel for good practices seeps into your body and bones.

Rulebooks can't enforce the rules. They can't alert you to violations. Experience alerts you to violations. The car will let you know. You'll know you removed the wrong hose when some slick, boiling fluid starts spewing from the engine. You remember the rule: "Never NEVER! remove that hose when the engine is hot." You can avoid mistakes and injury if you stick close to the master mechanic. He'll tell you if you start to do something dumb.

Whether we're repairing a car, playing an instrument, swinging a bat, tossing a free throw, or reading, the pattern is the same. A rulebook may contain standards of judgment, but a rulebook can't judge. Mature people, with senses trained to discern good and evil, teach us what to do and what not to do. Other people provide the brakes and checks that keep our reading on track and keep us from driving over a cliff. As you practice and listen to your mentor, you'll develop guidelines and rules. But they come later. Rules don't come first. Rules always come after a practice has begun.

For centuries, the church accepted Jesus and the apostles as model readers, learning to read the Scriptures, and everything else, by following their example and instruction. Teachers of the past weren't always good readers. They got things wrong. But their method was sound because they read in the Spirit.

For the past several centuries, that method has been mocked, even by many Christians. Modern "scientific" hermeneutics promises to teach us to read more accurately. It teaches us to reject childish allegorization and to pay close attention to the grammar and historical context so we can discern the hard facts of the case. Modern hermeneutics trains us to take fright at the "eisegesis" of the church's reading, its alleged habit of reading Jesus into the Bible instead of following the literal lineaments of the text.

Modern scholarship has made immeasurable contributions to our knowledge of the Bible. We know far more about the ancient contexts of the Hebrew Bible and New Testament than any previous age of church history. We have made great strides in grasping the languages of the ancient world. Archeological discoveries like the Dead Sea Scrolls have opened up forgotten features of the biblical world.

Plus, the church has always insisted on attention to the letter of Scripture, the grammar of the text, and its historical setting. Spiritual reading assumes the persons and events recorded in Scripture occurred in real time and space. Unless they are real, we are of all men most miserable. Modern scholars remind us to take the literal sense very seriously. To that degree, they, too, are gifts of the Spirit who model good reading. We take those warnings to heart and affirm the Reformers' correct insistence on the priority of the letter. The Spiritual reading I model here doesn't leave the letter behind. It plumbs the depths of the letter, which, we discover, opens out into glimpses of Jesus, frameworks for understanding the world. We seek to understand the text on the terms it sets for us. By the Spirit, the letter trains our senses to discern between good and evil.

At a fundamental level, though, modern biblical scholarship is a systematic, relentless, centuries-long experiment in quenching the Spirit. It replaces Jesus as Model Reader with a scientific, grammatical, or historical master. The Word is our food. It trains our senses and makes us mature. If we want to put away childish things, nothing is more crucial to the future of the church than repentance at this point. We must turn to get back in step with the Spirit, learning to read well by imitating the model reading of Jesus and His apostles.

READING WELL

Modern criticism of Jesus' way of reading hits home. Jesus seems to read the Hebrew Scriptures arbitrarily, and so do the other writers of the New Testament. *Are* they good readers or sloppy readers? Do they see what's in the text, or are they making things up? What, after all, does reading well mean?

Reading well doesn't simply mean understanding the words and sentences. Reading well isn't the ability to repeat what you've read. Everyone who is competent in a language can repeat what he reads. A good reader understands exactly what the text communicates, and he seeks to understand everything the text communicates. A good reader strives to understand accurately and fully, without sacrificing either to the other.

Or we might put it this way: A good reader hears the poetry of a text. We usually use poem and poetry to describe a particular kind of writing. Poems are written in lines and stanzas, have meter and rhyme, use devices like similes and metaphors and personification.

But all language has poetic features. The English word for poem comes from the Greek *poiema*, which simply means "a made thing." In this etymological sense, every text is poetic since it's built from the bricks and blocks and fasteners of language. Good readers notice everything about a text's construction.

Hard-headed realists bristle at nonsense like "my love is like a red, red rose" or "hope is a thing with feathers" or "shall I compare thee to a summer's day?" I'd rather you wouldn't, Mr. Shakespeare, says the realist. And, with all due deference to Rabbie Burns and Miss Dickinson, my love isn't a flower, and hope doesn't have feathers. Just the facts, ma'am. Just the facts.

But their hard-headed protests are as metaphorical as the poems they protest. After all, the sound "rose" isn't a flower either, the sound "feathers" never helped a bird fly, and the sound "breakfast biscuit" never stilled the rumblings of our morning borborygmi.

Every text is poetic because language itself is poetic. Metaphor happens every time we speak. It's the foundation of all language. I see my coffee mug next to my keyboard. I point to it—I'm doing it right now!—and say, "That is a mug." I identify an object on my desk with the sound "mug." But is the ceramic-container-for-coffee identical to the sound "mug"? How can an object "be" a sound? By what magic does my treasured coffee container come to be in a new form within the sentence I'm writing? How can an object be the visible markings m-u-g?

I can't explain the magic. It's a thing more to be adored than explained. But I know this: If metaphor is an error or a distortion of reality, everything we say is hopelessly distorted. Because metaphor lies at the base of all language.

We're the only creatures who do this kind of thing. Chimps signal to each other, Brazil's titi monkeys emit a range of sounds to locate predators, parrots mimic human speech, rats learn to identify letters on the doors of a maze. No other creature, though, uses metaphor. Only *we*, made in the image of God, have the creative power to say, "This (thing) is this (sound/visible sign)." We alone can make things in the world exist in a new mode within our speech. We alone are poets, God's *poiema*, mimicking the poetry of the divine Poet.

Paying attention to the poetry of a text isn't something we do in addition to getting the meaning. No matter how literal the text, we read it well only if we pay attention to the poetry—the way it's made.

Paying attention to the poetry means paying attention to word choices and the overtones and music of each word. Good readers pay attention to how words, like molecules, react and transform in the presence of other words. Good readers have read many texts and hear echoes of one text inside another.

Good readers have an ear for how motifs echo and reecho through the whole. Good readers read with all senses on alert, as if their lives depended on getting everything.

Let me try an experiment, or a game, to illustrate the magic of words. Let's start with one word:

robin

What's a good reader to get from that lonely, apparently unpromising word? At least this: A robin is a bird, proverbial harbinger of spring. "Robin" brings to mind the rusty red of the robin's breast feathers. Whatever might be added, we expect springtime, new birth.

Well, good. Let's add another word:

robin's eggshell

Well, that changes things. The definition of "robin" hasn't changed a bit, but the additional word picks out one aspect of "robin" and focuses our attention there. At the same time, it opens a range of new associations: Robin's eggs are sky blue, small, fragile, round, smooth. If we were already thinking spring when we read "robin," we're thinking it even more now since robins lay eggs in springtime. The sound and rhythm of the two words capture our ear. The phrase has a meter and nearly alliterates with different ranges of "s" (from a hard *z* to a softer *sh*).

OK, now we're getting somewhere. Let's add another:

robin's eggshell fine.

That's a surprise. We've been thinking of the properties of birds and eggshells, but now "robin" and "eggshell" modify the adjective "fine." Some things, perhaps, are ostrich-egg fine, which isn't very fine at all, or turtle-egg fine, which is leathery. Whatever this sentence is about, it has a different kind of fineness, similar to the fineness of a tiny bird egg. All we've thought about robins and eggshells still lingers in our minds when we add "fine." Whatever is fine, it's going to have some of the qualities of the bird and the shell—spring, delicate, perhaps even blue!

Let's end the suspense and quote the whole line:

> The day is robin's eggshell fine.
> ("Lake Ontario Park," Sadiqa de Meijer)

Well, I wasn't expecting that at all! Were you? A piece of china, a woman's skin and facial structure, or the sensibility of a delicate, rather nervous Victorian lady might be "robin's eggshell fine." For Sadiqa de Meijer, the phrase describes a day. We were right to detect a wisp of meter: This line scans as iambic tetrameter (unstressed-stressed, four times).

Notice what has happened. We started with one word. That one word is part of the English language and so already exists in the context of the whole set of English words. In English, this sound "robin" is a certain kind of bird. "Robin" belongs with other animal words, but its sound distinguishes it from other animal words. A robin is not-sparrow, not-hawk, not-alligator, as well as not-granite and not-shotgun.

Besides, "robin" has been used millions of times over the centuries and has picked up standard connotations. A good reader hears the reverberations of the word as it occupies its place in the context of the language, the history of English literature, the history of the world.

Then we added other words. We added more context. With each additional word, we performed some paradoxical magic. Each new word limited the scope of "robin." Adding "eggshell" drew our attention away from the bird, its color or feathers, to its egg. Adding "fine" put the delicacy of the eggshell in the forefront, rather than its color or shape. We could, after all, say, "His head was robin's eggshell round" or "Her eyes were robin's eggshell blue." Each new word, each additional bit of context, imprisoned the words and directed us down a particular path of reading.

At the same time, the additional context liberates and opens. Each new word opens up fresh connotations and possibilities. We may not have thought of fragile as a quality of "robin," but "eggshell" forced that on our attention. Robins aren't blue, but their eggs are.

The sentence offers a new glimpse of reality. I dare say none of you had thought to describe a day as "robin's eggshell fine" before reading that line of poetry. Now that you've read the phrase, you'll experience some days differently. Perhaps you'll be led to the thought that each day breaks as a new birth, as springtime, as fragile and as full of promise as a robin's egg. Perhaps you'll ask whether the poem's eggshell is whole or broken and be sobered at the thought that fine newborn days can so easily be shattered into a million little pieces.

Notice we've done all this without leaving the words behind for a moment. The marks on the page, with the attendant sounds and meanings, have been our guide at every step. As we've paid attention to the poetry of the text—to the way the line is constructed and to the materials it's constructed from—these six simple words have dazzled our ears and eyes and trained our senses to engage the world with new delight and insight.

We can also interrogate the line of poetry. What season is it? The line doesn't answer our question, but we infer it's spring. What kind of weather is it? We know it's fine, but "eggshell" hints at a brilliant blue sky with few or no clouds. "Fine" doesn't just mean "good weather" but suggests a cool tang in the air. I suspect it's morning.

I can't prove that it's spring, or that the sky is blue, or that it's morning. Perhaps the rest of the poem will clarify. With just this one line, a skeptic—perhaps you—might ask, "Haven't we read too much into the text?" Wouldn't we be better readers if we said, "No, we can't go beyond what's written. All we know about the day is that it's 'robin's eggshell fine,' whatever that might mean. Anything more is eisegesis"?

At the risk of insulting skeptical readers, the answer is, "No." A response like that comes from a very bad reader, a reader who thinks interpretation is no more than paraphrase. It comes from a reader with untrained poetic senses, a childish reader who wants to stay safe, a Peter-Pannish reader who never wants to grow up. To such readers, I can do no more than repeat the hermeneutical exhortation of Jesus, the Model Reader: "Have no fear."

A good reader is like someone with a well-tuned ear for music. A good reader hears the overtones and harmonies, the shifts in meter and instrumentation, that a casual reader misses. A good reader is not hearing things—no more than a trained music listener. A good reader notices what's on the page and catches the overtones, connotations, import, and implications of what's written. A good reader is so attentive to the text that he notices the thousands of traces of things that are virtually there. He's so attentive to what's there that he notices what's not there.

THE BIBLE AS POETRY

If all texts are poems, made-things, the Bible is too. We can be more definite. God wrote Scripture in a mode closer to poetry than to scientific or philosophical prose. The Bible is full of explicit poetry: the songs of the Pentateuch and Judges 5, the book of Psalms and the Song of Songs, long stretches of the prophetic writings. Each is a masterpiece of concentrated excess.

Take this, for instance: "Put me like a seal on your heart, like a seal on your arm," says the Bride in the Song of Songs (8:6). Seals mark things with the name of the owner. To say that the Bride seals the Bridegroom is to say that the Bride stamps her name on him. It's a love metaphor. She wants him to be hers.

But this line almost-says more than it says. If we remember the rest of the Song, we know there's mutual ownership: I am my beloved's, my beloved is mine (Song 2:16; 6:3). And if we read the Song as Yahweh's hymn of love to Israel, the scope of the image expands. Surprisingly, the Song emphasizes the Bride's ownership of her Husband, that is, Israel's ownership of Yahweh. Yahweh is Lord, yet He is so fully devoted to Israel that she owns Him. The Creator has freely decided He will not be God except as the Bridegroom of Israel.

His heart and arm are sealed. Heart because the Bridegroom's heart is captivated by the bride (cf. Song 7:5), arm because the arm symbolizes strength—the strength of Yahweh's arm stretched out against Egypt (Exod 6:6; 15:16; Deut 4:34; 5:15; 26:8), the strength of the everlasting arms that defend Israel

(Deut 33:17), the strength of the hosts of Yahweh (cf. Dan 11:6). The Bridegroom's strong arm, like His heart, belongs to the Bride.

"Love is as strong as death," Solomon adds, the very "flame of Yah" (Song 8:6; my translation). Israel's story is a story of a love as strong as *mot*, the god of death. Yahweh's jealousy is as possessive as *sheol* (Song 8:6), His flame too fiery to be quenched by many waters. Think of the waters that haven't quenched Yahweh's love: The waters of creation are no match for the Spirit. Yahweh blows the floodwaters, and dry land appears. With a breath, Yahweh divides the waters at the Red Sea. Yahweh's fire licks the drench from Elijah's altar. Yahweh reaches down to the roots of the earth to draw Jonah from the watery gates of Sheol.

Nothing stands in the way of the flame of Yahweh's love. On the contrary, everything is fuel for this fire and only makes the consuming Fire burn brighter, whiter, hotter.

John is the model reader of the Song, for he identifies Jesus as the glorified flame of Yah. Jesus has the keys to "death and Hades" (Rev 1:18). He's Love incarnate, the fire who is not consumed by many waters, the Lover who consumes death in pursuit of His bride. His death and resurrection are the great historical demonstration of Yahweh's passionate devotion to His Bride.

In those few lines, we hear the whole story of Scripture, which is the story of the world. And those few lines, read well, train us to face the waves and floods of life with confidence. Death stares us in the face, but we know His jealousy is harder than sheol. An epidemic unsettles everything, but this, too, is fuel for Yahweh's love. Scripture trains our senses to sense the world as it actually is.

You might admit that biblical poetry is a concentrated excess. But it's not just the poetry. Even the prose sections of Scripture are highly charged pieces of writing. We pay attention to details and muse on them in the light of the rest of Scripture. We try to hear the overtones and undertones, to pick up subtle shifts in rhythm and the little gestures that point us to other texts. And suddenly, with a flash of insight, we see how the jagged pieces of text fit together, which helps us to discern God's pattern in the fabric of the world.

Another example. What could be more boring and unfruitful than the genealogy of Judah (1 Chr 2)? But we don't have to read far before we recognize the brief stories told in Judah's genealogy as stories of death and resurrection.

Death intrudes early in the genealogy of Judah, Israel's royal tribe. The sons of Judah die because of their wickedness (1 Chr 2:1–4). Notably, this is the first time the Chronicler refers to God. When Yahweh appears, He comes not as Creator but as killer, as Judge and Executioner. God is a killer, especially of kings (Chr 10:14; cf. 2 Chr 36:17–18).

Er is so wicked that Yahweh puts him to death (1 Chr 2:3). None of Judah's other sons appear to have children. We know from Genesis that God put Onan to death too (Gen 38), and Shelah's line is (canonically if not historically) aborted. Judah gets a new lease on life through Tamar, his Canaanite daughter-in-law, who bears the twins, Perez and Zerah. The abortive line of Judah is revived through a gentile.

Then it happens again. Zerah's sons are listed then disappear (1 Chr 2:6–8), another abortive line. His descendants end with Achan/Achar, "the troubler of Israel, who violated the ban" (2:7) and was stoned. Zerah, whose name means "rising" and puns on the word for "seed," is not fruitful. Another false start; another blind alley for Judah.

Perez, the one who breaks through, has two sons, Hezron and Hamul. The Chronicler's genealogy focuses on the former, whose three sons are Jerameel, Ram, and Chelubai (1 Chr 2:9). Jerahmeel's line through Onam stalls three times over. One line goes from Onam to Seled, who "died without sons" (1 Chr 2:30). Another line from Onam goes through Jada to Jether, who "died without sons" (1 Chr 2:32). Sheshan (1 Chr 2:34) also has no sons, but his line is re-started through his daughter, whom he gives to an Egyptian slave, Jarha (1 Chr 2:34–35). Another death and resurrection for Judah; another renewal linked with the incorporation of gentiles.

What would Jesus the Model Reader make of this genealogy? As He tells the disciples on the road to Emmaus, everything speaks of Him, including the boring genealogy of His tribe. Jesus would tell them, "I am the Risen One, descended from the tribe of resurrection. In Me, Jew and Gentile are knit together, for my tribe is already the beginning of one new, united humanity."

Throughout this reading of 1 Chronicles 2, I've shifted back and forth between literal and figurative reading. Did Judah's line come close to dying out? Literally, yes. Does that foreshadow something about the tribe of Judah, the line of David, great David's greater Son? Yes again. Am I saying the text is both literal and figurative? That it has multiple senses?

Why, yes I am. And I really shouldn't have to defend my viewpoint. Most uses of language are literal and figurative. Am I, to refer back to an earlier sentence, really defending anything? Not literally. When I speak of defending my viewpoint, I operate within the common master metaphor that equates argument with war. To refer back a few pages, was the day literally fine? Yes. Was it literally a "robin's eggshell"? Nope. Days aren't eggshells. Does that mean the line is an incoherent train wreck? No. It means the poem mixed figurative and literal, just as we all do all the time.

We need to free ourselves from the deranged notion that a text must be either literal or figurative and that we have to read consistently one way or the other. The demand for consistency can only lead to absurdities.

Babylon is a great city and a great harlot (Rev 17–18). Which is it, John? If it's the city of Babylon, "Harlot" can't be literal. A city might be full of harlots, but the city itself cannot be a harlot. And it's not literally Babylon either. By John's day, Babylon wasn't a great power. Both terms are figurative. We can't take either one literally without talking nonsense.

Yet deciding that "Babylon the great harlot" is figurative does not mean that there's no literal city. Babylon refers, I believe, to a specific city, Jerusalem, that was literally conquered in AD 70. Yet, on the other hand, taking "Babylon" as a real city does not commit us to taking every detail of John's description literally. John sees Babylon dressed in scarlet and purple, wearing a name on her forehead, drinking blood from a golden cup. We don't need to ask whether cities have foreheads, or whether they can wear clothes, or where you find a city's hand to hold a golden cup.

Yet again, though figures, all of those details have some sort of literal force. The harlot city Babylon kills martyrs, spilling real blood. Her clothing and headgear indicate she's a priestess, and the city is the priestly city Jerusalem. With her idolatries and acts of unfaithfulness, Jerusalem truly is a harlot, albeit not literally so.

John's description is a blessedly bewildering mash of literal and figurative, and as readers we have the priestly-royal privilege of drawing lines and making distinctions. It's a mash of literal figures.

How do we make sense of a text like this? How do we know the difference between literal and figurative? There's no trick, machine, or manual. Start by refusing to polarize the two. Find a mature mentor who is willing to teach you to read. Under his guidance, cultivate a sacramental imagination that can see bread and body, water and Spirit, city and harlot, tree and man, both together at a glance, without division or confusion. And then, armed with a transformed imagination and alerted senses, learn to read.

THE SPIRITUAL READER

To read well, to read in the Spirit, we must cultivate the fruits of the Spirit. Spiritual reading doesn't take place outside us. If there's to be Spiritual reading, there must be Spiritual readers. And Spiritual readers are those who walk in the Spirit in everything. If you want to learn to read well, don't quench the Spirit. Walk in the Spirit. Pray for and practice the fruits of the Spirit. Read in the Spirit.

Love is the first fruit of the Spirit (Gal 5:2). Spiritual readers must read with love. We keep company with neighbors when we keep company with books. Books may be friends or enemies.

We're called to love both in the Spirit. When we love someone, we're attentive to his or her needs and desires. When we love a book, we are attentive to the poetry of the text. Reading in the Spirit, we don't drift from the page every three seconds to check our text messages. Reading in the Spirit, we don't forget the previous chapter when we get to a new one. The Spirit trains our senses to grasp the Bible accurately and fully.

Love is patient (1 Cor 13:4). Reading takes time. Reading in the Spirit, we don't jump to conclusions about what the author is saying. We listen with care to hear what's said and what's unsaid. The best reading, Robert Penn Warren once observed, comes not on the first or fifth or tenth reading but on the hundredth. We read best when we can "remember ahead," knowing the beginning and anticipating the end at every moment. We can do that only if we read, re-read, and re-re-read. We read well only in the patience of the Spirit.

Love is not arrogant (1 Cor 13:4). Reading in the Spirit, we humble ourselves before the author. We let him set the rules. Humility makes our reading playful; we play by the author's rules. When we make ourselves small, the text and the world are enlarged. Mature readers know how to be as children before the text.

The Spirit is the Spirit of creativity. Creativity isn't incompatible with submission to authority. On the contrary, humility is the only possible starting point for creativity. Pride is never creative, except of Pandaemonium.

We cannot produce anything absolutely *ex nihilo*. Though not creative as God is creative, we are creative. To be creative, we need to humble ourselves before the materials. A sculptor must submit not only to the characteristics of marble, but to the peculiar shape and features of this piece of marble.

Pianists and violinists and ensembles, like composers, are creative artists. Like all artists, performers submit to the material—the authoritative composition from the hand of the author. True, the notes on the page limit the creativity of the performer. If he is going to play this Bach fugue, he must play these notes, count out this rhythm, maintain this pace. But the limitation isn't really limitation. It's a necessary step toward freedom. We aren't playing Bach freely when we burst through the limits and play whatever notes we please. We're no longer playing Bach at all. As he humbles himself before Bach, the performer can create Bachian music. He limits himself to these notes so his music can stretch out to heaven.

Reading is creative in a similar way. We humble ourselves before the text and learn to perform it well. Following a guide, we enter the text and the world that it creates and get to know our way around. We accept its limits. Once we become familiar with the hallways, floor plan, and general layout, we're able to sniff out hidden passageways.

None of this takes place in isolation. The Spirit is among us, occupying the space between, not merely in each of us. The Spirit gathers. He weds and welds many into one without losing the unique contributions of each. As we noted at the start of the chapter, our senses are trained to read well, and we mature in our ability to read well, in conversation. Spiritual reading is reading in communion.

Literally communion. The dialogue that makes us good readers is a liturgical dialogue. We have Bible software and the internet and books galore. Pre-modern readers and teachers had the liturgy. They had the advantage.

Medieval monks spent their days in the scriptorium, copying and studying texts. They chanted the entire Psalter each week and listened to large chunks of the Bible during their hours of prayer. The Bible entered their souls through their eyes, but God's Word chimed in their ears, and they tasted it in their mouths.

Sadly, it's impossible to replicate that kind of experience in many Protestant churches. Many churches with "Bible" in their name have little Bible in worship. Their hymns contain isolated snatches of Scripture. The pastor reads a few verses for his sermon text, but otherwise the Bible is a closed book, unread and unheard. By a weird irony, many traditionally liturgical churches are more immersed in Scripture than Bible-believing Evangelical ones. You'll hear more Bible at a Catholic Mass or an Orthodox Divine Service than you will at many Bible churches.

The Bible is solid food, but you need to mature in the Spirit to digest it. Within the liturgy, Scripture brings us to maturity. To become a Spiritual reader, you need to take up and read. You need to take note and hear.

7

World

TO SEE YOUR POWER AND YOUR GLORY.
—PSALM 63:2

God is the Hero of Scripture, the main character and actor. He creates. He sends the flood. He calls Abraham. He rescues Israel from Egypt and clears Canaanites out of Israel's land. He crowns David and gives splendor to Solomon. He drives Israel into exile and brings them up again. In the last days, He comes in person to establish Himself as King and Savior of Israel and the nations, revealing Himself as Father, Son, and Spirit.

Yet the God of the Bible is the Creator and Ruler of the *world*. The Bible is about God-with-the-world, rarely about God-in-isolation. We learn many, many things about God, but we learn them through His interaction with creation. We know God in His effects.

The Bible's worldliness is a surprise to people who don't know much about the Bible—sadly, even to many Christians. They expect a book about spiritual things, eternity, and heaven. They expect a *religious* book in the attenuated modern sense that defines "religion" as private, individual piety. Some expect a book about God-in-Himself.

What they find instead is a book about human beings, about earth and time, about bodies—a *this*-worldly book. The Bible is about aging parents longing desperately for their first children, about sibling rivalry, about political clashes between God and kings, about war and conquest, about exile and return. People come expecting a book about heaven and find the Bible is of the earth, earthy.

Scripture's laws don't look spiritual. God tells Israel how to treat slaves and punish thieves and care for the landless poor (Exod 21–23). He gives detailed instructions to help priests distinguish varieties of skin disease (Lev 13–14) and spends an embarrassing amount of time on genital emissions (Lev 15). His law prescribes who may have sex with whom and the penalties for violation (Lev 18, 20). There are rules for worship (Lev 1–7), but they don't look very spiritual either, what with all the slaughter, dismemberment, entrails, blood, fire, vapor, and smoke.

The Bible's principal characters aren't monks or mystics or hermits or scholars but men of the world—shrewd sheiks, bold shepherds, deliverers, chest-thumping judges, priests, kings, and prophets. The women of the Bible are pious, but their piety is practical and political: They pray for children and for social revolution (1 Sam 2:1–11; Luke 1:46–56), lie to protect the innocent, and sometimes reach for a hammer and spike to split an enemy's skull. Israel's prophets don't do much in the way of calculating the timing of the rapture. They're intensely engaged in the politics of their day. They instruct and rebuke kings and deliver God's interpretation of current events.

For many, the New Testament seems to be a different, more agreeable sort of book. Jesus goes to isolated places for long nights of prayer. He tells His disciples to love one another, condemns the rich and tells them to give their goods to the poor, and encourages all to trust His Father's care. He teaches His disciples how to pray and seems to avoid the messy politics of first-century Judea.

That's more like it. That's what religion really is.

But it's an optical illusion. The Bible is mostly Old Testament, and we can't disengage the two Testaments without distorting both. Besides, the Gospels are mostly taken up with Jesus' public ministry of preaching, exorcism, healing, and teaching. His main message is a political one: "The kingdom of God is at hand." God is taking charge of the world, and He's doing it through Jesus; therefore, everyone, including rulers, had better get ready for a change of regime. Jesus provokes titanic clashes with the Jewish establishment, and the battle in the temple so enrages the leaders that they plot (successfully) to kill Him.

At some point, someone decided John's Gospel was the most spiritual of the four. Whoever made that decision hadn't read the Gospel very carefully. In chapter after chapter, Jesus performs a sign and then gets into a verbal war with Jewish leaders who object to what He's done (John 4–11). John is the most litigious, the most contentious of the four Gospels.

This is spirituality. Jesus is the One born of the Spirit (John 3:1–8). But it's not the kind of soft spirituality we expect if we're used to looking at Sunday school picture books or watching Jesus movies.

The earthly focus of the Bible continues right to the end. Revelation tells us more about heaven than the rest of the Bible combined (cf. chs. 4–5, 8, 15). But at the climax of Revelation, our attention is again drawn toward earth. Instead of ending with a vision of heaven, Revelation ends with visions of a heavenly city descending to earth (Rev 21–22).

Long ago, Christians developed the mental tick of ignoring the obvious, of switching registers, of raising our mindsfrom the earthiness of Scripture to heavenly and spiritual things. We've developed the habit of translating stories about barrenness and sibling rivalry and politics and war into stories about the lonely journey of the soul. We've insisted on turning the Bible into the kind of religious book we expect or want it to be.

But the surface story of the Bible is the story of the Bible. The Bible isn't a book about heaven or eternity or spiritual things. It's a story of heaven-and-earth, eternity-and-time, of the Spirit's formation and re-formation of matter. The Bible's content is mostly about the second term in each of those pairs. Most of the Bible's sentences and stories, most of its poems and prophecies, are about earth, time, and men and women with real bodies and souls.

The Bible doesn't turn us away from history but gives us a reading of history, God's own telling of the story of Himself-with-His-world. The Bible isn't about how we can go to heaven when we die. It's not about how we can escape the prison of this world. It's about the formation, deformation, restoration, and glorification of God's creation. It's the good news that heaven has invaded and conquered earth. We don't read and study Scripture so we can escape the world. Spiritual readers study to train our senses to understand the world and history more deeply.

Even when Paul exhorts us to raise our minds to heavenly things (Col 3:1–6), it's not for the reason we might expect. We focus on heaven because that's where Jesus reigns—Jesus, the Word made flesh, Jesus the God-man, Jesus with His glorified body. As soon as Paul directs our hearts to heaven, he gives instructions about how to live out our personal relationships on earth (Col 3:8–17). We don't leave earth behind when we raise our minds to heaven. We look ahead to earth's future. Heaven is where the future happens first. We turn to heaven not to escape earth but to contemplate earth's destiny. And we contemplate that destiny so we can pray and labor until His will is done on earth as in heaven.

WORLD AS WORD

When the Bible turns our attention to the world, it's *not* turning us away from God. His eternal power and divine nature are clearly seen in what He made (Rom 1:18-32). Creation comes from the God of eternal glory and is a temporal, created radiance of that glory. That's what the world *is*.

Everything in creation manifests God. He is light (1 John 1:5) and speaks light (Gen 1:4-6). He is brighter than the sun (Ps 84:11), which every day blazes like the divine Bridegroom across the sky (Ps 19:5). Every fire and every cloud reveal the God who appears to Israel in cloud and fire (Exod 13:21). His storm rests on Sinai and shoots lightning bolts as arrows (Ps 18:14). He is fiercer and stronger than a lion, gentler than a lamb. His Spirit flutters like an eagle (Deut 32:11) and a dove (Matt 3:16). His voice is like the sound of many waters, the roaring of the sea (Ezek 1:24).

Trees link earth and heaven, like the Son of Man who straddles sea and land (Rev 10:1–2). Dew evaporates in an hour, but while it lasts it sparkles like a precious gem, refracting divine glory. Clouds are airy nothings, yet God paints sunsets with them, so they gleam with His grandeur. Birds flit and sing like the angels of heaven, and the Creator shows His kindness by providing for the worms and roaches that slither and scuttle at our feet.

At the end, the world becomes transparent to the glory of God when in the new Jerusalem, God Himself replaces the sun and moon as light source (Rev 21:23). In the end, the world, matured into a heavenly city, will shine even more fully with the brilliance of divine glory. The Bible is the story of the world's advance from glory to glory.

Made in the image of God, men and women especially manifest the glory of God. He who made the eye sees; He who made the ear hears; He who made the mouth speaks (Ps 94:8–11). His arms and hands are strong to save (Exod 7:4–5). His feet rest on the circle of heaven (Isa 40:22).

Human artifacts and actions reveal God. He is a shield (Ps 84:11) and a fortress (Ps 18:10). His voice shakes the earth like a marching army (Ezek 1:24). He's like a man overcome with wine, who wakes suddenly and starts breaking things (Ps 78:65–68). Jeremiah complains that Yahweh is a deceptive spring, which promises refreshment but gives none (Jer 15:18).

Every time you see a human being, every time you see *anything*, you're encountering a revelation of God. God speaks. God speaks the world into being. Coming from His speech, the world echoes and answers the Creator. God speaks to the creature through the creature. Our speech is always a translation of

God's prior speech. If you don't see this, you're seeing an illusion and not the world as it is. If you don't see the glory of God when you peer outside your eyeballs, you're insane. You need new eyes, ears, hands, and a new nose and tongue. You need your senses healed, trained, and tuned to reality.

Sometimes theologians say the Bible's language is accommodated. God lisps to us as we do to infants because we can't handle anything more.

That's not entirely false. God is gracious in His speech. He speaks in a way we can understand. But for readers like the medieval Jewish philosopher Maimonides or the early modern critic Benedict Spinoza, accommodation means something different. For them, Scripture's language is inadequate or second-best. Many modern readers of Scripture say that talking about God as shield and sun is childish. It's not. It's the way God has chosen to speak about Himself. It's a fitting way for God to describe Himself because God originally created sun, sea, shields and everything else to shout and sing of Him. Even before He speaks of Himself as sun, the sun already speaks of Him. The Bible only reminds us of what is already true.

Maimonides and Spinoza and their Christian heirs also complain about the Bible's use of anthropomorphisms—descriptions of God in human terms. Some think these are childish too and say we need to outgrow them. Anthropomorphisms aren't childish. God describes Himself in human terms because humans are made in His image. God doesn't have eyes as we have eyes, but He sees. He doesn't have ears like ours, but He hears. Better, we should say, "He's the original, and we are the copies." He has the original ears, eyes, mouth, hands, arms, feet. Our bodily organs are glorious copies of God's more glorious powers.

We can't grasp Scripture without knowing something about the world. We can't understand what it means for God to be sun without knowing something about the sun. We won't quake at the Lord's thunderous voice (Ps 29) unless we've heard thunder. Our life experience trains our senses and so prepares us for the solid food of Scripture. It works the other way too. We can't grasp the world rightly without Scripture. Only the mature with trained senses can stand solid food, but Scripture trains our senses so we hear, see, touch, smell, and taste the world as it actually is. Spiritual reading of Scripture makes us good readers of the world.

As we saw in chapter 6, all language is inherently metaphorical. Every time we speak, we speak of the world as something else. We speak of flying things with the sound "bird" and fluffy-tailed climbing things with the sound "squirrel." The Bible teaches us how to speak rightly of the world. It teaches us to see everything as a finite form of God's infinite glory. Because everything is just that.

THREE-STORY HOUSE

The Bible's focus on earth is plain from the first chapters. As soon as we're introduced to God, we're introduced to His world: "In the beginning, God created the heavens and the earth" (Gen 1:1). The next sentence turns our attention to earth: "Now the earth was formless and void" (Gen 1:2). That's where our attention stays for the rest of Genesis 1 and into Genesis 2 and 3 and on through most of the Bible.

The whole Bible grows from the seeds planted in Genesis 1–3. The patterns, persons, and events of the early chapters of the Bible set the trajectory for the whole story. Every man is a variation on Adam, every woman a daughter of Eve, every environment an Eden or a ruined Eden, a wilderness. To read the Bible well, we have to have the first chapters firmly in our minds. That's the aim of the remainder of this book.

At the beginning, creation is nothing but dark *tohu wabohu*, "formless-and-void-ness" (Gen 1:2). Over the course of the creation week, God transforms all of those conditions. First, He calls light into existence to dispel the darkness; then He forms the formless; finally, He fills the empty form. He switches on the lights, builds the house, and then moves in the furniture.

He spends roughly the first half of the creation forming. God calls out into the undifferentiated darkness, "Let there be light," and there is light. He separates light and darkness so that they dance out nights and days (Gen 1:3–5). God gives creation a temporal form—its rhythm and harmonies.

Then He turns to forming space, which is primarily a hydraulic operation. He hauls water from earth up to heaven and then separates the waters above from the waters below with a firmament (Gen 1:6–8). At the beginning of Day 3, He divides the waters that remain on earth so that dry land appears (Gen 1:9–10). Creation is an art of boundary-making.

By the middle of the third day, God has created a three-story cosmic house. There's a firmament above, called heaven. Earth is beneath the firmament, and below the earth are the waters of the sea.

Throughout Scripture, the phrase "heaven, earth, and waters under the earth" means "everything in the visible creation." The Second Word prohibits Israel from making and bowing to anything "in heaven above, or on the earth beneath, or in the waters under the earth" (Exod 20:4). Yahweh is the One who "builds His upper chambers in the heavens, and has founded His vaulted dome over the earth" and "who calls for the waters of the sea" (Amos 9:6). He brings universal judgment when He shakes "the heavens and the earth, the sea also and the dry land" (Hag 2:6) or when He empties the earth of beasts, the sky of birds, and the sea of fish (Zeph 1:2–3).

When seven angels trumpet their trumpets, the Lamb burns the earth with fiery hail (Rev 8:8) then tosses a mountain into the sea that turns the ocean to blood (Rev 8:10). A star falls into the springs of water, poisoning the rivers (Rev 8:10), and when the fourth angel sounds, the lights of the firmament blink out (Rev 8:12). When all is said and done, each story of the cosmos has been demolished.

When all is going well, these zones of creation remain distinct and bounded. Heavenly waters stay in heaven, and the sea politely observes the boundary of the shore. When God removes the boundaries, the world returns to an undifferentiated primordial soup. Seeing the violence of the world, He removes the firmament barrier and lets deadly rain loose on the world in the flood. After forty days and nights of rain, with additional water bubbling up from beneath the sea, the world is back to its original state—a watery emptiness (Gen 7–9).

Sometimes the firmament cracks and crashes to the earth as giant hailstones (Exod 9:18–34; Isa 28:2, 17; Rev 8:7; 11:19; 16:21). Yahweh rips the veil of the sky as He comes to see, discern, and pass judgment, and to help and rescue His faithful ones (Isa 64:1). Jeremiah cuts to the chase. Heaven goes dark, and the earth quakes as the world slips back into its original formless-and-void-ness, the *tohu wabohu* that existed before God's voice pierced the darkness (Jer 4:23–26).

Every time you read about something happening to "heaven, earth, and sea" in Scripture, you're reading about a worldwide something. Every time you see the boundaries between heaven, earth, and sea dissolve, you're watching creation-in-reverse. God de-forms what He once formed.

Conversely, when God puts boundaries back in place, He's re-forming and re-creating. When flood waters top the mountains, Yahweh remembers Noah and sends a wind to uncover the earth (Gen 8:1). The Hebrew word for wind is *ruach*, the same as the word for Spirit. Genesis 8:1 is a replay of Genesis 1:2, with the Spirit-wind over the deep re-forming the world. When Israel is trapped at the Red Sea, Yahweh divides the waters to make a path of dry land (Exod 14:21–22), replicating the work of the third day of creation. He shakes down the old world of Egypt so He can form the new creation of Israel (cf. Ps 77:16–20).

The Bible teaches us to see the cosmos as a three-story house. Scripture attributes architectural features to the cosmos. Heaven has foundations (2 Sam 22:8), and so does earth (Ps 82:5; 104:5), laid by the Architect and Builder of creation (Isa 51:13). The earth is set on pillars (1 Sam 2:8; Job 9:6; Ps 75:3). The firmament is a starry dome over our heads (Amos 9:6).

Nations are small-scale creations, constructed by creative boundary-making. God sits as King on the circle of the heavens, and the king shines in the firmament of the people. The people are earth, and their enemies are the seas that threaten to overwhelm them. Israel especially is the people of land, and the gentile nations are often pictured as a surging, turgid ocean.

Yahweh sometimes allows the sea to flood the land (Isa 8:6-8), but then He speaks again, and Israel emerges as dry land from the midst of the sea. The micro-creation of Israel is de-formed, then re-formed.

God's various sanctuaries replicate the three-story structure of creation. With its three decks, Noah's ark is a small cosmos (Gen 6:16). The tabernacle and temple are divided into three zones—the court, the Holy Place (or nave), and the Most Holy Place (or, in King James English, the oracle). Each is a small cosmos, training our eyes to see the world as a cosmic temple.

These uses of the cosmic symbolism of heaven, earth, and sea clarify what's happening in various passages of Scripture. When Jeremiah says the world is slipping back into an empty void, he's not necessarily talking about the end of the physical universe. We have to look at the context. When we do, it's clear he's warning that Yahweh will demolish Judah's world, not planet Earth (Jer 4:22, 27–31).

Yahweh threatens to strip sky, land, and sea, but Zephaniah makes it clear He's stretching out His hand against Judah and Jerusalem (Zeph 1:1–6). The trumpets of the trumpet angels dismantle earth, sea, rivers, and land, but Revelation is about things that happened soon after John sees the visions (Rev 1:1–2). John isn't seeing visions of the end of the universe. He's seeing visions of the end of the old world.

To read well, we need to read bifocally, or trifocally, remembering that the world is a house, is a temple, is a political order. And then, having read Scripture, we need to see the world bifocally, seeing it as a stable or collapsing house, a glorious or a ruined temple. In this way, Scripture trains our senses to have contact with the world as it truly is.

FURNITURE OF CREATION

After the Lord forms the world into heaven, earth, and sea, He begins to fill it. In the middle of Day 3, He commands the earth to sprout vegetation. Day 4 fills the firmament with sun, moon, and stars. On Day 5, He creates swimming things in the sea and flying things that fly across the firmament and nest on the land.

On day 6, God calls land animals from the earth and creates man, male and female, in His image and likeness.

Genesis 1 isn't simply telling us that God created all these things. It shows us how these things interconnect.

On Day 1, God creates light, and for the first three days, light comes and goes without any light-giving bodies in the firmament. Presumably, the light comes from God Himself. (Where else would it come from?) On Day 4, God delegates this light-giving task to the sun, moon and stars. He gives them authority to rule the day and night (Gen 1:16), as He will later delegate authority to man to rule birds, fish, and animals (Gen 1:26). Heavenly lights rule from the sky as human beings rule on earth.

On Day 3, God calls up fruitful plants (Gen 1:11–12), and on Day 6, He commands man to "be fruitful" (Gen 1:28). We're to imitate the fecundity of the original fruitful things. On Day 5, God creates (Gen 1:21; Heb. *bara'*) great sea monsters, as He creates heaven and earth (Gen 1:1) and man (Gen 1:27; *bara'* used three times). By virtue of special creation, sea monsters and man are linked. Land animals come from the same earth as man, on the same day, and so are related to and symbolic of man.

Within the creation account itself, we're given hints of the associations of plants and man, of heavenly lights and man, of fish and man, of birds and man. The creation account gives the main coordinates for a way of looking at everything in creation as meaningful for us. The rest of Scripture fills this out, describing in more detail how the furniture of creation represents us, even as it manifests the glory of God. It all coheres in Jesus, who is both the glorious Creator and the imaging creature.

BIBLICAL BOTANY

Plants come from the earth bearing fruit in response to God's word (Gen 1:11–12) as man comes from earth and is commanded to be fruitful (Gen 1:28). Plants are the first fruitful things God calls from the earth. Types of men and women are symbolized by species of plants. Righteous men and women are like strong trees, planted by nourishing streams of water, bearing fruit and living long in the green of youth (Ps 1:3). The wicked aren't trees but chaff, the detritus of plants blown away by the wind (Ps 1:4), or grass, which withers and dies as soon as it's grown (Ps 92:7). Indeed, *all* flesh is grass (Ps 40:7–8).

Some people are thorn bushes (Gen 3:18), like Abimelech, who covets kingship only because, unlike the olive tree and the grapevine, he produces no delightful or useful fruit (Judg 9:7–15). Trees are different. Trees stand on the ground and stretch upright to heaven, just like human beings. Trees have trunks and arms and are topped with a bushy head of glory, just like human beings. No wonder kings are trees (e.g., Dan 4) because in their majesty they link heaven and earth. Trees are ladders to heaven. And thus, Jesus is the tree of life.

Great trees can come crashing down, reduced to stumps (Dan 4). The Lord sends woodsmen with axes to chop down the trees (Isa 10:1–19) and to turn temples to kindling (Ps 74:1–11). David's own house is chopped down to the roots, down to Jesse, as if David never existed (Isa 11:1), until Yahweh brings new growth, a new tree, from the old (Isa 11:1-5). Israel is an olive tree, its roots in the fathers and into which wild gentiles are grafted (Rom 11:11–24). As olive tree, Israel provides the oil that will illumine the nations, turning them into bright lamps burning with the Spirit.

The entirety of biblical history takes place among trees—Eden's tree of life and the tree of knowledge, the site of Adam's sin (Gen 2:16–17; 3:1–7); the tree of the cross (Gal 3:13) that springs up with new life in the resurrection so we can once again eat from the tree of life in a new Jerusalem (Rev 22:1–5).

This isn't poetic ornamentation on the biblical story. The substance of the biblical story runs through trees and plants. The Bible isn't showing us a "spiritual dimension" to the real world. It gives us the key to unlock the significance of the real world of plants. The trees of Scripture are real trees but bursting with meaning. Genesis 1 not only teaches us how to read the Word; it teaches us how to read the world.

SCRIPTURAL ASTRONOMY

Sun, moon, and stars are set in the firmament on Day 4 to rule day and night, to mark seasons and times, and to serve as signs. Human rulers are pictured as heavenly lights. Yahweh promises Abraham his children will be like the stars of heaven (Gen 15:5; 22:17; 26:4). This doesn't just mean he will have many descendants. It prophesies the status and quality of his descendants. Abraham will be the father of kings (Gen 17:6).

Sun, moon, and twelve constellations represent Jacob, Rachel, and the sons of Jacob (Gen 37:9–11). David's throne is like the sun before Yahweh (Ps 89:36). When we lift our eyes to heaven, we, like Abraham, see the story of our people.

When Yahweh returns after exile, Zion will no longer need the sun or moon. Yahweh will be their permanent light. Because Yahweh is Zion's Husband, because Zion reflects the light of God, the light that shines in Zion is "your light," turning Zion into the light of the world (Isa 60:19–20).

Because heavenly lights symbolize rulers, the blotting out or fall of lights represents the fall of kings and rulers and the collapse of a political order. "The stars of heaven and their constellations will not flash forth their light. The sun will be dark when it rises and the moon will not shed its light," Isaiah says (Isa 13:10). The collapse of outer space? No. The fall of Babylon (Isa 13:1).

"Immediately after the tribulation of those days the sun will be darkened, and the moon will not give its light, and the stars will fall from the sky, and the powers of the heavens will be shaken," Jesus says, quoting Isaiah (Matt 24:29). The end of the world? Nope. The fall of the temple and Jerusalem (Matt 24:1–3).

When the fourth angel trumpets, John sees "a third of the sun and a third of the moon and a third of the stars" are struck (Rev 8:12). End of the world? Not at all. A catastrophe that took place soon after John saw the visions.

This isn't mere metaphor. These are literal figures. Events are taking place—real catastrophes. And these catastrophes do mark the end of a world—the end of a temple order, or the end of a dynasty, or the end of an empire. When we read the Bible bifocally, through the double lenses of Genesis 1, we begin to see political events rightly: as cosmic, earth-shaking events.

All things in heaven hold together in Jesus. He is the Bridegroom-Sun, the bright morning star. He ascends to heavenly places to rule and to govern times and seasons. Creation reveals the glory of God, and Jesus is that glory.

ORNITHEOLOGY AND ICHTHEOLOGY

Birds were created on Day 5, along with swarmers of the sea. Insofar as they occupy the upper region of earth, birds are linked with heavenly lights and with angels, who are also winged. Though birds fly across the firmament, they are also earth-dwellers. They are, in fact, the first earth dwellers (Gen 1:22). Birds mediate between earth and heaven.

Birds manifest the Spirit (Gen 1:2). The Spirit hovers over the waters, undulating like a winged bird. The only other use of the verb is in Deuteronomy 32, where it describes the movement of a nesting eagle (Deut 32:11). The Spirit is "over the face of the deep"; on Day 3, Elohim makes plants "on the face of the earth"; birds fly "on the face of the firmament." Birds' wings image winged Yahweh ("I carried you on eagles' wings," Exod 19:4).

A dove brings an olive branch to Noah, a sign that new creation is emerging from the waters. The dove is a messenger/mediator that flies through the air to link Noah to the renewed earth. The scene again links birds with the Spirit: The dove hovers over the waters as the Spirit did (Gen 8:8–12). It's no accident that the Spirit appears as a dove at Jesus' baptism. The bird/Spirit analogy is baked into creation and knit into history.

Abram cuts covenant with animals and birds (Gen 15), confirming the promise of land and an abundant seed. The seed will be like stars and sand, which parallel the land animals and birds of the covenant ceremony. Sand : stars :: cattle : birds :: people : kings.

All Israelites are birds with tassels on the wings of their robes (Num 15:37–41). They are Yahweh's flock, also his bevy of doves and his kit of pigeons, sometimes his murder of crows. Israel is winged because it's a heavenly people, dwelling on earth but with a unique connection to heaven. Priests especially are linked with mediating birds as they move between earth and the heaven of the sanctuary.

Birds and fish form a Day 5 pair. Birds fly across the face of the firmament. Fish occupy the lowest space of earth, the sea. Because the sea represents the nations, fish represent gentiles. Big fish are big gentiles, like the Assyrian empire (Jonah 3) or Nebuchadnezzar of Babylon (Jer 51:34) or Pharaoh (Ps 74:13–14; Ezek 29:3). Jesus is the Fisher King. Unlike most Old Testament heroes, He eats fish and sends out His fishers of men on sea adventures (like Paul's) to reel in the gentiles.

Once we focus our eyes on birds and fish, we can fill out a political scheme based on creation. Fish occupy the lowest parts of the earth, beasts are on the land, and birds mediate between land and sky. That is, fish are gentiles, land animals are Israel, birds are angelic priests.

This symbolism is behind the use of birds in the Levitical system. Herd animals represent leaders, and flock animals represent members of the people. Poor people (Lev 5:7, 11; 12:8) and lepers (Lev 14:1–9) offer birds. Offerings of birds bring the marginal from the margins into the presence of God. This fits with the priest-bird symbolism. If lepers are marginal in being outside, priests occupy the other margin, standing as far inside as it's possible to be. Both margins portray the place of Israel in the world: a marginal nation chosen to bring the nations to the Creator.

ZOOTHEOLOGY

Land animals are at the center of human vocation. While the Lord gave man dominion over fish and birds, land animals are nearer to and more intertwined with human life. Most birds fly free, and most fish are outside human control. Many land animals have been domesticated.

God created some animals domesticated, the animals Scripture describes as "cattle" (*behemah*)—flock animals like sheep and goats, herd animals like bovines, domesticated work animals like donkeys and camels. Beasts are wild animals, which begin outside human rule but are brought under human control over time. In the first act of dominion, Adam previews the end by naming both cattle and beasts (Gen 2:20).

Adam's sin is an inversion of his proper relation to beasts and creeping things. Instead of taking control and protecting Eve from the serpent, he allows it to trick her into eating the fruit. Because of their subjection to a beast, Adam and Eve become beasts, clothed in animal skins as they leave the garden (Gen 3:21).

That animal clothing replaces the plant clothing, the fig leaf aprons, that Adam and Eve make for themselves. Animal skins are a blessing, covering the shame of human nakedness. Covering-by-animal is one of the keys to the Mosaic sacrificial system, where an animal is slaughtered and turned to smoke on the altar in order to cover or atone for sin. The whole sacrificial system is rooted in the created analogy between man and beast.

Different species of animals represent different kinds of people. Kings are supposed to be lions, ferocious protectors of their pride and dangerous to their enemies (Gen 49:9; Rev 5:5). Samson and David demonstrate their prowess by killing lions (Judg 14:5–9; 1 Sam 17:34–37). If they can kill lions, they can successfully battle Philistines. As the lion king, David gathers leonine warriors who share his strength and skill in combat (1 Chr 12:8).

Other men are violent scavengers, jackals who prey on the weak or sneak into abandoned cities to pick through the garbage (Isa 13:22; 34:13). Imagery like this could well be literal. During the coronavirus outbreak of 2020, wild boars and coyotes wandered through empty cities. When human society breaks down, wild animals move in. But the imagery is also symbolic. When the king is not a lion, predatory men roam freely, preying on their defenseless sheep.

Other people are serpents, who kill with the poison under their tongues (Pss 58:4; 140:3). The righteous who trust in the Lord mimic the Seed of the woman and crush the heads of the serpentine wicked (Gen 3:15; Ps 91:13). Groups of animals represent groups of people, which is why Abraham, Isaac, Jacob, Moses, and David start as shepherds and herdsmen before leading the flock of God (cf. Ezek 34:15, 17; Zech 9:16; 1 Pet 5:2). Other groups are like packs of dogs, roaming the streets and baring their teeth against the righteous (Pss 22:16; 59:6, 14).

A social taxonomy is built into the sacrificial system. Israel offers only domesticated animals—animals from the flock or herd. Animals for the sin offering are specified according to the offerer's status in Israel (Lev 4). A priest has to offer a bull (Lev 4:3), a leader a male goat (4:23), and a common person a female goat (Lev 4:28). Male animals represent leaders, and female animals represent the people of Israel, the bride of Yahweh.

The rules of clean and unclean animals also lay out a social taxonomy. Clean domesticated animals may be sacrificed and represent Israel as a priestly people. Many clean animals, though, cannot be offered on the altar, including "the deer, the gazelle, the roebuck, the wild goat, the ibex, the antelope and the mountain sheep" (Deut 14:5). These represent gentiles who worship Yahweh without becoming part of the priestly people. Israel may become one flesh with these animals by eating them just as they may have close communion with God-fearing gentiles.

On the other hand, some domesticated animals (donkeys, camels, pigs) and many wild animals (all predators, rodents) are unclean. Israelites are neither to eat them nor to touch their corpses.

The curse on the serpent is in the background: "On your belly shall you go, and dust you shall eat all the days of your life" (Gen 3:14). Man is made of dust and is cursed to return to dust (Gen 3:19). If the serpent is a dust-eater, he's a man-eater, an agent of the curse who drags Adam's children down to the dust of death. Land animals that walk in the cursed dust are serpentine, and Israel is forbidden to eat them. Animals with hooves to protect them from the curse-bearing dust are clean.

When David describes his enemies as strong bulls, lions, and dogs, his metaphor isn't arbitrary (Ps 22:11–21). Bulls are priests. Lions are kings and other civil rulers. Dogs are scavenging mobs. David is under assault from church, state, and the mob. The Psalm isn't a generic prophecy of the suffering of Jesus but a precise animal parable, for Jesus is the object of assault from precisely these three beasts.

Sometimes beasts become monstrous. John sees two beasts, one from the sea and one from the land (Rev 13:1–10). The sea beast is a gentile power, picturing Rome (cf. Dan 7:1–8), while the land beast is a Jewish figure, representing Jews who have sold their souls to Roman power. Together, empire and false church kill and devour the saints, just as Romans and Jews allied to destroy Jesus.

SEVEN DAYS

Creation is spatially structured as a three-story house—a residence for plants, heavenly lights, birds, fish, and animals. But creation isn't a static, motionless thing. Not for a nano-moment. Even its making takes time. God could have spoken the whole ordered universe into being with a word, but He chose not to. He instead built the world over the course of six days, capping His work with a day of rest and glory. Creation is made in movement, and it continues moving. It's not only an architectural wonder. It's a musical wonder, a billion-voiced symphony of harmonious moments.

Genesis 1 lays out the basic melody of history, a seven-note sequence that is repeated over and over in Scripture. It's the rhythm of creation because it's the rhythm of the Spirit, who is Himself a "seven" (Rev 1:4; 3:1; 4:5; 5:6). The Spirit who equips the Servant of Yahweh with seven graces (Isa 11:1–5) hovers over the waters of the deep. He initiates the rhythm of evenings and mornings, weeks, months, and years. Under the baton of the Spirit, time drums a seven-beat dance.

This is the root of typology. Typology isn't simply a way of reading. It's not simply the trick of spotting Jesus hidden like Waldo in unlikely texts. Typology is a theology of history.

God has habits. Nothing He does is ever exactly the same as before. No day of creation is identical to any other day. But there's a recurring rhythm as God takes, speaks, tears apart, rearranges, and pronounces good. And as the years roll by, He repeats the same actions. He takes hold of a corrupted world, undoes it in the flood, then remakes it. When Israel turns to idols in the time of Judges, Yahweh tears apart His sanctuary, sending part to Gibeah and the other part (eventually) to Jerusalem. When the temple is defiled, He dismantles it and sends it to Babylon so that it can later be returned to the land and rebuilt. Worlds end in a formless void, but then the Spirit breathes new life.

Types of Jesus aren't isolated pictures of a coming Messiah. We spot types of Jesus and the church in the Bible because the Bible and the history it records run in cycles. We spot types of Jesus because God keeps forming new Adams from the dust of the ground, building new Eves, setting them in new Edens, until He sends the Last Adam. We spot Jesus again and again because the Spirit keeps beating out his seven-day tempo.

Many Bible teachers say the number 7 is the number of fullness. That may be true but doesn't tell us much. And it's the wrong way to read the poetry of Scripture. It's a move from a concrete number (7) to an abstract quality (fullness).

Bible teachers make this move a lot. The desert represents testing. Lions represent strength or destructive power. White symbolizes purity. In each case, we move from something we can sense—a place we can survey, a color we can see, a number we can count, an animal that could rip us to shreds—to some quality that we can only think about.

The Bible doesn't work like that. It doesn't move from body to mind, or from matter to Spirit, or from concrete to abstract. Instead, the Bible connects one body with another—one thing, event, or person to another. We move from one concrete reality to another to another, seeing each in the light of the others. Scripture doesn't move us away from our senses but trains them.

The desert has specific qualities, but when a desert is mentioned in Scripture it evokes a set of specific episodes—Israel's journey from Egypt to the land, Elijah's retreat, John the Baptist, and Jesus' temptations. White doesn't represent some abstract quality but draws together the color of manna, the white skin of the leper, the white of a laundered garment, the white robes of the heavenly choir. Lion doesn't simply conjure a few leonine qualities but reverberates with prophecies and events throughout the Bible.

When Scripture employs sevenfold patterns, it isn't evoking thoughts of fullness or completeness. It's evoking thoughts of God's acts in creating the world. Sevenfold patterns are re- or de-creation patterns.

I. THE FIRST VERSE OF the Bible contains seven Hebrew words, and the second verse contains fourteen. Yahweh's Sabbath is recounted in a thirty-five word summary (Gen 2:1-3), and three of the sentences in that summary have seven words and include the phrase "on the seventh day" (vv. 2-3a). "Heaven" and "earth" appear together seven times in Genesis 1:1-2:4 (1:1, 15, 17, 20; 2:1, 4 [2x]).

II. YAHWEH'S INSTRUCTIONS FOR MAKING the tabernacle (Exod 25–31) are laid out in seven speeches, each marked by the words "God spoke to Moses, saying." God created the world through seven days of speech. He creates a new world, the tabernacle, by speaking seven times to Moses who, in obedience to the Word of Yahweh, makes a new world.

III. EACH ACTION OF THE PRIESTLY ordination ends with the phrase "as Yahweh commanded Moses" (Lev 8:4, 9, 13, 17, 21, 29, 36). The clause appears seven times, hinting that Aaron and his sons are being made "new men" through the ordination rite.

IV. SEVEN FEASTS ARE LISTED in the calendar of Leviticus 23. Each year cycles through a creation-week of appointed times.

V. THE LONG CENTRAL VISION of Revelation (Rev 4–16) is organized around a series of seven events: Seven seals open to seven trumpets, which climax in the outpouring of seven bowls. In each sequence, the world is undone, un-created, and returned to the formless void.

VI. SOLOMON'S WISDOM IS MANIFESTED in a sevenfold manner: his house, his food, the seating arrangements, the standing of his table servants, the attire of his table servants, his cupbearers, and the ascent into the house of Yahweh (1 Kgs 10:4-5).

VII. NO ARMY IN ISRAEL'S history is as well-equipped as Uzziah's, each warrior being issued a sevenfold panoply of offensive and defensive arms (2 Chr 26:14).

Whenever your eye lands on a list, whenever a phrase is repeated again and again, start counting. You'll often find a hint of Genesis 1 lurking in unexpected places.

Sevenfold patterns aren't mere literary devices. They describe God's characteristic way of working in the world. As we sense the rhythms of Scripture's sevens, we learn to sense the rhythm of our lives and the rhythms of the life of the world. Spiritual readers gain a good sense of rhythm and learn to read the rhythms of world.

THERE AND BACK AGAIN

Sevenfold plots, lists, and speeches are common in Scripture. So are chiasms. A chiasm is a way of organizing a text, whether a story, a speech, a letter, or a series of visions. In a chiastic text, the second half of the text repeats the first half in reverse order. Jesus uses chiasms with some frequency:

Sabbath
    was made for man
    not man
for Sabbath. (Mark 2:27)

Or,

Many who are first
    shall be last;
    and the last
first. (Matt 19:30)

That last one is especially neat, since the form exactly imitates the substance. Jesus says those who are first (Jews, leaders) will enter the kingdom last. In the course of the sentence, "last" and "first" trade places, which is *just* what Jesus is talking about.

Larger sections of Scripture are arranged in chiastic form. As many have noted, the flood is a large concentric text, centered on "Yahweh remembered Noah":

A. Violence in God's creation (6:11–12)
  B. First divine address: resolution to destroy (6:13–22)
    C. Second divine address: command to enter the ark (7:1–10)
      D. Beginning of the flood (7:11–16)
        E. The rising flood waters (7:17–24)
          GOD'S REMEMBRANCE OF NOAH
        E'. The receding flood waters (8:1–5)
      D'. The drying of the earth (8:6–14)
    C'. Third divine address: command to leave the ark (8:15–19)
  B'. God's resolution to preserve order (8:20–22)
A'. Fourth divine address: covenant blessing and peace (9:1–17)

Chiasms may seem odd and exotic, but they're very common in ancient literature. Every ancient rhetorical text includes a section on the use of chiasmus. But their frequency in Scripture suggests something more is going on. Chiasms aren't arbitrary ways of organizing texts. The chiastic pattern tells us something profound about reality.

Chiasms are there-and-back-again patterns. The text moves out, or up, to a climax and then returns back home. Along the way, things change. The end is never exactly like the beginning. The shire isn't the same shire when Bilbo returns. But there is a feeling of return. The whole Bible is a there-and-back-again story. God creates a world in 6 + 1 days and sets Adam in Eden. Adam seizes forbidden fruit and is driven from the garden out into the howling waste. Israel's history moves toward a crux, a literal crux: the cross of Jesus, the turning point of history.

From there, history runs in reverse: People estranged from God are made His table companions. The Spirit of Jesus gathers divided nations into one body. Lands turn fruitful; deserts become gardens. The world begins to mature toward the new Jerusalem until the heavenly city comes to rest on earth, a great garden city, better than the beginning—a city that is and is not Paradise restored.

Thomas Aquinas was right: Everything is encompassed by a movement of *exitus* and *reditus*, of going out from God in creation and returning to God in new creation. The Bible is full of chiasms because creation moves in a great chiasm.

CONCLUSION

Nothing in Scripture is merely literary. Everything, down to the design of a passage and the metaphors used, is instructive, designed to train us for every good work. Chiasms aren't mere literary devices. They mimic the shape of history and show that every episode follows the contours of the whole. Spiritual readers pay attention to every dimension of the poetry because we know every detail matters, even the least of these.

Solomon knew a lot about plants, stars, and animals. But we shouldn't think of him as a zoologist or botanist or astronomer in the modern sense. The Bible mainly teaches us to think with plants and animals. The Bible is an animal story about the serpent's temptation and Jesus the sacrificial Lamb, who ascends as the Lion of Judah to send the dove of the Spirit to hover over the world and form it into a new creation. It's a tale of trees, a star story, a treasure hunt, a fishing expedition, and a human story of mountains, cities, deserts, and adventures.

Spiritual readers learn to engage with the world through the Bible so that every thing and every moment becomes a sacrament for communion with the Creator. God gave the world to Adam as food. As the Bible heals us, as we become strong on its solid food, our eyes are dazzled by a continuous feast of glory.

As Spiritual readers, our senses are trained to use created things, interpreted through Scripture, to make sense of the world and our place in it. Do you know some bramble bushes? Maybe you go to church with some. Are your co-workers snakes or jackals? Better study Scripture to learn how to battle them.

Is your pastor a lion? I hope so. Are tyrants and wicked shepherds plotting together against the faithful? Read Revelation to anticipate the rest of the story. Are you stuck between Pharaoh's armies and the sea? Wait for it. Wait for the wind that will make a path of dry land.

As we learn the structural forms and plot patterns of the Bible, as we learn to engage history through the Bible, we gain a sense of where we are in the story. Is this a time of uprooting or planting, of breaking or building? Is it a time to gather or to scatter, to embrace or refrain? As we learn the Bible's recurring patterns, we learn to dance in rhythm with the world because the rhythm of the Word is the rhythm of the world.

8

Adam

JESUS STRETCHED OUT HIS HAND
AND TOUCHED HIM.
—MATTHEW 8:3

Jesus is Adam. That is one of the most obvious types in the Bible. Paul's overview of history has three main characters: Adam, Moses, and Jesus (Rom 5:12–21). Paul mainly compares and contrasts the first and Last. Because of one man's sin, death and sin enter the world and spread. Because of Jesus' one act of righteousness, life and righteousness triumph. Through one man's disobedience, many are made sinners. By one man's obedience, many are made righteous. Jesus undoes the doings of the first Adam.

Paul also appeals to the Adam-Christ connection when he teaches on the resurrection. Here Paul doesn't contrast unrighteous Adam with righteous Jesus. He contrasts created Adam with new-created Jesus. Adam has a natural body, made "from the earth, earthy." The second man is from heaven. Jesus doesn't become a living soul but a life-giving Spirit. At the last day, that transformation will happen to us. For now, we bear the natural image of the earthly man. At the resurrection, we will bear the image of the heavenly (1 Cor 15:45–49). Our present perishable, shameful, weak, natural body is sown as a seed so that an imperishable, glorious, powerful, spiritual body can sprout (1 Cor 15:42–44).

Though the Gospels rarely mention Adam, they're pervaded by the same Adam typology. Jesus calls himself "Son of Man" over seventy times (e.g., Matt 8:20; Mark 2:10; Luke 5:24; John 1:51). "What is man," Psalm 8 asks, "or the son of man?" The psalmist answers by paraphrasing Genesis 1: God crowns the son of man with glory and majesty and gives him rule over the works of His hands—sheep, oxen, and beasts, birds and fish (Ps 8:5–6). The Son of Man is Son of Adam.

In a vision, Daniel sees "one like a son of man" ascending to the Ancient of Days to receive rule, dominion, and a kingdom (Dan 7:9–14). That dominion once belonged to beasts—a winged lion, a lopsided bear, a winged leopard, and an indescribably ferocious monster (Babylon, Persia, Greece, and Rome). The Son of Man recovers the authority of Adam. Jesus the Son of Man is Daniel's beast-tamer.

Jesus' life parallels and inverts Adam's. He's born outside normal lines of descent, born of a virgin as Adam was born from untilled, virgin earth (Matt 1:23, 25). He's tempted by Satan to turn stones into bread. Jesus refuses, though He is fasting in the wilderness (Matt 4:1–11). Unlike Adam, He doesn't break the fast. Jesus' miracles undo the curse. With a touch or a word, He cleanses leprosy, straightens limbs, purges impurities, raises the dead. He restores glory to the deformed children of Adam. He wears a crown of cursed thorns to die on a tree (Gen 3:18) and suffers outside the gate, exiled from Eden (Gen 3:24). At his trial, Pilate presents Jesus to the mobs: "Behold the man" (John 19:5). Behold man. Behold Adam, cursed Adam, shamed Adam, soon-to-be new Adam, risen in glory.

ADAM IN EDEN

Jesus is Adam. That's obvious. But it can be misunderstood. It's misunderstood if we misconstrue Adam's original situation.

Christians sometimes assume Adam's situation is static. He's in Paradise with everything he needs. Why would he want to go anywhere else? We might think Eden is a lost ideal to which we will someday return. Salvation is a return to the beginning. Adam falls into a world of change and time. Salvation means rescue from time and change.

That's all wrong. Adam's not supposed to stay in Paradise. God commands Adam to be fruitful, multiply, and fill the earth (Gen 1:26-28). He can't do that if he stays in Eden. God commands him to subdue the earth and rule it (Gen 1:28). He can't do that by staying in Eden either. He's supposed to make the rest of the world like Paradise.

Adam's descendants share Adam's original vocation. We people the planet. We discover creation's powers and potentials, turn metals into flying machines and self-driving cars, plough and plant to make the land productive, carve stone into sculpture and organize sounds into symphonies, explore the depths of the sea and heights of the tallest mountains and hurtle out toward distant galaxies, tend forests and care for animals so our great-great-grandchildren can delight in the dazzling variety of God's creation.

God makes the world glorious. Creation *is* glory, a created radiance of the glory of God. Everything in creation reveals a facet of His beauty. Adam is God's agent to make it more glorious.

In this, Adam mimics his Creator. Even at the beginning, the world isn't changeless. Each day during the creation week, God remodels the world to make it better. Darkness isn't great, so He calls light into existence and calls it good. Day 2 dawns, and He's busy moving waters up and setting a firmament. As soon as Day 3 comes, He's not satisfied with what He's done, so He divides the waters below and summons the land to produce plants. That's good, but only until Day 4, when He does something brand new yet again. A lighted world is glorious. A lighted world with waters above and below is more glorious. A lighted world with heaven, earth, and sea is more glorious still. But a filled world is better than an empty one, so He spends the second half of the creation week filling it.

By the time Yahweh sits back to take His Sabbath delight, creation is more beautiful than ever. But this process doesn't end on the first Sabbath. God hasn't stopped nudging the world from glory to glory. Every day from Day 1 to this very moment brings something new.

As the image of God, Adam exists to remodel and fill, to keep the world moving from glory to glory. Our destiny is not a return to Eden. Our final home will be a city, adorned with the treasures of the nations (Rev 21:1–22:5). Paul says the same in 1 Corinthians 15:44: "If there is a natural body, there is a spiritual body." He doesn't say, "If there is a sinful body, there's a spiritual body." A Spiritual body doesn't merely reverse the effects of sin. A Spiritual body is a glorification of creation. Creation is designed to be glorified by Adam and his children. Glory is where creation is heading, whether or not Adam sinned. As children of Adam, we take and touch the world, break it down, and reassemble it to increase the voltage of its glory.

Along with the rest of creation, Adam and his children are created to be glorified. Human beings glorify and are glorified in glorifying. Human progress from glory to glory is one of the main threads of biblical history. As I mentioned in Part 1, James Jordan has said the Bible tells a triple story:

I. IT'S A STORY OF *sin and redemption*. God creates Adam and Eve. They sin and are condemned to death. God sends Jesus to rescue humanity from sin and death and restore us to communion with Him.

II. IT'S A STORY OF *holy war*. God creates Adam and Eve. God permits a serpent to tempt Eve. Adam is supposed to crush the serpent's head right then and there, but fails. History is God's centuries-long war against Satan and his seed. Jesus comes as the Seed of the Woman to conquer the serpent and to give us power to trample Satan underfoot.

III. IT'S A STORY OF *maturation*. God creates Adam and Eve as children. They serve in the garden, but they're supposed to grow up into king and queen, prophet and prophetess. Their sin interrupts and impedes their education. Under the Old

Covenant, God cares for Israel as a young child, training him toward adulthood. Jesus is the mature man and restores us to the path of maturity, so we and the world grow from glory to glory.

Each storyline hinges on the two Adams. The first Adam sins, but the Last Adam brings redemption. The first Adam is defeated by the serpent, but the Last Adam crushes his head. The first Adam is an infant, naked as a newborn. The Last Adam is the first fully mature man.

Many Christians get stuck on the first storyline: The Bible is redemptive history. That's true but too narrow. We'll miss much of what the Bible is about—and much of its practical force—if we don't recognize it's also a story of war and a history of the maturation of humanity. Spiritual readers discern the multiple layers of biblical history.

Paul doesn't limit himself to redemptive history. There's an interesting twist in Romans 5. He starts verse 17 with "if by the transgression of the one, death reigned through the one." We expect him to end the sentence with something like "so, by the righteousness of the one, life reigns through the one." We expect a transition from death into life.

That's not what he says, not exactly. The end of the sentence is "much more those who receive the abundance of grace and of the gift of righteousness will reign in life through the One, Jesus Christ." The reign of death hasn't given way to the reign of life. Paul doesn't even say the reign of Adamic sin has given way to the reign of Jesus. Rather, the reign of death has been overcome by the reign of those who receive grace and righteousness. The reign of death is succeeded by the reign in life of the justified. God overturns the regime of Adam by putting the saints on thrones.

This fits snugly in his presentation of the gospel in Romans. Paul doesn't summarize the gospel as justification by grace through faith. He summarizes the gospel as a royal announcement: It's good news "concerning His Son, who was born of the seed of David according to the flesh" and "declared Son of

God with power by the resurrection from the dead." The aim of the gospel is "to bring about the obedience of faith among the Gentiles, for His name's sake" (Rom 1:1–4).

Paul's gospel isn't just about rescue from sin. It's not only about forgiveness or our right standing with God. All of that fits into a larger, cosmic proclamation. The gospel is the good news that King Jesus now reigns, with the corollary good news that we reign with Him.

We can fill out the story of maturation by thinking about priests, kings, and prophets. Adam is placed in the garden to guard (Heb. *shamar*) and serve it (Heb. *'abad*) (Gen 2:15). "Serve and guard" is sanctuary terminology. Aaron is ordained to carry out the *'abodah* (service) of the sanctuary (Num 18:6–7). Priests are guardians. They *shamar* their priesthood (Num 3:8) and do "guard duty" (*mismeret*, from *shamar*) at the tabernacle (Num 3:31–32, 38).

In nearly every instance, the terms "serve and guard" apply to Levites. Levites and priests aren't identical. Aaron is from the tribe of Levi, but only his family serves as priests. The rest of the tribe helps the priests by doing the service (*'abodah*) of the sanctuary. Levites do guard duty (Num 1:53; 3:7–8, 28) and are authorized to kill intruders (Num 1:51; 3:10). Placed in the garden to "serve and guard," Adam is a junior-level priest, a Levite to the chief priest of the garden, the Angel of Yahweh.

Adam isn't supposed to remain a junior priest forever. He's to grow up into full priesthood and into kingship. That's what the two trees represent. The first tree, the tree of life, is freely available. Adam can eat of it any time, without restriction. He doesn't have to earn or merit life. Life—both biological life and life with God—is a gift given from the beginning, a gift to newborn Adam.

The other tree represents "knowledge of good and evil" (Gen 2:9, 17). In the Bible, this phrase refers to royal insight and the wisdom to discern and judge (2 Sam 14:17; 1 Kgs 3:9). We acquire royal discernment by experience as our senses are trained by life and by attention to the Word of God. The fruit of the tree of knowledge is solid food reserved for the mature (Heb 5:14).

Adam can't eat it yet because he hasn't been trained. Someday, after he's fought his battles and gained wisdom by subduing and ruling the earth, after his senses have been trained by the Word of God, his kingly status would be sealed by a feast at the royal tree. After passing the "taste not, touch not" test, Adam would be crowned and enthroned at his Father's right hand. The world would be given into his hands.

Instead, Adam seizes a royal privilege before the Lord gives it to him. He's not wrong to want knowledge of good and evil. He's not wrong to want his eyes opened. He's wrong to assume he's ready. He sins because he loses faith in his Father and becomes impatient. He lays hands on God's royal treasure before God is ready to open the treasure chamber. He just can't wait to be king.

Adam is to mature from priest to king and then to prophet. A prophet is a member of Yahweh's council (Jer 23:18–22) who overhears the decisions of Yahweh's court and delivers them to the people (1 Kgs 22). A prophet is a trusted advisor with the prestige to talk back to God (Amos 7:1–9). God discloses His plans to prophets and listens to their counsel.

From priest to king to prophet: That is the trajectory of humanity's growth toward adulthood. It's the trajectory of the Bible. During the Mosaic era, Israel is a priestly nation (Exod 19:6) with Aaron the High Priest as chief leader. The Mosaic order collapses at the end of the period of judges, and Samuel anoints Saul and David as kings. The priestly nation becomes a kingdom. The Davidic order also ends in disaster when the Assyrians and Babylonians invade and conquer the divided kingdom. Prophets already appear in the time of kings, but they take on a higher profile just before, during, and after the exile. Israel is a microcosm of humanity, encapsulating the maturation of the race until the Messiah arrives, who is priest, king, and prophet in one Man.

At many levels, our lives have the same shape. To play the cello, you first have to submit to strict disciplines (like a priest), focusing on how you bend your fingers, where to touch the strings, how to hold the bow. By practice, you gain mastery (king). Eventually, you forget your fingers and the bow because you now integrate and embody the disciplines. Bow and cello feel like extensions of your body. Now you can play. Once you're a master, you can become a teacher (prophet), imposing disciplines on young students until they become kings of the strings. Through these stages, your senses are trained until you can tell the difference between excellence and incompetence. Through practice, you develop a touch for the instrument.

Golfers and knitters, poets and painters, businessmen and accountants, mothers and midwives, pastors and politicians mature through a similar sequence. A well-formed life moves through these phases. Early on, we're priestly servants, children under discipline gaining skills, following instructions, obeying the rules. After the crisis of early adulthood, we emerge as kings, building families, answering the calls of vocations, gaining influence, issuing rather than obeying commands, passing judgments. Many see their achievements collapse in mid-life, but they come to new life with deeper, calmer wisdom, the ancient wisdom of prophets, who live on to advise priests and kings. As you read your experience through the lens of God's Word, you get in touch with the world.

Adam is a child. The Last Adam is the fully-formed adult. Every character of the Bible is somewhere between the first and Last, somewhere between first and final glory. So are each of us, stretched out between creation and new Jerusalem. For the story of the first and Last Adams is also our story, and we find our bearings by remembering our beginning and anticipating our end. Reading Scripture trains our senses to read our lives.

MANY ADAMS

Jesus is Adam. That can be misunderstood. It's misunderstood when we miss the force of Paul's term in 1 Corinthians 15:45: Jesus is indeed the "second man" (1 Cor 15:47). But He's described as the "last Adam" (1 Cor 15:45; *eschatos*). Jesus isn't just second. He's the final Adam. There are many Adams between Adam and Jesus.

The whole story of the Bible stretches out between the first and the Last Adam, but a chain of Adams links the two. Some mimic the first Adam in his sin, some anticipate the righteousness of the Last Adam, and some do each at different moments. Each man in Scripture needs to be seen bifocally through the double lens of the first and Last Adam.

Noah is an Adam. He lives in the tenth generation from Adam (Gen 5:1–32). During his life, the Lord de-creates the world, turning it back to the watery void that preceded His creative word (Gen 7:17–24). Noah is the father of the new humanity that emerges from that formless void. Despite man's propensity to evil, Yahweh doesn't give up on His original plan. He commands Noah to be fruitful and multiply (Gen 9:1) and gives him dominion over the animals as He did with Adam (Gen 9:2). After Noah emerges from the ark, the book of Beginnings revs up with more genealogies, showing that the race of Adam continues through the new Adam.

Abraham is also an Adam. After Yahweh scatters the nations from Shinar, He starts to form a new, united humanity within the old, divided humanity. He promises to make Abraham fruitful and to multiply him—that is, He promises to fulfill the vocation of Adam through Abraham's seed (Gen 17:20). Yahweh promises dominion. Abraham doesn't settle in the land himself, but the land is given to his descendants. Kings will be born from him (Gen 17:6, 16). Together, the promises of land and seed are a promise of a new Eden. Once the seed of Abraham is planted in the land, Yahweh promises to make them grow until the land becomes a garden, a fertile field.

"How can I know?" Abraham asks. Yahweh answers by telling him to perform a ritual (Gen 15). Abraham kills and divides several animals and lays the parts side-by-side to make a pathway between. Yahweh puts Abraham into a deep sleep (Heb. *tardemah*) and then passes through the pieces, flaming like a torch (Gen 15:12–21). Only one other man in Genesis falls into a "deep sleep"—Adam, when Yahweh takes a rib to build a woman (Gen 2:21–22). Adam goes into a deep sleep to receive the gift of a bride. Abraham goes into a deep sleep to receive the promised gift of land. Both foreshadow the Last Adam, who enters the sleep of death in order to receive a bride and inherit the ends of the earth.

Like Adam, Abraham speaks with his wife just after he wakes up. Sarah tells Abraham to father a son with her maidservant Hagar (Gen 16:2). Abraham does it: He "listened to the voice of Sarai" (Gen 16:2), just as Adam "listened to the voice of his wife" and took the forbidden fruit (Gen 3:17). In general Abraham is a model of faith and faithfulness, an obedient Adam. With Hagar, he repeats the fall and seizes the fruit of the promise before God's time.

Abraham is Adam in a deeper, more subtle sense. As the first man, Adam represents the human race. Whatever he does affects everyone who comes after. He's tossed from Eden, and so are his children and grandchildren. He's a representative head of the human race. Abraham plays the same role in relation to Israel. Yahweh loves Israel for the sake of Abraham, Isaac, and Jacob (Deut 4:37; 7:7–11). The father's actions determine the destiny of his children.

Because he's head, Abraham's entire life story anticipates the history of Israel. He's called from Ur into the land but soon finds the land is barren (Gen 12:10). Famine drives him to Egypt, where Pharaoh tries to seize Sarai until Yahweh touches him with plagues (Gen 12:17–18). Pharaoh sends Abraham out enriched (Gen 12:16); Abraham plunders Egypt. Once he's back in the land, Abraham gets sucked into a war that leaves him with military supremacy in the land (Gen 13–14).

In nearly every particular, Abraham's story matches Israel's. Famine? Check (Gen 41:50–57). Move to Egypt? Check (Gen 47:1–19). Oppressive Pharaoh? Check (Exod 1–2). Plagues? Ten checks (Exod 7–12). Departure with plunder? Check (Exod 12:36). Conquest of the land, including a battle with five kings? Check (Josh 10:1–15).

Abraham is a new Adam, and Abraham is a proto-Israel. Let's put these two facts into a petri dish and see what grows. I expect this: If Abraham is an Adam and if Abraham is the father of Israel, then Israel is a new Adamic people. The history of the seventy nations (Gen 10) is played out in miniature within Israel, which is also a collection of seventy (Gen 46:27). Spiritual readers discern the layers of Abraham's life as he embodies both Adam and Israel.

Moses is another good example of how the Bible layers Adams on top of each other. On the face of it, Moses is a new Noah:

- His basket is an ark (Exod 2:3, 5). The Hebrew word *tebah* is the same one used for Noah's ark (Gen 6:14–16).
- The waters of the Nile are waters of death (Exod 1:22), as are the waters of the flood. Moses, like Noah, passes safely through, untouched by Pharaoh, saved by baptism.
- Moses later leads a great company through deadly waters, a much larger company than the eight persons in Noah's ark.
- Moses leads Israel through the waters to a mountain. Sinai is a new Ararat (cf. Gen 8:4). The human race restarts from Ararat, and the new humanity of Israel cuts covenant at Sinai.
- At the foot of Sinai, Moses builds the tabernacle—Eden in tent form (see ch. 5)—just as Noah planted a vineyard after the flood.
- As soon as the tabernacle is finished, Aaron's sons defile it with strange fire (Lev 10) as Ham sinned and was cursed at Noah's vineyard (Gen 9:20–27).

Moses is a new Noah. Noah is a new Adam. Therefore, Moses is, indirectly, also another Adam. He's head of a nation, like Adam and Abraham. He has a priestly role, and he rules. Like Adam, Moses stands before the face of God, converses with Yahweh mouth-to-mouth (Num 12:6–8), and comes away horned with glory (Exod 34:29–34). To catch the full meaning of Moses' work, we need to see traces of Noah, which are refractions of Adam.

And Moses points to Jesus, the Greater Moses. Infant Jesus is saved from a murderous tyrant (Matt 2:1–12), passes through the Jordan as through the sea (Matt 3:13–17), endures trials in the wilderness (Matt 4:1-11), teaches Torah from a mountain (Matt 5–7), leads an exodus from the old world into a new creation (Luke 9:31), and ascends into the cloud of glory (Acts 1:6–11).

Moses' brother Aaron is an Adam too. The tabernacle is a new garden (see chapter 5), and Aaron and his sons are priestly Adams. Aaron draws near to Yahweh to stand and serve in His presence, something no man has done since Adam was driven from Eden. Priests eat the food of the sanctuary, the showbread on the golden table (Lev 24:5–16), as Adam was given the fruit of the tree of life. Aaron cares for the lampstand, a stylized golden tree, a burning bush (Lev 24:1–4), as Adam tended the trees of the garden. Adam was created a junior priest. Under the Mosaic law, Aaron and his descendants are restored to priestly service until Jesus comes as a better priest in the order of Melchizedek (Heb 7).

King David sees himself as an Adam. Yahweh's promise to David's dynasty goes beyond David's imagination. "Who am I, Lord God, and what is my house, that Thou hast brought me this far?" (1 Chr 17:16), David asks in astonishment. Yahweh's promise is not merely about David's immediate descendants but about "the distance" (1 Chr 17:17). And Yahweh's promise to David doesn't pertain only to Israel. It involves all humanity. Yahweh treats David as "a man of high degree" (1 Chr 17:17). The word for "man" is *'adam*, and the verb is *'alah*, "ascend." Yahweh regards David as "an Adam ascended" (1 Chr 17:17). By his elevation to kingship, to sonship, to membership in Yahweh's own household and family, David is a new Adam. Through David, Yahweh pledges to bring humanity as a whole to royal splendor and authority.

Like Saul, who preceded him as king (cf. 1 Sam 13–15), David is also an Adam in the negative sense. Chosen from his brothers, raised to kingship, granted victory after victory over his enemies, he risks it all for a one-night stand with a beautiful woman (2 Sam 11–12). Repeating the fall, David sees Bathsheba is good, takes, and tastes her. To cover his crime, he becomes a

Cain and kills her husband. Over the following years, his house and kingdom are wracked by the incestuous passion of Amnon for his sister Tamar, Absalom's murder of Amnon, Absalom's rebellion, and the rebellion of Sheba. David enjoys a moment of Edenic glory but loses it on one night. 'Tis like another fall of man.

As son of David, Solomon is Adam in royal mode. He rules a great people, fulfilling Adam's calling to take dominion of the earth. Kings come to hear his wisdom. He knows about plants and trees, animals, birds, creeping things, and fish (1 Kgs 4:33; cf. Gen 1:28).

Like his father, Solomon is a fallen Adam. His wisdom doesn't keep him from the folly of idolatry. In ancient Israel, kings are prohibited from multiplying gold, horses and chariots, and wives (Deut 17:16–17). Solomon breaks all the rules. He gathers horses and chariots, multiplies gold (1 Kgs 10:14–29), and, worst of all, marries many foreign women who turn his heart from Yahweh to idols (1 Kgs 11:1–13). David loses his kingdom temporarily because of his sin. Solomon's sins have more catastrophic results: Ten tribes embark on an exodus from the house of David (1 Kgs 12).

In the latter part of the Old Testament, many of the main characters are prophets: Elijah and Elisha in the northern kingdom of Israel, Isaiah and Jeremiah in the kingdom of Judah, Ezekiel and Daniel, exilic seers. Israel's prophets reach a stage of glory beyond the first Adam and anticipate the Last more precisely. Isaiah speaks obscure words to a deaf and blind people (Isa 6:8–13), as does Jesus (Matt 13:15). Jeremiah prophesies doom to the temple (Jer 7), as does Jesus (Matt 24). Jeremiah is attacked for telling the truth (Jer 38), like Jesus. Jesus' baptism recalls Ezekiel's vision of the glory chariot (Ezek 1; Luke 3:21–23), and Jesus the Son of Man fulfills the vision of Daniel.

None of these priests, kings, prophets, or heroes are identical to Adam. Each is unique. But each is modeled by some aspect of Adam, and each foreshadows some fold in the glory of the Last Adam.

IMPROVED ADAMS

Jesus is Adam. That may be misunderstood. We misunderstand when we fail to recognize there are many Adams. We misunderstand when we fail to see the progression from Adam to Adam. The many Adams are not merely repetitions of the first Adam. They're improvements. They're glorified Adams. God doesn't give up on His plan to educate the human race. Even in a world of sin, humanity matures from glory to glory. Before Jesus comes, Adams are trained by practice and God's word to discern good and evil.

Noah is a glorified Adam. Adam is allowed to eat plants (Gen 1:29–30), but Noah is given permission to eat flesh, though not blood (Gen 9:3–4). Noah is given royal authority to punish evildoers (Gen 9:5–7). Adam never does that. Noah builds an altar and offers the first ascension offering (Heb. *'olah*) in the Bible (Gen 8:20–22). Yahweh plants a garden for the first Adam (Gen 2:8). Noah, a second Adam, plants his own vineyard and enjoys wine, beverage of kings (Gen 9:20–21; cf. Gen 40:1–15; Ps 75:8; Jer 25:12–29). Adam is a junior priest, destined to become king. Noah is a king.

Noah's superiority to Adam is evident in the most misunderstood episode of Noah's life. After he drinks wine, Noah uncovers himself in his tent. Ham sees him and tells his brothers, who discretely cover their father (Gen 9:21–23). Many Christians think Noah is at fault: Noah the drunkard, Noah the flasher. That's not how Noah sees it. He pronounces a curse on Ham's son, Canaan, and blesses Shem and Japheth for showing respect (Gen 9:25–27). Whatever is going on here, Ham is the one at fault, not Noah. Noah plays a Godlike role, pronouncing curses against sinners—effective curses (compare Gen 3:8–19). Adam is made in the image and likeness of God. Noah images God more fully.

Abraham, too, is a matured Adam. We don't know whether Adam actually ruled animals or men, but Abraham has large herds and flocks and enough servants to raise a fighting force of 318 men (Gen 14:14). Adam defies God, but Abraham continually worships God at altars he sets up throughout the land

(Gen 12:7–8; 13:4, 18). Adam is impatient, touching and tasting the fruit before he is ready. Abraham shows some impatience, but mainly he trusts Yahweh to keep His promise even when it seems death has triumphed.

Abraham's and Sarah's fertility surpasses that of Adam and Eve. The original couple has children naturally, by the potency of flesh. The flesh of Abraham and Sarah is dead, but they trust Yahweh to raise new life from their dead bodies (Rom 4:16–21). When they receive their miracle child, Abraham willingly gives him back to Yahweh, trusting Him to raise Isaac from the altar as He raised him from Sarah's dead womb (Gen 22; cf. Heb 11:8–12). Abraham's life hints ahead to the resurrection life of the Last Adam, who gives His Spirit to bring the dead to life.

Abraham performs priestly tasks, building and worshiping at altars. He is also a mighty prince (Gen 23:6), ruling his household, conquering the land, taking dominion of animals. He's also a prophet (Gen 20:7), the first in Scripture. As prophet, he intercedes for Abimelech, whose house suffers a plague of barrenness after Abimelech seizes Sarah (Gen 20:2–6, 18), and he prays for Sodom (Gen 18:22–33).

Abraham's immediate descendants are also improved Adams. Both Isaac and Jacob own enormous flocks and herds (Gen 24:15; 26:14; 30:25–43), and Jacob has twelve sons and some daughters. They rule large households. Jacob is a perfect man (Gen 25:27) who overcomes the murderous hostility of his brother, Esau, and the manipulations of his father-in-law, Laban, in order to prosper. Joseph's suffering and glory point ahead to the Last Adam: Joseph's brothers hate and betray him; he is thrown into a pit and a prison but rises; he eventually becomes ruler of Egypt, second only to Pharaoh, and feeds bread to the world. Coming at the end of Genesis, Joseph partially overcomes the sin of Adam at the beginning of Genesis. Joseph is a sign that Yahweh will undo the first Adam's sin and send a greater Joseph, a Last Adam.

Genesis begins with three falls. Adam sins against God in the garden. His son Cain sins against his brother by killing him in the field (Gen 4:1–15). The sons of God, who are the descendants of Seth, intermarry with daughters of men, and their offspring fill the world with violence and wickedness (Gen 6:1–5). Adam is cast from the garden, Cain from the land, and in the flood the sons of God perish from the earth. Cain continues his father's assault on God by assaulting God's image. Adam is the original son of God (Luke 3:38), and the sons of God repeat his sin by seizing forbidden fruit: the daughters of men (female descendants of Cain). Cain and the sons of God are variations on an Adamic theme.

Abraham, Jacob, and Joseph invert each of these fallen Adams in turn. Abraham worships God and lives a life of patient faith: He turns Adam upside down. Jacob is an Abel who parries his brother's attacks and survives his assault: He upends Esau, a new Cain. Joseph resists the seductions of Potiphar's wife and brings life rather than death to the world: He's the true son of God. Abraham, Jacob, and Joseph are variations on a Last-Adamic theme.

Other Adams of the Old Testament are improvements on the first Adam. Despite sin, God remains faithful to His plan to glorify humanity. He's determined to train their senses so they become His mature children, sharing His reign over creation.

As a new Noah, Moses is a glorified Adam. He's not merely a priest serving in the garden; he's a prophetic architect. Moses "dies and rises" twice: in the Nile and at the Red Sea. Like Isaac, he's a risen Adam. Moses' powers are nearly Godlike. He is God to Pharaoh, while Aaron is his prophet (Exod 7:1). He performs potent signs and wonders in Egypt and the wilderness. With a touch of his rod, he brings death and life. In the beginning, Yahweh directly speaks the world into existence. He speaks seven times to lay out the plans for the tabernacle (Exod 25–31; see ch. 2), but Moses is the creative agent who actually makes the tabernacle. Hearing Yahweh's Word, gripped by the Word, Moses assumes some of the power of the Word. When his face shines with glory, Moses looks a lot like Yahweh.

Saul starts as an improved Adam, defeating the serpent-king Nahash (1 Sam 11:1–15; *nahash* means "serpent"). Instead Saul repeats the sins of Adam (by being impatient in worship; 1 Sam 13), Cain (by trying to kill his son Jonathan; 1 Sam 14), and the sons of God (by allying with Agag the Amalekite king; 1 Sam 15).

David sins too, but he also surpasses the first Adam. Adam is placed in a garden. David conquers and builds a city (2 Sam 5:1–12). David has discernment like an angel of God, knowing good and evil (2 Sam 14:17), and Solomon, too, is given knowledge of good and evil (1 Kgs 3:6–15). It's as if they've eaten the fruit of Eden's second tree. Adam is placed in a garden sanctuary; like Noah and Moses, Solomon builds himself a garden. Like Noah and Moses, David and Samuel are human "gods."

Israel's prophets are greater Adams. Adam never attains to prophetic stature. He never performs miracles like Elijah and Elisha, never speaks words to uproot and plant like Jeremiah, is never (so far as we know) caught up, like Ezekiel, into the glory to see Yahweh's throne. Each prophet is a sign that the Creator's plan to mature the human race is going forward. He continues to move the world from glory to glory.

That series of new-and-improved Adams comes to its climax in Jesus. He's the last Adam. That doesn't just mean His is the last name on a list of Adams. It means He's everything Adam is created to be. Jesus is a fully-human human, the first of His kind. As the *eschatos* Adam, He's head of a new humanity, of fully-human men and women. His touch heals broken humanity so we can finish Adam's work, so we can touch, take, and glorify creation.

Each Adam foreshadows the Last. Jesus is not only Last Adam but also a greater Noah, a son of Abraham, a new Moses, a priest better than Aaron, a conqueror like Joshua, a strongman like Gideon and a riddling Samson, a prophet like Samuel and Elisha and Jeremiah, a scribe of the law like Ezra, and a builder of cities like Nehemiah. Jesus sums up everything that went before. All Adams accumulate and cluster around Jesus. Every Adam is a piece of the mosaic. When assembled, they reveal the beautiful face of the heavenly King.

But they're accumulating even before Jesus arrives. Every new Adam not only builds on the first Adam but builds on others. Abraham isn't simply a new Adam; he's also a new Noah. Moses is a new Noah and a new Adam and points ahead to Samuel, David, and Elijah. Joshua is a conquering Adam and, as servant of and successor to Moses, anticipates the work of Elisha. Every prophet is not only a matured Adam but an improvisation on the great prophet, Moses.

To read well, we need to discern how every previous Adam is layered like Jesus. Each sums up everything that comes before Him, even as each anticipates the full-formed *eschatos* Adam.

IN THE LAST ADAM

Jesus is raised above all rule and authority and power and dominion. He's above every name and fills all things (Eph 1:21–23). He has completed the Adamic vocation to fill and rule.

Jesus will complete Adam's vocation in and through us, in concrete, historical reality. We are seated with Jesus in heavenly places (Eph 2:6). Not, "We will rule," though we shall. We rule now. Not, "We rule spiritually," which is to say, not really. No, we really rule. We rule all things. All things are yours. Everything is your servant. Everything belongs to Christ, and you are members of Christ's body. You are heirs of the world (1 Cor 3:21–22). Everything you touch belongs to you because it belongs to the Last Adam, and you are in Him. Everything you touch is sanctified by the Word and prayer (1 Tim 4:4–5). Whatever's holy becomes God's possession and ours because He shares all He has—Himself above all.

We sometimes read the Bible's drama of the first and Last Adam as something that takes place outside of us, as if we're spectators. Adam messes everything up. Lots of Adams come and go. Jesus puts everything back together. Curtain falls. A great show.

But an Adam is a representative head of a people. Adam is the head of the whole human race. Jesus is the Last Adam, head of all things for the church. United to Christ, we are the new humanity. The whole history of the world comes to its climax in Jesus, and because we're in Jesus, it comes to a climax in us, His church.

All the Adams reach fulfillment in the *totus Christ*, the whole Christ, who is both head and body. The *eschatos* world has arrived in the *eschatos* Adam, and we are His. It doesn't arrive in some invisible, spiritual form. The end arrives in communities of real men and women and children. It arrives in our rites of baptism, in our meals of bread and wine, in our prayers and praise, in the communion we have with one another in Christ, in our service for the life of the world. We are the last men, the last women, the people of the future. The end arrives in us.

All previous Adams accumulate and cluster around us. In Christ, we are Noah, navigating the ark of the church through stormy waters. In Christ, we are children of Abraham, sons and daughters born of the Spirit. In Christ, we are Israel-Jacob, wrestling with God and man and limping in triumph toward the promised land. In Christ, we are Moses, passing through the sea, enduring the howling wilderness, hearing and teaching the Word of God. In Christ, we are kings in the line of David, sons of the prophets who receive the Spirit to see visions and dream dreams. In Christ, we have matured, our senses trained to discern good and evil. The mosaic doesn't just picture the head. It's a full-length, whole-body portrait. We are that body.

Each Adam is an archetype that helps us make sense of our lives and our place in history. We follow the examples of these Adams because we are disciples of the Last Adam, in whom all types cohere. Is the world filled with violence and evil? Are the storm clouds gathering for a global flood? Be Noah in the greater Noah; build the ark and plan your future vineyard. Do you cry out under the heavy hand of a Pharaoh? Is a tyrant hunting you and your children? Be Moses in the greater Moses; deflect Pharaoh's hand until you can march out of Egypt. Has the Lord graciously set the faithful on thrones? Be David, doing justice and righteousness; rule with Solomonic wisdom by the Spirit of the One greater than Solomon. Are you in exile? Have you been forbidden to pray? Dare to be a Daniel.

This is what the gospel is all about. Jesus comes not merely to rescue us from sin, certainly not to rescue us from the world. Jesus doesn't come as the Last Adam to cancel the original

Adamic task of ruling and filling. The Last Adam comes to accomplish the vocation of the first. In Him, we are priestly servants, royal judges, prophetic advisors. In Him, we're fruitful to fill the earth. In Him, we subdue and rule the earth, glorifying the glorious creation until it is nothing but the heavenly city of God. In Him, we've grown up.

"Adam and Christ" is the substructure of the gospel. But we need to get it right. Not, "Jesus saves, and in addition Jesus is King." Rather, Jesus saves as king. Salvation is Jesus becoming king and sharing His kingship, His new-Adamic reign in life. In Him, we take up the book and find our stories in His. In Him, we take the world until it's transfigured according to the pattern of the book.

9

Eve

MY PERFUME GAVE FORTH ITS FRAGRANCE.
—SONG OF SONGS 1:12

The creation of Eve is startlingly novel. Nothing else remotely like it happens in the creation account. Nothing.

It's startling because it's God's response to something that's not good (Gen 2:18). Yahweh repeatedly declares the creation good—light is good, the division of earth's waters is good, plants are good, fish and birds are good, animals are good, *everything* is good. Then suddenly, "It's not good for the man to be alone." As the kids say, "Bam!"

It's startling, too, because of the way Yahweh makes the woman. When Yahweh wants light, He orders light, and light shines. When He wants plants, He talks to the earth and tells it to be fruitful (Gen 1:11–12). When He wants fish and birds, He says, "let the waters team" and "let birds fly on the face of the firmament" (Gen 1:20–22). He summons land animals from the earth with a word (Gen 1:24–25).

Adam's creation is different. Yahweh doesn't speak from a distance but digs in the clay, forming the *'adam* from the *'adamah*, the human from the humus. He makes Adam a living soul with a kiss of life (Gen 2:7). With Adam, Yahweh takes a hands-on approach.

When Yahweh prepares a companion for Adam, we expect Him to do something similar. He could call a woman from the ground. He could mold her as He did Adam. Instead, He goes through an elaborate process. He puts Adam into a deep sleep, removes a rib, closes the flesh, and "builds" (Heb. *banah*) the woman from the rib (Gen 2:21–22). It's a startingly violent, intrusive way to make a woman.

Why? Why the sleep? Why the rib? Why the elaborate procedure?

We can come up with various answers. Eve is the first living being to come from another living being, the first soul born from a soul. She's born, as it were, from a male womb. Or we might note the movement from one (Adam) to two (Adam and Eve) to one (flesh). Eve comes from Adam because she's going to return to Adam in a unity glorified by diversity. As many have pointed out, Eve is taken from Adam to symbolize the intimacy between husband and wife.

Almost universally, the church fathers interpret the passage as a type of Christ. Like everything else in Genesis—like everything else in the Bible—this account is about Jesus. Eve comes from Adam's side as a preview of the church's birth as the Bride of Jesus, given life by the water and blood that come from Jesus' side (John 19:34). The water signifies baptism, and the blood points to the wine of the Eucharist. The Bride is made by water and blood from the Bridegroom. Augustine pithily sums up the tradition: "Eve was born from the side of her sleeping spouse, and the Church was born from the dead Christ by the mystery of blood which gushed from his side" (*Contra Faustum*, 12.8).

We can press the point: Jesus is the temple who is torn down on the cross (John 2:19–22). When pierced, He becomes a source of living water, like the temple of Ezekiel (Ezek 47:1–12). Women are often associated with wells and water (Gen 21:19; 24:11; Exod 2:16–21; Prov 5:15; John 4:7-38). The flow of water from Jesus the temple is the Eve that comes from the cut in the Last Adam's flesh. It's the stream of children that come from the marriage of the Last Adam with His Bride.

You might regard these readings as fanciful. You might turn up your nose in disgust. If so, you need your senses trained. You need to learn to read in the Spirit. The church fathers make sense of Genesis 2.[1]

Let's think about Adam's deep sleep. The word isn't the normal one for sleep, and it's used only one other time in Genesis (Gen 15:12), when Yahweh confirms the covenant bond with Abraham. Abraham's deep sleep is part of a sacrificial, covenant-making procedure. Abraham is an Adam, who will be fruitful, multiply, fill, and rule the land through his royal descendants. We can infer this: The first Adam's deep sleep is also a covenant-making, sacrificial procedure. Through it, Yahweh forges a marital covenant between Adam and Eve.

The creation of Eve is the first sacrifice. When Israelites offer sacrifice, they bring an animal, kill it, divide it into pieces, and turn it to smoke on the altar. Sacrifice isn't over when the animal is killed. Through fire, the animal is glorified and ascends to Yahweh. Sacrifice is a movement through death to glorification. So, too, with Adam. He's put into a death-like sleep. He's divided into two pieces. When he wakes, he finds Eve, his glory (1 Cor 11:7). The creation of Eve is Adam's sacrificial passage through death to glory. For the woman is the glory of the man. Adam to Eve is the first step in the Bible's story of glorification.

Death-to-glory is just what's happening to Jesus at the cross. He doesn't go into deep sleep. He dies. His body is opened so that blood and water rush out. He dies so that He will be raised and will build a Bride through the work of His Spirit, in the water and in the blood.

The church fathers are right. They read in the Spirit. Their senses were trained, so they became kings of interpretation. Jesus *is* Adam. Eve *is* the church, formed from the side of the Last Adam.

Now that's a big deal. If the Bible is the story of the first and Last Adams, it's also the story of the first and Last Eves. It's the

[1] The next few paragraphs overlap with parts of chapter 13.

story of the first woman, made from the side of the first Adam. It's the story of the church, the *eschatos* Eve, formed from the cross and resurrection of the heavenly Adam. It's not just the story of God or the God-Man. It's the history of God-and-the-world, Jesus-with-His Bride.

This talk about Eve is liable to the same misunderstandings we noted when we talked about Jesus as Adam. We're immature readers if we jump from Adam to Jesus as if Jesus were no more than a second Adam. There are many Adams. We're also immature readers if we jump from Eve to the church. There are many Eves, and the church embodies all of them in one way or another. Each Eve is a piece of the mosaic. When it's completed, we find it's a wedding picture of a Bride, robed in white, prepared for her Husband.

MOTHER OF THE LIVING

Eve is a complex character. She's the bridal glory from Adam's side. As such, she enhances the glory of the garden. The Song of Songs is a poetic recovery of Edenic eroticism, portraying a love of mutual possession (Song 2:16; 6:3; 7:10) fired by the flame of Yah (Song 8:6–7). In the Song of Songs, the Bride is a watered garden (Song 4:12–15) with flowers, trees, and fruit (Song 2:1; 7:7–8). Adam is commissioned to guard the garden. As soon as Eve is added, he guards her too.

The links between glory-bride and garden form the background for much of the feminine symbolism in Scripture. Solomon's temple has a face (1 Kgs 6:3), ribs (1 Kgs 6:5, 8), and shoulders (1 Kgs 7:39). The language makes it clear that already in the Old Testament, the temple is humaniform.

Not merely humaniform, but *femino*-form. Yahweh God took a rib from Adam, and Solomon's temple is surrounded by ribs. Yahweh God closed the flesh underneath, the same word translated as lowest in 1 Kings 6:6. Yahweh God built (Gen 2:22; Heb. *banah*) a woman for Adam, and 1 Kings 6 uses the same verb repeatedly (vv. 1, 2, 5, 7, 9, etc.). Israel's sanctuaries are feminine buildings, which Yahweh the Bridegroom enters for Sabbath delight.

Solomon is a new and greater Adam. He knows good and evil (1 Kgs 3:9, 11–12). He has dominion over the land (1 Kgs 4:21, 24). He speaks of plants and categories of living souls (1 Kgs 4:33–34). In 1 Kings 6–7, Solomon shows himself a superior Adam again: In the beginning, Yahweh God builds a bride for Adam. Solomon, the greater Adam, builds a bride-house for Yahweh.

At the end of the Bible, the garden-temple-bride nexus reappears. New Jerusalem has cubic dimensions, like the Most Holy Place (Rev 21:16). Revelation adds another layer. New Jerusalem is a temple-city (Rev 21:2, 10) as well as a "Bride adorned for her husband" (Rev 21:12), gleaming with the glory of God (Rev 21:11). Her arrival brings the marriage supper of the Lamb to its consummation (Rev 19:9–10).

Eve is the first mother and, therefore, mother of all the living (Gen 3:20), as her name indicates: *chavvah*, Eve, is a pun on *chay*, "life." As mother, Eve is essential to the vocation the Lord gives man as male and female. Adam can't be fruitful and multiply and fill the earth on his own. Dominion isn't a male vocation. I've used the phrase "Adamic vocation" earlier in this book, but that's not entirely accurate. It's a human vocation—Adam-and-Eve-ic. The world must be peopled, and that requires both fathers and mothers.

Eve, not Adam, receives the promise of a Seed who will crush the head of the serpent (Gen 3:15–16). The Lord places enmity between *Eve* and the serpent, and the Deliverer is described as her child, not Adam's. The woman fights the serpent by giving birth to the head-crushing Savior.

Eve is, of course, also the one who succumbs to Satan's temptation and, so, is a paradigm of the fallen woman. According to Paul, the serpent attempts to seduce Eve (2 Cor 11:1–3) so that her children will serve the serpent rather than the Creator. Eve rightly discerns the tree is good for food and has the power to make one wise. But she is deceived by the serpent (Gen 3:13; 1 Tim 2:14) into seizing and tasting the fruit before it's offered. She can't wait to be queen.

The fault is Adam's. God reveals the prohibition of the tree of knowledge directly to Adam, prior to Eve's creation (Gen 2:15–17).

Adam is supposed to guard her from the serpent's assault. After all, he's with her during the temptation, cowed by the serpent or waiting to see what happens (Gen 3:8).

Eve is Bride and mother, sinner and, in a sense, savior, as the mother of the future serpent-crusher. Every woman of the Bible captures one or another aspect of Eve's person and history. And every woman in history lives between the first Eve and the Last, as every man is suspended between Adams. Spiritual readers sense the scent of Eve in the Bible's women.

SEDUCTRESSES AND WHORES

Eves are often tempted or assaulted by serpentine figures. When Abraham takes Sarah to Egypt, Pharaoh tries to take her into his harem (Gen 12:14–15). Abimelech does the same (Gen 20:2). A later Pharaoh tries to stop Hebrew women from having male children. He's a serpent, who kills to prevent the birth of a seed who would crush Egypt's head (Exod 1:8–22).

John sees a woman in the sky, in labor to give birth to a son. Nearby, a dragon waits to devour the newborn child (Rev 12:1–4). It's a snapshot of the history of the Old Testament: Israel is the woman, enduring a centuries-long labor to give birth to the Messiah, always threatened by serpents who seek to devour. The Old Testament is a long birth story with many complications.

Eve is tempted. Other Eves tempt. Sarah encourages Abram to have a child with Hagar. As Adam "listened to his wife" and ate, so Abram listened to his wife and took his concubine (Gen 3:17; 16:2). Potiphar's wife is a hyped-up temptress who tries to seduce Joseph, strips his robe, leaves him naked and shamed, and accuses him of trying to rape her (Gen 39:6–18).

Lady Folly in Proverbs is another hyped-up Eve. She isn't deceived; she's a deceiver. She isn't seduced by the serpent; she seduces. Dressed like a harlot, boisterous and forward, she seizes a passing simpleton, kisses him, and lures him to a bed covered with Egyptian linens and spices. She promises a torrid night of love and freedom from detection because her husband is off on a business trip (Prov 7:10–20). She entices the fool with promises of stolen water and secret bread (Prov 9:15–17). Her victims are so naïve that they don't realize her house is a gateway to Sheol (Prov 7:22–23; 9:18). Eve herself isn't Lady Folly, but Lady Folly is a corrupted Eve, a prostituted bride.

Eve is the original model for prostituted Israel. At Sinai, Yahweh enters a marriage covenant with His people Israel. He rescues Zion, feeds and cares for her, clothes her with porpoise skin sandals, and puts a ring on her nose. Yet she turns from her Husband and chases every idol, every passing penis (Ezek 16:1–22; 23:1–49)."You are a harlot with many lovers," Yahweh scolds Judah. She pollutes the land with idolatrous harlotry (Jer 3:1–5). As she is taken to exile, her nose, once adorned, will be cut off (Ezek 23:25). The jewel on her nose will be replaced with a hook as she's led like a beast to a strange land.

Some women in the Bible are actual seducers. Lot's daughters get him drunk and sleep with him so the human race will continue past the destruction of Sodom. Their sons, Moab and Ammon, are a persistent threat to Israel (Gen 19:30–38).

Some women look like seducers but prove otherwise. Tamar marries two sons of Judah, each of whom dies because of his wickedness. Judah is supposed to give her his youngest son, Shelah, so she can have an heir in Judah's line, but he delays. To secure her right, she dresses as a prostitute and sleeps with her father-in-law. When Judah finds out, he wants to execute her until he realizes he's the father. Then he knows "she is more righteous than I" (Gen 38:26). Tamar doesn't just want a son in the line of Judah. She wants her children to share the inheritance of Abraham, Isaac, and Jacob, which they do: Tamar ends up in the line of Jesus, the son of Judah, the son of David (Matt 1:3).

Ruth is a Moabitess, a child of Lot's incest with his older daughter. At times, she looks just like her ancestress. Like Lot's daughter, she approaches a man at night—a man who has been drinking, a man who addresses her as "daughter." She lies at his feet (perhaps a euphemism for genitals) and asks Boaz to spread his wing over her (Ruth 3:6–13), a marital gesture. Typical Moabitess, we might think, but Boaz sees the truth: "you are a woman of excellence" (Ruth 3:11), a model of the excellent wife (Prov 31:10–31). She's bold to the edge of scandal in order to become a new Eve, mother of the head-crushing Last Adam (Matt 1:5).

Tamar and Ruth are types of Israel, the Bride of Yahweh. They are brash Eves, like the beloved of the Song of Songs. The Bride of the Song is not a nice girl. She doesn't remain within the polite confines of social convention. Her lover comes to her door, oiled with perfume, and the aroma drives her mad (Song 3:6). Her escapades in the streets (Song 3:1–5; 5:2–8) look suspiciously similar to Lady Folly's. She is untamed in her passion for her Bridegroom. And she's black, burned by the sun (Song 1:5–6). Solomon's beloved has the untamed, exotic beauty of a black goddess. In this, Solomon resembles Moses, who has a Cushite bride (Num 12:1–2). The Bride of the Song is like Mary Magdalene, a scandalous woman (Luke 8:2) who desperately seeks Jesus and finds Him in a garden (John 20:1–18). She is an Eve who mistakes Jesus for Adam the gardener.

We catch a whiff of allegory: Yahweh doesn't choose His Bride from the domesticated, prim ladies of the city. Yahweh chooses a beautiful, unpredictable Bride to make her Queen at His right hand. Yahweh chooses the shrew.

MIRACLE MOTHERS

Eve is the mother of all living, the first woman who gives birth to the first sons and daughters (Gen 4). All other mothers in Scripture are new Eves.

Like Eve, they labor under the curse: "I will greatly multiply your pain in childbirth; in pain you will bring forth children" (Gen 3:16). Rachel is an Eve who dies in tears as she gives birth to Benjamin (Gen 35:5–8). Scripture is about the triumph of life over death, and women are the heart of the story. Many new Eves have trouble getting pregnant. By Adam's sin, death is unleashed on the world (Rom 5:12–21), and death takes hold of the source of life, the mother's womb. But where death abounds, life abounds all the more.

Yahweh promises Abraham seed like the stars of heaven and the sand of the seashore, along with a land of milk and honey. When Abraham first enters the land, there's a famine (Gen 12:10). Even before that, we learn that Sarah is barren (Gen 11:30). Death blocks Yahweh's promises and Abraham's Adamic destiny. If Abraham is to be a new Adam, Sarah needs to become a new Eve. Yahweh the Creator can overcome dead wombs. He makes the wilderness blossom like a rose. He opens Sarah's womb and gives her a son (Gen 21:1–7). The Abrahamic promise comes to fruition when Sarah becomes fruitful. The vocation of humanity moves forward through a new Adam and a new Eve.

Another generation, another dead womb, Rebekah, the wife of Isaac, is barren too. Again, the Lord brings life from the grave. He secures the destiny of Abraham's children (Gen 25:21). Jacob is surrounded by fertile women—Leah, Leah's maid Zilpah, and Rachel's maid Bilhah. Rachel herself is barren (Gen 29:31) until Yahweh remembers her, removes her reproach, and gives her a son, Joseph (Gen 30:22–24), the son who will preserve his whole family alive by giving out grain in Egypt. Yahweh's plan for Israel continues because Rebekah and Rachel, like Sarah, become new Eves.

At crucial junctures in Israel's history, Yahweh repeats the wonder. The Hebrew women in Egypt aren't barren, but their children are stillborn by Egyptian policy. If Israel is to be redeemed from slavery, if they are to inherit the land Yahweh promised Abraham, He will have to bring life from dead wombs. He raises Moses from the waters of death, the Nile where Hebrew boys had been drowned (Exod 1–2). By their cunning, Moses' mother, Jochebed, and his sister, Miriam, cheat death to deliver the future deliverer. The Nile's death waters become the womb of a new world.

At the end of the period of the judges, Yahweh again intervenes—twice—to open closed wombs. Manoah's wife is barren, a cursed Eve like Sarah (Judg 13:2). Throughout the annunciation scene, she is called the woman or Manoah's wife (Judg 13:2, 3, 6, etc.; *'ishshah*, "woman" or "wife," is used 14 times). She is another Eve, the woman, the original *'ishshah*. She bears Samson, one of the head-crushingest of Israel's heroes, whose name connotes sunshine because his advent is a new dawn for Israel.

At nearly the same time, pious, beleaguered Hannah visits the tabernacle at Shiloh. She not only bears the shame of barrenness but has to put up with the mockery of her husband Elkanah's second wife, Penninah. Hannah asks Yahweh to open her womb and give her a son and promises to dedicate her child to Yahweh's service. She gets what she asks, a son whose very name means God hears: Samuel (1 Sam 1; *shama'* + *'el*).

Samson and Samuel are Yahweh's one-two punch that KOs the Philistines. Together, they prepare the way for the coming of the kingdom and dynasty of David. Because the woman and Hannah become Eves, the whole nation of Israel moves from death to life. And behind the woman and Hannah, readers whose senses are on the alert will glimpse the shadow of Eve, mother of all living.

Sarah, Rebekah, Rachel, Manoah's wife, Hannah—all are portraits of Yahweh's corporate Bride, Zion. Zion, too, is a barren woman. When Yahweh's Servant comes, Zion begins to stir, and sound is the first sign that she's alive. "Shout for joy, O barren one, you who have borne no child; break forth into joyful shouting and cry aloud, you who have not travailed" (Isa 54:1). Jerusalem's homes and streets have been empty, silent as graves. But when the Servant bears away sin and prolongs His life, Zion breaks into song.

She sings because she's no longer alone. The barren woman has become a joyful mother of children. Yahweh tells Zion to embiggen her tent because her house will once again be filled with children, her courts once again teem with worshipers. Zion is raised from death to become mother of the living (Isa 54:1–3).

Mothers sometimes consume children rather than give them life. When the curses of the covenant intensify, when cities are besieged into famine, even the most refined and delicate woman eats her offspring (Deut 28:54–56; Lam 2:20). This is not a gruesome symbol. It actually happens. During Aram's siege of Samaria, two women ask King Jehoram of Israel to settle a dispute about eating their babies (2 Kgs 6:24–31). It's a macabre reprise of Solomon's judgment of the prostitutes (1 Kgs 2:16–28).

Zion becomes a cannibal mother, eating her children's flesh and drinking their blood through economic abuses and injustices (Isa 10:1–4; Lam 4:10; Rev 17:7). Zion imitates Sheol, who, like the barren woman, never says, "Enough" (Prov 30:16). Zion becomes the anti-Eve, anti-mother of the dead. If old Zion can turn cannibal, so can new Zion, the church, which has been known to chew up and gobble down her best children.

WARRIOR BRIDES

Eve is the mother of the Seed who crushes the serpent's head. Mothers and sisters shout with savage joy when that happens. Miriam leads the women of Israel in song and dance, boasting that Yahweh hurled Pharaoh and his horses into the sea (Exod 15:1–21). The women of Israel praise David after he bashes and removes Goliath's head (1 Sam 18:1–9). Heaven praises the Lamb after He and the martyrs overthrow Babylon (Rev 19:1–6).

Women don't just praise the head-crushers. The Bible records redemptive history, the story of sin and salvation. It's a story of maturation as Adam grows up to the Last Adam, from glory to glory. It's also a story of God's holy war against Satan. It may come as a surprise that the women of Scripture are as crucial to the holy war as they are to God's victory over death. A surprising number of Eves don't praise head-crushers; they are head-crushers.

Deborah and Barak lead the armies of Israel against Jabin, king of Canaan, and his general, Sisera. Despite having 900 chariots (Judg 4:12–13), Sisera gets routed from the field because Yahweh fights for Israel. Escaping on foot, he passes by the tent of Jael (wife of Heber, the Kenite), who offers to hide him. She gives him milk and covers him with a blanket. As soon as Sisera falls asleep, she pulls out a mallet and drives the tent peg through his temple (Judg 4:17–22). Like the woman at Thebez, Jael is Eve and her Seed rolled into one, a warrior bride who herself bashes the serpent's head and is celebrated in Deborah's song (Judg 5).

Abimelech, son of Gideon, kills all seventy of his brothers on a single stone (probably as sacrifices) and declares himself king (Judg 9:1–6). When Shechem rebels, Abimelech takes his revenge (Judg 9:22–45). He's a violent, vicious man. He has a mentor. "Abimelech" means "my father is king," and, sure enough, Gideon was a king in all but name. He assembles a harem (Judg 8:30) and makes an ephod that leads Israel into idolatry (Judg 8:22–27). Abimelech continues Gideon's trajectory toward standard-issue ancient kingship.

Until Abimelech meets his match. During a battle at Thebez, he gets too close to a tower, and a woman rolls a millstone off the top, which hurtles down to flatten Abimelech's head (Judg 9:50–57). Abimelech has all the military gear and soldiers, but a lone woman stops him with a tool for grinding grain. Like Jael's, this woman's weapons are household tools. You can do this at home.

While Judah is in exile, Haman plots to destroy the whole Jewish nation. Mordecai puts the Jews in peril because of his stubborn refusal to bow to Haman, which is similar to Queen Vashti's refusal to appear before King Ahasuerus. Fortunately, there's an Eve at the court: Esther, a female savior, who appeals to the king, tricks Haman into revealing his duplicity, and wins the day for Israel. By the end of Esther, Mordecai is elevated to the place vacated by Haman (Esth 10). An Adam takes the throne because of the courage and heroism of an Eve.

Jesus is the child who plays by the adder's hole (Isa 11:8). He is the Seed who tramples the serpent and drives him from heaven (Rev 12:5–12). But the victory belongs to the Last Adam's Bride as well as to Adam. Jesus tells His disciples they will toy with snakes (Mark 16:18; cf. Acts 28:3), and Paul tells the Romans they will crush Satan underfoot shortly (Rom 16:20). In all these passages, a Spiritual reader recognizes the new Eve, the church, who joins her Bridegroom in overthrowing Satan.

Jael points to another dimension of this typology. The Bible's warrior women use deception. Sarah and Abraham deceive Pharaoh and Abimelech by telling them half-truths about their relationship (Gen 20:8-13). Tamar deceives Judah to trick him into giving her an heir and a share in the line of Abraham (Gen

38). The Hebrew midwives lie to Pharaoh to protect infant boys (Exod 1:15–22), and God is so pleased with them that He gives them households. Michal, daughter of Saul and wife of David, lies to her father to protect the future king (1 Sam 19:11–17).

Rahab is one of the most complex Eve figures in the Bible. A prostitute, she seems primed to be a false Bride, a figure of idolatrous Israel. Instead, she proves faithful. When Joshua's spies show up at her inn/brothel, she confesses her fear of the God of Israel. Forty years after the exodus, Jericho is still panicked about Yahweh (Josh 2:8-11). Rahab wants to be on Yahweh's side, and she's willing to renounce the king of Jericho to join the winning team. She protects the spies, hides them on her roof, and then sends the local soldiers off in the other direction on a wild goose chase (Josh 2:1–7).

"Shame, shame on Rahab," tut the commentators. "She's right to protect the spies, but she shouldn't have lied." The Bible never breathes a word of criticism. Instead, Rahab's whole house is rescued; she marries into Israel and, like Tamar and Ruth, wins a place in the genealogy of Jesus (Matt 1:5). She's a model woman of faith (Heb 11:31), comparable to Abraham as an example of the harmony of faith and works (Jas 2:14–26). Rahab's story shows what faith *is*: public, active loyalty to the God of Israel.

Our senses should be attuned enough to catch a whiff of Eve. The first Eve was deceived by the serpent and ate the forbidden fruit. New Eves reverse the process and deceive serpents and Satans. It's the symmetry of Yahweh's justice. Eye for eye, tooth for tooth, life for life, lie for lie, a lie leading to death overcome by a lie leading to life.

The Bible's Adams are often strongmen and warriors. Abraham fights a war. Moses leads Israel in battle, and so do Joshua and Gideon and Samson and Samuel and David. But the best warrior-Adams are the ones who learn to use the tactics of the warrior Brides. One of the remarkable things about David is how frequently he uses deception. He's the greatest Adamic warrior because he fights like an Eve.

MARIAN CHURCH

Mary is the new Eve in person. She gathers all the great women of Scripture into herself. She doesn't listen to a serpent but receives Gabriel's unexpected news with a simple, "Behold the bondslave of the Lord" and "May it be unto me according to your word" (Luke 1:26–38). The first Eve is promised a Seed to crush the serpent's head, but Mary gives birth to that Savior.

Though not barren, Mary is a new Sarah, a new Rebekah, Rachel, Hannah. She's a virgin, yet the Spirit overshadows her to give her the miracle Son. Her Son is the true Isaac, born of Spirit, not flesh—a new Jacob, the true Israel. Jesus, Son of Mary, is a riddling warrior like Samson, a prophet like Samuel.

Like Hannah, Mary sees her son's birth as the catalyst for revolution in Israel. The Lord will throw down the high and lift those in the dust. He fills the hungry and sends the rich away empty. He remembers and fulfills His promises to Abraham (Luke 1:46–55; cf. 1 Sam 2:1–11). Israel comes alive again because of Mary's miracle Child.

Mary receives the same accolade as Jael—most blessed among women (Judg 5:24; Luke 1:42)—because she gives birth to the Seed of the Woman who crushes the serpent's head once and for all. She is the greatest of the warrior women.

As the Last Eve, the Bride of the Last Adam, the church is corporate Mary. Barren though we may be, the Spirit makes us fruitful. The church is called to be virginally pure yet also a mother. The church is a warrior Bride, called to join her Husband in battle, called to take up millstones and hammers to crush heads and slay giants. With our senses trained by Scripture, we can see the church as Mary, laboring until Jesus is born among us (Gal 4:19).

QUEEN OF HEAVEN

Paul makes it clear that Adam and Eve are figures for Christ and the church. That's the theological basis for his exhortation to husbands and wives (Eph 5:22–33). The great mystery is that marriage discloses Christ and the church. Paul expounds the

Christ-church relation by quoting Genesis 2: The two shall be one flesh.

To say the church is Eve is to say the church lives in intimate communion with her Husband, submitting to His authority, living as one flesh in one Spirit with Him. The church is the Bride of the Song of Songs. Aroused by the aroma of her Lover, she is relentless in pursuing His company. That should be you.

But Eve isn't merely a figure of intimate communion. To say that the church is the *eschatos* Eve is to say the church is a helper suitable to the *eschatos* Adam. The Last Adam is the King who rules all things and fills all things. The church is the Queen at His right hand to share His throne, majesty, and authority. We are Miriam; we are the women of Jerusalem, dancing and singing at the victory of our Moses, our David.

The Last Adam is the Priest who serves in the house of His Father. The church is the Levitical priestess who assists Adam in His priestly work. The Last Adam is the liturgical Leader; the church is the Bride who speaks in response. The Last Adam is the Prophet with access to the council of God, the Prophet who brings the indictment against the world and who petitions the Father. The Last Eve is the prophetess, a new Miriam and Huldah, who hears, reports, and intercedes.

The church is Eve glorified. At the beginning of the Song of Songs, the Bride is despised—an outcast oppressed by her brothers, blackened by the sun. By the end of the Song, she has become not just a beauty but a cosmic beauty: "Who is this that grows like the dawn, as beautiful as the full moon, as pure as the sun, as awesome as an army with banners?" (Song 6:10). By the end of the Song, she receives the name "Shulammite," a feminine version of the name "Solomon" (Song 6:13). Through the course of the Song, she is conformed to her lover. She becomes the feminine version of the King. The Song is about the Solomonification of the Bride. That's you too.

That's the promise of the gospel. We are made one-flesh with the Last Adam by His Spirit and so are conformed to Him. We become the bridal version of Jesus, the feminine form of the new humanity. Our perfume is the aroma of the Last Adam, the aroma of Christ—to the world, an aroma of life and death (2 Cor 2:14). Humanity began as a man, Adam. When the progress from glory to glory is complete, when the new humanity reaches full maturity, we will be Eve, bridal Jerusalem. For the woman is the glory of the man.

That's a wonder. But our senses should be alert to a still greater wonder.

Before Eve's creation, Adam is simply "Adam." He receives his name from his origin: Taken from the *'adamah*, he is *'adam*. Adam is of earth, earthy. He speaks for the first time when he sees Eve. He names himself, but he doesn't name himself Adam. He doesn't call the woman Adamah because she was taken from Adam. Rather, he calls her woman, *'ishsheh*, because she was taken from him, the man, the *'ish*. Both words are derived from the Hebrew word *'esh*, "fire." Once Eve appears, Adam is no longer simply a man of earth. He's a man of fire. He becomes a burning altar. After he sees Eve, he's lit.

Guys know what this is like. We're lit for life by the woman we love. Jesus knows it too. Jesus is the Last Adam, the church the Last Eve. Like the first Adam, the Last is lit by His Bride.

Here's the final wonder: The Son has bathed in the glory of the Spirit from everlasting to everlasting. And yet He is glorified and enflamed by the beauty of His Bride. He is intoxicated with her perfumes as she arises as a sweet-savor. Jesus has entered into glory. But like the first Adam, He won't enter into the fullness of His glory until His Bride is with Him—a spotless Bride without blemish or wrinkle, a heavenly Bride who is also a city and a temple, a mother and a Queen. Jesus will not have all His glory until He has you and me in glory with Him.

10

Eden

HIS FRUIT WAS SWEET TO MY TASTE.
—SONG OF SONGS 2:3

The lights dim. The first shot is a dusty, windswept road. Tumbleweed rolls and bounces across the screen.

Quick: What kind of movie is this? When the camera pans around to show a settlement, what kind of buildings are there? If the camera pans to the landscape, what will it look like? How do you know?

The camera saunters into a small town. It moves toward a doorway with two swinging half-doors. Music drifts from within. What kind of business is this? What kind of music do you expect? What other sounds will you hear? What will you see when the camera pushes inside? How will people be dressed? What will they be doing? How do you know?

Suppose you hear one of Beethoven's late quartets. Are you surprised? Why? Suppose the camera moves inside to reveal a set of elegantly dressed people watching a Shakespeare play. Will *that* surprise you? Why?

Suppose someone walks out the door. How will he be dressed? What sort of footwear will he have? If the doors swing open and U.S. Supreme Court Justice Ruth Bader

Ginsburg or Pope Emeritus Benedict XVI or the Dude from *The Big Lebowski* walks out, will you laugh? Why?

Another film, another opening scene: A cloudy night with only a glimmer of moonlight. A bolt of lightning flashes and illuminates a house. What kind of house is it? How do you know? What if you see Pope Benedict or the Dude peering from a window? Will you laugh?

We don't think twice about guessing what's going to happen in a movie. We've become accustomed to the conventions of filmmaking. We know the house illumined by the lightning flash will be a Victorian mansion, probably rundown, likely with a scary turret. Directors of short films depend on this. They only have thirty minutes and need to set our expectations very quickly. Fortunately, they only need five seconds of film. Like a sidewalk caricaturist, the director sets a scene with a few strokes of his pen. He can do that because we know the formulas: Dusty road + tumbleweed = Western. Stormy night + old house = thriller.

If you don't know these tricks, you'll be lost. It'll take you a few minutes to get your bearings. Finally, it dawns on you: "Ah, yes. This is the Old West. That is the sheriff. Oh, and that brassy lady in the frilly dress runs a brothel." A practiced movie-watcher has his senses trained. He knows all this instantly.

If you haven't developed a taste for the conventions, you won't notice when they're being violated. Ruth Bader Ginsburg comes out the saloon doors, and you shrug, "Hmm. Interesting." It's only jarring or humorous to viewers expecting someone else—John Wayne, Clint Eastwood, Brad Pitt, or some other square-jawed tough with a badge. If you don't know the conventions, you don't just miss a nuance. You miss everything. If you don't know what fits, you won't sense that Justice Ginsburg doesn't fit. You won't know there is a joke, and you certainly won't get the joke.

The premise of this book is that Scripture has its own conventions, rooted in the early chapters of Genesis. Adam is the conventional male figure, and his vocation and actions set the pattern for the men who come after—Noah, Abraham, Jacob,

Moses, Aaron, the judges, Samuel, David, Solomon, Elijah, Isaiah, and on and on till the advent of the Last Adam.

If you don't know Adam thoroughly, you won't spot the meaningful variations on the theme. You won't recognize Noah as an improved Adam. You won't realize that Yahweh's promise to make Abraham fruitful is a promise to fulfill Adam's vocation in Abraham's seed. You won't see the Adamic features of Aaron the priest. You won't sense that Solomon has what Adam doesn't, namely, knowledge of good and evil. You won't recognize the prophets as Adams who have reached a stage of maturity that Adam never reached.

Most importantly, if you misconstrue how Jesus is the Last Adam, you'll miss the heart of the gospel. You might think Jesus comes to whisk us from earth to heaven. In fact, the gospel presents Jesus as the Last Adam, who has fulfilled the human vocation and is now fulfilling it on earth, by His Spirit, through the church. If your palate isn't trained to savor the Adams of the Bible, you won't have any good sense of who you are: a priest, king, and prophet, co-member of a community of priests, kings, and prophets joined to the great Priest, King, and Prophet.

Eve is the main female character, paradigm for the women of the Bible. As mother of the living, she sets the pattern for the Bible's miracle mothers—for Sarah, Rebekah, Rachel, Hannah, and the wife of Manoah. As sinner, she lurks behind the seductresses of Scripture. As mother of the serpent-crushing Seed, she's the model for the warrior women. Eve is deceived by the serpent, but other Eves—the Hebrew midwives, Rahab, Michal—gain victory *by* deception.

Spiritual readers sense Eve's presence in all her myriad transformations and variations. Like a sommelier, a Spiritual reader tastes the hints of Eve in the story of Mary and the history of the church. Though there's an element of play in Spiritual reading, it's not an aesthetic or literary diversion. We discern the conventions of Eve so we can grasp the story of Scripture, which is the story of each of us and the story of the world.

The Bible has conventional, recurring characters. It also has conventional scenes: city, wilderness, temple, field, vineyard. If you want to learn to read well, you need to familiarize yourself with the conventions—the typical settings that recur throughout the Bible. Like all biblical themes, these conventional scenes all have their roots in the original scene, the garden of Eden.

I have sometimes given students a "pop culture" survey to test their knowledge of movies, music, and TV. They do scarily well. Some remember advertising jingles and silly sitcoms from *my* childhood. Then I give them a Bible trivia quiz, asking them to identify the daughters of Zelophehad or give the weight of Goliath's armor or identify Jeremiah's birthplace. On that test, they typically do—I put it delicately—less well.

My punch line is this: Earlier generations of Christian students and intellectuals treated the Bible as their "pop culture." Without concordances, much less search engines, they had the whole Bible at their fingertips. I imagine Origen riffing away on snatches of the Bible, as today's teens and twenty-somethings can fill hours with movie quotes or pop song lyrics. And my exhortation to them and to you is this: The Bible needs to become *at least* as second nature as pop culture.

GARDEN, VINEYARD, TEMPLE, CITY

The Bible sometimes refers directly to the garden of Eden. When Yahweh restores Zion, He makes it like Eden (Isa 51:3). The prince of Tyre is Adam or the serpent in Eden (Ezek 28:13). Pharaoh is such an immense, majestic tree that all the trees of Eden are jealous (Ezek 31:9), but Pharaoh will be cut down just like lesser trees (Ezek 31:18). After Yahweh brings Israel from exile, He gives His people new hearts and puts His Spirit in them, so the wasteland again becomes an Eden (Ezek 36:35). Joel prophesies of a locust plague that turns an Edenic land into a burnt-over district (Joel 2:3).

Scripture refers to gardens. Even without the name Eden, the allusion is clear. Lot chooses to live near Sodom because at the time it's "well-watered everywhere ... like the garden of the Lord" (Gen 13:10). Moses reminds Israel they're entering a land watered from heaven, where they don't have to use a foot pump to irrigate their vegetable gardens (Deut 11:10). Giving water from heaven, Yahweh Himself ensures that Canaan remains a garden-land.

Jehu pursues King Ahaziah of Judah through the "garden" gate of Samaria (2 Kgs 9:27), a hint that Ahaziah is a fallen Adam driven from Eden. Later, the garrison of Jerusalem flees through the same garden gate as Babylonians flood into the city (2 Kgs 25:4). Godlike Ahasuerus throws a banquet in his palace garden (Esth 1:5) and later pronounces judgment against Haman, a Satan, near a garden (Esth 7:7-8).

If Judah keeps the true fast and true Sabbath, they will flourish like a garden (Isa 58:11), as righteousness and justice spring up like plants (Isa 61:11). Jesus prays in a garden as He begins to re-open the gate of Eden (John 18:1). After His resurrection, Mary Magdalene mistakes Him for the gardener (John 20:15), a mistake that reveals the truth: Jesus is the Last Adam.

A vineyard is a special form of garden. Noah plants a vineyard after the flood (Gen 9:20). Yahweh uproots Israel from Egypt and plants her as a vineyard, which He hopes will produce wine to delight God and man (Judg 9:13; Isa 5:1-7). When it produces bad fruit, He tears down the wall and leaves it to be trampled by unclean beasts (Ps 80:8–13). Israel is to be a new Eden. She becomes a wilderness.

Orchards are Edens (Song 4:13; 6:11). So are groves of trees (Josh 24:13) and forests (Isa 29:17; 32:15–19). During Solomon's reign, every family in Judah has its own vine and fig tree (1 Kgs 4:25). Canaan is Edenland, each man an Adam, every woman a fruitful vine (Ps 128:3), every plot a little outpost of Eden.

Gardens, vineyards, orchards, and groves don't occur naturally. They're planted, cared for, and cultivated. Yahweh sets the example by planting the first garden. As His images, human beings plant and tend gardens too.

Cultivated gardens can mature into something more solid, permanent, and glorious. When Yahweh renews the land, He also causes "cities to be inhabited, and the waste places to be rebuilt" (Ezek 36:33–35). Zechariah envisions the ideal future as a city with peaceful streets filled with laughing children as the elderly look on (Zech 8:1-5). John's final vision is of a city that looks a lot like Eden—tasty fruit, tress of life, water, purity (Rev 21:22–22:5).

These aren't visions of a *return* to Eden. They're visions of a *built-up* Eden, an urban Eden, the world subdued so as to become a garden-city. Even the most pastoral prophecies of Isaiah envision a new-and-improved Eden. Lions lying with lambs, bears and oxen grazing together: This is a world *after* Adam's task is complete, when humanity has tamed the beasts (Isa 11:1–10). This isn't the world of the first Adam but of the Last.

Revelation adds another dimension (Rev 21:1–22:5). New Jerusalem isn't a garden or simply a city. It's a garden-city and also a *temple*. It's a house for God and the Lamb, a house for His images, the saints who populate the city.

Genesis 1 and 2 already anticipate the temple of new Jerusalem. Creation is a temple-building project. The tabernacle and temple are world-models, and, reasoning backwards, we conclude the world is a temple. God builds a cosmic house in three zones, and the tabernacle and temple have three zones. After forming and filling, God places His image in His house, a sign of His presence. At the end of the creation account, Yahweh is enthroned in rest in His cosmic house.

The garden is also a temple. Every other sanctuary in the Bible is modeled after the garden. Each sanctuary is a well-watered place. Every one is a place of festivity. Yahweh speaks with Adam in the garden, and each sanctuary is a dwelling place for Yahweh, centered on Yahweh's Word. After the fall, cherubim guard the garden (Gen 3:21), and every sanctuary in the Bible is adorned with figures of cherubim and guarded by human cherubim, the priests and Levites (Exod 26:18–22; 1 Kgs 6:23–35).

World, garden, and temple overlap and interpenetrate. If we read of a garden, we should also taste the hints of a fruitful land and the temple and the world itself as potential garden. When we examine the details of the tabernacle or temple, our senses need to be trained to spot elements of a glorified garden.

We need to learn to read at several levels at once: The natural (garden, land), the liturgical (temple), and the civic (city) all mirror each other. We can fold in the bridal imagery from chapter 4 because cities and temples and gardens are feminine spaces.

Let me give you a for-instance. Is the Song of Songs a love poem (marital)? Is it the king's paean to the beauty of his land (natural)? Is it about the temple (liturgical) or the city (civic)? The answer is yes. In some portions, Solomon the king celebrates features of the land and the glory of his people. At other times, the erotic dimension is at the forefront. Throughout, Solomon draws on the imagery of the temple. As a poem, the Song is all about all of them.

"Our couch is luxuriant! The beams of our house are cedar, our rafters, cypresses," says the Bride near the outset of the Song (Song 1:16-17). She's describing the trysting place where lovers meet. But the description alludes to the temple. The temple is paneled with cedar of Lebanon (1 Kgs 6:9-20); Solomon builds a house of the forest of Lebanon, and his throne hall is paneled with cedar (1 Kgs 7:7). Cypress, too, is one of the materials of the temple (1 Kgs 5:8, 10). The word translated as luxuriant means "green" (*ra'anan*), and the temple is a forest or grove, an interior space conceived as a natural place (cf. Psa 52:8; 92:14). Though man-made, it's a green world where people flee for refuge and renewal. There, Israel finds apples to taste, the fruit of her beloved (Song 2:3, 5).

There are competing green spaces throughout Israel, idolatrous shrines under every green tree (Deut 12:2; 1 Kgs 14:23; 16:4; 2 Kgs 17:10), where Israel plays the harlot (Jer 2:20; 3:6, 13). All the while, the green space of the temple is there, Yahweh's own cedar-and-cypress grove where He promises to make love to His Bride on a green couch.

The poem refuses to be pinned down. It relentlessly mixes the natural, the liturgical, the marital, and the civic. Spiritual readers develop the refined taste to savor and distinguish all the flavors.

None of this is mere imagery. The overlapping garden-temple-land-city allusions point to the vocation of mankind and the purpose of human history. Adam has a task in the garden and a task in the world. The two tasks are connected because the garden-temple sets the pattern for the cosmic temple. The garden is the template (pun initially unnoticed), the little taste of heaven that anticipates what Adam will achieve on earth. Adam's task in the world is to glorify the world until it's a civic Eden and a dwelling of God.

This is Israel's task as well. Yahweh gives them a good land of vineyards and orchards and olive trees they didn't plant, a land of cities they did not build (Deut 6:10–15). They build the garden-sanctuary in the land and are called to transform the whole land into a temple. As a priestly people, they guard the garden-land. As a royal people, they extend the garden into the corners of the land.

Man's vocation and history's meaning are woven into the literary fabric of Scripture. History is the gardenification of creation, the Edenification of the planet, the new-Jerusalemification of the cosmos, the templeization of the original cosmic temple, the heavenization of earth.

WILDERNESS

Adam is created to subdue and rule the earth until the cosmic temple becomes a garden-temple. Instead, he disobeys and turns the world into a wasteland.

The desert is everything the garden is not. In the wilderness, there is no water (Exod 15:22; 1 Kgs 17:1–7; Ps 63:1). Instead of fruitful trees, there are brambles and cacti. There's no food, and after forty years the only food available doesn't taste so great (Num 21:5).

There are animals, but they're wild and uncooperative toward human beings—jackals (Ps 44:19; Isa 35:7), ostriches (Isa 43:20), wild oxen (Num 23:22), and donkeys (Job 6:5). There are predators and scavengers—lions (1 Sam 17:34–37; Jer 4:7), leopards (Jer 5:6), wolves (Jer 5:6), vultures (Isa 18:6), bears (2

Kgs 2:24), tree snakes, and hawks (Isa 34:13–15). The desert isn't a place for human beings, and those unfortunate enough to be cast out into the wilderness don't thrive or exercise dominion. The desert is the un-garden.

Cities are civic expansions of the garden, but cities, too, can be reduced to wilderness. Zion becomes a wilderness, Jerusalem a desolation (Isa 64:10). Isaiah's mission lasts until Yahweh the Judge empties out the cities of Judah (Isa 6:11). Israel's enemies leave Jerusalem in ruins (Ps 79:1) and break the city's walls and fortifications (Ps 89:39–40). Yahweh threatens to demolish Moab (Isa 15) and Damascus (Isa 17). He turns fortress cities into ruinous heaps (Isa 37:26). Wild gentiles trample the vineyard.

Sometimes Israel's own leaders do the trampling. Yahweh tells Jeremiah that He's just completing what Israel's shepherds started. Before Yahweh judges Judah, the leaders have already turned the garden city into a wilderness and made Yahweh's "pleasant field a desolate wilderness" (Jer 12:7–13). Under Yahweh's judgment, the city is reduced to the *tohu* and *bohu* that preceded Yahweh's forming and filling (Isa 34:11).

You can tell a city has become a wilderness when you find hyenas in the towers and jackals wandering through palaces (Isa 13:22; Jer 10:22; 49:33). Instead of vineyards, olive groves, or fig trees, a wilderness city is full of thorns and briers (Isa 34:13). You know a city is on its way to being undone when it's unpeopled (Jer 2:15; 4:7; 9:11).

Temples can become desolate too. If Israel doesn't keep covenant, Yahweh threatens to rip apart His own house until not one stone is left on another (1 Kgs 9:8). Psalm 74 laments the destruction of the temple by axe-wielding pagans Ps 74:1–11), who chop down the temple as if it were a "forest of trees" (Ps 74:5). Nebuchadnezzar burns Solomon's temple, but Israel had made it abominable long before. Ultimately, Yahweh tears down what He builds, cursing Israel for her infidelity. That warning is central to Jesus' ministry: Not one stone will be left on another because the house is filled with desolating abominations (Matt 24:1–2, 15).

The good news is that Yahweh is in the habit of bringing life from death. He is, after all, the Creator. Once there was nothing, then something. Once there was a watery wasteland in utter darkness. Then the Spirit and Word illumined, formed, and filled the world of glory we inhabit. If the Lord can bring something from nothing, everything from *tohu vabohu*, He can make the wilderness fruitful, rebuild cities, raise up His ruined house, and re-ascend to His throne. When our senses are trained by Scripture, we'll see graveyards as wombs, rubble as material for a new temple, dry bones as a future army.

This story of death and resurrection recurs again and again in Scripture and history. Yahweh brings Israel from Egypt, then leads them into a howling waste—without water or food, without fields to plant or harvest, without shelter. Many Israelites look longingly back to slavery in Egypt, which from a hazy distance looks a little like Eden. Then Yahweh brings water from the Rock (Exod 17:1–6; Num 20:1–13), enough water to sustain two million people. He rains bread from heaven (Exod 16:1–7) and quail for the grumblers in the mixed multitude (Exod 16:8–21). He protects Israel from her enemies and leads her through the wilderness in a pillar of cloud and fire.

When the prophets look back to the exodus, they see Yahweh turning the wasteland into a garden. He turns the arid wilderness into pools of water (Ps 107:35; Isa 41:18). He makes the desert rejoice and blossom like a rose. Carmel, Lebanon, and Sharon are among the most fertile areas of ancient Israel, but Isaiah says the Lord will give their glory to the desert (Isa 35:1–3). When He pours out the Spirit who hovered over the emptiness at creation, He turns a barren land into a fertile field and the field into a forest (Isa 32:15–16). The vineyard returns, and Yahweh comes to taste the wine.

The prophets who look back to the exodus expect Yahweh to do it again. The God who delivered Israel from Egypt will deliver them from the Philistines. He brought them from Egyptian bondage, and He will lead them back from Babylon. He gave them a land full of gardens, orchards, groves, vineyards, and cities. Those may be in ruins, but He will bring it all back again. Edenland will be restored. Where there has been nothing, Yahweh will spread a banquet to dazzle Israel's eyes and delight Israel's tongue.

Yahweh gives hope to Israel's desertified cities. Barren Zion will be filled with children (Isa 54:1). Disfigured, ruined Jerusalem longs to be made new. When Yahweh returns, He glorifies His Bride. She will no longer be tossed like a ship on a turbulent sea but set firm on a solid foundation of gems and precious stones (Isa 54:11–12). Zion will be adorned as a Bride in her sparkling gown. She'll become a crystal city with foundation, gates, and walls of rubies and sapphires. She will be set in the firmament, a sapphire pavement under her feet and a sun shining within her (Isa 54:11; 60:1–3). And Zion the jeweled city will be utterly safe (Isa 54:13–17).

Zion becomes a harlot. The city once full of justice becomes a haven for murderers. Her rulers are rebels and thieves, lovers of bribes. Instead of defending orphans and widows, mother Zion devours them. Innocent blood is on her hands. When the Servant has come, Zion will again become a "city of righteousness, a faithful city" (Isa 1:26). Because of the Servant, the Righteous One, she will be established in righteousness, and Yahweh will silence all the blasphemy against Himself and all the slanders against Zion. By building His crystal city, He justifies His Bride: "This is the heritage of the servants of the Lord, and their vindication is from Me, declares the Lord" (Isa 54:17).

This repeated melody comes to a crescendo with Jesus. He announces the end of the temple and city. Jerusalem will be desolated. He also promises a new temple. He raises the temple of His body in three days, and fifty days later He pours His Spirit to fill the new temple of the church. Jerusalem has become Babel, mother of harlots (Rev 17). But a new Bride comes, formed and adorned in heaven, descending to earth (Rev 21–22). The New Testament is also a story of desolation and renewal, of desertification that gives way to gardenification.

Let me sum all this up with a chart:

	NATURAL	LITURGICAL	CIVIC	MARITAL
POSITIVE	Garden/land	Temple	City	Bride
NEGATIVE	Wilderness	Ruined temple	Empty city	Harlot

The Bible doesn't sharply distinguish between these zones of life. A healthy city can be pictured as a garden or a faithful bride. An idolatrous temple can be described as a wilderness or a harlot. The Bible has an intricate, built-in pattern of imagery, rooted in creation, rooted in the opening chapters of Genesis with Adam, Eve, and Eden.

I remind you again: This isn't literary ornamentation. Jerusalem really does have a temple with orchards and gardens. Jerusalem really is destroyed. Nebuchadnezzar really burns the temple. I imagine some wild animals actually prowl the ruined buildings and unkept yards. It all actually happens. And it happens again in the first century when the Romans assume Babylon's role to flatten Jerusalem.

The restoration is real too. After seventy years of exile, Cyrus sends the Jews back to the land. Joshua and Zerubbabel re-erect the temple (Ezra 6:13–16), and Nehemiah rebuilds the city walls. Isaiah's prophecies come to pass. Cyrus gives them gold and other treasure, cypress and cedar, to restore the temple (Isa 60:6, 9, 13). Kings minister to Israel, and foreigners help rebuild their walls (Isa 60:10). Yahweh really re-plants what He uprooted. Jesus builds a new temple, a new kind of temple of living stones, from the debris of the old.

Even prophecies that don't seem literal have a literal force. The parallel lines at the end of Isaiah 60:5 compare "abundance of the sea" to the "wealth of nations." The background, as we saw in chapter 2, is the consistent use of the sea as an image of the gentile world (cf. Jer 6:22–23). Isaiah promises that when the Jews return to the land, they'll go fishing. gentiles will rise from the sea to worship Yahweh and bring their sunken treasures to Zion to adorn and maintain the house of Yahweh. Israel will taste and eat of the delicacies of the gentile sea.

Christians often spiritualize prophecies like this. Yahweh's restoration of Zion pictures regeneration. God vindicating Zion portrays justification by grace through faith. Building up Zion represents going to heaven when we die. Many believe the Old Testament was oriented to the earth, while the New Testament directs us to heaven. The Old is about bodies; the New is about souls. The Old is about external things; the New moves inside.

None of that fits the Bible. Spiritualized reading isn't Spiritual reading. They're nearly opposites. From beginning to end, the Bible is about this world. It's a book about God by being a book about God-and-the-world. It's a book about heaven, but only insofar as it's about heaven-and-earth. Guided by the Spirit, Spiritual readers learn to discern the inner workings of the world and its history.

Imagine you live in ancient Israel and hear Isaiah or Jeremiah or Ezekiel. What do you think they're talking about? It's clear they're describing what's happening to Jerusalem, the capital city of the Davidic dynasty. They prophesy its destruction and reconstruction. They describe a series of actual events under the literal-figures of wilderness and garden, of desertification and Edenification. They predict and recount political events—the destruction and restoration of a *polis*, a city. A Theopolitan reading of Scripture won't miss the *polis*.

The prophets clarify the biblical meaning of salvation. It doesn't just have to do with forgiveness and communion with God. Salvation is the restoration and glorification of broken creation. Saved people are restored to God's favor. But they're also restored in their relations with one another and with the world. Saved people form the body of Christ, knit together as a new humanity by the Spirit. Saved people become new Adams and Eves equipped by the Spirit to be fruitful, multiply, fill, subdue, and rule the earth.

New Testament passages that talk about a ruined temple and city are just as this-worldly as the Old. Jesus prophesies the destruction of Jerusalem and the Second Temple in AD 70 (Matt 24; Mark 13; Luke 21). The city John sees is about a real polity, the church, the heavenly city that is already being built on earth.[1]

In the Bible, salvation is this-worldly. It takes a communal, political form in the church. It takes the form of a communion of real men and women and children who serve their neighbors, stand for justice, pray and praise, hear the Word, and taste the bread and wine of the Lord's table. Where you see that, you see salvation taking form in the here and the now.

TRACES OF EDEN

Let's go back to those movie scenes. How much of a Western film do you need to see before you know it's a Western? Not much. A few seconds of footage and you're in. If you want to thicken the atmosphere and reach for an Oscar, you can start with an endless scene at a railway station, silent except for the unremitting drip-drip of rain water from the roof onto a gunslinger's hat.[2]

How much does a biblical writer need to evoke Eden or the anti-Eden of the wilderness? Zion or the rubble of ruined Zion? The temple or the charred remnants of the temple? If we're biblically literate—as attuned to the Bible as we are to the movies—the answer should be, "Not much." A few strokes of the pen, a few seconds of film, and we know exactly where we are.

What's in Eden? Eden is on a mountain (Ezek 28:13–14). There are trees and two special trees at the center, with fruit (Gen 2:9). A river flows from the land of Eden and through the garden, splitting into four rivers (Gen 2:10–14). There are animals, which Adam names (Gen 2:18–20), and people, eventually a man and a woman. Soon enough, there's a serpent at the tree, tempting Eve (Gen 3:1). And after Adam sins, there are cherubim at the gate, guarding the way of return (Gen 3:24).

[1] See Part 1, ch. 1.

[2] I'm describing the opening scene of *Once Upon a Time in the West.*

Sometimes, we find all or most of these features together. The temple is built on a high place, Mount Moriah (2 Chr 3:1). It's possible there were groves surrounding the temple, but we know for sure the temple is lined with cedar and the floor covered with cypress. The two bronze pillars at the door are designed like giant lilies (1 Kgs 7:15–22). There's no gold in Eden, though there was gold downstream in the land of Havilah (Gen 2:11). In the temple, the gold has been transported up to Eden to adorn the sanctuary. There's the stylized almond tree of the lampstand. There's no fruit in the temple, but there's bread and strong drink and wine for libations—plant products transformed by labor into food.

The temple is a well-watered place like the garden of God (Gen 13:10). In the court is a great bronze sea set on the backs of twelve bronze oxen, and ten water stands form a stream of water flowing from God's house out to the world (1 Kgs 7:23–39). There are animals in the temple courts—oxen, sheep, goats, and birds turned to smoke as a soothing aroma before Yahweh (Lev 1–7). There is an Adam, the priest, and his helpers, the Levites. Cherubim are carved into the cedar walls of the temple, and two gold cherubim form Yahweh's throne in the inner sanctuary (1 Kgs 6:23–32).

Cities also share many of the features of Eden. Ancient cities are often on mountains, and they need to have water sources. There are animals, trees, food, and people. Ancient kings boast of their elaborate gardens and parks (cf. Eccl 2), and even the sleekest modern cities have their Central Parks, their Hyde Parks, their Yoyogi Parks.

But the Bible doesn't always provide full-scale portraits of Edenic scenes. It doesn't have to. Like the filmmaker, the biblical writers trust us to pick up a whole scene from one or two hints.

The Bible is full of high places that touch the floor of heaven: Sinai, Ebal and Gerazim, Pisgah, Zion, Moriah, and Olivet, the upper room where Jesus has a new covenant feast with the

Twelve. Each is a recapitulation of Eden. And so are all the mountain-like things in the Bible. Altars are mountains. Towers are mountains. Temples are mountains. Pillars are mountains; some even have Edenic flora on their capitols. The biblical writers don't have to put up a blinking sign to announce, "This is a new Eden!" A brief reference to a mountain is enough for the attentive reader to know where he is.

Isaac's servant meets Rebekah at a well (Gen 24:10–21). Jacob first meets Rachel at a well and rolls away the large stone at the well's mouth (Gen 29:1–12). Moses fights off the surly shepherds who pester the women at the well in Midian so that Jethro's daughters, including his future wife Zipporah, can water their flocks (Exod 2:15–22). On his way to be anointed as king, Saul meets women going to draw water; soon, Saul will be "in-lawed" to Israel (1 Sam 9:11–14). In Samaria, Jesus meets a woman at a well and discusses her marital history (John 4).

A man, a woman, and water. Where are we? We're not in a Western or a Gothic horror film. We're in Eden, and Isaac, Jacob, Moses, Saul, and Jesus are all Adams finding their Eves in a well-watered place.

Or try this: a tree, full of green leaves, fruit hanging, near a river. It's Psalm 1, where the psalmist uses the image of the tree to describe the righteous man who chews over Torah day and night. Psalm 1 places us in Eden: The righteous man is a tree of life and establishes a little Eden around him. So does the righteous woman, an Eve, who is a fruitful vine at the corners of her house (Ps 128:3). The psalmist doesn't need to sketch the whole picture to make his point. He assumes we know our way around. He trusts us: When we see a tree and water, our senses should leap back, and forward, to the tree of life.

The negative environments don't need to be spelled out in detail either. "You will be like an oak whose leaf fades away," says Isaiah 1:30. You don't need any more to infer what kind of setting you're in: The tree is dying. Its leaves are brown. Perhaps there's no water. We're somewhere on the path of desertification. The following line seals it: "as a garden that has no water" (Isa 1:30b).

A filmmaker doesn't need a widescreen shot to evoke a ruined city. A coyote scrabbling at a garbage will do the trick—or an unweeded yard, or peeling paint on the siding of a once-luxurious home, or a crumbling stone wall. Biblical writers evoke scenes of civic ruin with passing references to jackals and wild animals in houses (e.g., Isa 13:22), to desert animals or plants in what should be a civic garden. Jerusalem's water supply is poisoned by wickedness (Jer 6:7). When we see that, we sense we're in anti-Zion. Wild beasts and birds of prey inhabit the city, feasting on corpses (Jer 7:33). We're in a fallen Jerusalem. Yahweh lets loose adders and serpents in the city (Jer 8:17). We're back in Genesis 3.

And the biblical writers don't have to paint a detailed canvas to speak of the restoration of Eden, of the city, of the temple. A change in plant and animal life is enough to evoke the renewal of creation. Because of the sins of Judah, the land is filled with thorns and briars (Isa 32:12–13), and emptied, a haunt for wild donkeys (Isa 32:14). It will not remain so forever. The wilderness will not remain wilderness; the briars and thorns will not remain briars and thorns. When the Spirit comes, everything turns around; everything changes (Isa 32:15). The wilderness will become fertile, and the fertile field will explode into a forest. Where injustice and oppression reign, righteousness will spring up, and the fruit of righteousness will be peace, security, quietness, and confidence. Instead of wild donkeys, the land will be full of herds of cattle and domestic beasts of burden.

CONCLUSION

Jesus is Adam. He fulfills the vocation of Adam to fill, subdue, and rule the earth. The church is Eve, a helper suitable to the Last Adam, tasked to join Jesus in filling, subduing, and ruling creation. Eden is the down payment of a glorified world. Adam is created to transform the world into an Edenic temple-city. He fails and instead turns Eden into a wasteland. The Last Adam reverses the process, so the earth is renewed, the city rebuilt, the temple purified. Jesus accomplishes all that and then sends us out to finish up the task.

Spiritual reading trains our senses to see this cast and this plot over and over within Scripture, in never-exact repetitions. Spiritual reading trains us to see this cast and this plot in our lives and our world. Barbarians breach the walls of Rome to loot the city, and Augustine knows he's living through a biblical story. He knows the city's end isn't the end, so he writes a visionary book that prepares the church for the world after the world's end. English settlers land on the shores of North America and see before them a wilderness that needs to be Edenified. (Tragically, they view Native Americans as Canaanites.) A pandemic rages across the globe during the spring of 2020, a pestilence like those predicted by Jeremiah and the prophets. Cities go silent, work stops, and weddings are canceled. We sense that a world is ending. But we face it with hope because we know God always makes new Edens spring up from the wastelands.

Theopolitan reading is about more than reading. Theopolitan reading is inextricably linked to the Theopolitan vision of the church's mission and the Theopolitan reading of history. Spiritual reading is necessarily political reading, ecclesial reading, missional reading. Jesus is the Last Adam. We the church are the Bride, the new Eve, at His right hand. As we read the Bible as a story of Eden given, Eden lost, Eden regained, Eden glorified, we're reading about ourselves, our mission, the mission of the Last Adam and His Bride.

Conclusion: On Reading

THE GLORY OF KINGS
IS TO SEARCH OUT A MATTER.
—PROVERBS 25:2

Perhaps you've gotten excited about new possibilities for reading Scripture. With me as your mentor and model, you're ready to dive in and notice things in Scripture you hadn't noticed before. I hope so.

Perhaps you're a pastor beginning to prepare your next sermon, a Sunday school teacher working on a lesson, or a plumber, nurse, designer, electrical contractor, landscaper, carpenter, or mom who wants to enrich your personal Bible reading and your family worship. You're ready to start. What do you do?

It's been my mantra from the interlude on: What you do first is find a guide and stick with him or her. You need teachers, mentors, other people. You need to apprentice yourself to a master reader. Sometimes, the master will be the author of a book, rather than a friend or pastor. It's better, though, if you can find a live mentor so your reading can mature in its natural setting of communion and conversation.

It's been another mantra: Your senses are trained when you follow Jesus the Teacher, who is also Jesus the Host of the banquet. If you want to become a king who searches out the secrets of Scripture, join a church where the worship is drenched with Scripture, a church that communes each week at the Lord's table, a church faithful in evangelism, discipleship, service. Spiritual reading happens in Spirit-filled churches.

I'm not being coy. Those things are essential.

Still. You want to know what to do when you sit down tomorrow for your morning Bible reading. You flip the pages and start reading. You want some rules or guidelines, at least some suggestions. What should you notice? What should you pay attention to? Your senses are on the alert: but for what? There are four corners of the earth, four winds of heaven, four corners of the altar, and four Gospels. Therefore, pay attention to four things:

I. WHAT THE PASSAGE *says*. Who does what to whom? Where is this event taking place and when? What happened just before this, and what happens after? What was said in the previous chapter, and what is said in the next chapter? Pay attention to the letter. *Always* follow the letter, and let the Bible set the terms for your reading. Pay attention to how the writer says what he says, the turns of phrase and allusion, the metaphors and similes. How does this verb or noun, this metaphor or allusion, throw your mind to another section of Scripture? How are the two passages similar and different?

II. WHAT THE PASSAGE SAYS about *Jesus*. Everything in Scripture says something about Jesus. Everything in the *universe* discloses something about Jesus, the Creator Word in whom all things cohere. How does the passage send you back to Adam and Eve in Eden or to one of the many other Adams and Eves and Edens? How does it project you forward to Jesus and the church in the world? How does the *way* things are said point you to Adam or Jesus? What does the passage teach you to *believe* about God, Jesus, humanity, the world? Pay attention to what the Bible says about *faith*.

III. WHAT THE PASSAGE SAYS about *you* in Jesus. Everything in Scripture is about Jesus. You are "in Christ Jesus." So everything in Scripture is about *you*. The whole church is "in Christ," the Body and Bride of Christ, one flesh with Him. If the whole Bible is about Jesus, it's also about the *church*. How does the passage reach back to Eve or the many Eves of Scripture? How does it launch you ahead to think about the Last Eve, the new Jerusalem? What does the passage tell you about yourself as a member of the church, part of the Bride of the Last Adam? How does it teach you to understand your experience, the condition of the church and the world, in the light of Christ? What does it teach you to *do*? Pay attention to what the Bible teaches about *love*.

IV. WHAT THE PASSAGE SAYS about *your future* in Jesus. Everything in Scripture is about Jesus. Jesus came and will come. He is the Alpha *and* the Omega. Everything in Scripture teaches about Jesus and His future. And you are in Him, so everything in Scripture tells you something about *your* future. Every passage says something about the future of the church and the world. Ask how the passage takes you back to Eden, to gardens, vineyards, garden-cities, and temples. How does it reach forward to new Jerusalem? What does it teach you to *hope* for?

As you read, the Spirit and Word will work to conform you—your heart, your mind, your will, your imagination—to the living Lord Jesus. Scripture is the food that nourishes you in faith, hope, and love. As you read, you become a gloss on Jesus the Word, a living epistle of God's love and justice, a king or a queen whose senses are trained to discern good and evil.

You're ready now. *Tolle lege*. Take up, read. And *labete phagete*. Take, eat.

Part III

Theopolitan Liturgy

Interlude: On Liturgy

I should warn you: Part 3 offers unusual content on liturgy. It doesn't do some of the things you might expect it to do. It isn't designed to answer "Should we or shouldn't we?" questions: Should we use leavened or unleavened bread? Should we serve wine in little plastic cups, or use glass, or drink from a common cup? Should the pastor wear a white or a black robe or no robe at all? Should we baptize and commune babies or not? Should we dunk, pour, or sprinkle? Should we use an organ or a band? Should we sing old hymns or praise songs? I have views on all those questions, and I'll occasionally express and defend my views along the way. As every pastor knows, those questions need to be answered. But I don't answer them. Part 3 isn't a how-to manual.

It's not about liturgical history either. It's important to know how the church has worshiped through the centuries. Much of the liturgical scholarship of the past century has focused on the history of worship. But that can miss the main point. History isn't the most important thing to know. I'm a Bible-thumper at heart, so I believe it's far more important to know what the Bible says about liturgy. That's what these chapters are about.

Every Christian agrees the Bible is critical. In practice, though, many Christians cobble a liturgical theology and practice from slivers of Scripture—the gospel accounts of baptism and the Last Supper, a few chapters of 1 Corinthians, scattered snippets from other epistles, and perhaps Revelation. These fragments are barely enough to answer the "Should we or shouldn't we?" questions. They aren't close to sufficient if we're trying to develop a rich biblical theology of worship.

The following chapters use a larger and more varied pallet. I dip my brush into Genesis, Exodus, Leviticus, Chronicles and Kings, Psalms and the Song of Songs, as well as the Gospels, Pauline Epistles, and the Apocalypse. As a result, Part 3 provides a thicker, more complex biblical framework for thinking about the liturgy as a whole and for answering the "Should we or shouldn't we?" questions that need to be answered.

I admit that my approach leaves many questions open. It may frustrate readers who are looking for quick answers. That can't be helped. The liturgy needs to be shaped by the Word of God, but we can't do that well unless we know what the Word of God actually says about liturgy.

CREATION, CULTURE, LITURGY

I can make things a bit easier. I can give away the gist of that framework up front. I'm going to break a basic rule of comedy: I'm going to start with the punch line. I'm going to tell you exactly what Part 3 is about before you read it. If you're the kind of person who's inclined to skip interludes, you'll be at a disadvantage. Come to think of it, if you're reading this, you aren't the kind of person who skips interludes.

Here's the theme: *Theopolitan Liturgy* explores the analogies among and the intertwinings of three levels of reality:

I. Creation

II. Culture

III. Liturgy

Each chapter explores some feature of created reality, expounds how human culture moves in the grooves of this created reality or distorts this reality, and then explains how Christian liturgy corrects, redirects, glorifies, and completes these features of created and cultural reality.

To see how this works, I need to explain I mean by liturgical. Creation and culture aren't material realities that need to be spiritualized. Creation and culture aren't a secular cake awaiting a liturgical icing.

Creation and culture are *always, already* liturgical. Creation emerges from a divine liturgy and lives, moves, and has its being as liturgy. Culture is liturgical all the way down. Liturgy is baked into the cake, not just for Christians, but for everyone: liturgy crystallizes culture, and culture is the flowering of liturgy. We're liturgical girls and boys living in a liturgical world.

After the fall, we don't stop being liturgical. We become *idolatrously* liturgical. We enact perverse liturgies. That puts us at odds with the design of creation and, worse, with the Creator. It misshapes our cultural worlds.

Jesus dies and rises to restore and glorify creation and culture. His Spirit condemns the perverse liturgies of culture and puts them right. Through the Christian liturgy, the Spirit restores us to *proper* liturgical forms. The liturgy *is* creation and culture being put back in right order.

That's it. That's the punch line. I suspect it's obscure. Let me elaborate.

THEOPOLITAN VISION

I am the president of the Theopolis Institute, a think tank and educational ministry in the heart of the Bible Belt, Birmingham, Alabama. At Theopolis, we use the tag line: "Bible. Liturgy. Culture." It's all over the place—on the website, our stationary, the business cards I always forget to carry with me.

The punctuation is misleading. The list isn't over when we get to Bible; it's not "Bible, *period*" or, for you Brits, "Bible, *full stop*." Bible and Liturgy aren't finished without the "Culture" bit. The whole point of the tagline is that these three are inseparably united.

Without the Bible, the church doesn't know what do to in her liturgy. In fact, there would be no liturgy at all, since the Word read and preached is essential to Christian worship. Instead of a period, we might have written this: We learn how to worship from Scripture. The Bible makes the liturgy.

But it works the other way too. Bibles might exist even if no churches gathered for worship. But the Bible can't do all God intends it to do unless it's read, proclaimed, and taught in the liturgy.

The Bible is God's Word to God's people. As I explained in Part 1, the church isn't an invisible entity. It's a real-world communion of men, women, and children. That visible communion is the family of the Father, the body of the incarnate Son, the temple of the Spirit.

Gathering and dispersal is the systole and diastole of the church's life. She's the people of the Triune God whether she's gathered for worship or dispersed into the world. But it's in the liturgy that she is publicly, visibly what she in fact is: the family of the Father, the body of the incarnate Son, the temple of the Spirit.

The Bible convicts, commands, encourages, and teaches each of us individually. It does all that when we read silently in privacy. But God gave the Bible to His *church* to build the living temple of saints. God's Word comes from God through His ordained leaders for the church. It's God's community-constructing speech. It's the Bridegroom's love letter to His Bride.

If we only read the Bible silently in private, God will never speak His Word to His people. Studied in private, the Bible doesn't do its temple-building work. The Bible can't be all it's supposed to be outside the liturgy. God wants to speak to His people, *gathered* as His people.

Plus, the Bible isn't merely spoken *to* us. It's given to be spoken *by* us. The Bible is fulfilled when it's turned into prayer, praise, song, dialogue. That happens in the liturgy.

So we can't separate Bible from liturgy. Yes, Christian liturgy must be biblical. If it's not biblical, it's worse than useless. God hates it. But we also have to say the Bible becomes fully operative in the liturgy. The Bible determines what we do in the liturgy. But the liturgy shapes how we read and apply Scripture.

And we can't leave "Culture" dangling out there at the end of the tagline. At Theopolis, we believe churches transform culture when they're shaped by biblical liturgies and liturgical biblicism. Living water flows from the living temple to renew everything from the land to the sea of gentiles (Ezek 47).

But it works the other way too. Inevitably, culture comes *into* the liturgy.

What do I mean? In this book, I'm using culture in a broad sense. It doesn't mean high culture or art. It refers to beliefs, habits, customs, rituals, things, norms—a people's entire way of life.

Cultures assume, enforce, and teach norms. They prescribe how we should behave, how we use our bodies meaningfully. *Do* stand to show respect. *Don't* burp at the dinner table. Thou shalt not kill, commit adultery, steal, bear false witness.

Cultures are patterned environments of material things. A group organizes the space where it lives and moves. It puts up walls to keep out invaders. It puts up walls to keep out invaders. It plans cities, builds roads, develops architectural styles. It establishes legal barriers to prevent baddies from prospering. It produces artifacts, tables and chairs, teacups and wine glasses, computers and conference tables, machines with their assembly lines, bombs and bombers. It produces consumable goods, food and drink and clothing and, in some cases, thousands of varieties of sporty footwear.

Cultures coordinate time. They set aside special occasions, holidays when the norms of the culture are celebrated, when the heroes are remembered. They give shape to work and rest.

Perhaps most obviously, cultures are linguistic. If you're an English speaker, you know you're deep in a foreign country when you can't read any of the road signs and no one can give directions in English.

All these cultural habits and institutions pre-date the arrival of the gospel and the church. Cultures have languages before the missionary comes to town, though missionaries have often created written forms of an existing language. Before the missionary builds a chapel or celebrates Christmas, a culture has organized their space and time. Before the church sings the first hymn or paints the first crucifixion scene, the culture already has artistic and musical artefacts and styles.

All these exist before and outside the liturgy, and all come into the liturgy, in one way or another. The church uses an existing language, gathers in whatever space the culture provides, and adjusts to the time-keeping of the culture.

This looks like a problem. If a pre-existing culture infiltrates the liturgical heart of the church, how can the church *transform* culture? If the city of God is always partly city of man, how can it be an *alternative* to the city of man?

It might seem best to raise the barricades to keep cultural contaminants out of the sanctuary. Do the liturgy in Latin since nobody outside the Vatican and classical schools speaks it. Use the same musical, artistic, and architecture styles wherever the churches go. That's the safest option, it seems, because it ensures the liturgy will transcend the particularities of culture.

I'm poking at Roman Catholics in that last paragraph, but we see similar impulses in some branches of Protestantism. Protestants sometimes reduce the cultural contribution to a bare minimum: Use the language of the surrounding culture, but strip all art from the church walls and windows, and keep out all the musical instruments. That way, the liturgy won't be cultural. It will be *purely* liturgical.

Culture infiltrating is a *potential* problem, yes. The church is always at risk of becoming a mirror image of the earthly city instead of an outpost of the heavenly city. She must resist conforming to this age. We live toward and according to the standards of the age to come. Some cultural customs, habits, and artifacts must be expelled from the church's worship.

At bottom, though, the infiltration of culture into the liturgy isn't surprising or problematic. In fact, it's key to understanding not only the relation of liturgy and culture but to understanding the liturgy itself.

Liturgy and culture don't occupy different worlds. Rather, each inhabits the other: Culture finds a place in the liturgy, and the liturgy inserts itself into culture. It's what theologians call a perichoretic relationship. The Bible shapes the liturgy, but the liturgy shapes the way we read the Bible. Liturgy transforms culture, but only because the culture has been brought into the liturgy to be transformed.

Liturgy shouldn't put up impenetrable barriers to culture. That's sure to make the liturgy culturally irrelevant. Rather, liturgy is culturally transformative only *because* it's permeable to culture.

LITURGY AS CHRISTIANIZED CULTURE

How does this work? Think about language, which I'll talk about at more length in chapter 12. The church uses the culture's pre-existing language in her liturgy. But she uses it to say new things. She uses the existing language to call on the Father through the Son in the Spirit. She uses the existing language to announce, Jesus is Lord. She uses the existing language to say, "Love your enemies."

An existing language enters the liturgy, but the liturgy doesn't leave the language intact. By putting the language to Christian uses, the church refreshes and restores it. She fulfills the original purpose of the language, which is to be a medium of communion between God and human beings, and a means of edifying communication among human beings. Liturgical language is language in the process of being redeemed.

If liturgy and culture inhabited different worlds, we'd need to build something to bridge the gap. We'd be tempted to alter the liturgy to make it relevant to the culture. If culture already inhabits the liturgy, things look quite different. As we'll see throughout Part 3, every fundamental component of culture is always already inherent in the liturgy. We don't need to build a bridge if there's no chasm.

The Eucharist serves as a paradigm case. Bread and wine are cultural products, grain and grapes transformed by human labor, technology, and ingenuity. They exist before they become elements of the church's liturgical feast. The liturgy takes up these cultural products and puts them to a new use. In the liturgy, these common foods become means of communion with the Father in the Son by the Spirit. Through the liturgy, the Eucharistic assembly becomes a preview of new Jerusalem, the city from heaven.

In the Eucharistic liturgy, all of *creation* is summoned into the presence of God. In the liturgy, all of *culture* is summoned into the presence of God. In the liturgy, the created and human worlds are brought back into right relation with God.

We can apply that Eucharistic logic to all the other features of culture, which are taken up as features of liturgy. The time of the liturgy is *God's* designated time, the Lord's day. The place is, ideally, a church building, designed and decorated to focus our hearts, minds, and bodies on the work of worship. Our bodily actions aren't just meaningful, but meaningful to God. In most Christian churches throughout history, ministers have worn liturgical clothing to mark their office, a liturgical transfiguration of culture.

The words we hear are words of God, either directly from the Bible or a pastor's words based on the Bible. We speak and sing words from Scripture or words inspired by Scripture. As we do this, language is redeemed by its insertion into the liturgy. Liturgical music expresses our joys and laments. It shapes our moods. What's happening in the liturgy is something deeper: Music—a product of cultural transformation of creation—is tuned toward God. Music is fulfilled as a sacrifice of praise.

The liturgy doesn't leave culture behind, not for an instant. Everything in the liturgy is cultural, and every cultural element is transformed liturgically. Everything we are and produce—space, time, speech, action, clothing, music, art—is directed toward its ultimate end, our entry into the glory and joy of God.

This is why the liturgy is culturally transformative. It's not that we commune with God and *then* head out to start transforming the world. The world is transformed *in* the liturgy. We keep liturgical time, which changes our time-keeping. We hear and speak Bible, and *right there in the liturgy* we begin to talk differently. We break bread and drink wine, and *right there in the liturgy* agricultural and cultural products are put to new uses.

This world—this real-life cultural world—is the material of the liturgy, which the liturgy transforms into an effective sign of the coming city of God. The liturgy *is* culture transformed, culture being Christianized. Creation and culture are taken up to become *liturgical* culture.

The chapters that follow examine some of the coordinates of Christian liturgy, which are also the coordinates of human life as such—place, dialogue, sacrifice, time, and joy. Each chapter shows that creation itself is liturgical. Space is created as a temple, language exists for dialogue with God and one another, life is a sacrificial movement of death and resurrection, time is choreographed for liturgical dance, and the world exists to give us a share in the joy of the Father.

Cultures inescapably manifest these created patterns. All cultures organize time and space, use language, offer sacrifice, encourage hope for some form of final bliss. Since Adam, cultures distort these created patterns. We tell lies, brutalize one another in sacrificial slaughter, organize time and space unjustly, hold out hope for false joys. Cultures are idolatrous, perverse variations on the liturgy of creation.

If it is biblically formed, the liturgy enacts the truth about the world. It concentrates creation and culture—space and time, language and sacrifice, joy and feasting—in order to usher creation and culture toward its ultimate fulfillment in the city of God, the heavenly Jerusalem.

Here's the punch line of this little book: The Liturgy is *itself* the first transformation of culture. The Liturgy *is* culture transformed into kingdom.

11

Place

LORD, YOU HAVE BEEN OUR DWELLING PLACE
IN ALL GENERATIONS.
—PSALM 90:1

Some Christians are put off by the word liturgy. It conjures up images of dank churches full of dull people bumbling and mumbling their way through inexplicable rituals. A liturgical church is, by definition, a dead church, murdered by vain repetitions. If we're merciful, we'll give it a dignified burial.

Liturgy means irrelevance. Only a hidebound traditionalist likes liturgical forms. Liturgical churches pathetically preserve a past that was pretty lame to begin with.

If you want energy and life, you need to find a church with a praise band and a light show. That's where you can *worship*.

So it seems to many Christians.

If that's what you're thinking, I know where you're coming from. I grew up in a liturgical church. The worship was dull and slow. We mumbled our way through. We had no idea why we were doing what we were doing.

I loved parts of it, but I fled at my first opportunity. At twenty, with the brash omniscience of youth, I renounced liturgy with all its pomp and show.

Over the following years, with the help of friends and collaborators, I turned back to liturgy. I'm a convert, or a re-convert. I now believe the church should have a repetitive order of worship, done pretty much the same every week, with pre-written prayers and dialogue, weekly communion, candles, pastors in white liturgical robes. I now believe, in short, the church should worship with an old-fashioned liturgy.

My reasons for re-converting were partly historical. I learned the church's worship has been liturgical until the day before yesterday. The early church developed liturgical forms rooted in the temple and synagogue liturgies of Judaism. The Eastern and Western church pursued distinct trajectories, but both used set forms of prayer and worship. Nearly every Reformer wrote at least one liturgy. Prayer books aren't Catholic. They were introduced at the Reformation.

Non-liturgical Christian worship developed in the centuries after the Reformation. They're an aberration. And non-liturgical is a ruse anyway. As historian Lori Branch points out, non-liturgical churches develop rituals, though they don't always notice. Their rituals are, paradoxically, "rituals of spontaneity."

Even if a church doesn't use a prayer book or print a bulletin, its services fall into repeated patterns. It's pretty much the same thing every week. That's not a criticism. It's good to have liturgical habits. It's the way God wants us to worship. It's the way we're made.

The historical case for liturgy is convincing, but history isn't the most important factor in my re-conversion to liturgy. The *Bible* is. History isn't our ultimate standard for worship or anything else. The *Bible* is.

After all, not everything the church has done in worship is good. Orthodox Christians venerate icons, which the Second Word forbids (Exod 20:4–6). The medieval church largely excluded lay people from the liturgy.

Protestant worship is, I believe, closer to Scripture, but it isn't perfect either. Some Protestant churches wrongly strip art from the place of worship, and some wrongly believe musical instruments are prohibited. Many Anglicans kneel to receive communion, an odd posture if you're eating a celebratory meal. Besides, Protestants differ on all sorts of liturgical issues. Five hundred years after the Reformation, we still can't agree on what happens in holy communion or whether or not to baptize infants.

Unless we have a standard *beyond* history, we can't sort through the good, the bad, and the ugly of the church's liturgical history. Scripture is that standard. It tells us how we're to worship, warns us about false forms of worship, and infuses everything in the liturgy.

I think Christian worship should look a lot like a traditional Lutheran, Anglican, Methodist, Catholic, Orthodox, or Reformed service. But I don't think those are best because they're Lutheran, Anglican, Methodist, Catholic, Orthodox, or Reformed. I think they're best because they're *biblical*.

In this book, I'll try to make a *biblical* case for a form of worship that looks a lot like those liturgical services many find so boring. I'll try to get you excited about liturgy by unveiling a little of the Bible's stunning theology of worship.

Let's get something straight at the beginning: Liturgy isn't a marginal issue in Scripture. It's *the* issue. God created the world as liturgical space, and He intends to fill it with joyous, eternal worship. Liturgy is the Alpha and Omega of the biblical story. It's the reason God created human beings and everything else.

To talk about liturgy, we have to talk about everything. Liturgy stretches from creation to the eschaton and to the ages of ages. Amen.

COSMIC TEMPLE

During the first half of the creation week, God forms a three-story house—heaven as the roof above, earth as the main floor, the sea as the flooded basement. He spends the second half of the week filling the spaces—with plants, heavenly lights, fish and birds, land animals, and man and woman. After six days of labor, the Lord takes His rest, enthroned on the circle of heaven, delighting in His work.

By the end of the week, God has built a temple. A temple is a dwelling place for a god, and God created the world as His house. Creation is a sanctuary for God's image.

Why think that the cosmic house is a *temple*? Genesis 1 never says that. Are we reading into it? The reason becomes clear when we look at other "creation stories" in the Bible.

Yahweh's instructions concerning the tabernacle are a creation story. They're laid out in seven sections (Exod 25–31), each beginning with the phrase "and Yahweh spoke to Moses." The speeches mimic the creation week. Yahweh speaks *seven* times, and the seventh speech is a Sabbath command (Exod 31:12–17).

The construction of the tabernacle also mimics God's work in creation. First Moses sets up walls, curtains, and covering, *forming* the tabernacle (Exod 40:17–19). Then he places all the furniture, *filling* the tent with the altars, the table, the lampstand, and the ark (Exod 40:20–33).

At the climax, Moses ordains Aaron and his sons as priests, new Adams in the new creation of the tabernacle (Lev 8–9). With His house built, His furniture in place, His servants installed, Yahweh takes His throne above the cherubim in the Most Holy Place. He enters Sabbath (Exod 40:34–38; Lev 9:23–24).

Here's what we learn from Exodus: The design of the tabernacle is described in seven speeches. Its construction mimics the form-and-fill action of God's creative work. The tabernacle is a sanctuary, a dwelling place for God.

From here we can reason backwards: If the tabernacle is a new creation, then creation is the original tabernacle. If the sanctuary is like creation, then creation is a sanctuary.

Creation is an ordered world. The Bible shows it's a particular kind of order, a *temple* order. Creation is a cosmic temple.

As a temple, the universe is a stage for a cosmic liturgy. All the furnishings of creation are directed toward worship. God speaks light into existence to order day and night. On Day 4, He places lights in heaven to mark seasons and appointed times (Gen 1:14). With its rhythm of evening and morning, new moons and solar year, heaven is a liturgical clock, ticking out times of worship.

God fills His temple with liturgical materials and utensils. He creates a watery world, calls plants from the ground, forms animals from the earth. Every one of these things is destined for inclusion in worship. As soon as they're spoken into existence by the mouth of God, created things are vessels of God's house, choreographed into a liturgical dance.

The first liturgy is the liturgy of the world.

IMAGE, PRIEST, TEMPLE-BUILDER

Here we have to make things a little more complex. God doesn't create a steady-state world that remains the same from beginning to end. God creates a world of change and movement. He creates a world that will undergo a *history*.

The initial temple isn't supposed to stay just as it is. It's going to change. It's supposed to get better. It's eventually going to be a glorified city-temple. And human beings are the ones who make it better. The cosmic temple is the platform for a cosmic liturgy. The cosmic temple also provides the materials and time for the development of human culture. Culture is the bridge from the first to the final temple.

Ancient temples are homes for a god or a pantheon. At the climax of a temple-building project, the architect-king sets a god's image on its pedestal in the inner sanctuary. Ancient peoples know the god is present because his image is present.

The living God sets the pattern. He does it first. He builds and furnishes a house. At the climax, He sets His image at the center: Man, male and female, in the image and likeness of God (Gen 1:26–28).

Adam and Eve are signs of the Creator's presence in His cosmic temple. By placing them in His world, the Creator claims the universe as His own. Setting His images in His house, He pledges to share His temple with them.

The images of the Creator are, of course, drastically different from the images of false gods. As Psalm 115 says, idols are blind, deaf, and immobile, incapable of smell or speech. Those who worship dead gods die. Idols aren't just dead. They're deadly.

Like the God they image, Adam and Eve have eyes to see, ears to hear, noses to smell, hands to grasp, feet to walk. Adam is a *living* being, the living image of the living God.

This is the foundation for the Second Word Yahweh speaks at Mount Sinai (Exod 20:4–6). He forbids Israel to make images to venerate and serve because the Israelites are *themselves* images. The only images of Yahweh in Israel's sanctuaries are human images: the Aaronic priests and the gathered people.

As living images of the Creator, Adam and Eve are caretakers of the cosmic temple. Creation is a temple, and everything in it is designed as a liturgical vessel. But the world is fulfilled in liturgy only through *us*, priests of the cosmic liturgy. Through men and women, all creation is directed toward worship as we direct creation and all our work in creation toward the end of praise. Created things come to fulfillment as they nestle into the liturgy.

Sometimes created things come directly into the liturgy. We baptize with water, plain ol' H_2O. Most often, creation enters the liturgy only after it has been changed, glorified by labor. We turn creation into culture, and we present creation and culture to God in liturgical fulfillment.

This is clear at the end of the Bible, John's vision of new Jerusalem. The city is a glorified garden (Rev 22:1–5). It's also a sanctuary, a cubic Most Holy Place expanded into civic space (Rev 21:1-8). In Revelation, creation is fulfilled as new creation, a completed, glorified cosmic temple. Scripture begins with an initial cosmic temple. It ends with a vision of the final cosmic temple, finalized by our cultural contribution.

The final cosmos is filled with praise. As Revelation 5 opens, John sees a book at the right hand of the One Enthroned. No one can open it, and John laments. If the book remains unopened, God's purposes will not be completed.

Then the Lamb appears. Jesus ascends to take the book, and His ascension touches off radiating, concentric waves of praise: first the living creatures and angelic elders near the throne, then other angels, then "every created thing which is in heaven and on the earth and under the earth and on the sea" (5:13). That is to say, *everything*.

The world won't end in a climate change apocalypse. The world won't end in world war. The world ends in worship, neither a bang nor a whimper but a shout and song of praise.

From cosmic temple to cosmic temple-city: This is what history is all about. God seeks worshipers. He seeks to unite all things into a universal act of worship, and He will find what He seeks. Human culture—the realm of our making and doing—is the bridge between the first and final temple, between creation and new creation. Through us, the world becomes what it's created and destined to be.

I realize this may sound a bit mistily mystical, so let me give some examples.

Trees glorify God by their sheer existence, but they're fulfilled when human beings transform them into musical instruments to accompany song. Creation is transformed into culture, which is brought into the liturgy. In particular, trees are made into musical instruments that bring praise to God.

Do the very stones worship God? Yes. But they're fulfilled as stones by being incorporated into the liturgy. Israel mines gold to make a cover for the ark of the covenant. They dig up gemstones, polish them, and set them in the breastplate of Aaron. Rocks are hewn from a mountain to become walls of Solomon's temple, or of a Gothic cathedral. Again, creation transformed by culture becomes a liturgical offering.

Grain yearns for self-sacrifice, to be cut, ground, baked into bread, eaten. Every young grape dreams of being crushed, fermented, and relished at a feast of wine. All food longs to be incorporated into the covenant feast, where the Bride communes at her Husband's table. Bakers make the dreams of grain come true; vintners fulfill the ambitions of young grapes. The general movement of creation to culture to liturgy is evident in the Eucharist: grain and grapes are transformed into bread and wine, which become the stuff of Eucharist.

Shepherds and herdsman care for animals, so they're able to enter worship. Not all are chosen, but every newborn lamb longs to be transformed to smoke on Yahweh's altar. Sons of the herd come to fulfillment by giving their blood on the altar for atonement.

This is what *things* are for: to become vessels of the liturgy. This is what *human beings* are for: to glorify the cosmic temple by transforming created things into vessels of praise. This is where *everything* is headed: At the last, all the treasures of the nations will adorn new Jerusalem, the completed cosmic temple (Rev 21:24).

Pay attention because this is crucial: The liturgy doesn't spiritualize material things. It doesn't turn a secular world into a sacred one. Creation is liturgically designed. It has a liturgical destiny. It's liturgical all the way down. When we worship, we unveil creation's origin and history's hidden destiny. The liturgy anticipates the way the world ought to be and *will* be.

PATTERN ON THE MOUNTAIN

We keep making things more complicated, but we haven't quite captured the complexity of the situation. Let's think a little about a specific feature of culture: the organization of space.

Every culture organizes space in one way or another. We draw boundaries and property lines, build walls for houses and factories, erect fences, plan the streets and neighborhoods that make up our cities.

Cultures don't organize space in the same way. Think of the difference between the Shambles in York and the wide sidewalks of old Greenwich Village; between the winding streets of Rome and the geometric grid work of a Midwestern American city; between the makeshift crush of an African shantytown and the elbow room of an American suburb.

We organize space because we're made in the image of God the Builder. With Wisdom at His right hand (Prov 8:22–31), Yahweh lays the foundations of the earth (Ps 104:5; Isa 51:13), sets up pillars (Ps 75:3), and stretches out the curtain of heaven (Ps 104:2; Isa 40:22).

Made in His image, human beings are builders. We, too, set boundaries, lay foundations, stretch out roofs. Yahweh plants a garden for Adam, but Noah himself plants a vineyard. Yahweh builds a cosmic sanctuary, and later Moses pitches Yahweh's tent and Solomon constructs His temple.

Noah, Moses, and Solomon are new and better Adams because they're builders. But no builder is as great as the Last Adam, who constructs a lasting city, the city whose Builder and Maker is God (Heb 11:10), the church whose gates withstand hell's assaults (Matt 16:18), the bridal city Jerusalem.

Adam is created to glorify God's cosmic house. He's created to organize created space to honor God. But how does he know how to build? How does he know what a glorified cosmic temple looks like? Where are the blueprints?

Genesis 2 tells us: The *garden of Eden* is Adam's blueprint. God provides a 3D model to guide the formation of human space. What the garden is, and what happens in the garden, sets the tone for what happens in the liturgy of the world.

Your Sunday School teacher probably told you Adam and Eve lived in a beautiful garden, full of fruit trees and tame animals. That's almost true, but misleading. When God creates the world, it's marked off into *three* areas, and these three areas have different purposes.

At the center of creation is the garden, on the eastern edge of the larger land of Eden ("east in Eden," Gen 2:8). So there's a garden, and there's a land. Outside Eden, God makes other lands. One of them is named: Havilah, where there is gold (Gen 2:11–12). If you wanted to draw a map, you'd mark three areas: garden, land, and world.

Adam and Eve have different tasks in each zone. The garden is the place of worship. How do I know that? Genesis doesn't say it, but the rest of the Bible implies it. Once again, we can think backwards by looking at the garden-like features of the temple and tabernacle:

- The temple is built on a mountain, Moriah (2 Chr 3:1). Eden, too, is on a mountain (Ezek 28:12–14).
- The tabernacle and temple have golden lampstands molded to look like trees. At the door of the

temple, Solomon sets up two giant bronze pillars with capitals like lily blossoms. The cedar walls of the temple are carved with palm trees. All these are reminiscent of Eden, with its real trees with real fruit and flowers.

- Yahweh promises to meet Israel at the tabernacle and temple, and He meets Adam and Eve in the garden.

- After Adam and Eve are driven from the garden, Yahweh sets cherubim at the gate to keep them out (Gen 3:24). We don't hear about cherubim again until Yahweh tells Moses to put cherubic figures on the ark of the covenant (Exod 25:8–22) and weave them into the tabernacle curtains (Exod 26:1, 31). Why would Yahweh tell Moses to put cherubim in the tabernacle unless it's a new garden?

- Adam is placed in the garden to serve and guard (Gen 2:15). In the Old Testament, those verbs describe the work of Levites and priests (Num 1:53; 3:8–10; Deut 10:8). Adam serves as guardian priest of the garden of God.

Of course, the tabernacle and temple are built *after* the fall. That's why only priests can go in, and only partway. Under the Torah, even Israel isn't ready to re-enter the presence of God. Aaron and his sons are new Adams in a new garden, but Israel the new Eve can't draw near. Israel's sanctuaries are garden settings in a post-fall world.

If the garden is a temple, it's a scale model of creation as a whole. God creates a cosmic temple; He plants a garden-temple. He wants the former to become like the latter. The garden previews the destiny of the universe, which will one day resemble Eden (Rev 22:1–5).

God makes other places too. Outside the garden, Adam and Eve don't worship in a direct way. They have a different task. God blesses them to multiply and fill the earth, and to subdue and rule it (Gen 1:28). They don't need to subdue the garden. It's already subdued. What they need to subdue is the rest of the world. But if the garden doesn't need to be tamed, it does need to be *adorned*.

Here's what's supposed to happen: One day Adam ventures down the river Pishon from Eden to Havilah and sees shiny things on the ground (Gen 2:10–12). "Those are pretty," he thinks. "I'm going to take one home." Then he thinks: "That's glorious, like the glory of the Lord. I'll take some back to the garden and pretty it up a bit."

Adam is subduing and taking dominion over the earth. He discovers new things and uses them to make the glorious world more glorious. He discovers new things to glorify the garden-temple of God.

Adam is a priest in the garden. He's a king in the world, filling and ruling with Eve his queen. His work in the world outside is oriented toward the garden. He works so he can offer the fruit of his labor in worship.

But remember: The creation isn't designed to stay as-is. Even before sin, Adam and Eve are supposed to change things. God tells them, "Be fruitful, multiply, and fill the earth." As human beings spread over the earth, they can't all gather in the garden of Eden for worship. What do they do?

They set up *other* places of worship. A temple goes up in Havilah. Adam and Eve's children follow the Tigris and set up a sanctuary in Assyria. They plant a garden on the Euphrates. Eventually, if everything goes well, there will be places of worship on the shores of what we call the South China Sea, along the banks of the mighty Mississippi, in the jungles of Africa.

What do these sanctuaries look like? Adam's descendants will set up sanctuaries to resemble the garden of Eden, the original pattern on the mountain. As human beings take dominion over the earth, they plant and build new Edens everywhere they go. Two millennia on, the world will be dappled with lush sacred parks in the middle of every city around the world. Ten millennia on, and the world will be well on its way to becoming entirely a garden-city.

The first Eden sets the pattern for other sanctuaries. It also sets the pattern for the *world*. The multiplied gardens aren't supposed to be green oases in a howling brown wilderness. They're supposed to be gardens of worship in an increasingly gardenified world.

There are fruit trees in the sanctuary and orchards and vineyards outside. Adam names animals in the garden, and shepherds tend animals in their fields. Adam meets Eve in the sanctuary, and their children establish homes and families. The garden is an enclosed space, and outside the garden they build houses, towns, and garden-cities. Beautifying a beautiful creation, we fulfill the destiny of the cosmic temple. Through our cultural labor, we form creation as a home for God.

What about the third zone of creation, the *land* of Eden? What's that for? It's not like other lands. It's the land where God's garden is, and so it belongs to God in a unique way. It's a kind of holy land in the original creation.

We know the land of Eden is on higher ground than the garden. A spring springs up in Eden and flows through the garden (Gen 2:10) to become four rivers. The garden is somewhere between the highest spot in Eden and other lands.

Eden is the throne-land, where Yahweh rules. Adam and Eve start out in the garden, with Adam as priest leading Eve in serving God. But they're created to become kings. As they subdue the world, they ascend to the high place of Eden to rule alongside the Creator. Like the world, the land is to resemble the garden. Adam and Eve are called to transform the land.

Three zones: garden, land, world. Three assignments: worship in the garden, enthronement and rest in the land, and conquest and rule in the world. This is how the space of the original creation was divvied up.

As Adam and Eve's children spread out from Eden, they carry this map with them. Wherever they go, they're to plant garden-sanctuaries for worship and set up places for rest and rejoicing. Wherever they go, they're to remake the world according to the pattern of the garden. Their cultural labor moves the initial temple of creation toward its fulfillment as new creation.

To sum up, we've got to put two things together here. On the one hand, God gives Adam and Eve the garden as a *model* for the world. Man's purpose is to transform creation into sanctuary or, to say the same thing, to transform creation into God's garden-city. History is the gardenification of creation. Or the "Edenification." Or the New-Jerusalemization. You get the idea.

On the other hand, the garden serves as Adam and Eve's place of worship. It's the first liturgical space.

Add these up, and we draw a crucial conclusion about worship and liturgical space: Liturgy and liturgical space model the future creation. What we do in the liturgy is what we hope will one day happen everywhere at all times. Liturgical space serves as the template for transforming the world. Our worship space should anticipate what the world will eventually be. When we enter, we should sigh and think, "Ah, yes. Someday the whole world will look like *this*."

DIS-PLACEMENT

Almost immediately, of course, it goes badly wrong. Adam sins in the garden (Gen 3), Cain sins in the field (Gen 4), and the sons of God intermarry with daughters of men in the world (Gen 6). Adam fails in worship; Cain assaults his brother rather than guarding him; the sons of God compromise their witness by allying with the wicked.

Adam is made and placed in the garden (Gen 2:7–8), in the presence of God. After he sins, he and his wife are cast out to the east, and the way of return is guarded by cherubim with flaming swords (Gen 3:24). Since Adam's sin, man is *dis*placed.

And the displacement continues. After Cain kills Abel, he's cast out of the field, forced further east, further from the face of God, out to the land of Nod (Gen 4:16). When sons of God marry the daughters of men, the world is filled with violence, and God sends a flood to cast out everyone except Noah and his family.

Adam is created to turn the world into a garden, to glorify the cosmic temple. Instead, his sin kicks the first domino that eventually de-creates the world, turning it back to watery emptiness. Instead of a worldwide garden, Adam's descendants leave behind an endless waste. Devastation reigns over the world.

Adam's descendants are builders, but their construction is a form of destruction. Cain builds a city, but it's founded on the blood of his innocent, faithful brother (Gen 4:17). Cain's city is the first of the Bible's many wicked cities, of which Babel is most famous.

The men of Babel refuse to spread over the earth, raise a tower to connect earth to heaven, and build a city in defiance of God (Gen 11:1–9). Babel's tower is a sanctuary, but an idolatrous one. The city aims to unite mankind in rebellion. In Sodom, the town square isn't a place of welcoming hospitality. Instead, strangers are subjected to homosexual assault (Gen 18). While Israel is in Egypt, Pharaoh builds storage cities by beating down the people of God (Exod 1).

Israel is no better. Gibeah is Little Sodom (Judg 19). Late in his reign, Solomon turns idolatrous and Pharaonic, builds shrines to idols, and so provokes an exodus of ten tribes (1 Kgs 11–12). Isaiah calls Jerusalem "Sodom" because Zion, like Sodom, abuses the poor. The bridal city becomes a harlot (Isa 1:10–31). In Isaiah's day, wealthy Israelites add field to field to keep their brothers at a distance (Isa 5:8–10). Jeremiah calls the temple a den of thieves (Jer 7), and on his tour of the temple, Ezekiel finds it's as choked with idols as any pagan temple (Ezek 8–11).

Jesus echoes Jeremiah in His lament over Jerusalem, the city that kills prophets. He warns the city walls will be dismantled, not one stone on another. What the priests fear comes to pass, as the Romans take away the Jews' place (John 11:48). Displaced, man forms spaces of violence, injustice, and oppression. Our cultural efforts don't form a bridge from Eden to new Jerusalem; more often, they form a bridge to hell.

Of course, this isn't ancient history. All over today's world, men and women damage God's cosmic temple. Man still organizes space in insolent disobedience to the Lord of the temple.

We build grand temples to Satanic idols. Today, tens of millions are displaced by war, persecution, or other forms of injustice and violence. We exploit creation until forests are charred deserts. We zone our cities to keep untouchables and undesirables on the far side of the tracks, while those who can afford it live in safe complacency within their gated, well-policed neighborhoods. Our spaces don't express love of God and neighbor, but blasphemy and hatred for strangers.

After Adam's sin, the spatial structure of the original creation is still in place. Human life is still organized around three spaces with their three activities: worship in the garden, rest in the home and throne land, dominion in the world. But in every place, human life is corrupted: Idols occupy gardens; abuse is rampant in homes; war, rivalry, and greed devastate the world. After Adam's sin, men and women are displaced, without true sanctuary. We're strangers in God's cosmic temple, searching for a place to call home.

GARDEN IN THE WILDERNESS

God doesn't leave us without a witness. He gives Adam a model home. After Adam's sin, He keeps giving models to shape our work within His cosmic temple. In a world turned to desert, God gives us gardens of hope. In a world of displacement, *God gives places*.

These places are redeemed spaces, spaces where the world is in the process of being recreated, where the liturgical vessels of creation are being put to their proper, liturgical uses. These sanctuaries are God's answer to Babel and Sodom. Instead of raising a defiant tower toward the sky, these sanctuaries descend from heaven, made according to a heavenly pattern to connect heaven and earth (Exod 25:9, 40; Heb 8:5).

At these places, Yahweh is present in glory. Strangers aren't raped, but welcomed. Slaves, the poor, and the weak share a feast with the free, the rich, and the strong (Deut 12:12, 18; 14:29; 16:11, 14). *Here* is a place for the displaced.

These sanctuaries are products of human labor. They're cultural artifacts, full of cultural artifacts: Altars, tables, lampstands, the ark, bread, beer, wine. But they're products of *Spirit-led* labor (cf. Exod 31:1–11; 35:30–35), and so they're outposts of new creation.

In the sanctuaries, the rebellious organization of space is reversed. Space is put to its proper use as space for worship. In the sanctuary, creation transformed into culture is fulfilled in liturgy. The sanctuaries give a small glimpse of creation's destiny to be fulfilled as God's cosmic temple.

Israel's sanctuaries are sacred places, made holy by the glory of the Lord (Exod 29:43). For Israel, sacred means off-limits. Like the garden, the tabernacle and temple are prohibited places, guarded by cherubim. Only consecrated priests are allowed to enter Yahweh's house. Israel isn't yet holy enough to enter the holy space.

It's important to emphasize again: Liturgical space isn't spiritual space in a secular world. Liturgical space is *rightly-ordered, rightly-used space* in a displaced world. Liturgical space is where the future city is taking form within the cities of men. Liturgical space is future space present in the present.

In the Old Testament, God's place doesn't stay in place because people keep spoiling it. First, God's place is the garden. Cain and Abel have to bring their offerings to the gate of the garden because they can't get in. Later, Abram sets up altars throughout the land (Gen 12:7; 13:4, 18; 22:9).

After the exodus, Yahweh instructs Israel to pitch His royal tent at the foot of Sinai. In the early days of Samuel, Philistines attack and leave the tent in tatters (1 Sam 4–6). For a century, Israel worships in two places—the tent for the ark, which David eventually takes into Jerusalem (2 Sam 6), and the Mosaic tabernacle, which ends up at Gibeon (1 Kgs 3:3–5).

Solomon puts the pieces back together and builds a permanent house for Yahweh, the temple on Mount Moriah. But Israel abuses that house, so Yahweh sends in Nebuchadnezzar to rip it apart and cart it away in pieces to Babylon. Joshua and Zerubbabel build a new temple, and Ezra and Nehemiah complete the Lord's house by extending it to the edges of the city. Jerusalem becomes a holy city, an urban temple, anticipating the final temple from heaven. But the second temple doesn't last either. Before the apostles die, not one stone is left on another.

So, where's the place of worship? Where's the garden in the wilderness of the world? Eden? Bethel? Sinai or Shiloh? Gibeon or Moriah? It keeps moving. There's no permanent place for worship. That's a problem. If there's no liturgical space, there's no redeemed space. Can displaced humanity find a place if God keeps moving?

Plus, all these places are a long way from almost everyone. Suppose you're an Ethiopian who wants to worship the God of Israel. You can pray from anywhere. But you can't enter fully into worship without making a long trek to Jerusalem. If you're a eunuch in the court of Queen Candace (Acts 8), you can afford the trip. If you're a peasant, you can't.

That distance is a problem. Yahweh is the Creator. He's the source of all good. He's the God of Eden, who offers the fruit of the tree of life. He's the God of Sinai, who speaks words of life. If you want to *live*, you need to get close to Him. But He's a long way away. Even if you get to His house, He might not be there anymore. While you were traveling, He might have moved from His polluted house to Babylon.

But there is something constant: *Yahweh*. Wherever and whenever people call upon the name of the Lord, He's there. He's there in Eden, walking among the trees. He appears to Abram and Jacob, and they build altars. He comes down in a fiery cloud on Sinai, and His glory fills the completed tabernacle and later the temple. When Yahweh casts Israel into exile, Yahweh goes into exile with them (Ezek 8–11), sharing the curse He Himself imposes on His people. Can Israel sing Yahweh's song in a strange land (Ps 137)? Sure, because the living temple is with them.

Where is the place of worship? *Yahweh* is the place of worship. He's the garden in the wilderness of the world. Generation after generation sings Psalm 90: "Lord, thou has been our hiding place in all generations" (v. 1).

All the places of worship in the Bible reinforce this truth. They're architectural representations of the glory of Yahweh.

It's as if Yahweh's luminous glory cloud precipitated as fabric, wood, gems, gold, silver, bronze—as if the uncreated splendor of God took solid shape in blocks of stone and slabs of wood.

This truth becomes more fully evident in the new covenant. Since Jesus died and rose, there has been no single earthly sanctuary. The *people* are the temple, made of living stones (1 Pet 2:4–8). *We* are God's house, which means *we* are the created glory that manifests the uncreated glory of God. And it means that wherever the people gather, *there* is liturgical space because the Lord God Almighty and the Lamb are our temple (Rev 21:22; cf. John 4:15–26). The living God makes room for us *in Him*.

The liturgy is an entry into *this* place, the place that is God Himself. That tells us something about how the liturgy should run. In many churches, worship begins with an invocation of God's name: "In the Name of the Father, and of the Son, and of the Holy Spirit." That's God's welcoming invitation, a sign He *wants* you to come into His house. It also announces a *destination*. You enter a church building, but that's a portal to the heavenly sanctuary. It's a gate into the true temple, the Father who dwells in the Son. By the Spirit, they dwell in us and we in them.

Worship, in short, has a Triune shape. By that, I don't merely mean Christians worship the Triune God—the Father, Son, and Spirit; the One enthroned, the Lamb, and the seven Spirits who are the eyes of the Lamb. That is the God we worship. But we need to think more deeply. Christians don't toss up prayers and praise toward a Triune God who lives at a great distance in heaven. Christian worship is worship *within* the Trinity. Gathering as church, we gather *in* the Triune God.

We are in Christ, joined to the Son by the Spirit who is poured out on and in us. As the Father is in the Son and the Son in the Father, so they dwell in us by the Spirit (John 17:21). And we dwell in them. We are incorporated into the Triune communion.

That Triune fellowship is an eternal communion of prayer, communion, praise, mutual glorification. The Father glorifies the Son with the glory of the Spirit, and the Son glorifies the Father by the same Spirit. The Father humbles Himself to exalt the Son, and the Son to exalt the Father. The Father praises the Son through the Spirit, and the Son praises the Father in the same Spirit. The God who creates the universe as a cosmic temple is *Himself* an eternal divine temple. God is a dwelling for God. In Christ, He invites us, displaced sons of Adam, to share *His* place.

Our prayers aren't merely ours but are joined to the prayers of the Son as He cries "Abba" to His Father. Our wordless groans are carried by the Spirit, who groans within us in unutterable laments (Rom 8:18–25). When we praise the Father, we join the Son's praise. When we honor the Son, we are caught up by the Spirit in the Father's glorification of the Son.

Christian worship is never—it *cannot* be—a merely human activity. Christian worship is always our incorporation into the eternal liturgy that is the life of the Triune God.

GARDENIFIED CHURCHES

God is our liturgical space. In an ultimate sense, He's all we need. The church can worship in catacombs and caves if she needs to. God will hear and delight in our praises. He is redeemed space, the one safe place in a world of displacement.

But the church has never been satisfied with catacombs and caves. She's built buildings for worship. Biblically, that's the right instinct. The liturgy redeems place and therefore should take place in places. So the church has rightly sought to make the reality of God's presence public, visible in the world. Whenever the church has the freedom to build, she has carved out spaces for liturgy. Following Scripture, she tries to reflect God's glory in stone, glass, and wood. This isn't merely pragmatic, a matter of convenience. It's part of the church's mission, as we redeem culture by redeeming space.

Some Christian traditions describe churches as sacred space, but that phrase is liable to be misunderstood. As I said above, in Israel "Sacred" is a "No Entry" sign. Israelites can't enter the temple because the temple is holy and they're not.

The Christian church doesn't have *any* sacred spaces in this sense. Jesus opened the way and brought us all in. He tears the veil that separated the sacred space from the outer court. In Him, we're all saints, holy ones, because we're united to Jesus through baptism. Every believer has access to the heavenly sanctuary; all are in Christ, at home in the eternal communion of Father, Son, and Spirit. *We* are the glory that consecrates the Lord's house.

Under the new covenant, places are consecrated in the way everything else is: by thanksgiving, the Word, and prayer (1 Tim 4:4–5). Every saint consecrates everything he receives with gratitude and prayer. Every congregation makes a church building holy by giving thanks.

But holy things aren't forbidden things and holy spaces are no longer closed spaces. Christian churches shouldn't be designed to exclude or to communicate that the laity is further away than the clergy. Like the bread of the Lord's Supper, a church building is a "holy thing for holy people."

Christian churches have been, and should be, Bible-made-buildings. Like Eden, the tabernacle, and the temple, churches have often been built on an east-west axis, with the congregation facing east, enthroned with Christ and awaiting the sunrise from on high. They should resemble the garden of God. The roof vault looks like the ribs inside a ship because the church is Noah's ark on the dangerous seas of the world. Christian churches have been, and should be, architectural embodiments of God's glory. Cathedral spires soar up toward heaven. Stained glass windows rainbow the sunlight. Statues and pictures of heroes and saints remind us we worship with the dead as well as the living.

Christians who built such churches understood what they were doing. They understood the creation as a temple. They knew culture is the bridge between the initial and the final temple. They put their cultural skills, styles, tools, and materials to use in building churches that anticipate the new heavens and new earth, the heavenly temple-city. They seasoned the world with sanctuary-gardens, outposts of new creation. We should continue their work. If you walk into church and groan, "I hope the new creation is *nothing* like this," something is badly wrong. We aim at a gardenified world. Gardenify the liturgical spaces first.

The Scriptures are written for our edification, Paul says. Israel repeatedly spoils her places of worship. By her idolatry, injustice, sin, and hypocrisy, she pollutes Yahweh's places and He abandons them. He doesn't automatically stay with the church either. We don't trap him in our cathedrals, no matter how glorious they are. If a church persists in sin, Jesus removes the lampstand, which plunges the church into darkness. He will spit us from His mouth (Rev 3:16). Cathedrals can become hollow shells, or worse, synagogues of Satan.

Liturgical space is where the Spirit is redeeming created place, where He's remaking the world's space into a glorified cosmic temple. But He doesn't redeem our places if we defy Him. Liturgical space isn't worth anything if we quench the Spirit. The liturgy won't do its culture-transforming work if we grieve the Spirit of the liturgy. It calls us to faith, dogged allegiance to King Jesus.

But: As we keep in step with the Spirit, liturgical space spreads across the planet—space devoted to the worship of God, redeemed space that begins to redirect all space toward its intended purpose, space used the way the whole creation is designed, and destined, to be used. As liturgical places multiply, the world is increasingly gardenified. It increasingly comes to resemble what it will be: new Jerusalem, the garden city that descends from heaven.

12

Dialog

THEN GOD SAID, "LET THERE BE LIGHT";
AND THERE WAS LIGHT.
—GENESIS 1:3

Remember those dank cathedrals with the dull repetitions I mentioned at the beginning of chapter 11? They're not just dank and dull. They're also very, very quiet, hushed even.

Not *completely* quiet, mind you. If you time-traveled with The Doctor back to a medieval French church, you'd hear a *few* things. Priests and monks chanting psalms. A priest reading Scripture and whispering the *Hoc est* ("This is") at the altar, confecting bread into the body of Christ. If you time-traveled to the right century, you'd hear a sermon, maybe from an itinerant friar.

But you'd notice something about the sound. It's almost all in Latin. That's strange, because the people speak French or some precursor of French. All over Europe, all Catholic churches sound the same. Whether you step into a church in England or Poland or Norway, the priest is speaking Latin.

There's something attractive about that, of course. Today, you can visit two churches in the same town, from the same denomination, and the worship services can be entirely different. A little uniformity is a good thing.

Mostly, though, it's a bad deal to have a Latin liturgy for people who don't speak Latin. The faithful gather in the presence of the Lord, and He speaks in an unknown tongue. No wonder medieval Christians turned to relics and statues and other objects of devotion. God wasn't talking much.

You'd notice another thing too: The congregation doesn't say much either. They don't know Latin, so they can't chant along with the hymns. They can't understand the Scripture readings and wouldn't recognize the "Hoc est" even if they could hear it.

Some of them learn a few snatches here and there. They learn to recognize some Bible words. If there's a sermon, it's in the vernacular, so they can follow along with that. If they attend Mass often enough, they'll pick up some of the phrases of the altar liturgy. Even so, they don't speak. Worship isn't a dialogue.

There are theologians out there who will tell you hushed reverence is the way Christians participate in the liturgy. They might quote Habakkuk: "The Lord is in His holy temple. Let all the earth keep silent before Him" (Hab 2:20). Silence, they'll say, isn't exclusion. Silence is what makes worship spiritual. Quietness is next to godliness.

There's a place for silence in the Christian life and the liturgy. But the accent of Scripture is entirely in the opposite direction. The God of the Bible *speaks*, and worship is a dialogue between the speaking God and His listening, and speaking, people.

LITURGY OF THE WORLD

Remember from the last chapter: God created the world as a cosmic temple, Adam as priest, and everything else as a vessel of a cosmic liturgy. History is a cosmic liturgy. The *word* is at the center of the liturgy of the world. History begins with a word from God, and at every moment everything is sustained by the word of the Lord.

Genesis 1 introduces God to us. What do we learn about Him? First we find out He's the Creator of heaven and earth. Then we learn He is or has a Spirit. We're only three verses in when He speaks His first words: "Let there be light." "God speaks" is one of the very first things we learn about Him.

He keeps talking until there's heaven above, earth beneath, waters under the earth. He keeps talking until heaven is filled with lights, the sea teems with fish, birds fly over the face of the sky, and animals, creeping things, and men and women are multiplying on the face of the earth.

He speaks to the earth, and it sprouts grass and trees. He speaks to the fish and birds and animals, and they multiply. The Creator is King, who rules His creation through His word, by issuing decrees.

When God first spoke creation into existence, there was nothing there to respond to Him. He didn't find light lurking in a seedy bar and ask it to come out into the open to dispel the darkness. He said the word "Light" when there was no light, and then there was light.

There's no more fundamental reason for the existence of the world than God's Word. There isn't some more basic essence or nature that determines that the world is and what it is. God's *word* is the foundation.

It's not quite accurate to say things exist to respond to God. More profoundly, we exist as response to God's almighty summons. Light doesn't have the power to be light on its own. Without the divine "Let there be," light isn't. It doesn't exist and then respond to God. Its very existence is a dialogic response that is possible only because of the Creator's word. God's first word enables creation to respond.

Now that things exist, things respond to God's word. But they are what they are and continue to be what they are because they are engaged in a dialogue with the Creator.

This is how the world works, even now. Every morning, He commands the sun to repeat yesterday's performance. Every evening, He tells the sun to descend in a burst of glory, so the moon and stars can take their place on the darkened stage of the sky.

His voice splits cedar trees, makes the earth shake, bursts out in flame, makes the deer calve and strips the forest bare

(Ps 29). He commands the angels who are His ministering spirits (Ps 91:11–12).

Why is there something rather than nothing? Because in the beginning, God called things into existence. Why do things continue to exist rather than blipping out of being? Because God *keeps* speaking them.

Man is His primary dialogue partner. He creates mankind and immediately starts talking to us. He gives Adam a command and comes back to see if he's obeyed it. He confronts Cain with his sin and warns Cain's brothers not to take vengeance. He tells Noah He's about to flood the earth and gives him a plan for a saving ark.

He talks to Abraham, Hagar, Isaac, and Jacob. He speaks to Moses at the burning bush and to Israel at Sinai. He speaks to Joshua and Gideon and David and Solomon. Prophets speak because the "Word of Yahweh" places words in their mouths.

When He's not talking, He communicates in other ways—through Joseph's dreams and visions, through Solomon's dreams, through Daniel's ecstasies.

He speaks as God. His words manifest His character. His words are true. He speaks with authority (and not as the scribes). His words are powerful. They accomplish what He intends. He speaks to enter into intimate communion with us.

Since God's words are the words of God, we should respond to them as such. When He makes a promise, we should trust it. When He says something is true, we should believe it. When He commands, we should obey. When He summons us to rejoice in song, we sing.

God speaks in many portions and in many ways. Our lives are surrounded and infused with His words. We are made to answer; we are made *as* an answer to His creative word. We answer in the portions and ways His words demand.

Everything in our lives is shaped by how we answer His words. If we trust His promises, He proves trustworthy. If we believe what He says, we won't be disappointed. If we obey His commands, we walk in the way of life.

We often do the opposite. He promises, but we doubt. He asserts, but we disbelieve. He commands, but we disobey. Doubt, disbelief, and disobedience lead to frustration and death, eventually eternal death.

Every moment of life and our final destiny in life are determined by our response to the Lord in the liturgy of the world. It's determined by how we answer the word of the Lord. It's determined by our performance in the dialogue of life.

That doesn't just apply to individual men and women. It applies to families, nations, and churches too. The future of a nation depends on whether or not it responds rightly to the word of God. Rulers should honor the King, and He shatters the ones who don't (Ps 2). The same goes for churches. In His messages to the churches of Asia (Rev 2–3), Jesus warns He will remove the lampstand from unrepentant churches. The future of a church depends on its responsiveness to God's word.

This is the liturgical movement of history, the liturgy of the world: God speaks, human beings and communities respond faithfully or not, and their future is determined by that response.

That destiny is the result of a further word from God. He *initiates* the liturgy of history by speaking. He *ends* the liturgy of history with a word of final judgment. History—and every segment of history—is suspended between God's first and final word.

We can see this pattern in the creation week. God speaks light into existence and speaks again to call it good. He speaks to divide waters above from waters below, and water from land, and then speaks again to pronounce it good. He speaks plants and heavenly lights, fish and birds and land animals, then speaks His approval of what He has made.

Each of us and all peoples are suspended between word and word. God speaks, humans and nations answer, and He speaks a second word of evaluation and judgment.

He commands Adam (Gen 2) and then curses after Adam disobeys (Gen 3). He tells righteous Noah to build an ark, and, when Noah obeys, He saves him from the flood (Gen 8–10).

When Abram believes His promises, He judges Abram as righteous (Gen 15). He enters into covenant with Israel, promising to bless their obedience and threatening to curse their unfaithfulness with exile (Lev 26; Deut 28). He instructs kings (Deut 17) and takes ten tribes when Solomon violates every royal command (1 Kgs 11–12).

He commands Pharaoh to let Israel go, and when he refuses, He sends plagues and Passover. He summons Assyrians and Babylonians to discipline Israel, but when they overstep their mandate, He punishes them for their pride (Isa 10).

Nations and individuals don't succeed or collapse by accident. God doesn't speak a first word then leave things to take their "natural" course. History is surrounded and embraced by His speech. He speaks the first *and* the last word. The word of the Lord is the Alpha *and* the Omega of creation's and humanity's history.

Creation exists by the power of the word. Creation moves and changes by the power of the word. Everything that is exists as a dialogic being, as a response to God's speech.

The liturgy of the church takes place within this cosmic liturgy of the world. The church's liturgy isn't a retreat from this world. The church's liturgy concentrates the liturgy of history. In the church's liturgy, we carry on a properly ordered dialogue within the dialogue of creation and history.

LITURGY OF THE WORD

The God of the Bible is a communicative God, and not just in relation to the creation. He's an eternally communicative God. John draws back the veil to reveal this at the beginning of his Gospel. God the Creator has a Word who is "toward" Him, a Word who is God. This Word created the world (John 1:1–5).

God doesn't start conversing when He makes creatures to converse with. He is an eternal conversation. From forever to forever, the Father has spoken His Word by the breath of His Spirit. The Father cannot speak His Word without hearing the Word speak back. So, from forever to forever, by the same Spirit, the Word responds to the Speaker.

God doesn't happen to speak. He doesn't happen to converse. He is Word. His life, the Triune life, is an eternal trialogue.

Now, if you go to visit this God in His house and He doesn't say anything, you know you're being left out. You know there's a conversation going on because there's always a conversation going on, and you're not part of it.

Think of it this way: Your best friend invites you to dinner, but his family spends the evening speaking Obenglobish. Unless you're in on the joke, you'll feel frustrated, confused, left out. You'll suspect your friend is playing an elaborate trick.

God hasn't played an elaborate trick. He doesn't invite us to His house and sit in sullen, stern, or sanctified silence throughout our visit. He invites us so that He can speak to us.

It's even better than that. The conversable God doesn't speak from a great distance. He doesn't speak from behind a veil. He's removed the veil and invites us in. He ushers us into the new sanctuary, heaven itself. He gives us access to the ultimate temple, which is "God and the Lamb" (Rev 21:22).

Let me say it more forcefully: In worship, *we're brought into the Triune conversation*. We're in the Word, the incarnate Son, Jesus the anointed King. In and with Jesus, we speak to the Father by the Spirit. Through Jesus and His Spirit-breath, the Father speaks to us. Our words to God and His to us are folded into the eternal trialogue of the eternally conversable Triune God.

It's no accident that throughout the Bible, worship is a response to God's word, a dialogue between the Lord and His people:

As we saw in chapter 11, the Garden of Eden is the original micro-cosmic sanctuary, the place where Yahweh commands Adam and then returns to evaluate Him, to bless or to curse.

When the flood subsides, Yahweh commands Noah to come out of the ark, along with his family and all the animals. Noah answers by building an ark altar and offering ascension offerings from every clean animal. When Yahweh smells the soothing aroma, He promises never again to curse the land and to maintain the regular cycles of the seasons (Gen 8:13–22). The sequence is: Yahweh commands; Noah obeys and makes offerings; Yahweh promises.

When Abram first enters the land on his journey from Ur, Yahweh meets him at Shechem and promises to give the land to his descendants. Abram responds by building an altar. Abram camps between Bethel and Ai, builds an altar, and calls on the name of Yahweh (Gen 12:4–9). The sequence is: Yahweh commands and promises; in response, Abraham obeys and builds altars and calls on Yahweh. Abram's worship is a dialogue with the God who promises.

Moses is the first man to stand on holy ground (Exod 3:5) when Yahweh appears to Him at the burning bush. The entire scene is a conversation between the Lord and Moses, at the place where Yahweh will later cut covenant with Israel.

Sinai is a covenant-cutting event. Following the Lord's instructions, Israel assembles at the foot of the mountain to offer ascension offerings and sacrifices. Yahweh thunders out the Ten Words, then reveals His commandments and statutes to Moses. When Moses brings the word from the mountain, Israel shouts, "All the words Yahweh has spoken, we will do" (Exod 19:1—24:3).

David writes psalms and assigns others to write psalms (e.g., Asaph). Most of the psalms are written in two-line verses designed to be sung antiphonally, that is, in dialogue:

> Yahweh, how my adversaries have increased! Many are rising up against me. (Ps 3:1)
>
> The voice of Yahweh shakes the wilderness; Yahweh shakes the wilderness of Kadesh. (Ps 29:8)
>
> Whoever secretly slanders his neighbor, him will I destroy;
> No one who has a haughty look and an arrogant heart will I endure. (Ps 101:5)

After Solomon finishes the temple, he dedicates it with a series of offerings. But the heart of the temple dedication is a long prayer (1 Kgs 8; 2 Chr 6) about future prayer. Solomon asks Yahweh to respond to prayers directed toward the house.

Whatever Israel suffers—famine, drought, defeat, invasion, exile—Solomon asks Yahweh to hear them when they turn to the house for healing. He even asks Yahweh to answer gentiles who trust Him. In response, Yahweh promises to place His eyes, ears, and heart in the house. He will hear and see, and He will answer. Solomon's temple is a house of prayer for the nations, where distressed people can seek relief in response to Yahweh's promises. It's a place of healing conversation with the conversable God.

Once Israel settles in the land, most of Israel's liturgical life doesn't take place at the tabernacle or the temple. Men are required to travel to the central sanctuary three times a year, for Passover, Pentecost, and the Feast of Booths. They don't go to the sanctuary every week. Holy convocations happen every Sabbath (Lev 23:3), but they happen in local assemblies scattered throughout the land. No animal offerings are permitted at these synagogues. Priests and Levites, who live in towns throughout Israel, teach Torah, lead prayers, and lead singing. By the time of Jesus, we know what the synagogue liturgy looks like. It's a dialogue, just like every example of worship in the Bible.

LOVE SONG

Leviticus looks like an exception to the rule. Instead of a personal dialogue between Yahweh and Israel, Levitical worship consists of complicated, mostly silent, rituals.

That's a misperception. The book of Leviticus itself is made up almost entirely of Yahweh's words to Moses. Israel performs rites of offering, priests carry out priestly service, and Israelites observe purity regulations in response to Yahweh's word. Israel's ritual actions speak back obediently to God's speech.

Ritual is always a form of communication. A giddy young man gives a love-struck young woman a diamond ring. He's doing nothing new. He's following a ritual script repeated hundreds of millions of times across the centuries. It's old and repetitive, yet the script still shouts love, longing, and lifelong commitment.

In Leviticus, worship is still dialogue: Yahweh instructs Israel how to approach Him; then Israel answers by doing what He commands; then Yahweh smells the soothing aroma and is pleased. God invites Israel to His house, and Israel speaks back with acts of sacrifice, in blood, fire, and smoke.

The romantic example I gave a couple of paragraphs back isn't accidental. Yahweh is Husband to Israel. The Sinai covenant is their wedding service, and the tabernacle is their honeymoon tent. Liturgical rites maintain communion between Yahweh and His Bride.

That's what the Song of Songs is about. Modern Christians read the Song as a celebration of erotic love, and it is that. But it's *first* an allegory of Yahweh's love-play with Israel.

Temple imagery is all over the Song. The lovers' hideaway is made from cedar and cypress, the woods of the temple (Song 1:17). The Bride is a lily (Song 2:1), and lily designs are part of the temple décor (1 Kgs 7:19, 22, 26). The Bride is without blemish (Song 4:7), smooth and silky as a sacrificial offering.

At the center of the poem, the lovers enter a garden to feast on one another (Song 4:16–5:1). In this garden sanctuary, each gives him/herself to the other, just as, in the Levitical system, Israel offers herself as food to Yahweh and Yahweh gives life to His bride. The reality of mutual consumption becomes even more pronounced in the Eucharist. We're incorporated into Christ, "eaten" into His body, even as we feast on His flesh and blood. We in Him, He in us, made one flesh as Bridegroom and Bride.

Together the lovers are consumed with a love strong as death and jealous as the grave, fueled by the very flame of Yah, the flame that is Yah (Song 8:6–7). The lovers are consumed in the sacrificial flame of Yahweh's love.

The Song's dialogues are dialogues of mutual admiration and praise. "Your love is better than wine," says the Bride (Song 1:2). "Your love is better than wine," responds the Bridegroom (Song 4:10). "Most beautiful among women," says the Bridegroom of his Bride (Song 1:8). "My beloved is outstanding among ten thousand," answers the Bride (Song 5:10). When the Bridegroom is absent, the Bride searches in desperation, willing to suffer humiliation to be restored to communion.

This *is* the liturgy. It's the liturgy of the world because the entire history of humanity is the Lord's romance with His Bride, His daring rescue that leads to a real-life, eternal happily ever after. It's the liturgy of the church, which is a dialogue of mutual admiration and praise.

The liturgy of the church encapsulates the liturgy of the world, acting it out on a small scale. The liturgy isn't a retreat from the world. It's a place and time when the dialogue of the world is done *right*, and it sets the pattern for our speech and dialogues outside the sanctuary. It's a place and time when the Bride responds in love to the Bridegroom.

We come to the door of the Lord's house, and He welcomes us with, "Come, my sister, my bride, most beautiful among women. You are altogether beautiful, without blemish, my darling, my bride." We answer with praise of our Bridegroom. "How handsome you are, beloved, and so pleasant. My beloved is like a young gazelle or stag on the mountains." We sing songs of communion: My beloved is mine, and we are His (Song 2:16). We are our Beloved's, and He is ours (Song 6:3). We are our Beloved's, and His desire is for us (Song 7:10). We are mutually intoxicated by one another's love-wine, mutually consumed in the fire of Triune love.

You think liturgy is slow, repetitive, dull? It's the opposite. It's as exciting as sex. *More* exciting, since the communion of the Triune God with His Bride is the original communion of which sexual union is a copy. A splendid copy, for sure, but not the first game of love.

The upshot is plain: Wordless worship isn't *too* liturgical. Wordless worship is an *abandonment* of liturgy because Christian liturgy is a dialogue of love.

DIALOGUE REDEEMED

Man is made in the image of the God of Scripture, and so we are communicative creatures. Yahweh places Adam in the garden to name the animals, to assign linguistic labels to other creatures. When God presents Eve to Adam, the man bursts into poetry (Gen 2:23).

From Eden on, our interactions with one another take place primarily through the medium of language. Husbands speak to wives and parents to children. Employers speak to employees, and employees talk back. Legislators write laws; judges issue decisions; kings, presidents, and prime ministers give speeches. Voters and protesters cheer or jeer in response.

Language is *the* fundamental cultural reality. Languages distinguish one group from another. The French are French because they speak to one another and name the world Frenchly. The Nuer interact Nuerly, Xhosa click the world in their Xhosan way. America and Britain are, so the quip goes, nations divided by a common language.

Language is the first common practice of every group, the one that makes all other common practices possible. Markets function only if sellers and buyers can communicate. What force can laws have if they're written in an unknown language? It's hard to get a bowling team together if bowlers don't speak the same language. If they have no language in common, each will be bowling alone.

The architect has to speak to the general contractor and the general contractor to the crew. If they can't communicate, the project will be left in ruins like Babel's unfinished tower, lonely on the plain of Shinar. Even the solitary painter in his studio has to communicate to get supplies, to present his works to buyers or museum curators, to seduce his models.

Talk is cheap, sure. But it's indispensable. Everybody's gotta talk. We can't live without it.

Our speech to one another is supposed to be a response to the speech of God. God says, "Speak truth in love" (Eph 4:15) and "Lay aside falsehood, and speak truth to your neighbor" (Eph 4:25). If we respond rightly to His word, our words to one another will build communities of truth and love, cultural habits and institutions that embody hope and justice.

But we *don't*. We don't speak rightly back to God, and so we don't speak rightly to one another.

After Adam sins, Yahweh comes to the garden to speak to him. It doesn't go well (Gen 3:8–13). Yahweh calls Adam to appear before Him, but Adam is hiding among the trees in fear and shame. Confronted with his sin, he doesn't confess, but blames Eve and ultimately blames God.

Everything's upside down. Instead of responding to a call to worship, Adam slinks out from hiding. Instead of confessing, he targets the closest scapegoat. The dialogue doesn't end with benediction but malediction, with Yahweh issuing curses against the serpent, the man, and the woman. It's the Bible's first liturgy, but it's twisted. It's an *anti*-liturgical dialogue.

When Adam's dialogue with God gets spoiled, so does his dialogue with his wife, his sons, his eventual neighbors. He submits to the serpent, whose wickedness is linguistic wickedness. Human speech becomes diabolical, full of lies, half-truths, seductions, temptations, threats, hatred, and anger. We speak like the serpent, with forked tongue.

Speech is corrupted, and so are all the common practices that rely on speech. Patterns of common life and the institutions that carry communities become infused with lies, slander, gossip, boasts, blasphemies. Husbands accuse wives instead of defending them. Parents denigrate children, and children defy parents. Sellers deceive buyers. Legislators write unjust laws, judges favor the rich or the poor, presidents and prime ministers manipulate public opinion through slick media campaigns.

The world comes under the dominion of the father of lies.

The God who creates by Word *re-creates* by Word. The eternal Word becomes flesh in order to redeem man and society. He enters our linguistic disorder to put it back in order so that our speech to God and one another is what it ought to be, restored to truth, love, hope, and justice.

Here's where the liturgy comes in. The liturgy of the church restores language so that it becomes what it's intended to be: a medium of dialogue with God and one another, the common practice that facilitates other common practices. By putting our fragmented language together again, the liturgy of the heavenly city repairs the common life of the earthly city of man.

The liturgy doesn't do this by inventing a new language. Liturgical speech isn't a religious version of Esperanto. The liturgy uses the common language of the worshiping people, which exists before it becomes a liturgical language. The Bible is translated to become a viable liturgical Bible. It uses the syntax, grammar, and vocabulary that's already there.

The church can force things. Missionaries can teach English or French to Korean, Indian, or Peruvian converts to make them worship in the missionary's tongue. That's happened often enough. But the church is called to be Pentecostal, speaking the one gospel and praising the one God in every tongue under heaven.

All human languages are broken. They've been used to lie and blaspheme. The liturgy, like the Word Himself, takes up the dilapidated language of fallen humanity. It assumes language to redeem language, so it can turn our heap of broken images into the language of Zion.

The liturgy puts an existing language to work in a new way. Pastors preach Scripture to teach people the truth about God, the world, themselves. Over years, decades, and centuries, God corrects our mis-naming and teaches His people to name the world properly. The liturgy reorients existing languages so they begin to speak rightly in response to God's speech.

New vocabulary must be added: words for sin, the cross, resurrection, the heavenly city. New names are added to the stock of names: Adam, Abel, Abraham, David and Solomon, Josiah, Jeremiah, Jesus. New sentences are uttered: "God so loved the world that He gave His only Son." Converted worshipers sing and speak in *their* language to praise and thank the Creator, who is Father, Son, and Spirit. Tongues once used to praise Marduk or Zeus or Allah become instruments of righteous praise, directed to the living God.

In the liturgy, language does what language is created to do. In the liturgy, the language is redeemed and fulfilled as it's *Christianized*, infused and corrected by the Scriptures. The liturgy doesn't just *lead* to the Christianization of language. It's the first Christianization of language, which anticipates the final transformation of language in new Jerusalem, the un-Babel when people of every tongue will be united in praise to the Lord and the Lamb.

The liturgy performs this magic by the power of Word and Spirit. The church may abandon Scripture and turn her liturgy into an echo of the diabolical dialogue of the world. That doesn't redeem language but degrades it more deeply. The church can carry on the dialogue of the liturgy while defying the Spirit of the liturgy. Then the Spirit of Pentecost takes flight, and the church is just another outpost of Babelic confusion.

To redeem language, the liturgy must be reformed and refreshed, again and again. It must be called back, again and again, to Scripture. It must be carried out by people who walk in the Spirit to follow the Lord Jesus.

But a liturgy infused with Scripture performed by people filled with the Spirit—*that* is an agent for the redemption of the world. As I said in the Preface, culture is the six-day bridge between creation and eschaton. Liturgy orients culture toward its ultimate purpose. In the city of God, liturgy is the seventh-day initial transformation of culture, redirecting damaged words toward their proper end.

DIVINE DIALOGUE

Through most of the church's history, Christian worship has been just the kind of dialogue I've been describing. A priest or minister is ordained to speak Christ's word to the people, and the people respond as the Bride. You hear the minister's voice, but he doesn't speak his own words. Jesus authorizes him to speak, and the words he speaks *ought* to be the words of Jesus. The liturgy might look like a dialogue between minister and people. In reality, it's a dialogue between Bridegroom and Bride. It's the church's participation in the trialogue of Father, Son, and Spirit.

To illustrate how this works in practice, I'll run through a standard Lutheran liturgy. You can find the same dialogic patterns in Anglican, Methodist, Catholic, Orthodox, Reformed, and other liturgies. This *is* the church's historic liturgy.

Many of the specific phrases, songs, prayers don't come directly from the Bible. They could be different. But any liturgy shaped by the Bible is going to look something like this. It's going to be a dialogue between God and His people, organized around Word and Table.

The conversation begins as soon as the congregation assembles. After a procession, the minister greets the baptized people in the Lord's name: "In the Name of the Father, and of the Son, and of the Holy Spirit." The people respond with "Amen."

It's a word of welcome. It's also a word of new creation. The minister speaks the word of the eternal Word. Through him, the Word that summoned the world into existence summons the church into being. Through the minister, the Word gathers a new-created humanity in the midst of fallen humanity.

Having called us to worship, the minister calls us to confess our sins. To commune with the Bridegroom, the Bride needs to enter His presence fragrant with the fragrance of the Bridegroom. She needs to freshen up.

The call to confess is again a dialogue:[1]

> M: I said, I will confess my transgressions unto the Lord.
>
> C: And thou forgavest the iniquity of my sin.
>
> *Ps 32:5*

Minister and people then kneel to confess their sins before God and one another, with these or similar words:

> Almighty God, our Maker and Redeemer, we poor sinners confess unto thee, that we are by nature sinful and unclean, and that we have sinned against thee by thought, word, and deed. Wherefore we flee for refuge to thine infinite mercy, seeking and imploring thy grace, for the sake of our Lord Jesus Christ.

Notice what's happening here: English is being used to admit our sin and disobedience before a holy God. A language

---

[1] In the following, "M" stands for "Minister" and "C" for "Congregation."

that was already in development before the gospel arrived is deployed to express humble contrition. Every time an English-speaking congregation confesses sin, it contributes to the redemption of the language and moves the world toward its final glory.

After confession, the minister pronounces absolution; that is, he assures the people that their sins are, in fact, forgiven:

> Arise and hear the good news! Brothers and sisters who have been baptized into union with Jesus Christ, God Himself promises you the forgiveness of the Father, the victory of the Son, and the glory and empowerment of the Holy Spirit. Believe this, and rejoice.

Remember, this isn't the minister's promise. It's not his opinion. He speaks for the Son, who speaks the words the Father gives Him. When the minister says, "Your sins are forgiven," you should take it as God's address to you. Don't trust the minister. Trust God.

And rejoice. After the people respond with an "Amen," the liturgy kicks into high gear with a series of sung responses. The *Kyrie Eleison* ("Lord, have mercy"), the *Gloria in Excelsis* ("Glory in the highest," an ancient hymn of praise), the *Te Deum* ("We praise you, O God") together constitute an ascension in song.

Having humbled ourselves in confession, the Lord raises us to glory. We climb the heavenly Zion to join angels and saints in joyful assembly (Heb 12:18–24). Heaven and earth join in a universal dialogue in God's cosmic house. We anticipate the final Zion, when there will be no words but words of praise. Filled with praise, the church is the heavenly city, present now in part with hope for a future fullness.

One of the traditional dialogues is the *Kyrie*, a Trinity-shaped set of petitions and pleas for mercy. A simple version is

M: Lord, have mercy upon us.

C: Lord have mercy upon us.

M: Christ, have mercy upon us.

C: Christ, have mercy upon us.

M: Lord, have mercy upon us.

C: Lord, have mercy upon us.

Sometimes the *Kyrie* is more elaborate[2]:

M: In peace let us pray to the Lord.

C: Lord, have mercy.

M: For the peace that is from above,
and for the salvation of our souls,
let us pray to the Lord.

C: Lord, have mercy.

M: For the peace of the whole world,
for the well-being of the churches of God,
and for the unity of all,
let us pray to the Lord.

C: Lord, have mercy.

M: For this holy house,
and for them that in faith, piety, and fear of God
offer here their worship and praise,
let us pray to the Lord.

C: Lord, have mercy.

M: Help, save, comfort, and defend us, O God,
by thy grace.

C: Amen.

The minister has conducted us from the foot of the mountain to the peak. Using the keys of the kingdom, he's unlocked the door of the Lord's house and led us into the inner chamber,

[2] This is taken from *Service Book and Hymnal* (1958), 18. Many other prayerbooks and hymnals also have it.

where the most intense communion happens. Every step has been a small dialogue setting up for the climactic dialogue in preaching, prayer, and feasting.

Churches have traditionally introduced corporate prayers with a snippet of dialogue:

> M: The Lord be with you.
>
> C: And with thy spirit.
>
> *1 Tim 4:22*

It's a small gesture, but profound. With this exchange, minister and people form a communion of prayer in the Spirit. Through the Spirit, in fact, minister and people enter the communion of the Triune God. The church's dialogue is folded into the eternal conversation of love that is Triune life.

FORMED BY THE WORD

At the mountaintop, the Lord speaks directly to us in readings from the Bible. Many churches use "lectionaries," an annual cycle of Scripture readings. Each week, the lectionary prescribes an Old Testament, an Epistle, and a Gospel reading.

The assigned readings correspond to the season of the church year. During Advent, Old Testament readings are prophecies of the Messiah or the new covenant. Epistle readings are prophecies of the Lord's coming or the final judgment. Gospel readings include Jesus' Palm Sunday entry to Jerusalem, Jesus' Olivet Discourse (Matt 24), or narratives about the incarnation. Through the lectionary, the dialogue of the liturgy is tuned to the time of redemption, the life, death, and resurrection of Jesus the Messiah.

At the end of each reading, the minister says, "The word of the Lord," and the congregation responds with gratitude: "Thanks be to God." Another small but profound gesture. God often speaks to comfort and give hope. But His word is also a sword (Heb 4:11–12). His word breaks into our hearts to dig up hidden sins and bring them to light. He speaks terrifying judgments that chill the bones. And yet, *no matter what word He speaks*, no matter how shattering or startling, the liturgy trains the church to say, "Thank you." It's more than etiquette. It's a confession of faith: Even when He kills us, God intends good. He intends to raise us to new life.

This is another moment in the redemption of language and culture. God initiates the dialogue of history and of the liturgy. Our response should always be grateful obedience. Often, it's grumbling disobedience. Here, at least—here in the liturgy—we say what we should when God speaks. We say, "Thank you."

Sunday's "Thank you" sets the tone for the rest of the week. When God speaks in the world, in the midst of difficulties in family or at work, in the midst of our doubts and fears, we repeat Sunday's "Thank you." Thus the liturgical dialogue reshapes the dialogic patterns of daily life.

When we don't, when we grumble or close our ears, Sunday's "Thank you" stands in judgment. We go back to church the following week, again hear God's word, again say, "Thanks be to God." If we're paying attention, it should be a moment of self-examination and repentance. Sunday's "Thank you" is the measure of our everyday speech in the dialogue of life. Sunday's "Thank you" in the heavenly city tests our speech in the earthly city.

In the sermon, the minister speaks the Lord's word more pointedly to a specific congregation. If he's doing his job, he'll stick to the text. He shouldn't be telling stories or commenting on the World Cup. He should be delivering the word of God to the people of God. Through the readings and preaching, the word comes into its own. The written text becomes a living voice. Through the text read and taught, the Spirit of Jesus speaks to the churches (cf. Rev 2–3).

There's a lot of talk these days about formation and about the liturgy's role in forming virtuous men and women. Scripture teaches the liturgy is formative, but in a more direct way. We're deformed because we worship idols. We need to be formed into worshipers. That's what the liturgy does. If it conforms to God's will for worship, it's an act of true worship, and those who participate are worshipers.

Everyone who participates in Christian liturgy worships the true God. They pray to the Father of Jesus, praise the Triune God, hear the word of God, and gather at the table of Jesus Christ.

Of course, not everyone who participates in the Christian liturgy worships the true God *truly*. Some are cunning conscious hypocrites. Some desperately doubt. Some are more devoted to idols than to the true God. Done rightly, done biblically, the liturgy shatters false worshipers to raise them up as true worshipers. The liturgy is the work of the Triune God. It's the Father's work on us by His two hands, the Son and Spirit. Through the acts, gestures, words, and rhythms of the liturgy, the Spirit is calling us into fellowship. Through the liturgy, God is making worshipers.

It's especially through the word that the liturgy makes worshipers. Husbands who spend the week abusing their wives hear Paul's words: "Husbands, love your wives as Christ loved the church" (Eph 5:22–33). Children who resent their parents hear God say, "Children, obey your parents" (Eph 6:1). Employers who abuse their employees are confronted by the Torah's demands for justice. Slumlords who prosper on the suffering of the poor hear the severe words of Isaiah: I hate your new moons. Stop this trampling of my courts. Your hands are covered with blood (Isa 1).

Suppose they hear all this and *still* don't change? Even then the Spirit works on them, convicting them of sin, righteousness, and judgment (John 16:5–8). No one can participate in a faithful Christian liturgy without being formed like clay into a worshiper or hardened into a brittle vessel that will eventually be shattered. No one walks out unchanged.

As I've said before, this happens only when the liturgy is thoroughly biblical, saturated with Scripture. Worship forms worshipers only if they are confronted by the word, sing the word, dialogue in the word, eat and drink the Word at the Lord's table.

Lack of emphasis on the word has been one of the glaring weaknesses of "liturgical churches." They have pomp and ritual and sacrament and mystery. They have awesome cathedrals and chapels. They have colorful vestments, pungent aromas, transcendent choral music.

Without the word at the center, none of this is effective. Wordless liturgy can form aesthetes. It can make traditionalists. It can make Pharisees. It *can't* make worshipers who carry on the liturgy of life in faith. It can't do what the liturgy is intended to do—redeem language and redirect it toward the new creation. I'll repeat myself: The problem with "liturgical churches" isn't that they're *too* liturgical. Insofar as they sideline the word, they aren't liturgical enough, for the liturgy is God speaking to and feeding His people.

LOVE FEAST

Traditionally, the Eucharist also begins with a series of exchanges between minister and people. Bridegroom and Bride speak words of love as they approach their love feast and their marriage supper:

> M: The Lord be with you.
>
> C: And with thy spirit.
>
> M: Lift up your hearts.
>
> C: We lift them up to the Lord.
>
> M: Let us give thanks to the Lord our God.
>
> C: It is meet and right so to do.

Once again, minister and people form a communion of prayer in the Spirit prior to the Eucharistic thanksgiving. In the *Sursum Corda* ("Lift up your hearts"), the church acknowledges it ascends to heaven for the communion meal. By giving thanks, the church acknowledges it's a moment of Eucharist, thanksgiving.

Of course, the Eucharist isn't our only moment of thanks. The liturgy of thanks expresses the church's culture of gratitude.

"In everything give thanks," Paul says (1 Thess 5:18). And again, "always give thanks for all things" (Eph 5:20). Saying thanks at the Lord's table trains us to receive *everything* with thanks (1 Tim 4:4–5).

We're inclined to grumble. Complaint becomes habitual. Ingratitude is institutionalized in media, political, educational systems devoted to critique. Contemporary culture is designed to foster discontent. The Eucharistic liturgy challenges cultural habits and institutions and infuses the lives of Christians and churches with perpetual thanks. It Christianizes culture by filling our mouths with the words of God: "O give thanks to the Lord, for He is good" (Pss 106:1; 107:1).

This dialogue marks off the Eucharist from the prior "liturgy of the word." The distinction between liturgy of the Word and liturgy of the table can go wrong. It might lead us to think there are two liturgies, one where the Lord *speaks* and the other where He *feeds* us. We might think that He speaks on earth, and we ascend only when we come to the Lord's table.

Many liturgies give that impression. The liturgy of the word is detachable as a self-standing service. Some churches do a Eucharistic liturgy only on special occasions. That's a mistake. There's only one liturgy, a liturgy of Word-and-Table, a liturgy of communion in Word and food. And after the confession and absolution, the whole liturgy takes place on the mountaintop, in heavenly places.

Every Sunday is a feast day. Every Lord's Day is Eucharistic. Every Sunday, liturgy should be a liturgy of Word *and* Sacrament. God's people have always worshiped at tables. So should we.

To avoid the idea of divided service, it's best to move the *Sursum Corda* to the beginning of the liturgy, right after the confession and absolution. That way, it'll be clear that the word is a heavenly word, just as the table is a heavenly table. Churches that keep the *Sursum Corda* in its traditional place need to make it clear that the liturgy isn't divided and that the whole service occurs in heavenly places. The whole liturgy, from the call to worship through the Eucharist, is a single divine dialogue.

God has spoken. The Father has spoken words about the Word through the Spirit. God has fed us. The Father has given us the body and blood of His Son through the Spirit. Now God is ready to let us go. He speaks one final word, the good word of Benediction, ending the service with the same Triune name that began the service.

> The Lord bless you and guard you.
>
> The Lord make His face to shine upon you
> and be gracious to you.
>
> The Lord lift up His countenance upon you
> and give you His peace.
>
> In the Name of the Father, and of the Son
> and of the Holy Spirit. Amen.
>
> *Num 6:24–26*

The liturgy anticipates the final order of things. The liturgical dialogue puts our dislocated language right. In the liturgy, we hear God's word afresh and respond the way we ought to respond, with loving thanks. But the liturgy doesn't stand alone. The liturgy of the church sets the standard for the liturgy of the world. The dialogue of worship needs to shape the dialogue of our lives, society, politics, and culture. Having spoken right speech with the gathered city of God, we're to speak rightly when we return to the city of man.

CONCLUSION

God speaks. That's a wonderful thing. He's not silent. He's not left us in the dark about His plans or His demands. He lets us know what's on His mind. He doesn't tell us everything, of course. But He tells us everything we need to know.

God speaks, and God is *spoken to*. That's *also* a wonderful thing. We can imagine a God who is so austere, so transcendent, that He cannot be approached or addressed. He'd be like the unknown god of the Athenians (Acts 17). They know he's there, but they don't know anything about him. They can't be sure he hears their prayers or receives smoke signals from their altars.

God is spoken *to* because God's life is an eternal conversation of Father, Son, and Spirit. In the Trinity, God is the speaking God, the Father who utters the Word in the Spirit. In the Trinity, God is the spoken-to God, the Word who speaks back to the Father in the Spirit.

Dialogue is the shape of Christian worship because the liturgy conforms to God's own life. It's the shape of Christian liturgy because the liturgy takes place *within* the Triune life, as the body of the Son hears the word of the Father and speaks back in the Son.

When it is a dialogue in the Word, carried out by a people walking with the Spirit, the dialogic structure of worship forms a communion of worshipers, a liturgical city. More profoundly, it forms a communion between the worshipers and the Worshiped. Thus the Lord uses the liturgy to redeem our twisted languages and transform them into the language of the kingdom.

13

Sacrifice

GOD ... SEPARATED THE WATERS WHICH WERE BELOW THE EXPANSE FROM THE WATERS WHICH WERE ABOVE THE EXPANSE.
—GENESIS 1:7

Pop quiz: Who offers the first sacrifice in the Bible? If you answered "Cain" or "Abel," you're awfully close. But close isn't the same as right. There's a sacrifice before Cain and Abel were even born. In fact, there are several. These are easy to miss, but they're essential for understanding the purpose and shape of biblical sacrifice.

GLORIFICATION BY SACRIFICE

In Genesis 1, God judges things "good" seven times (Gen 1:4, 10, 12, 18, 21, 25, 31). More good things appear in Genesis 2—the fruit of the trees in the garden (2:9) and the gold of the land of Havilah (2:12).

Just when we're getting into the rhythm, He suddenly shifts gears. "It is *not* good" (Gen 2:18). The thing that's not good is Adam's solitariness. Why does it matter if Adam is alone? Why is *that* the one not-good thing in creation?

We might think Adam needs a friend. But God is with him, offering all the friendship he could hope for. We might think that Adam needs help to fulfill his mission. That's true, but he can carry out a lot of his work of dominion using his own muscles and training animals.

One thing he *can't* do without another human: Be fruitful and multiply. Adam alone is Adam fruitless. Alone, Adam can't reproduce or fill the earth. As God designed the world, another male human won't do the trick either. Adam isn't biologically equipped to be fruitful on his own. Double Adam, triple Adam, keep adding Adams until there's an unimaginable number of Adams, and they still won't be fruitful. Guys with guys can't make more guys.

Adam needs a helper who corresponds to him (Gen 2:18). That helper has to be like him but can't be *exactly* like him. To multiply, Adam needs another human who is similar with a difference. He's a man and needs a woman. Or, in the original Hebrew, he's an *'ish* who needs an *'ishshah*.

Reproduction is one important reason why Adam needs a partner. But it's not the most basic reason. Remember chapter 1, where I said the garden is the original human *sanctuary*, the holy place where God meets with Adam, where they converse and where Adam is supposed to eat in the presence of God. When Yahweh says, "It's not good for man to be alone," He's talking about the *garden*: "It's not good for Adam to be alone, *in the sanctuary*." Adam does need a partner to multiply and fill the earth. He also needs a partner for worship. He needs a *liturgical* helper.

Once we see that this is the issue in Genesis 2, the rest of the story takes on fresh meaning. Adam inspects the animals, but none is a "helper corresponding to him." For a long time, animals serve as mediators in Israel's worship. But from the beginning, it is not so. Yahweh gives Adam a *human* partner so they can commune with the Creator.

Remember how God makes that human partner? Adam doesn't find her among the animals. Yahweh doesn't dig into the ground and mold a woman, as He molds Adam. Instead, Yahweh puts Adam into deep sleep, a death-like, coma-slumber. While Adam is asleep, the Lord removes a rib and builds a woman from the rib. When Adam wakes up, he knows he's found his helper. He recognizes her as a sister: "bone of my bone, flesh of my flesh" (Gen 2:21–23).

There it is! *That's* the sacrifice. Did you miss it? Let me go through it more slowly.

Adam is put into a state near death, and his body is divided in two. That's what happens to animals offered on the altar. They're slaughtered, and their bodies are dismembered. (The other man put into "death-sleep" is Abram, who has a vision after dividing animals to cut covenant with Yahweh [Gen 15].)

For Adam, division isn't the end of the story. Adam is divided into two pieces, but the final aim is to reunite as "one flesh" with the woman made from his rib (Gen 2:24). He's divided in two in order to enter a higher state of unity.

"The woman," Paul says, "is the glory of the man" (1 Cor 11:7). Proverbs speaks of an excellent wife as a crown to her husband, raising him to royalty (Prov 12:4). Adam passes through death and dismemberment to be glorified. He dies in order to rise in a new form. He dies and rises to become king.

That's what sacrifice *always* does. We moderns rarely see an animal butchered. We think meat is naturally shrink-wrapped, ready for the shelves. It can be traumatic for us to see an animal slaughtered. We can't get past the violence.

That's not the focus of biblical sacrifice. Of course, the animal dies, as Adam "dies" in the garden. But that's only one moment of sacrifice. Sacrifice is a pathway, a *movement* through death to new life. In sacrifice, we die to one state so we can rise in an exalted state. Adam is a seed that must go into the ground to die before it can bear fruit (John 12:24). So are we.

Notice: This early sacrifice isn't an animal sacrifice. It's a *human* sacrifice, the death-and-division of Adam to become a new and improved man, Adam-and-Eve. That sets a trajectory toward the final sacrifice, the death of Jesus on the cross, which brings forth a new Eve, the church, from His spear-pierced ribs (John 19:34).

Once we see sacrifice in Genesis 2, we can see how sacrifice is built into the structures of creation and undergirds history.

Adam's surgery isn't the first sacrifice. *Creation* is a sacrificial procedure.

To form the world, Yahweh divides light and darkness and choreographs them in a dance of day and night. He separates the waters above and below and divides the waters below to form dry land. He separates a portion of the earth (*'adamah*) to form an *'adam*. At every stage, it's division-and-reunion. The creation week is a week of sacrifice.

History moves in sacrificial rhythms. God wipes out the world in the flood, sends Noah through death-waters in a coffin-ark so that he can rise as a new Adam doing Godlike, royal things—planting a vineyard, confronting his son Ham (as Yahweh confronted his son Adam), declaring curses (Gen 9:20–27).

Yahweh tears Israel from Egypt, leads them through the Red Sea, and brings them to Sinai where He elevates them to be His royal priesthood. He tears Israel from the land, sends them to the grave of exile, then raises them up (cf. Ezek 37) into a new and better covenant (Jer 31).

This is *your* life too. You started life in the cozy comfort of your mother's womb, but then you got squeezed out, screaming. You died to the womb to come alive in the world. Then you had your first day of school, your first date, your wedding, your first child, your first grandchild, the death of your mother and father. Each of these crisis moments is a small death that shatters the world as you know it. If life carries on at all, it carries on with a new, unknown horizon. No wonder life can be terrifying. You're constantly dying to *this* to come alive to *that*.

You *live* sacrifice. You live it *every day*, and so does the world. Each day descends into the darkness of night, into sleep, death's second self, until morning breaks like the first morning, the blackbird speaks like the first dawn, and you wake to a new creation.

Division to reunion, death to resurrection, grave to glory—that's the way the world comes to be and the way the world works. It's the sacrificial movement of creation, life, and history. Sacrificial liturgy doesn't introduce an alien pattern into the world. It runs along the grain of a sacrificial cosmos.

COVERING

Creation, including the creation of Eve, constitutes the first and foundational sacrifice. But there's another sacrifice in the first chapters of the Bible. And it brings out other essential dimensions of sacrifice and liturgical life.

After Adam and Eve eat the fruit of the tree of knowledge, they recognize they're naked and sew fig leaf aprons to cover their shame (Gen 3:7). Those aren't effective coverings. They're as lame as Adam's excuses and blame-shifting.

Adam and Eve can't provide covering for themselves. God has to give covering, and He does. He provides animal skins (Gen 3:21). In order to get animal skins, Yahweh has to kill and skin some animals. How appropriate: The Lord performs this first post-fall sacrifice as He offers the final sacrifice, the self-sacrifice of the Lamb.

What can we learn from this first animal offering?

Sacrifice produces a covering. That's what the word atone means (Heb. *kaphar*). To make atonement is to cover. Why do Adam and Eve need covering? Adam and Eve want protective covering. They don't want to be exposed naked before the Lord. They don't want their shame displayed. Sacrifice covers sin, so sinners can appear in the presence of God without shame. Sacrifice covers us, so we don't have to cower among the trees of the garden. Like Jacob, we come to our Father wearing the skin of the Firstborn so that we can receive His blessing (cf. Gen 27).

Animal coverings represent a demotion. Adam and Eve listen to the voice of a serpent rather than the voice of the Lord. They obey a beast, and so they're clothed like beasts. They serve the creature and descend into animality. But there's a plus side. Clothing marks identity and status. Priests and kings wear robes. Prophets like Elijah and John the Baptist were known for their distinctive clothing. Covered with vestments, we're invested with prestige. Coverings cover. Coverings also *glorify*.

Sacrifice has both of these effects at once. On the one hand, it covers our sin and shame and makes us acceptable to God. On the other hand, it installs us as priests and kings. Adam leaves the garden robed in an animal skin because he is the forgiven prince of creation, son of the Creator King.

There's more about sacrifice in Genesis 3. After Adam and Eve are expelled from the garden, Yahweh sets cherubim at the eastern gate, armed with flaming swords to prevent Adam's return to the tree of life (3:24). The message is clear: If you want to eat the fruit of the tree of life, you'll have to slip past the cherubim. They're hard to slip past. Cherubim are full of eyes, watching in every direction all the time (Ezek 1:18; 10:12). Try slipping past *that*.

If you're *really* determined to get back to Eden, you can try another tack: Charge straight for the gate. That plan doesn't pass the cost-benefit test. If you charge the gate of Eden, the cherubim will swing their fiery swords, and you'll be cut into stew meat and turned to smoke. There's no way to survive. You'll hesitate to charge the gate unless you're pretty confident you'll rise from the dead on the other side.

Those cherubim represent a problem. Inside Eden are all God's gifts. He offers life. He offers the wisdom of the tree of knowledge. *He* is present. In Eden, you can find all the treasures later deposited in the ark—food, word, a shepherd. The only catch is that you can't get in without being killed. Stay out, and you can't get to the tree of life. So you die. Try to get in, and cherubim kill you. So you die. It looks pretty hopeless.

Sacrifice is the solution to that dilemma. Sacrifice is the Lord's gracious alternative to the choice between the certain death of exclusion and the certain death of re-entry. Sacrifice enables us to enter the garden to enjoy its gifts. Sacrifice assures you you'll live again after passing by the cherubim.

Instead of being left out in the grave, instead of being cut down by cherubim, you can send in an animal substitute. By entering the altar, the animal goes through Eden's gate, suffers the cherubic sword and fire, and ascends as soothing aroma to Yahweh.

Sacrifice is a gate liturgy. Sacrifice is the ritual path of return. Sacrifice cuts a way through death to glorified new life. Through sacrifice, we can return to God in what the Bible speaks of as a covenant, a committed union of love. In the garden, Adam "dies" and rises to a new life. Outside the garden, sacrifice enables his children to experience the same progress from glory to glory.

There's one last thing we learn about sacrifice from Genesis 3. We return to the garden to *eat* in the presence of God. Sacrifice is a gate liturgy, and the gate is the entry to a banquet hall. Sacrifice is a *food* rite.

That's actually implied by the Hebrew verb for "sacrifice," *zavach*. It means specifically "to slaughter for a meal" or "to butcher." Whenever the Old Testament uses the term sacrifice, it implies a feast.

To say biblical worship is sacrificial is to say that it takes place at a table. *All* worship in the Bible takes place at a table. In the old world, Israel worships at altar-tables where animals are turned to smoke. Now in the heavenly city, we gather at the Lord's table where the Father gives us the body and blood of His Son through the Spirit. Biblically speaking, worship without a meal isn't worship at all. It's missing the crucial piece of furniture—a table—and the crucial liturgical materials—bread and wine.

What have we learned about sacrifice from Genesis 1–3?

- Sacrificial division and reunion, death and resurrection, are built into creation.
- Sacrifice is a movement of glorification by death-and-resurrection.
- Before there are animal sacrifices, there's a *human* sacrifice—Adam put into death-sleep to produce a bride. Human sacrifice is the original, and the final, form of sacrifice.
- Sacrifice covers, covering shame and conferring glory. By covering, it allows us to enter the presence of God.

- A worshiper enters the presence of God through a substitute who suffers death on his behalf.
- Once in the presence of God, worshipers eat and drink and rejoice together. The sacrificial substitute gives himself as food for a feast.

Everything else the Bible teaches about sacrifice—the complex Levitical system of offerings, the sacrifice of Jesus, the sacrificial praise of the temple and the church—all of it builds on the foundation of Genesis 1–3.

Above all, everything else the Bible teaches about sacrifice builds on this basic truth: *God* performs the first sacrifices, and He does it to glorify the creation and to cover and glorify us. In that, we already see the gospel because the God who performs the first sacrifice also offers the last. God is the Alpha and Omega of sacrifice.

SACRIFICE BEFORE SINAI

God creates by sacrifice. He forms Eve and the union of man-and-woman by sacrifice. Made in the image of this God, human beings are sacrificial creatures. Along with place, language, and time, sacrifice is one of the constants of human life. We reshape a sacrificial creation into sacrificial culture.

Ancient peoples performed various rites of animal or human sacrifice. Every ancient Greek home had its hearth fire not only for cooking but for domestic sacrifice. Temples were built on the central acropolis of ancient Greek cities, houses for the gods and places for sacrificial festivity.

Ancient political life was infused with sacrifice. The Greek citizen assembly was called to order by the sacrifice of a pig. If a city established a colony, it would carry sacred fire from the home city to light the hearth fire of the new city, because a city couldn't be a city without a place for civic sacrifice.

Romans offered sacrifices before battles and to celebrate victories. Shakespeare knew his Romans. His Julius Caesar asks a priest to examine the entrails of an animal before he enters the Senate on the day of his assassination. It's just the thing superstitious emperors did.

When Yahweh instructs Israel to offer animals on altars, He doesn't invent a new custom. It's already pervasive. From Egypt to Babylon and Assyria, from China and Persia to the Inca and Mayan empires, sacrifice was a central rite of all ancient civilizations. All of them were children of Adam and Noah and continued the sacrificial customs of Eden and Ararat.

But God isn't accommodating to human custom. Ultimately, ancient peoples sacrifice because they're children of a sacrificial Creator, who baked sacrifice into the bread of creation. As we have seen throughout this book, culture reflects and builds on the patterns of creation, whether faithfully or unfaithfully.

Since Adam's sin, cultures build defectively, perversely. In most ancient cultures, sacrifices are offered to false gods, what Paul describes as demons (1 Cor 10:20). Idolatrous sacrifices offer false paths to life, atonements that are no better than fig leaves. They don't enhance life, but destroy it.

Yahweh instructs Israel how to sacrifice to redeem this universal cultural practice. In Israel's sacrificial liturgy, He redirects sacrifice back to its true end—glorification, entry into Eden, covering and communion with the living God.

True and false sacrifices appear together early in the Bible, in the account of Cain and Abel (Gen 4). For Cain and Abel, sacrifice is a gate liturgy. They are born outside Eden, and they can't draw near to God without being cut down by the cherubim. They bring their offerings near to send a substitute past the angelic guardians.

We typically have a childish, Sunday-school idea of what happens between Cain and Abel. We imagine two teenagers who each build an altar and make a solitary offering. It's much more likely they perform their sacrifices in public. Nearly all sacrifices in the Bible are public events. Abram sets up altars all over the land of promise to lead his company of perhaps a thousand men, women, and children in worship (with 318 fighting men, Gen 14:14). All of Israel's sacrifices take place in public at the altar of the sanctuary.

We should imagine Cain and Abel doing the same. Cain approaches the gate of Eden with his company of worshipers. Abel gathers his clan in the same location. When Abel brings his animal near, the cherubim send out fire that consumes the offering, a sign that Yahweh accepts it. Cain sets out his vegetable offering, but there's no fire.

That's why Cain becomes angry, envious, ultimately murderous. He's been publicly shamed, and by his kid brother. God acknowledges Abel but not Cain, and *everybody knows it.*

Cain is the first murderer. Before he's a murderer, though, he's a false worshiper. His hatred arises from a conflict over worship. We think politics are the source of history's wars. In fact, liturgy is the secret core of political history.

Why does God accept Abel's offering but not Cain's? Abel offers animals, imitating Yahweh's first offering. Cain, a "servant of the ground," offers vegetable offerings. Later, Israel offers grain offerings, but they're always *added* to animal offerings. One of the lessons of the first sacrifice is this: Without the shedding of blood, there's no atonement (Heb 9:22). Blood alone *covers.*

There's another reason. Every ritual has what Dru Johnson calls a "biography." The ritual isn't just what happens at the sanctuary. It includes the whole backstory of how the worshiper acquires the offering, how he lives outside the sanctuary, how he treats his wife and children and employees and parents on the day of sacrifice.

If a worshiper steals a neighbor's lamb for an offering, Yahweh doesn't accept it. Even if the animal is without blemish and the worshiper goes through the right liturgical motions, the offering is tainted. God evaluates the offering on the basis of its entire biography.

You can't bring an acceptable offering if your hands are filled with innocent blood (Isa 1:1–18). Your offering is tainted if you abuse your employees or ignore the needs of the hungry, naked, homeless, and poor. You can't pretend your offering expresses love for God if you spend your life hating your brother. Acts of sacrificial worship can't be disconnected from the whole life of the worshiper. Israel repeatedly forgets this. They think they can cover evil lives with a blood-and-smoke screen of sacrifice. Yahweh sees right through it and sends prophets like Jeremiah to condemn it (Jer 7).

God doesn't accept Cain's offering because it isn't liturgically correct. More important, the Lord rejects his offering because he hates his brother (1 John 3:10–12).

SACRIFICE OF KINGS

Noah is the next person to make an offering. After the flood, he sets up an altar and offers all kinds of clean animals. Yahweh smells the soothing aroma and promises never to curse the ground again (Gen 8:20–22).

This is new. Both Cain and Abel offered *minchah* offerings (Gen 4:3–4). A *minchah* is "tribute," homage from an inferior to a superior. Subject kings bring *minchah* to their overlords. Noah offers an *'olah*. The Hebrew word means "to go up," and the offering represents ascension. For the first time, we learn that sacrifice ascends into the Lord's presence as an *aroma*.

Noah's *'olah* also tells us something about Noah. Yahweh has undone creation, turning it back into a formless and watery void (cf. Gen 1:2). Noah emerges from the ark like Adam from the ground, head of a new human race, a second Adam, called to multiply, fill, and rule the earth (Gen 9:7).

But Noah doesn't go back to the starting blocks. He's a new and *improved* Adam. Unlike Adam, he's allowed to eat flesh (Gen 9:3–4). Unlike Adam, he has authority to punish evildoers (Gen 9:5–7). Yahweh planted the first garden and set Adam in it. Noah plants his *own* garden, a vineyard, and enjoys the first wine (Gen 9:20–21). Having gone through the sacrificial death-and-elevation of the flood, Noah naturally presents elevation offerings.

Yahweh intends for Adam to become a king. But Adam fails as a priest, and his path to kingship is blocked. The children of Cain become kings, but they're brutal tyrants who fill the earth with violence (Gen 4:16–24). It takes another creation, and another Adam, for a righteous king to appear on earth. Noah offers ascension offerings because *he* has ascended. He offers ascension offerings to acknowledge there's a higher, heavenly King.

Yahweh's sacrifice in Eden produces coverings. Noah's ascension offering produces an aroma (Gen 8:21). When Yahweh gets angry, the Hebrew Bible says his nose burns. By turning an animal to smoke, Noah calms Yahweh's burning nose. The ascension offering covers God's anger. It covers Noah, so he bears the aroma of the substitute (cf. 2 Cor 2:14).

When Yahweh smells the aroma of the ascension, He makes a covenant with Noah and, through Noah, with the world (Gen 9:8–17). He promises never to curse the ground again and to maintain the cycles of time—days and nights and seasons (Gen 8:22). Yahweh maintains the order and movement of creation in response to Noah's offering. Yahweh makes a covenant pledge in response to sacrifice. Throughout the Old Testament, He renews His covenant when He smells the fragrance of Israel's sacrifices. Sacrifice restores the covenant relation between Yahweh and His creation. Sacrificial liturgy is a liturgy of covenant-cutting and covenant-renewal.

When Noah ascends through the sacrificial animal, Yahweh promises a world at peace. As his name promises, Noah brings rest to the world (Gen 5:29) and anticipates another King who will ascend to Sabbath glory as Prince of Peace.

LITURGICAL CONQUEST

Noah is born in the tenth generation from Adam. Abram is born in the tenth generation from the second Adam, Noah. Both reboot the human race. Noah starts the human race over again after the rest are wiped out. Through Abram, Yahweh begins to renew the human race from within after the nations are scattered from Babel. Both renew the human race through sacrificial liturgy.

Noah is the first man to erect an altar, a miniature holy mountain where he communes with God. Abram builds altars everywhere he goes (Gen 12:7–8; 13:4, 18; 22:9), setting a pattern for his son Isaac, who builds an altar and digs a well (26:25).

Abram dies before he receives his inheritance, the land of promise. But as a sojourner, he consecrates the land as a place of worship. He leaves a liturgical trail from Shechem to Bethel to Ai, locations of Joshua's later conquests. He offers sacrifices from stones piled in the land so that Joshua can later offer Jericho as a civic ascension offering.

This is the sequence: First Abram makes the land a place of worship, then Yahweh hands it to his descendants. It's still the sequence for the church: Missionaries don't grab power when they enter a mission field. They start with a liturgy of word and sacrament and worship in faith until the Lord gives the land.

The first redemption of a land or nation takes place in the liturgy, and from there it radiates to the polity. Liturgy isn't a retreat from mission or political combat. Liturgy lays the foundation for mission and is on the front lines of the church's war. Liturgy is the first form of the heavenly city, the first redemption of a land or a people.

Like Noah, Abraham offers an ascension offering, on Mount Moriah (Gen 22:2–3, 6–8, 13). Initially, Isaac is the offering, but at the last minute, Yahweh intervenes to substitute a ram. Like Noah, Abraham ascends to kingship. Elevated by his obedience to God's command, he becomes a great father by his willingness to offer his son. Because of his obedience, the Lord confirms he will inherit the land and become the father of kings.

Later at Sinai, Yahweh lays out detailed instructions for the *'olah*, the ascension offering. He tells Israelites to bring a "son of the herd" (Lev 1:5). Every worshiper is an Abraham, offering a substitute son on the altar. Abraham's offering is the background for Passover, where Israelites offer lambs or goats as substitutes for their firstborn sons. By enacting the liturgy of the *'olah*, a worshiper is incorporated into the history of Abraham and Exodus. The ritual realizes a past event in the present and points toward the future.

Abraham gives up his son and receives him back, resurrected (Heb 11:19). Abraham offers his future to Yahweh, and it comes back to him renewed. Those who wish to save their future will lose it. Those who lose their future for Jesus' sake will find it. Sacrifice to the living God is an act of radical discipleship, a giving-up in hope of getting-back, a passage through death to new life.

Abraham makes his offerings among nations that have their own forms of sacrifice. His sacrificial liturgy is a moment of true sacrifice in a world filled with idols. At Abraham's altar, sacrifice is done the way sacrifice ought to be done: as worship of the true God, the God of creation and covenant, who covers sin and raises His faithful worshipers to thrones.

SACRIFICE UNDER TORAH

"Where there is a change of priesthood, there is also a change of law" (Heb 7:12). In Hebrews 7, law means "rule for priestly succession." The writer is talking about the change from old to new covenant. The Aaronic priests qualify for priesthood by flesh, by birth into the line of Aaron. Jesus becomes priest by resurrection, by the power of an indestructible life.

But the principle of Hebrews is broader. The law of succession isn't the only thing that changes. The laws of worship change too. Every time there's a change of priesthood, there's a liturgical revolution.

That's what happens when Israel arrives at Sinai. There's a change in priesthood, and the liturgy receives a radical makeover.

Prior to Sinai, there is no special caste of priests. Noah, Abram, Isaac, and others serve at altars. Perhaps their sons assist. After the exodus, Yahweh chooses Aaron and his sons to serve at the altar and to keep His house. They offer Yahweh's bread on His altar-table. They trim the wicks of the lamps and refill them with oil so the light doesn't go out in Israel. They burn the incense of prayer. They bear the sins and impurities of Israel so that they can be removed on the Day of Atonement. They guard the sanctuary from intruders.

Priests are servants of Yahweh's royal house, and Yahweh chooses Aaron as priest at the same time He instructs Israel to build a house where He will dwell in glory.

Abram entertains angels, including the Angel of Yahweh. But the Angel of Yahweh doesn't move into Abram's neighborhood. At Sinai, Yahweh does just that. Israel lives in tents in the wilderness, and in the middle of their camp is Yahweh's tent. For the first time since Eden, human beings live in proximity to the Creator.

And, for the first time since the fall, human beings slip past the cherubim. They can't go *all* the way in. Lay Israelites have to stay in the courtyard, and priests are limited to the Holy Place. But the Lord's house is nearby, and He opens it for hospitality, for eating, drinking, and rejoicing (Deut 12:1–7).

If God comes close, you can't just keep up business as usual. Israel's liturgy has to change. Because Yahweh is close, Israel has to be concerned about purity. Normal bodily processes suddenly become dangerous.

- Certain meats become unclean (Lev 11).
- Women are unclean after childbirth (Lev 12).
- People with skin disease are unclean, and so are mildewed clothing and houses (Lev 13–14).
- Men become unclean because of genital emissions, and women are unclean during their menstrual periods (Lev 15).
- Even within marriage, sex makes both man and woman unclean (Lev 15:18).
- Touching a dead body, even being in the same room with a dead body, makes you unclean (Num 19).

To draw near to the sanctuary, Israelites have to be clean. Usually, they only have to wash their bodies and clothes and wait for the evening sacrifice. Sometimes, purification rites are more elaborate (cf. Lev 14; Num 19).

Because Yahweh is close, Israel also needs new forms of sacrifice. Like Cain, Abel, Noah, and Abraham, they still bring ascension offerings (Lev 1) and tribute offerings of grain (Lev 2). But new forms of sacrifice are introduced:

- Through the blood rites of the purification or sin offering (*hatt'at*), the priests cleanse the altars and the house from defilements of sin and uncleanness (Lev 4:1–5:13).

- Through the trespass offering (*'asham*), the priests compensate for aggressive, high-handed sins and for intrusions on holy things and holy space (Lev 5:14–6:7; 7:1-10).

If Israel's sins pollute Yahweh's house, He'll abandon it (Ezek 8–11). Israel offers these offerings to keep the sanctuary clean and to ensure that Yahweh sticks around. When Yahweh moves into Israel's neighborhood, He makes sure they have the tools they need to keep Him close by.

The other new offering is the peace offering (*shelem*). Like the purification and trespass offerings, the peace offering is never mentioned until Israel gets to Sinai (cf. Exod 20:24; 24:5). Unlike the purification and trespass offerings, the peace offering isn't for maintenance. It's a festive sacrifice that always culminates in a meal. It's the one offering an Israelite worshiper can eat.

In the Old Testament, the word sacrifice refers specifically to the peace offering. While Israel was in Egypt, Yahweh tells Pharaoh to let Israel go to sacrifice in the wilderness (Exod 3:18). He wants to bring Israel out of Egypt to *feed* them. That's the goal of the exodus: Yahweh bares His mighty arm so Israel can join Him for a party at the mountain.

The peace offering is a vision of a redeemed world. It depicts the world as it ought to be: God's people gathered with Him to enjoy the fruits of creation in His presence. In a world filled with tables of demons, the peace offering is an invitation to share in the table of the Lord. The peace offering, in short, is an Old Testament form of the Lord's Supper.

We can be more specific. There were three types of peace offering: Votive offerings fulfilled vows; free will offerings were expressions of praise; thanksgiving offerings (*todah*) showed gratitude for a specific blessing. The *todah* is the closest analogy to the Lord's Supper: It's a thanksgiving meal, accompanied by prayers and songs of thanks (Pss 69:30; 107:22; 116:17).

In introducing these new offerings, Yahweh also specifies ritual procedures. For the first time, we learn *how* to do an ascension offering, a tribute, a peace offering. There's a skeletal structure that runs across all the animal offerings:

I. THE WORSHIPER PRESENTS an animal and *leans his hand* on its head. By this gesture, the worshiper identifies with the animal and ordains it to represent him as it approaches Yahweh's presence.

II. THE WORSHIPER *slaughters* the animal. No one can pass the cherubim at Yahweh's gate without dying. The animal takes the curse of death as a substitute for the worshiper.

III. SLAUGHTER ISN'T THE END of the rite. After the worshiper kills the animal, the *priest sprinkles blood* on the altar. Blood purifies, turns away death, and opens doors.

IV. ONCE THE ALTAR IS SMEARED with blood, the priest dismembers the animal and places it in the *fire*. Yahweh lit the fire from His own fiery being (Lev 9:24; Deut 4:24). Entering the fire, the animal enters Yahweh's presence. More, the animal is changed into smoke and fire. This isn't punishment. It's transfiguration, even deification, like Adam being glorified into Adam-and-Eve. This is the aim of the animal offerings: Through the animal, the worshiper unites with the God who is a consuming fire, whose love is an eternal flame.

V. ALL ANIMAL OFFERINGS are food rituals. At the end of a sacrifice, someone *eats*. Sometimes only Yahweh eats. Sometimes only the priests join Him. Sometimes the worshiper joins the priests to feast with Yahweh.

I've taught my kids and grandkids a chant to help them remember this:

Lay the *hand*

Slay the *beast*

Spread the *blood*

Burn the *flesh*

Eat the *meal*.

You've got to do it rhythmically, accenting the italicized syllables, or it doesn't work. Preferably while stomping your feet.

This sacrificial sequence gives a skeletal order of service for Christian worship, the fulfilled sacrificial ritual:

I. WE ENTER THE PRESENCE of Yahweh only through our substitute, the Lord Jesus. We lay hands on Him as our priest.

II. GOD ACCEPTS US, but we still sin, and we should confess them. When the church gathers, she should confess her sins as a body. When we confess our sins, the Lord cleanses us from all unrighteousness (1 John 1:9–10). The minister declares we are forgiven.

III. WE ARE DISMEMBERED by the Word, the sword of the Spirit that divides soul and spirit, joints and marrow (Heb 4:11–12).

IV. BY WORD AND SPIRIT, we're incorporated into the fiery presence of the Lord, transfigured into His image.

V. HAVING ASCENDED to the throne, we're seated as kings at the Lord's royal table.

Each offering follows the same basic ritual but differs from the others at a crucial point:

I. THE PURIFICATION OFFERING (*hatt'at*) highlights the blood rite (Lev 4). In the other offerings, the priest dashes blood against the side of the altar. But the blood of the purification offering has to be smeared on the horns of the altar and poured at the base of the altar. Sometimes the blood is taken into the Holy Place and smeared on the horns of the golden altar.

II. THE ASCENSION OFFERING (*'olah*) highlights the burning (Lev 1). The entire animal is burned. No human being eats any of the meat. It all belongs to Yahweh.

III. THE PEACE OFFERING (*shelem*) emphasizes the meal (Lev 3). Non-priests are only allowed to eat meat from the peace offering.

When you put these in order, you have this sequence: purification, ascension, meal. And this is precisely their order whenever they are performed at the same time (Lev 9:1–7; Num 6:13–20; 2 Chr 29:20–36). First the worshiper is purified, then he ascends, then he feasts in the Lord's presence. This is also the order of the original covenant-making ceremony at Mount Sinai (Exod 19–24). Israel cleanses themselves at the foot of Sinai. Then Moses ascends to receive the law. Finally, representatives of Israel eat and drink on the mountainside.

Translated into New Testamentese, purification, ascent, meal mean this: Confession and cleansing, ascent to receive the word, communion; mourning for sin, instruction in the way of life, thanksgiving and dismissal. That's the structure of biblical worship and the basic structure of nearly every Christian liturgy throughout history.

If our worship services don't look like that, we're not worshiping biblically. If we don't confess our sins at the beginning of the service, we shouldn't presume to go through the gate. If we don't get cut apart by the sword of the Word, we can't be put together again. If we don't end the service with a meal, what's the point of coming in the first place?

The Lord loves obedience and mercy more than sacrifice (1 Sam 15:22; Matt 9:13; 12:7, 33). When Israel offers sacrifices with blood-stained hands and sin-stained hearts, the Lord rejects them (Isa 1). The church can go through all the proper motions, conform to all the rubrics, say all the right words and do all the right gestures, and *still* offer a putrid stench instead of a soothing aroma. The *forms* of the liturgy are acceptable only if they conform to God's word. We *performers* of the liturgy are acceptable only if we walk in faith, obedience, compassion, love, humility, and justice.

God doesn't want the blood of bulls and goats. He delights in contrite hearts (Ps 51:17; Isa 57:15) and the sacrifice of the open ear (Ps 40:6-8), worshipers attentively obedient to His every word. He wants our liturgical sacrifice to express a sincere offering of our hearts, bodies, and lives.

POLITICAL SACRIFICE

Viewing Christian worship from the perspective of Levitical sacrifice helps us see the depths of the liturgy and its cultural and political impact. We might think Sunday is only a teaching time or an opportunity to get an emotional jolt from the music. In fact, we're doing in reality what ancient Israelites did in symbol. Adam's "sacrifice" in Eden is the first sacrifice, and it is a human sacrifice. Israel replicates that sacrifice figuratively, using animals. Jesus offers the first true sacrifice, a voluntary *human* sacrifice, by which He passes through death and ascends to the Father.

After Jesus, *because* of Jesus, sacrifice is humanized. It's humanized in the church. In the liturgy, we replicate Old Testament figurative offerings in reality; our offerings are like Jesus' offering, real human self-sacrifices. It's blood, fire, and smoke, dismemberment and bodies rising from the dead. It's a meal where we eat the God-man so that He lives in us and we live in Him. We do in the open what Israel did under the shadows.

Sacrifice is also humanized politically and culturally. Liberal societies fool themselves into thinking we can do without sacrifice. The Roman Senate began with animal sacrifice, but not the U.S. Senate. No President or Prime Minister reads entrails; at least none admits to it.

Liberalism claims to order society without reference to God or gods. Politics is about human power and doesn't need to establish any sacrificial connection with the powers of the cosmos. Liberalism says we can have progress without catastrophe, that we can rise to glory without dying. Liberals believe in resurrection without a cross.

We think life can go on without death. To prove it, we shove death and the dying into closed clinical spaces where we don't have to see or think much about them. We resist self-sacrifice. Self-preservation is the highest good.

This is all a trick. Liberal societies still demand sacrifices. Not animal sacrifices, of course, but *human* ones. Modern liberal societies are Christianized enough to humanize sacrifice. They aren't Christianized enough to imitate Jesus' self-sacrifice. Instead, they demand sacrifices to human deities like the nation and the people or abstractions like Freedom and Democracy.

Totalitarian regimes are also modern sacrificial machines. They demand total sacrifice from their subjects, plant Killing Fields, and slaughter millions so that a "new man" can rise from the wreckage. They conquer and kill not just to extend territory but to fulfill their dream of a classless society, of Jew-free national socialism, of the utopia *du jour*.

The early church entered a world flush with sacrifice, and the modern church is no different. Wherever the church goes, she encounters a world organized by sacrifice, with its own idolatrous gestures, its own false atonements, its own empty promises of glory and life.

The church preaches the gospel and calls the nations into union with Jesus' self-sacrifice to the Father. She calls the nations to offer true sacrifice, a sacrifice of witness and praise like the sacrifice of Jesus.

She calls the nations into the realm of redeemed sacrifice, that is, into the liturgy. The church's liturgy re-orients the sacrificial habits of the world toward the true sacrifice of the kingdom. It puts sacrifice back in sync with the sacrificial patterns of God's creation. In the liturgy, sacrifice is being Christianized so that the sacrifices of the cities of men may be redeemed and reoriented toward the sacrifices of the heavenly city.

After Jesus, we have only a few choices. Sacrifice has been humanized, and societies will either cling to the sacrifice of Jesus enacted in the Eucharistic liturgy or will invent fresh forms of human slaughter and turn history into a charnel house. We face the choice between the peaceful sacrifice at the Lord's table or the violent sacrifices of secular order.

The Eucharist remakes the world because it redeems the perverse sacrifices of the world. Had Idi Amin, Stalin, or Pol Pot repented and taken a place at the Lord's table, their lives of brutal slaughter would have been redirected from their idolatries. Joined to the sacrifice of Jesus, their perverse sacrifices would have been corrected and, for the first time, they would have participated in a true human sacrifice.

SACRIFICE OF PRAISE

The liturgy redirects secular human sacrifice into the true human sacrifice of *praise*.

From Sinai to the end of the Old Testament, Israel's worship follows Torah. They offer animal and grain offerings at the Lord's house and keep the cycle of feasts laid out in Exodus, Leviticus, and Deuteronomy.

But there are dramatic changes along the way. As we saw in chapter 1, the tabernacle is ripped apart and never rebuilt. Instead, the Lord raises up Solomon to build a new sanctuary, the temple.

More importantly, Yahweh directs David to reorganize Israel's worship. He reorganizes the priesthood, dividing the descendants of Aaron into twenty-four clans, which serve two-week stints at the temple. The most interesting change has to do with music. David is the sweet psalmist of Israel. He composes hymns and invents musical instruments. He also creates a musical culture in Israel. Before Solomon builds a temple of stone, David has orchestrated a living temple of song.

Priests blew silver trumpets at the tabernacle (Num 10) and at Jericho (Josh 6). Otherwise, they seem to be a quiet clan. Along come Israel's kings, and suddenly there's music everywhere. Saul knows he will become king when he meets a band of prophets singing and playing music, and he joins them (1 Sam 10:5–6). David sings and plays while he's on the run from Saul (Ps 18; 52; 54).

Everywhere, kings make and inspire music. When a king takes his throne, his people sing and play music. Kings ascend to their thrones on the praises of the people, like the Lamb whose appearance in heaven sparks thunderous song (Rev 5). Music is a royal art. To sing, you must rule your body and breath. To make a musical instrument, you have to take dominion over a portion of creation and shape it into something beautiful that makes beautiful sounds.

Music is a militant art. In preparation for the temple, David and the leaders of the army establish a permanent orchestra and choir (1 Chr 25:1). The military's involvement is noteworthy, a signal that temple music is part of Israel's arsenal. When the Moabites and the Ammonites attack Israel during Jehoshaphat's reign, he puts the special forces in front of the army—the Levitical choir, who sing destruction to their enemies (2 Chr 20). Martyrs go to the stake and the arena singing (Rev 14). Song equips worshipers psychologically, spiritually, and physically for Spiritual war. A church that sings together fights together. As the city of God sings, we offer true sacrifice in cities of false sacrifice.

Song is prophetic too. Singers prophesy (1 Chr 25:1) because the Spirit of prophecy inspires song (Eph 5:18–19). When martyrs sing, they glimpse their future vindication. When we sing of God's victory before it happens, we enter into that victory yet to come.

Priests are the main music-makers in Scripture. Once David becomes king, he brings the ark of the covenant to Jerusalem in a procession led by priestly musicians (1 Chr 15:16). After he installs the ark in its tent, he arranges for continuous musical worship (1 Chr 16), which is incorporated into the temple (1 Chr 25).

David doesn't just add a new dimension to Israel's worship. Something more profound is going on. A change of priesthood sparks a liturgical revolution. Sacrificial and priestly terminology is transferred to song. Music becomes a form of priestly service (1 Chr 15:2). As Levites once carried the furniture of the tabernacle, so now they bear the Lord in song (1 Chr 15:22, 26). Music becomes a form of priestly work (1 Chr 6:31–32; 23:25–32).

Priests guard the sanctuary. Music now takes over that function as a guardian of tradition (1 Chr 25:8). Singing Psalm 78 or the Song of Moses in Deuteronomy 32, Israel preserves her corporate memory and hands it over to a new generation.

Sacrifices are memorials before Yahweh (cf. Lev 2:2, 9, 16). A memorial reminds *God* of His promises so He will continue to keep them. Like the rainbow after the flood, a sacrifice calls on Yahweh to keep His word to Israel. In the temple liturgy, song becomes a form of memorial (1 Chr 16:4). As Israel sings of Yahweh's heroism, she calls Him to be the hero again and again.

It's hard to exaggerate the importance of David's innovations. It's a step toward the new covenant when we no longer slaughter and burn animals at all. Augustine said animal offerings were figurative offerings. The real sacrifice is always human self-sacrifice, pre-eminently that of Jesus. As he prepares for the temple worship, David introduces the true form of sacrifice, sacrifice fulfilled in song. We now offer sacrifices of song because the King has come.

The Spirit is the music of God and inspires song (Eph 5:18–19). We sing in and by the Spirit, and it would be a contradiction to sing in the Spirit while also grieving Him. Just as Yahweh hates Israel's offerings when they're mingled with oppression, so our songs may be drowned out by the cries of orphans and widows we abuse. The Father closes His ears to the songs of lying lips. He recoils when we have the smell of death on our breath (Ps 5:9).

LOVE DUET

David's liturgical innovations have some uncomfortable implications for worship. Think of how central sacrifice was to Israel's worship. Pretty central, right? Then think: Song is introduced to accompany animal offerings and then takes over the place of animal offerings. Then think: Perhaps *music* should be as central to Christian worship as sacrifice was to Israel's worship.

Few churches face up to this implication. A church that wouldn't think of hiring a pastor without a seminary degree will farm out the music to anyone who can read music or carry a tune. Churches that pay careful attention to the doctrinal content of the words often pay scant attention to the musical quality of the notes. Some churches ride the wave of tradition, singing golden oldies whether or not they're good oldies. Churches with contemporary worship get tossed to and fro by waves of fashion.

If song is our form of sacrifice, it deserves more attention, time, expertise, training. If song is our form of sacrifice, we should devote considerable effort to learn the songs of Scripture, the Psalms and other canticles that have been the primary songbook of the church for two thousand years.

Temple song has another important implication for worship. Sacrifice pervades Israel's worship. It's what Israel's worship *is*. *Christian* sacrifice should pervade Christian worship, and that means the service should be *sung*.

We saw in the last chapter that worship is a dialogue, a communion in speech between Jesus and His Bride. Spoken dialogue is good. A spoken liturgy sounds a little like boot camp, with the recruits standing straight and answering every bark from the commander with a firm "Hoo-Ha, Sergeant!" A sung liturgy is *better* because it captures the erotic dimension of the liturgy. Friends speak to one another. A drill sergeant shouts at his troops. Lovers *sing*. Jesus the Bridegroom calls a man to sing His love song to His Bride.

Are you a pastor who croaks through the hymns and keeps his voice down? There are options. Take the time and make the effort to learn to sing. Find a cantor to lead the church's singing. At least aspire to make the liturgy a fully sacrificial dialogue, that is, a dialogic sacrifice of *song*.

EUCHARISTIC SACRIFICE

We can't leave sacrifice without addressing one more topic more directly: The Lord's Supper. Is it, or is it not, a sacrificial meal? That's a question that divides the church. Catholics say, "Yes." Protestants typically say, "No." Few ask what sacrifice means.

From the start of this chapter, we've seen sacrifice isn't only or mainly about killing and dismembering. Sacrifice is a ritual movement through death to new and better life. It's the progress of Adam to Adam-and-Eve, of Noah through the flood into a new creation, of Israel escaping Egypt through the death-waters of the Red Sea. It's the passage of Jesus through cross and grave to His Father's right hand.

If the question is, "Is Jesus crucified all over again at the Supper?" the answer is clear: No, of course not, and few, if any, teachers in the church have ever taught anything that crude. If the question is, "Do we pass through death into new life in union with Jesus at the Supper?" the answer is "Yes."

The Eucharist is a memorial of Jesus' death, a reminder to the Father of His self-offering. The Eucharist is a sacrifice of praise. But it's more: It renews our union with Jesus' death and resurrection, a union forged in baptism (Rom 6:1–14). As we participate every week in the Eucharist, we pass again and again from death into new life. As we eat and drink Christ's body and blood, we're conformed to his sacrifice, so our entire life becomes reasonable service, a liturgy of self-offering in which we, like Jesus, are priests of our own self-sacrifice. As we share this sacrificial meal, we're made over into martyrs, willing to shed our life's blood in faithful witness.

14

Time

THEN GOD SAID, "LET THERE BE LIGHTS IN THE EXPANSE OF THE HEAVENS TO SEPARATE THE DAY FROM THE NIGHT, AND LET THEM BE FOR SIGNS AND FOR SEASONS AND FOR DAYS AND YEARS."
—GENESIS 1:14

The creation account reads like the rubrics of a prayer book. Day after day, God runs through the same series of actions:

God speaks.

God names.

God sees and pronounces it good.

During the first three days, God divides. On Day 1, it's:

God speaks light.

God sees the light is good.

God divides day and night, and sets them in a sequence.

God names light "day," and darkness "night."

Then Day 2:

> God speaks a firmament.
>
> The firmament separates waters above and below.
>
> God calls the firmament heaven.

Then Day 3:

> God speaks in order to separate waters and land.
>
> God names the dry land "earth," the waters "sea."
>
> God sees and pronounces it good.

After that, God starts filling the heaven, seas, and earth. He calls plants to sprout on earth, speaks the sun, moon and stars into the firmament, summons the waters to teem with swimming things and the earth and heaven to be filled with birds, makes land animals, creepers, and man from the ground.

Over and over, God repeats the same series of actions: speaking, making, seeing, judging; speaking, dividing, naming, pronouncing. Each day is a variation on the theme. The days aren't identical, but they're repetitive.

The creation week gives us a shadowy glimpse of the Trinity as God (*'elohim*) speaks His Word while His Spirit hovers. God speaks to start a day, and God speaks back to Himself to end each day. Creation comes to be through a divine liturgy as God, the Spirit, and the Word speak and speak back, call and respond. Creation emerges from the trialogue of Father, Word, and Spirit.

By the end of the week, God has created a full world of space and time. True, Genesis 1 doesn't use the word "time." It uses words like "light" and "darkness," "day" and "night," "evening" and "morning." Without using the word "time," Genesis 1 describes what we mean when we say "time." God's rhythmic work of creation sets creation's temporal rhythms ticking and tocking.

God establishes the rhythm of the day on Day 1, and every day follows the pattern. Evening and morning, Day 1. Evening and morning, Day 2. Evening and morning, Day 3. You get the point. It keeps going until it's "Evening and morning, *yesterday*." Like God's own creative work, the world moves in a pattern of non-identical repetition.

God creates liturgically. His actions are liturgical. And creation dances a liturgical dance of evenings and mornings, light and dark.

Scholars sometimes talk about liturgical time as if it's a species of time imposed on the natural time measured by the motion of the sun, moon, and stars. The Bible doesn't present things that way. The motion of sun, moon, and stars is *itself* a liturgical motion, a heavenly liturgy.

Liturgical time isn't a spiritual or religious layer on top of real time or scientific time or clock time. Time *is* liturgical, created in liturgy and choreographed by the divine Liturgist. It's liturgy all the way down.

APPOINTED TIMES

I'm not speculating or playing with words. The Bible actually uses liturgical language to describe creation's temporal movements.

Initially, God oversees creation's time directly (Gen 1:3–5). For three days, light follows darkness, and darkness follows light. But the light doesn't come from sunrise, and the darkness doesn't follow sunset. There's a simple reason for that: There's no sun. Wherever the light comes from, *God* is orchestrating it.

Then on Day 4, He makes created lights—the greater light of day, the lesser light of night, and the stars (Gen 1:14–19). He's been keeping time Himself, but after Day 4, He gives *creatures* authority over time. For three days, the Creator is Lord of time all by Himself. After Day 4, He *delegates* the rule of time. Sun, moon, and stars become the first created time lords.

Sun, moon, and stars have critical physical, biological, and cultural functions in the universe. All life on earth depends on the sun. The moon drags the tides to and from the sandy shore. Stars help sailors navigate the wine-dark seas.

Those *aren't* the purposes mentioned in Genesis 1. Heavenly lights separate day and night (Gen 1:14). That's what *Yahweh* has been doing in the first part of the creation week (Gen 1:4, 6). Now He empowers created things to take up this divine task. Heavenly lights also govern the day and night (1:16). Again, God delegates authority to creatures to rule creation, to participate in creation's own fulfillment. Even before man and woman were placed on the earth, the earth had creaturely rulers.

Sun, moon, and stars are also created "for signs, seasons, days and years" (Gen 1:14). Days and years is pretty straightforward. We know the day is over when the sun sets. We track months by phases of the moon. When the sun returns to springtime position in relation to the Zodiac, a year has passed.

Signs are less obvious. Astrologists today look to the heavens to suss out the future, but sane people know that's bogus. Still, God creates the heavens to communicate. In the Bible, people *do* see signs in the heavens, and the heavens do speak. Even if we can't predict the future by looking at stars, the heavenly lights signify: "The heavens are telling of the glory of God, and the firmament is declaring the work of His hands" (Ps 19:1).

For my purposes, the most important term is "seasons" (Heb. *mo'ed*). The Hebrew word doesn't refer to the cycle of winter, spring, summer, fall. It means "appointed times" and usually refers to the times of Israel's festivals (Exod 13:10; 23:15).

How do ancient Israelites know when to celebrate Passover? Passover happens on the night of the first full moon after the beginning of spring, the vernal equinox. The month of Passover is the first month of Israel's liturgical year (Exod 12:2), and other feasts are dated by counting from Passover. Israelites know appointed times because they look at the night sky. The heavens are tracking seasons.

Israel doesn't read this liturgical meaning *into* the sky. They don't make it up. God *creates* the sky as a liturgical calendar. Sun, moon, and stars exist to indicate the appointed times. Created time is liturgical, and Israel's time ticks and tocks along with the movements of the universe.

The phrase *appointed* time is important. Think of an appointment for a meeting or, even better, a date" Yahweh sets times when He promises to meet with Israel, marked by heavenly lights. He sets dates with His Bride, when she visits His house to commune with Him. *Mo'ed* is the word for "meeting" in the phrase "tent of meeting" (Exod 27:21; 28:43; 29:4, 10; etc.). God's tent is the place where He keeps appointments, where Israel gathers at the appointed times. Creation is designed to make sure Israel's timing is right, to keep them from showing up in an untimely way.

We'll look at Israel's cycle of feasts below and think about how it's transformed into the Christian calendar. For now, just notice this: Creation is organized liturgically. The sun, the vast galaxies of stars, the light of the silvery moon, are set up to show the Bride when she can be with her Beloved.

SABBATH

There's another hint that created time is liturgical time: Day 7, the Sabbath. Yahweh completes His work, rests, blesses and sanctifies the day (Gen 2:1–3). Exodus later calls this day the Sabbath, a pun on the Hebrew word for seven that means ceasing (Exod 20:8–11).

The Sabbath isn't just a day of ceasing. It's a day for celebration. Yahweh completes His work. He's said all the week that creation is good. At the end, He says it's very good (Gen 1:31). A job well done, and Yahweh takes time to delight in it. He enters into His joy.

Sabbath is also a day of enthronement. As we saw in chapter 1, the tabernacle is a small replica of creation. After Moses completes the work of building the tabernacle, Yahweh descends from Sinai to take His throne above the cherubim in the Most Holy Place (Exod 40:34–38). After Solomon "completes" the microcosmic temple, Yahweh fills the house with His glory (1 Kgs 8:10–11). Sabbath is for ceasing. Sabbath is also a day of royal splendor.

Each day of the creation week includes a mini-Sabbath. Yahweh establishes the pattern of day and night and then works within that pattern. He does something new each day and ceases each night. Like the week, each day is divided into work-time and rest-time, time for labor and time for joy. Each day has a Sabbatical, liturgical structure.

The Sabbath connects the liturgy of God's cosmic time with human time-keeping. There's nothing in the earth or sky to indicate that our time should be organized in units of 6 + 1. But it's not arbitrary. We observe weeks as well as days, months, and years because God sets the pattern in the creation week. God's days are rhythmical, and His weeks are rhythmical. So are ours.

Some theologians think men and women start keeping Sabbath as soon as they're created. From Adam, they say, human beings work six days and rest on the seventh, following Yahweh's example. We don't know for sure whether or not early humans ceased from their labor on the seventh day. They *may* have, but the Bible never tells us. I suspect they didn't. Adam is supposed to join Yahweh in enthroned rest as prince of creation. Because of his sin, like Israel later, he doesn't enter into rest (Ps 95; Heb 4).

Noah's name means rest. He brings rest to the world (Gen 5:29). We're not told that he keeps Sabbath, but we *do* know he becomes a king after the flood. He's given authority to execute murderers, and he enjoys the wine from the vineyard he plants. Wine is a Sabbatical, royal drink. Noah the rest-bringer becomes Noah the king. Sabbath probably isn't a creation ordinance. It's more likely a postdiluvian institution.

But the first *explicit* reference to human Sabbath-keeping doesn't occur until after the exodus. Pharaoh imposes an oppressive uniform time on Israel, an identical repetition of work-work-work, work-without-rest. After the exodus, Israel still has to work for their food, but not much. Yahweh provides miraculous food, manna from heaven and water from the rock. They don't have to plant, tend, and harvest. They gather. That's it. Yahweh opens His hand to satisfy their souls' desires.

That minimal work is ordered by God's pattern in the creation week. Yahweh forbids Israel to gather on the seventh day (Exod 16:22–26) and promises to provide seven days' worth of manna in six days. For the first time, human beings dance their weeks alongside Yahweh.

Israel's Sabbath-keeping is a continual reminder of her deliverance from Pharaoh. It's an *effective* sign of that deliverance, a sign that does what it signifies. So long as Israel keeps Sabbath, Israel's time is *actually* different from Egypt's time. Yahweh delivers Israel from Pharaoh's anti-liturgy of restless labor to enter His liturgical rhythm. This is what the exodus is for: to reorder Israel's time-keeping so it conforms to the Creator's. It's what salvation *is*: entry into a new time.

Keeping Sabbath is an act of faith, a confession of Israel's utter dependence on Yahweh. They have to trust Yahweh to provide two days' worth of manna on the sixth day. Some don't trust him and go searching for manna on the seventh day (Exod 16:27–30). Even after they enter the land, they keep Sabbath because they're still utterly dependent on His blessing to enjoy the fruits of the earth.

Sabbath is also a sign of Israel's glorification. They aren't just *freed* in the exodus. They're *exalted*, elevated to become Yahweh's treasured possession, His royal priesthood (Exod 19:5–6). They begin to share Yahweh's Sabbath enthronement as they share Yahweh's rest.

Every Sabbath after the exodus, Israel gathers for a holy convocation" (Lev 23:3), enthroned again with Yahweh their Master. Ancient Israelites don't spend every Sabbath at the tabernacle or temple. That would be impossible. Danites living in the far north of Israel would spend half the week traveling to Jerusalem and the other half returning, just in time to head back to the temple. They wouldn't do any work to rest *from*. No, Israel has holy convocations every Sabbath, but they don't happen in one location. Levites are scattered in cities throughout the land, and there are Levitical and priestly cities. Every Sabbath, Israelites assemble in synagogues all over the land to praise Yahweh, learn Torah, and pray.

Most ancient peoples don't follow this rhythm. They have their own calendars, their own patterns of time-keeping. They keep appointed times with their idols. Like the Egyptians, they work without rest, or at least force their slaves to work without rest. Their holidays don't celebrate the mighty acts of Yahweh, the living God. Idolatrous time-keeping facilitates false worship and becomes an instrument of abuse. Throughout the ancient world, time is out of joint.

Except in Israel. By conforming to Yahweh's weekly routine, Israel keeps time with the time of creation. Israel's liturgical time becomes an echo of creation's original time. They're put in sync with the time of the cosmos. By celebrating God's mighty act in the Exodus, Israel's time keeps time with the time of redemption. Israel's liturgical calendar is the redemption of time.

We find again the same pattern we've seen in earlier chapters when examining place, language, and sacrifice. God creates a liturgical world, and man lives, moves, and has his being in the liturgical grooves cut by creation. After Adam's sin, cultures take on distorted shapes, which are put back in shape when God delivers sinners and incorporates them into His liturgical community. As it's done in obedience to God's Word, liturgy redeems time as, over years and centuries, it smooths the crooked time of the nations into a created image of the Creator's time-keeping.

EIGHTH DAY

Most Christians don't worship on Saturday, at the end of the week. Jesus rises from the dead on the day *after* the Sabbath, on the first day of a new week. In a sense, it's a return to the origin. Adam is created on the sixth day, so his first full day of life is the seventh day, Yahweh's Sabbath. Jesus is the new Adam, restoring time's original balance. Jesus restores the priority of rest.

But Jesus doesn't restore the old. He doesn't turn the clock back to the beginning. Jesus' resurrection happens on the "eighth day" (John 20:26; cf. Exod 22:30; Lev 12:3), a day that bursts out of the calendrical constraints of the old creation. Jesus' resurrection inaugurates a new calendar.

The Lord's Day isn't identical to the Sabbath, but it is the designated day of worship. On this day, heaven and earth join. On this day, the Lord invites us into His house, calls us to join Him at the peak of heavenly Zion. On this day, He speaks to us and feeds us. The Lord's Day isn't just another day. It belongs to the Lord as His day of enthronement and judgment, which has become our day of enthronement.

Every time we assemble for worship, we declare a new Adam has arrived, bringing a new time and a new creation. We don't just say it's true. It is true as we assemble in the Spirit on the day of Jesus. Our worship is an entry into the new creation. We taste the final day already now, experiencing the new creation in the midst of the old.

Worshiping on the eighth day, we don't merely work in order to reach a day of rest. We do that. But the church's week goes the other way: We *start* the week in rest. We begin our work from a position of enthroned victory.

The peace, rest, and glory of the first day infuses the whole week. As Karl Barth said, a man who prays on Sunday will pray throughout the week. A man who gives thanks on Sunday will live a life of gratitude. A man who rejoices in the Lord on the Lord's day will see every day as a day of the Lord, a day of joy. Each Lord's day, we taste the last day, and the taste lingers through and spices up our work days.

On the Sabbath, Israel already shares in Yahweh's enthronement. But they don't share fully. No one, not even the high priest, goes into Yahweh's throne room—the Most Holy Place—and climbs up to sit above the cherubim. Our Priest has done just that because Jesus the Priest is also Jesus the King. He offers Himself once for all, rips the curtain of the temple, and processes upwards in glory to share His Father's throne.

He doesn't do it alone. Jesus has taken our flesh to make a way *for us*. He's above all rule and authority, enthroned in heavenly places. Because we're in Him as His body, so are wewe're in the heavenlies too (Eph 1:21–23; 2:6). He makes us kings and priests and shares His throne, which is His Father's throne, with us, His Bride (Rev 3:21). The Lord's day isn't a "break" from the turmoil of daily life. On the Lord's day, the Lord sifts and judges us, declares His royal word, gives us our marching orders. On the Lord's day, *we* sit on thrones to declare, judge, rule. Nothing affects the world so much as what the church says and does in our prayers, praises, and proclamation on the Lord's day.

Remember what I said about the sun, moon, and stars a few pages ago? God delegates authority to the heavenly lights to govern time. But they don't keep governing time. God gives *man* that authority.

It starts happening already in the Old Testament. In Genesis 14:1, we read about the "thirteenth year of Chedorlaomer." Huh, how'd *he* get his name on a year? Throughout Israel's monarchy, time is named by the names and numbers of kings. As Israel slides toward exile, we enter the times of the gentiles, when gentile emperors imprint their names to time periods (e.g., the "days of Nebuchadnezzar"). You see what's going on? At first, sun, moon and stars rule time. Once kings come into the picture, they take over. They govern time because they're like lights in the heavens and stars in the firmament.

That's all preparation for the new era that comes with Jesus. Jesus comes in the fullness of time. As God-Man, He is Lord of ages, who has inscribed His name on our calendars (I'm writing in *AD* 2019) He graciously shares His status with us. *We're* in the heavens, shining like stars (Phil 2:15). We are sons, exalted with Jesus above the angels (Heb 1:1–13). Once heavenly lights ruled time. *We* are the new time lords.

We here means we Christians or "we members of Christ's body." Jesus separates the times. But we're with Jesus, and so this is *our* time too. We can abuse this authority, lording it over time as if we were autonomous. We can make a relentless 24/7 news cycle, an Egyptian system of work without rest. All human lordship must submit to the decrees of the High Lord. But that potential for abuse doesn't change the reality: We're the heavenly clocks of the new covenant.

Christians used to know this. Christopher Page has described medieval Christendom as a soundscape. A medieval traveler knew he was back in the Christian world when he stopped hearing muezzins calling the hours of prayer and started hearing the chiming of bells. Bells clanged out liturgical hours with their giant iron tongues. They called the faithful to the Mass every Lord's day. In Christian Europe, liturgical time became the governing time for a whole civilization.

If we're the time lords, we don't determine when to celebrate feasts by looking at the phases of the moon. Paul goes apoplectic when Christians submit to the elementary things in the heavens (Gal 4:8–11; Col 2:16). As time lords, we have authority to decide when and how to celebrate. We must organize time obediently. We can organize time well only if we have the tunes of creation and redemption running in an endless loop through the ears of our soul. But we've grown up, and God has given us the authority to shape time.

ISRAEL'S CALENDAR

The creation week establishes a weekly rhythm of work and rest, labor and liturgy. Yahweh sets the liturgy of time and later invites Israel and us to dance along.

The week isn't the only pattern of liturgical time built into the creation. As we've seen, the Lord creates the sun, moon, and stars to mark years, months, and appointed times as well as to govern day and night. God creates a world that sways to multiple rhythms.

Virtually no culture marks only days and weeks. Every thirty days or so, we start a new month. When we have passed through twelve moon-cycles, we say we've grown a year older. Day-night, day-night; week after week after week; month follows month follows month; and years crawl and then sprint by.

When God lays out Israel's liturgical calendar, it matches that complex created rhythm. He invites them to share His Sabbath every week. But He also instructs them to mark the beginning of each month (Num 28:11–15) and to punctuate years with an annual cycle of feasts (Exod 23:14–17; Lev 23; Deut 16).

On the first day of every month, the priests offer extra offerings at the sanctuary. They offer two male lambs every day and two more every Sabbath. At the beginning of each month, they offer even more—two bulls, a ram, and seven lambs (Num 28:11–15).

Three times a year, there are bigger festivals. At the beginning of the liturgical year, in spring, all Israelite men are required to appear before Yahweh to celebrate Passover and the week-long Feast of Unleavened Bread. From Passover, they count seven weeks, and when they get to fifty days, they keep Pentecost, also called the Feast of Weeks. That takes place in the third month of the liturgical year.

The seventh month is the final month of the liturgical calendar, and it's jammed with festivity. The month begins with a special new moon feast called the Feast of Trumpets (Lev 23:23–25). On the tenth day, Israel fasts while the high priest performs the rites of the Day of Atonement, to purify the sanctuary and re-start the priesthood (Lev 16; 23:26–32). From the fifteenth to the twenty-second day, Israel celebrates the Feast of Booths, also known as the Feast of Ingathering (Lev 23:33–44).

We could spend a lot of time studying these feasts, but I'll confine myself to a few general points. Israel's feasts follow the natural cycle of the agricultural year. Passover and Unleavened Bread take place at spring planting, Pentecost is a first fruits festival, and Booths is a harvest feast. By observing these feasts, Israel acknowledges Yahweh as the Lord and Giver of life. He makes the earth fruitful.

The feasts also mark key events in Israel's history. Passover, of course, commemorates Israel's liberation from Egypt (Exod 12–13). Pentecost celebrates Israel's arrival at Sinai, the cutting of the covenant, and the giving of the law. Israel lives in booths during the Feast of Booths to remind them of their forty-year campout in the wilderness (Lev 23:42–43).

Every year, Israel lives through the founding events of her history all over again. It's a great teaching tool. Going through the rituals of Passover, Israelite children ask what it's all about, and their parents have a chance to retell the story of the exodus (Exod 12:25–27). They don't just tell the story but *re-enact* it.

It's more than a teaching tool. The feasts are memorials (Exod 12:14), like the offerings on the altar and the rainbow in the cloud. Feasts remind Yahweh of His promises. As they commemorate Passover, Israel asks Yahweh to liberate them from other enemies—Midian, Philistia, Babylon. As they keep the feast of Pentecost, they call on Yahweh to keep the Sinai covenant.

The festival cycle also points ahead to Israel's future and the world's. As a harvest feast, the Feast of Booths expresses Israel's hope that the Lord will gather the nations into His house. It's hope performed as liturgy. During the week of the Feast of Booths, the priests offer a total of seventy bulls on the altar (Num 29:12–38). Seventy is the number of nations (Gen 10). The Feast of Booths anticipates the time when gentiles will offer themselves as living sacrifices to the God of Israel.

The natural and historical dimensions of the feasts overlap and interpenetrate. Passover is the beginning, a planting of Israel among the nations. Pentecost is first fruits, Israel the covenant people as the first harvest of nations. Booths represents the full harvest, not only of Israel but of the gentiles.

Once again, we see liturgical time isn't alien to real time. Time is inherently liturgical, and the specific liturgical calendar of Israel tracks with and enhances created liturgical cycles. The liturgical calendar is a calendar of *new* creation.

Early in Israel's history, Yahweh Himself lays out Israel's annual schedule of feasts. Later Israel's leaders *add* festivals to the calendar. After the Lord delivers Israel from Haman's plot, Mordecai establishes the annual festival of Purim (from Hebrew *pur*, meaning lot) to commemorate this great deliverance (Esth 9:20–32). During the intertestamental period, the Maccabees defeat the Syrian king Antiochus Epiphanes and recover Jerusalem. They institute the Feast of Dedication, known as Hanukkah, to celebrate the victory. Jesus celebrates the feast (John 10:22), so He must have thought it legitimate.

Given what we've seen, this isn't a surprise. Israel's leaders have the authority to organize the calendar. After all, they're on their way to becoming lords of time.

In its annual calendar, Israel stands in contrast to the nations. Her year is Yahwehized, fashioned both by created rhythms and by Yahweh's just and merciful works. Not so the gentiles. Their annual calendars celebrate the great moments of their own history, including festivals to their false gods. Their calendars take no notice of their Creator or His works. In a world of broken time, Israel alone keeps time faithfully.

But Israel doesn't exist merely to stand in contrast. Israel calls the nations to worship Yahweh. As that happens, gentiles reorder their time, adding celebrations of God's acts to their own time-keeping. As they conform to Israel's liturgical time, their time begins to be redeemed, reoriented toward God's past works and His future harvest of nations. They begin to redeem the times.

THE CHURCH'S YEAR

For most of her history, the church has followed Israel's example in keeping an annual as well as a weekly liturgical cycle. Like Israel's calendar, the church calendar marks specific events of redemptive history: Christmas celebrates the birth of Jesus, Good Friday commemorates the cross, Easter celebrates the resurrection, and Pentecost gives thanks for the gift of the Spirit.

The New Testament doesn't mention any of these Christian feasts, and some Christians think it's wrong for the church to observe any feast besides the weekly Lord's Day. Since it's not commanded, it's forbidden. But we aren't children any more. Our calendar isn't controlled by the sun, moon, and stars. We don't need direct revelation from God to schedule times with the Bridegroom. We're in heavenly places with Jesus as time lords. The church's leaders, like Mordecai, have authority to establish feasts and commemorations in keeping with the model of Israel's calendar, which is laid out so carefully in the Bible.

So the church has arranged the whole year around the life of Jesus. The Western church's calendar begins late in the calendar year with Advent (Coming or Arrival), a four-week season of preparation before Christmas. During Advent, the church meditates on the many ways the Lord comes. We remember Israel's longing for the advent of the Messiah and renew our longing for His final advent.

Christmas, of course, celebrates the human birth of the Son of God. It's followed by several weeks of Epiphany (Manifestation), which focus on events that radiate Jesus' Messianic vocation and power—His baptism, the wedding at Cana, His miracles and healings, the Transfiguration.

After Epiphany comes Lent, a forty-day period of fasting devoted to meditation on the suffering and death of Jesus. Lent climaxes in Holy Week, which walks through the final week of Jesus' life, His Last Supper (on Maundy Thursday), and His trials and death (on Good Friday).

Some churches observe Holy Saturday, the day when Jesus lies dead in the tomb. After the fast of Lent and Holy Week comes the glory of Easter. Easter isn't a single day but lasts through the whole of the forty-day period until Ascension. It takes weeks to grasp the joy of resurrection.

Ascension Day has been under-celebrated throughout the history of the church. Most churches recognize it, but it doesn't get the emphasis it deserves. As Jesus tells Pilate, He's born for the purpose of becoming a king. The gospel is the announcement that Jesus is the Davidic king (Rom 1:1–4). Ascension is the climax of the gospel narrative and should be celebrated as such.

After Jesus ascends, He gives His coronation gift to His Bride. That gift is the Spirit, who unites the church with Christ, animates the body, gives gifts to the members so each can serve and edify the whole.

The Sunday after Pentecost is Trinity Sunday. The whole of the church calendar unveils the Trinity. The Father sends the Son at Advent and Christmas, and the Son manifests the glory of the Father during Epiphany. He offers Himself as a perfect sacrifice to the Father on Good Friday, and the Father rewards His self-offering by raising Him from the dead. Ascended to His Father, he receives the Spirit, whom He pours out on the disciples.

Jesus comes from the Father to reveal the Father and then returns to the Father. Jesus receives and gives the Spirit, who unites us to Jesus so we can go to the Father. Father to Son to Spirit, who catches us up in the Son's movement to the Father.

As we observe the church year, we are brought into this Triune movement. The rhythms of historical time are incorporated into the rhythms of Father, Son, and Spirit. In the liturgical calendar, our time is taken up into the life of the Trinity.

DAILY OFFICE

Many churches have danced another liturgical dance, the tiny dance of the day. In the early centuries, some churches gathered several times a day for public prayers. Days began with Matins and ended with Vespers. With the rise of monasticism, the daily cycle of prayers disappeared into the cloistered confines of the monastery. Instead of morning and evening prayers, monks kept a twenty-four-hour cycle that included eight times of prayers. No one with a day job could keep up. Monks prayed on behalf of everyone else.

Some Protestant churches attempted to revive the daily office for lay Christians. In the *Book of Common Prayer*, there are services for Matins and Evensong (Vespers), and these services are observed in Anglican churches around the world. Sadly, the daily office has largely disappeared from many parts of the church.

It should be revived. The daily office has biblical roots. At the tabernacle and temple, priests begin each day by offering an ascension offering, establishing a communion of prayer between heaven and earth. They end each day with an evening offering (Num 28:1–8). The offerings cohere with the temporal rhythm of the creation week, with its evenings and mornings. Each day becomes a day of new creation, a new stage in the Creator's work of forming and filling.

Under the law, these daily offerings affect everyone in the entire land, including those far from the central sanctuary. An Israelite who becomes unclean has to wash himself and wait till evening to become clean (e.g., Lev 15:5–11). Why wait till evening? Because his impurity is removed by the evening offering. By "baptizing" himself, he participates in the cleansing effect of the offering.

As long as the temple stands, the apostles observe these hours of prayer. Peter and John heal a man as they come to the temple at the ninth hour for prayer (Acts 3:1).

Christians today have a daily habit of prayer. They pray, read Scripture, or meditate privately or with their families every morning and evening. That's good. But it's better for a church to *gather* daily, morning and evening. It's better for worship to be public. It's better for daily time, as well as weekly and annual time, to be organized liturgically.

Few may show up to daily offerings of prayer. It doesn't matter. Jesus promises to be present where two or three are gathered. And if Jesus is there, the church has all she needs to commune in dialogue with her Lord. Her prayers, like the offerings of Israel, spread out to affect the world around her. Her prayers aren't just for her but for "all sorts and conditions of men," for rulers and nations. Her public daily prayers have public effects.

Following the example of Israel, following the apostolic precedent, we keep a liturgical calendar, including daily offices, to ensure that time is thoroughly Christianized, from top to bottom, from the year down to the day.

TIME TURNED CHRISTIAN

I can hear the objections. Isn't this esoteric and irrelevant? What difference does the church calendar make? Shouldn't we be thinking about more important things? If we want the gospel to change the world, shouldn't we focus on mission?

Such objections are superficial. Few things are more important to a culture than its time-keeping, and there can be no more fundamental cultural change than a change of time. The Christian calendar *is* a missional issue. It's all about transforming the city of man into an image of the future city of God.

Calendars record history before textsbooks, and calendars retain history longer than history journals. Change the calendar, and you change the way time is experienced and organized. Change the calendar, and you change the rhythm of life. Add Martin Luther King Day, and you've embedded the Civil Rights movement in American government, public education, entertainment. Turn Christmas into Winter Holiday, and you've de-Christianized one part of the year. Think of the epochal change when the Roman world acknowledged that Jesus, an obscure Jew, was the crux of the ages. Think of what it would mean for China to adopt a Christian calendar: A billion people and more would enter the Christian era.

The gospel alters and redeems time. God enters time so that through time, He saves and glorifies the world. Because of Jesus' death and resurrection, time isn't progress toward death. Death is swallowed up by life. Time moves toward resurrection.

That change of times lies at the heart of our calendars, in the distinction between "Before Christ" and "Anno Domini," "In the Year of our Lord." BC counts down, like a bomb about to detonate. AD moves upward toward eternity.

Every revolutionary movement in the modern world has attempted to start time over again. French Revolutionaries tried to renumber from 1789 as Year 1. Russian Revolutionaries rebooted time in 1918. They tried to turn the time of Jesus into a parenthesis. Jesus won. As I write this paragraph, France and Russia date their letters and laws with *AD* 2019, along with much of the rest of the world.

These movements were obviously heretical, implicitly denying Jesus is Lord of time. But this denial takes more subtle forms. Virtually every culture follows some annual calendrical pattern. In the United States, the Fourth of July, Independence Day, celebrates the sacred nation. In France, it's Bastille Day. In England, Guy Fawkes Day is about England's deliverance from Spain and the Papacy.

Days of remembrance are central to national identity. When we celebrate national holidays, we renew our commitment to the nation and its ideals. Holidays move us emotionally. It's hard for an American to watch fireworks and listen to the National Anthem without getting a lump in his throat.

Love for country is good. But the nation can displace the church in our order of affections and commitments. If we're to hate our father and mother to follow Jesus, we surely must be prepared to hate fatherland and mother country. The church is the Christian's primary community. Christians are citizens of *that* nation, residents of the *heavenly* city. While we're also citizens of other cities and other nations, the church claims our primary loyalty and love because it is the body of our Lord

Jesus. Baptismal water is thicker than blood, and the church, born of water and the Spirit, is bound as one body more firmly, more substantially, than any nation born of fire and blood.

That means the church calendar must be the Christian's primary calendar. When the church molds her time-keeping to the world's time-keeping, she becomes worldly at a fundamental level. The temporal rhythm of her life becomes worldly. The church calendar is a political and cultural and missional issue, a test of the faithfulness of the heavenly *polis* against its earthly challengers.

Because the church is an outpost of the heavenly city on earth, she must mark time differently. Her holidays must mark the great events of her history, which are the great events of world history. If we don't observe a liturgical calendar, we leave the twisted times of the nations in place. If we don't have a liturgical calendar, time isn't shaped by the life, death and resurrection of Jesus. If we refuse a church calendar, time isn't recognized as the time of Father, Son, and Spirit. In short, if liturgical time doesn't redeem time, time is unredeemed. If we let the world make the calendar, we're denying that Jesus matters. We're denying that He's Lord of time.

The liturgical calendar corrects the disjointed time-keeping of the world. The liturgical calendar is time-keeping conformed to God's work and will. When the church keeps the rhythm of redemptive history, redemption is inscribed on the temporal foundation of life. A church that keeps the liturgical calendar begins to Christianize time, keeping time in tune with the time of creation that will be fulfilled in the endless day of new creation.

15

Joy

WHEN THE MORNING STARS SANG TOGETHER
AND ALL THE SONS OF GOD
SHOUTED FOR JOY.
—JOB 38:7

Remember how I described liturgy at the beginning of the book? Slow, repetitive, boring, boring, boring. Dead. And deadening.

That's how many Christians experience liturgy. Churches are often at fault. Some liturgies *are* deadening because they teach you to treat yourself like dirt. You grovel when you come in. You grovel during confession. The sermon is designed to make you grovel some more. You crawl to the communion rail to choke down a wafer and a sip of wine. Then you're sent out to invite other people to come grovel along with you. You might stand and sit, but you feel as if you spend the whole service on your knees, if not flat on your face.

Don't get me wrong. There's a place for abject confession and repentance. There are moments for kneeling and prostration. Every service should include a confession of sin, when it's best to kneel. But you don't come to church to stay on your knees. You lower yourself before the Lord so He can exalt you. You're kings in the King. It's the Lord's day, the new covenant day of enthronement. The liturgy should be fit for kings.

It's the Lord's day, the fulfillment of Israel's Sabbath. On this day, we enter the Lord's own Sabbath, which is a day of joy and satisfaction. Yahweh ceases because He's finished. Ceasing, He enjoys the delights of what He's made.

In an important sense, our rest isn't like that. We're *never* finished. No matter how hard you work during the week, you never get *everything* done that needs doing. No matter how long you live, you'll leave unfinished projects scattered around your workroom or desk.

Yet the Lord invites us to rest anyway. Long before we're finished, the Lord tells us to rejoice *as if* we're finished. There's a promise in that: By instructing us to cease from work, He promises He'll give us time to complete the tasks He assigns to us. He promises us all the time we need.

We should take a liturgical lesson from all this. On His first Sabbath, Yahweh entered into satisfied delight in His work. For us, the Lord's day is a day of joy, a day to take delight in God's work for us. If we imitate the Lord's own Sabbath, it should also be a day for delight in our own work.

Some Christians are reluctant to discuss their work on the Lord's day. They fear they might contaminate the holy day with profane conversation. That's exactly wrong. The Lord's day isn't a sacred island in a secular world. It's a taste of the future in the midst of the present. On the Lord's day, we touch the day when our work comes to fruition in a new heavens and new earth. By talking about work, we're linking our labor with the great cosmic movement of history, from the first to the final temple.

The Lord's day gives a taste of new creation because it's a Eucharistic day. On the Lord's day, we eat bread and drink wine, products of human skill and work. Grain and fruit plants are the first products of earth (Gen 1:11). Eucharistic bread and wine are glorified grain and fruit, the first products of new creation.

As a Eucharistic day, the Lord's day is a day of joy, gladness not glumness, delightful not dour.

As we've seen throughout Part 3, creation sets the pattern for human life and culture. God shapes space, and we form spaces within His cosmic temple. He speaks the world into being, and our social and cultural lives are ongoing, intergenerational dialogues. He divides and reunites, constructing creation by sacrificial labor, and sacrifice is at the heart of human society. He sets the world's temporal rhythms, and every culture puts its own stamp on time.

Sabbath is also an inescapable feature of culture. I don't mean that every culture observes a day of rest. They don't. Israel was unique in the ancient world, and the church has a unique weekly pattern too. But Sabbath isn't just rest. It's joy and satisfaction. It comes at the end of the creation week and is the end toward which God works.

Every culture mimics God by offering some hope for future bliss. That hope may be for the nothingness of Nirvana, an escape from suffering, or eternal life with a bevy of nubile virgins. The hopes aren't necessarily religious. Modern cultures encourage us to find our bliss in material wealth, peace of mind, an ever-expanding economy, being left alone to do our own thing. Marx dreamed about the end of social classes and the extension of individual freedom so everyone could be a manual laborer in the morning, a philosopher in the afternoon, and an artist in the evening. In practice, Marxism hasn't been so benign.

Promises of joy motivate individual and collective action. Why were so many willing to die in two World Wars? On one side, many died for a dream of world domination. On the other side, many died to protect their way of life, their freedom, their prosperity. Why do people work themselves sick with eighty-hour weeks at the office? They're seeking some joy, perhaps the joy of the work itself, perhaps the joy of a large bonus, perhaps the joy of notoriety. Alone and together, we live toward what we think will bring us to bliss.

Since Adam's sin, human hopes are distorted and perverse. Cultures inculcate joy in things that cannot bring joy. They direct our hopes to things that are finally hopeless. The liturgy exists to redirect our hopes and joys toward their proper object because the liturgy directs us to find our joy in the joy of the Lord of Sabbath. The gospel calls us into a liturgy of life that's a liturgy of joy.

SEEKING WORSHIPERS

This is one important thread of Paul's letter to the Romans: God turns idolaters into worshipers who enter His kingdom of joy.

At the outset of the epistle, Paul describes a world descending into chaos (Rom 1:18–32). Men turn their sexual desires from women to other men, and women burn with unnatural lust for other women. Their minds are darkened and depraved. People are dominated by greed, envy, violence, strife, lies, malice. They slander, boast, resent their parents, hate one another. They know God hates these things, but they keep doing them. They become so perverse that they praise those who defy God.

It's a bleak picture, but where does it start? It starts with worship. God makes Himself known in creation, but men suppress the truth. They know God but don't honor Him as God or give thanks. They know God's power and divine nature but venerate images of birds, animals, and creeping things. When men turn to idols, God gives them over to sexual confusion. When they persist in sexual perversions, God gives them over to social and moral chaos.

Corruption of the sanctuary, the place of worship, leads to corruption of the home, of marriage and sexuality. And from the sanctuary and the home, death flows out to fill the world with corruption. Sanctuary, home, world, these three. But the beginning of these is the sanctuary.

As Paul explains and expounds it in Romans, the gospel is good news about the restoration of proper worship, which reorients the home and the world. Jesus the son of David has been raised by the Spirit to become king (Rom 1:1–4). He rules to enact God's justice (Rom 1:17–18). He gives the gift of righteousness so men and women will worship His Father.

Abraham is the model. He believes God and is reckoned righteous. He believes God's promise to make him the father of nations and to give him seed through Sarah. By believing that God can call what is not as though it is, he gives glory to God (Rom 4:20). While the rest of the world turns to idols, Abraham is the father of worshipers because he is the father of believers.

Because of Adam's transgression, sin and death reign (Rom 5:12–21). By one act of obedience, Jesus triumphs over sin and death. Those who receive righteousness reign in life through Jesus (Rom 5:17).

How are you freed from sin and death? By dying and rising with Jesus in His death and resurrection, a union that occurs at baptism. Those who die in the waters of baptism are freed from the Adamic reign of death (Rom 6:1–7). Baptism extracts us from the world of Adam and brings us into the body of Christ, the people who are united by the Spirit to the incarnate Son. Within the church, the Spirit sanctifies the baptized so that we become true worshipers. Through baptism, God releases our bodies from our slavery to injustice. Paul uses the liturgical language of presentation to describe what the baptized do with their bodies. Instead of dishonoring our bodies by idols and sexual sin, we "present [our] members as instruments of justice to God" (Rom 6:13). By offering our bodies in worship, we bring the justice of God to reality.

From Paul's perspective, the entire life of the Christian and of the church is liturgical (Rom 12:1–2). We are to present our bodies as living sacrifices. This, Paul says, is our "liturgy" (Greek *latreia*) guided by the word (*logike*). Christians enact the liturgy of life by using our spiritual gifts for the benefit of the whole body (Rom 12:4-8). Our liturgy is a life of love, diligence and fervor, prayer, perseverance, generosity, hospitality, unity of mind (Rom 12:9–16). If we're doing the Christian liturgy of life, we renounce vengeance. We never pay back evil for evil but overcome evil, including evil empires, with good (Rom 12:17–21; 13:1–7).

Paul describes a *corporate* liturgy, the civic liturgy of the *polis* of God. In this city, in this kingdom, what matters isn't food and drink but righteousness, peace, and joy (Rom 14:17). The gospel calls people from the darkness and chaos into the Spirit's joy. That is, it calls us from idolatrous worship into the Christian liturgy.

JOY IN THE SPIRIT

What kind of people does God want? What kind of people does the liturgy produce? The Son pours out the Spirit to bring out the fruits of the Spirit: love, joy, peace, patience, kindness, goodness, faithfulness, gentleness, self-control (Gal 5:22–23). Those fruits should characterize members of the body of Christ. Those practices set the tonality of the church's corporate life.

Joy is the most immediate and evident effect of the Spirit's advent. Filled with the Spirit, Mary rejoices in God the Savior (Luke 1:47). When the seventy return from their mission, Jesus rejoices in the Spirit (Luke 10:21). Jesus goes to the cross "for the joy that was set before Him" (Heb 12:2). After Pentecost, the disciples are "continually filled with joy and with the Holy Spirit" (Acts 13:52). The members of the church are to imitate the apostles and Jesus, clinging to the word "in much tribulation with the joy of the Holy Spirit" (1 Thess 1:6).

In every dimension, the liturgy means joy. Liturgical space is the space of joy. When Yahweh planted Israel in the land, He chose a place to set His name, where Israel would gather to "eat, drink, and rejoice" before Him (Deut 12). Joy infused the temple dedication and followed Israel as they returned to their tents (1 Kgs 8:66).

During the feasts at the sanctuary, Israel enjoyed Yahweh's blessing on their labor and the produce of their hands so they would be altogether joyful (Deut 16:15). In His presence, at His house, is the fullness of joy (Ps 16:7).

The dialogue of the liturgy is a dialogue of love between Jesus the Bridegroom and His Bride the church. It is also an ecstatic dialogue of joy. The Bridegroom rejoices over us as a mighty man over his bride and calls us to enter His joy (Zeph 3:17). The liturgy is a journey into joy. The Latin Mass begins with Psalm 43: "*Introibo ad altere dei*," and the people respond with "*Ad Deum qui laetificat juventutem meam*." "I will go to the altar of God / to God who is the joy of my youth." The Bridegroom, anointed with the oil of joy, calls the Bride to His house:

> But let all who take refuge in You be glad, let them ever sing for joy; and may You shelter them, that those who love Your name may exult in You. (Ps 5:11)
>
> Sing for joy in the Lord, O you righteous ones; praise is becoming to the upright. … Sing to Him a new song; play skillfully with a shout of joy. (Ps 33:1, 3)
>
> O clap your hands, all peoples; shout to God with the voice of joy. (Ps 47:1)
>
> Shout joyfully to the Lord, all the earth. (Ps 100:1)

Exiled from the land, David longs to rejoin the throng in procession to the house of God so He can join his voice to the "voice of joy and gladness" of "a multitude keeping festival" (Ps 42:4). If the ministry of condemnation (2 Cor 3) came with joy, how much more the ministry of righteousness. For we have not come to another Sinai, a fearsome mountain that cannot be touched. We have come to the heavenly Zion, with its joyous assembly of angels and saints (Heb 12:18–24).

Every step in the liturgy's procession is surrounded by joy. We arrive and enter with thanksgiving and praise. We confess, and the minister pronounces absolution. In deliverance from guilt, there is joy: "Deliver me from bloodguiltiness, O God, the God of my salvation; then my tongue will joyfully sing of Your righteousness" (Ps 51:14). Confession and absolution moves us from lament to laughter, from sackcloth to song.

Having been cleansed, we ascend into heavenly places on the wings of song as we sing from the songbook of Scripture, the book of Psalms:

> Let them also offer sacrifices of thanksgiving, and tell of His works with joyful singing. (Ps 107:22)

> Let Your priests be clothed with righteousness, and let Your godly ones sing for joy. (Ps 132:9)

Because the Lord has rescued David from his enemies and lifted him above his enemies, he offers sacrifices in His tent "with shouts of joy" (Ps 27:6). He wants to sing for joy under the wings of the cherubim (Ps 63:7). The sacrifice of song is a sacrifice of joy and a sacrifice that induces joy and makes singers joyful. In the music of the church, joy compounds joy in a spiral that ascends to become a sweet sound in the ears of the Father. We sing in the Spirit, who is the Spirit of joy.

Joy is lively. Joy is active. When we rejoice, we don't mumble or mutter. We shout and sing at the top of our lungs. When we rejoice, we move, clap, sway, dance. Joy doesn't belong down down down down in my heart. Joy grips my body, my tongue and hands and feet. Clothed in the Spirit, my body rejoices. What should liturgy look like? Don't think grim and proper Presbyterians. Think African Anglicans. Think Brazilian charismatics. Don't quench the Spirit. Don't bottle up the joy.

God speaks through Scripture and in preaching, and the church rejoices at the voice of the Shepherd because His testimonies are "the joy of my heart" (Ps 119:111). The Word of the Lord is a source of joy, more than riches or spoil after a battle (Ps 119:14, 162).

At the peak of the mountain, God speaks to us and feeds us. His table is a table of delights, a feast of wine, and in the Bible, wine means joy. The wine of Jesus' blood offers genuine gladness, unlike the deceptive wine of the world. In the Song of Moses (Deut 32), Moses says that the vine of Israel grew from a cutting from Sodom's vine, from the vineyard of Gomorrah. Such vines produce only bitter fruit or worse—venom from dragons (*tanniyn*; vv. 32–33). Isaiah picks up the image when he complains about the worthless grapes produced by the vineyard of Jerusalem (Isa 5:1–7). Not coincidentally, Isaiah has earlier charged that Jerusalem has become Sodom (1:9–10; 3:9). The wine of Jerusalem's feasts is the poisonous wine of the serpent (cf. 5:11–12).

Always, there's wine and there's wine: There's the wine of the dragon, the serpent that poisons; and there's the wine of the One who was lifted like the Bronze Serpent, struck, and killed. Only the latter wine lifts up the heart.

Bread and wine are things, created things transformed into cultural artifacts. These things bring us joy. And bread and wine stand for all other things. We rejoice in the Lord, but that joy in the Lord takes the form of delight in His gifts, *all* His gifts.

Because we find joy in Eucharistic bread and wine, we also find joy in the plate that holds the bread and the chalice that contains the wine. We rejoice in the table and the pulpit and the windows and the paintings or banners. Dismissed from the liturgy, we go out in joy—to find joy in pots and pans, trees and flowers, mountains and sunsets, sleek cars and powerful smart phones, joy in a husband or a wife, children or siblings, friends and neighbors. We find joy in all God's gifts, which means we find joy in *everything* because we have nothing we have not received (1 Cor 4:7).

We cannot find joy in *abusing* His gifts. There's joy in sex, but no joy in adultery. There's joy in a family feast, but no joy in a house full of bickering, back-biting, and strife. There's joy in material goods, but no joy in greed or a life devoted to Mammon.

After eating, the church is sent out. The Bride rejoices in the presence of the Bridegroom, and she goes out rejoicing, to spread joy to the whole earth. Nations are called to join the joyful assembly (Ps 66:1; 67:4), and even creation is summoned to join in (Ps 65:13). The church's mission is to live joyfully, inviting the world into joy.

We enter with joy, receive forgiveness with joy, ascend with joy, hear with joy, feast with joy, depart in joy. The liturgy welcomes the sad, sad world and leads it to the joy of God. The liturgy confronts the false and fruitless joys of the world and reorients them to the One in whom there is fullness of joy. Cultures always aim at joy but miss their target. Over decades and centuries, the liturgy redeems culture by redirecting its quest for bliss. Liturgy redeems because it's a culture of joy.

As I've emphasized again and again, there's no magic here. The liturgy doesn't *automatically* bring true joy. In some churches, the liturgy is quite joyless. And we can't expect to thrill in the Spirit's joy unless we are walking in the Spirit. A quenched Spirit, a grieved Spirit, doesn't elicit joy but rather witnesses against us, convicting us, along with the world of sin, righteousness, and judgment. If we want the liturgy to be a journey to joy, the church and each member must trust and obey the Lord who is Spirit.

JOY IN SORROW

All this joy may strike you as Pollyannish or even cruel. What right does the church have to rejoice in a world of sex abuse and slavery, hunger and homelessness, sorrow and terror and cruelty? How *dare* we?

Christian joy doesn't ignore the evils of the world or the anguish of existence. Christians, after all, follow a crucified Lord, who instructs us to take up our own crosses to follow Him. Jesus experienced the full range of weakness and woe.

But here's God's commitment to His people: Sorrow *never* has the last word. Darkness *never* triumphs over light. The light comes into the world, and darkness *cannot* overcome it. After darkness, light. After the grave, resurrection.

This is one of the key lessons we learn by singing the psalms of lament. They begin with the most poignant descriptions of human pain ever written. David is driven from his home. He suffers physical deprivations and pain. His friends betray him, and, worst of all, it seems Yahweh has abandoned him. Before the end of the Psalm, the mood turns. David remembers the Lord's promise. He may not yet be delivered, but he's certain he will be. Yahweh's promise is enough. He prepares a table in the midst of enemies (Ps 23:5), assuring David he will look in triumph on his foes (Ps 59:10).

Singing the Psalms, we sing the Lord's promises of joy. Even in the midst of sorrow, we rejoice in the coming joy. The very fact that Jesus enters our sorrows transforms our sorrows. The Good Shepherd is with us in the valley of the shadow. Jesus is Lord of the grave so that whether we live or die, we are the Lord's. Jesus went to the cross for the joy set before Him. But more: The cross is the beginning of His ascent to the Father. It's the first step in His journey to joy. Joy comes at the end, but the light of the destination shines on the path.

And so it is in the liturgy. The liturgy gives us a taste now of the kingdom to come. In the liturgy, we glimpse endless day. In the liturgy, we experience now the joy of resurrection and the eternal marriage feast of the Lamb. We gather with broken relationships, failed hopes, frustrated dreams. We don't leave behind our sorrows any more than we leave behind our language and culture. As the liturgy transforms our language and culture, so it brings our sorrows into the joy of the Spirit.

JOYOUS MISSION

So the liturgy is joyful. Liturgical culture is joyful culture. But *so what*? What does that have to do with anything? How does joy advance the mission of the church? How does a joyful liturgy in the city of God transform the city of man?

Let's start with a baseline answer: The city of God isn't merely a city of moral uprightness. The liturgy doesn't aim to form merely "virtuous" people. Obsession with the minutiae of law is Pharisaical, not Christian. The church can build a "Christian" culture that's an empty shell. All the forms and patterns are right, but there's no life.

Joylessness is a mark of deep trouble. If a community is Christian, it must be enlivened by the fruits of the Spirit. If a culture is transformed by the church's ministry in the Spirit, it must manifest the work of the Spirit. Where the Spirit is, there is joy, and the faith of joyous Christians is contagious.

For Western Christians, there's a contextual reason to emphasize joy. Nietzsche complained Christians have no joy. We shouldn't dismiss this comment just because Nietzsche was an enemy of the church. To the extent it's true, it's a fundamental indictment. If the Spirit brings joy, a joyless church must be Ichabod, bereft of the Spirit of glory and joy.

Outside the church, many are desperate. Life is stale, flat, unprofitable, meaningless. Nothing delights. Nothing causes wonder. It's same old, same old, same old, till the last syllable of recorded time. We can identify various causes for the ennui of the contemporary mood. We're over-saturated with stimulation. Technology is partly to blame. We've lost confidence in institutions. We have no heroes. We cynically think everyone's on the make.

At heart, though, the joylessness of modern life reflects the joylessness of the church. The church is the light of the world, radiating the light of Jesus by the Spirit among the nations. The church is the place of joy; the liturgy is the time of joy. If there is no joy at the center, there will be none at the edges. If there's no joy in the sanctuary, no joy will flow out. If the redeemed culture of the liturgy isn't joyous, nothing will be.

THE LORD'S SERVICE

Joy is a gift of the Spirit. The liturgy is a journey to joy because it's the Spirit's work. From beginning to end, the liturgy is God's work in and for us.

God always initiates worship. He calls us into His presence, a place where we wouldn't dare go without an invitation. Every worship service should begin with an acknowledgement that He gets things rolling. Every worship service should begin with a call to worship, an invocation of His name: "In the Name of God the Father, God the Son, and God the Holy Spirit." With this summons, the minister also names our destination because our liturgical journey is a journey into the Triune life, the communion of eternal joy.

If we stop there, we've misunderstood the liturgy. Liturgy isn't Deist. It's not that God kicks things off and then leaves us to muster up the strength for the rest of the work. God is the primary actor throughout the liturgy, from start to finish. *He* calls us into His house. *He* forgives us. *He* speaks to us. *He* feeds us. He feeds Himself to us, as the Father gives the body and blood of the Son through the Spirit.

The liturgy is primarily God's action, not ours. No wonder it's a time for rejoicing.

That's true in an obvious way. Ever since Adam honored the serpent above God, we've all been idolaters, worshiping and serving the creature rather than the Creator (Rom 1). We worship rightly only because the Spirit turns us from idols to the living God. The liturgy is utterly dependent on God's work *in* us.

But the liturgy is also God's work *for* us and *towards* us. The liturgy is the Lord's service, not primarily because we serve Him but because in the liturgy *He serves us.*

This is true under the law, though God parcels out His gifts less lavishly. Think about Israel's worship. They're permitted to enter the courtyard of the sanctuary but can't enter the Holy Place, where there's bread, light, and incense. The priests can enter the Holy Place, but even they're excluded from the Most Holy Place, God's throne room.

The ark of the covenant is the one piece of furniture in the Most Holy Place (Exod 25:10–22). At the top of the ark is the cherubim throne of Yahweh, where He sits above the wings. Beneath the throne is a box, covered inside and outside with gold, a treasure chest. In the treasure chest are the tablets of the law, inscribed by the Spirit-finger of God; a jar of manna; and the staff of Aaron that budded and blossomed (Heb 9:4).

These are God's treasures, the treasures King Yahweh offers to His people: the bread of life, the wisdom of Torah, the guidance of a priest—food, word, and a shepherd. All these treasures are under the Lord's throne, but no one can go in to get them. Not the lay Israelite, not the priest, not even the high priest. Yahweh's treasures are locked away in His inner vault.

UNTIL ...

Until Jesus comes. Jesus offers Himself as a final sacrifice. He passes through death to resurrection life. He goes behind the veil into the throne room. He passes through the firmament and enters the original sanctuary, the heavenly one (Heb 9:11–22; 10:19–22).

He isn't a suppliant approaching the throne. He's the Conqueror, who takes the throne.

Jesus isn't descended from Aaron. He's from the tribe of Judah, not Levi. He's not qualified to enter the earthly temple. But He *is* a priest. He's a priest after the order of Melchizedek, qualified not by fleshly descent but by resurrection (Heb 7).

As a priest in the Melchizedekan order, Jesus enters a better sanctuary, the heavenly one. He doesn't come in through the blood of an animal; He sprinkles His own blood. He doesn't have to offer sacrifices again and again; He offers Himself, the sacrifice of complete obedience, once and for all.

Jesus doesn't stop His priestly work with His death on the cross. Jesus doesn't stop being Priest when He rises again, or ascends. He "ever lives" as priest, to make intercession, to lead us in worship, to be the chief singer of the choir of God (Heb 7:25).

Now, at last, there's a priest who won't stop being priest because He can't die. Now, at last, there's a sanctuary that won't be dismantled or move away because it's safe in heaven. And now, at last, we can receive the treasures God has stored up for us in His house. Having ascended on high, Jesus gives gifts to men (Eph 4:7–13), distributed through the Spirit, who equips the members of the church with gifts to edify the entire body.

Through the Spirit, we receive the true manna from heaven, the body and blood of the Lord Jesus. Through the Spirit, God speaks His word and so reveals His living Word. Through the Spirit, the minister guides us with the rod and staff of the Good Shepherd. Through the Spirit, He gives life, wisdom, and glory.

This is what happens in the Christian liturgy. We're no longer at a distance, out in the court. We gather in the throne room. Jesus is with us by His Spirit, and Jesus gives away His gifts. He girds Himself as He did in the upper room, and *He* serves *us*. Through the Spirit, He gives the gift of bread, the gift of word, the gift of a shepherd. In, with, and under all these gifts, the Spirit gives us the gift of joy. Food, word, shepherd: These gifts are joy incarnate.

Am I waxing mystical? In a sense, yes. Since God is active in the liturgy, there are things happening we can't explain. There's a kind of liturgical magic as the Lord takes up our places, our words, our sacrifices, our time-keeping and transforms them into anticipations of the heavenly city.

Culture isn't Christianized in the liturgy by some sociological process or ministerial manipulations. It's Christianized because it's touched by the magical finger of God.

Still, we can think about it concretely. If you were an Israelite in the temple courts, you'd never see bread set out on the table of showbread, much less manna from the ark. You'd never see the lampstand, much less the tablets of the law. You might glimpse some priests, but they'd keep disappearing through the veil and then reappearing.

Now, what do you see when you enter church? Okay, what *should* you see? There's a Bible up on a lectern—the completed word. Bread and wine are laid out on the table—manna. There's a man wearing a white robe at the front, leading worship—the pastor-shepherd. That can mean only one thing: You're *in*! You've entered the heavenly Most Holy Place. You're inside the ark of God.

What you *shouldn't* see is a barrier between you and the Bible. You shouldn't see a rail dividing the Lord's table from the congregation. You shouldn't see anything that sends the message you're on the outside. Because you're *not*. You're as far inside as you can get. You're in the throne room, and your Father is there with His Son and Spirit, to feed you, to speak to you, to guide you through the valley of the shadow.

You aren't just inside an earthly sanctuary. By the Spirit, heaven and earth join in the liturgy. You don't come to Sinai any more, with all its thunders and terrors. You *have* come—not will, but *have*—to another mountain, to the heavenly Zion (Heb 12:18–24). When you enter the church building, you're entering heaven. That's where the liturgy takes us, right into the throne room, into the presence of eternal joy.

This is at the heart of the good news of Jesus. The gospel announces Jesus the priest has entered the heavenly sanctuary and opened up a way for us to follow. The good news is that all the treasure of the throne room is distributed freely to Jesus' loyal disciples. The gospel is the good news of an open sanctuary. The gospel is an inherently *liturgical* gospel and so is inherently a gospel of joy.

You might be thinking, "Are you saying we go to church to *get* something from God? I thought we were supposed to *give* something to Him—praise, honor, glory. I thought worship was supposed to be *God*-centered."

If you're thinking that, you're catching the drift. That's just what I'm saying: We gather in the presence of God to *receive* His treasures. We go to church because of what we can *get* there. We gather in His presence because we want Him to share His joy.

Of course, there's a bad way to "go to get." If you go to church to get an emotional high, that's not healthy. If you go to church to have an experience, you're likely to be tossed around by your emotions. If you go to church because you think it's socially advantageous, you must be living in the 1950s.

But think about it: Do you *really* think that you have something to give to God? *Really*? If so, repent. You *don't*. You have nothing you haven't received. You have nothing He needs. Outside of church, we know that we can't do anything without God's grace. We can't believe, obey, trust, love, display the fruits of the Spirit without the Spirit's work in us. Let's stop being pious. Let's be real: You can't breathe, digest, urinate, defecate, or pump blood through your veins without the power of the Spirit.

Somehow, when we enter the church building, we become giddy Pelagians who think we can muster up something from our own riches. We think that we can bring treasures of our own and present them to God.

We *do* present ourselves as sacrifices (see chapter 3). But we do that only as a response to His gifts and treasures. That response is *itself* a gift. The liturgy is just like everything else: We give only because we have first received. We love because He first loved us. We rejoice because we receive joy.

That's God-centeredness, a proper God-centeredness, a *Triune* God-centeredness. The Triune God isn't glorified by keeping glory to Himself. The Father is glorified as He glorifies the Son in the Spirit, and the Son is lifted up by honoring the Father through the Spirit. We are properly God-centered, *Triunely* God-centered, when we receive the treasures He offers, when we accept the glory and joy of the Father so that we might glorify and delight Him and share His glory and joy with the world. We gather for the liturgy in order to receive the Father's gifted Spirit, who is the gift of joy.

Conclusion: On Liturgy

What have we discovered? We've discovered things about creation. Creation is a temple. Life is a dialogue. History moves in a sacrificial pattern of death and renewal. God created timekeepers to mark the appointed times when we enter the joy of the Bridegroom.

We've learned where creation is headed. One day, the new heavens and earth will be a civic temple, the heavenly Jerusalem. Life is dialogue, and one day we will all be Moses, who speaks to Yahweh mouth-to-mouth. The dialogue of history will be fulfilled in the Bridegroom's eternal kiss. One day, the sacrificial pattern of death and renewal will give way to endless life. One day, sun and moon will fade before the glory of God and the Lamb. One day, there will be joy, only joy, to ages of ages.

To say all that is to say *creation* is liturgical all the way down. To say all that is to say God moves creation toward a liturgical consummation.

We've learned things about culture too. Culture inescapably moves in the liturgical grooves of creation. Mimicking the divine architect, we build and adorn places within the place of creation. Made in the image of the Word, we carry on a dialogue within the cosmic dialogue between Creator and creation. Human history replicates the sacrificial movements of creation, and political communities are founded on and for sacrifice. We give communal shape to the created rhythms of time, setting aside moments to eat, drink, and rejoice.

To say all of this is to say that *culture* is inherently liturgical.

Teach me how you build, how you speak, what you will die and kill for. Show me your calendar and tell me the wellspring of your joy. Teach me this, and I will learn your culture. That is: Teach me your liturgy, so I can sing and sway along.

Liturgy crystallizes culture. Culture is the flowering of liturgy. Culture is liturgy stretched out into life. Culture is the liturgy of everyday life.

Culture is the bridge between beginning and end. God created a good but unfinished world and made us as His images to finish it. Through our building, speech, sacrifice, timekeeping, and joy, we glorify the creation. Through our cultural labors, creation moves toward consummation. Through *us*, the Spirit broods over the dark abyss and calls it into light.

We've learned things about the effects of sin. Since Adam sinned and brought death into the world, cultures have run at cross-purposes to the Creator and His creation. We build and adorn shrines to idols—Zeus and Molech, but also France and America and Mother Russia. We build to keep Untouchables and African Americans on the other side of the tracks. Our built culture, our organization of space, offends God. It doesn't glorify but perverts the good creation.

Human lies replace God's truth. Tyrants hard and soft force their subjects to immolate themselves to brute and mute idols of blood and soil and the Proletariat. Liberals and dictators rule time without honoring Jesus, Lord of ages. We're dazzled by the works of our hands and are seduced into seeking our joy in them.

Since Adam's sin, all the created patterns of culture—place, language, sacrifice, time, joy—are twisted. If there's going to be a cultural bridge from creation to consummation, culture has to be put right. Unless something is done, the liturgy of creation will dissolve into a formless void or a temple of terrors.

The gospel announces that something *has* been done. The Father sent the Son to live, die, rise, and ascend to harmonize culture with creation and the Creator and to direct it toward glory. The Father and Son poured out the Spirit to reestablish the created fit between God's works and ours. The liturgy is the Spirit's work to accomplish that mission.

Creation's liturgy stretches toward liturgical consummation. Human culture bridges the time between. But culture is a bridge from Jerusalem now to Jerusalem not yet only when it's purged and transfigured by incorporation into the divine service. A biblically-formed liturgy done by Spirit-filled and Spirit-led disciples *is* the first redemption of culture. Specifically:

Place: Creation is a temple, designed to grow from glory to glory until it becomes new Jerusalem. When we build a church for the worship of God, we're turning creation to its intended end. A gathered church, a church building that is a cultural product, anticipates the fulfillment of creation in the eschaton.

Dialogue: Language exists so God can speak to us and we can speak back. It exists so we can speak to one another in God, and speak from generation to generation. The liturgy uses language as it's designed to be used. It calls us into dialogue with the primary Speaker, which renews our speech to Him and one another.

Sacrifice: The sacrifice of praise unmasks the pretense of liberalism to live beyond sacrifice and subverts the violent sacrifices of ancient and modern despotisms. In the liturgy, we offer true human sacrifice, so that we may offer ourselves as witnesses in daily sacrifice.

Time: God created the heavens as a liturgical clock, but Adam's children put time out of joint. The liturgy re-orders our time, so our time-keeping is shaped by the life, death, resurrection, and ascension of Jesus, stamped with the rhythms of Triune life.

Joy: At the end of creation week, God enters into His joy and intends to invite us to share His joy. After Adam, we pursue false joys and pleasures. In the liturgy, we're re-directed from counterfeit joys into the delights of God, so that we can enjoy the creation as God's gift.

Liturgy doesn't stand outside the world. It takes place in the world. Or, better, the world, the true world and the new world, takes place and takes form in the liturgy. Liturgy transforms the world as it takes up creation and culture so they become a foretaste of the kingdom.

Part IV

Theopolitan Mission

Interlude: On Mission

Part 4, "Theopolitan Mission," is a companion to Part 3, "Theopolitan Liturgy." They're twin meditations on the relationship between liturgy and culture.

Part 3 explains how the liturgy is the initial Christianization of culture. Existing languages, customs, methods of time-keeping, uses of space, forms of sacrifice, symbols and social habits, gestures and rituals are brought into the liturgy to be transfigured by Word and Spirit. Latin and French and English become liturgical languages, refreshed by the poetry and truth of Scripture. Time is Christianized by church calendars and public space by church architecture. Social relations are transformed by rituals of communion that gather people from every tribe, clan, family, and race at a common table. Liturgy is the first transformation of culture. Liturgical culture is culture Christianized.

Part 4 moves in the opposite direction. In the following pages, I explain how the liturgical life of the church flows out as a rushing, mighty river to wash away sin-corrupted institutions and ways of life. The liturgy is a spring of the Spirit to refresh the world.

This section of *Theopolis Fundamentals* winds together three threads. The first is an exploration of human making. We make things because we're made in the image of a God who makes things. We image the Creator in our creativity, and in our creative making we also make ourselves. Since Adam, our making is damaged by sin. Instead of making good things, we mis-make; instead of beautifying creation, we corrupt it as we make sophisticated fig leaves to screen us from the scrutiny of God.

But God is faithful to us and to His creation. He won't let us ruin His world. He sends His Son, the Last Adam, to make a new creation. Jesus' first task is to remake sinners. We're remade as makers by becoming members of His body. The first thing we make is ourselves. By the power of the Spirit, we members of the body build the very body that we are; in Christ, we the Bride build the Bride. Through us, the remade humanity, Jesus fulfills His second task, remaking the creation. By His Spirit and His Word, at His table and among His people, Jesus restores us to right making so we can flow out to remake and glorify creation.

The second thread is about Noah and his ark. Noah is the first godly maker in Scripture. He obeys God's instructions for construction. Because it's made according to God's design, the ark is a vessel of salvation that preserves a micro-world of human beings, animals, birds, and creeping things. It contains the seeds of a new world, which are planted in the new earth after the flood. By building and filling and sailing the ark, Noah ascends to kingship. He's an artist and a craftsman and a gardener, a glorified Adam.

Jesus, the Carpenter of Nazareth, is the last and greater Noah. He builds a living ark from the crooked timber of humanity. By His Spirit, we build ourselves into a saving vessel, where the human race is safe from condemnation. Like Noah's ark, the ark of Jesus contains the treasures of the old world, which are the materials for a new world. As the world is repopulated and renewed by the humans and animals on the ark, so new cultural and political worlds continually emerge from the ark of Jesus' body, His Bride, the temple of His Spirit.

Thirdly, I fill out this meditation on making, mis-making, and right-making by attending to the book of Acts, the great missionary narrative of Scripture. The apostles lead an evangelistic campaign. They announce Jesus as King and establish churches in Jerusalem, Judea, Samaria, and the ends of the earth. Each church is an outpost of the heavenly sanctuary, a temple of the Spirit. By adopting the customs of the apostles—apostolic teaching, the breaking of bread, communion in Spiritual and material goods, continuous prayer—the church challenges and defeats the Satanic powers that rule the world. Because they're courageous witnesses, the apostles take over the Roman ship of state and pilot it through stormy seas, preparing a place where Jesus reigns. In short, the church's mission is the mission of man: to build God's temple in the world, then to remodel the world after the pattern of the sanctuary.

I worry that some parts Part 4 are abstract, but my aim is practical. If you're a Christian and a member of the church, the mission of Jesus is your mission. You're made to be a maker, remade as a maker when you were baptized into the Last Adam. Your witness, worship, and service build the body of Christ. Through your life and labor, Jesus restores and glorifies creation. It may seem little, but it's not. You've been enlisted into a construction project, than which none can be greater. So follow Solomon's counsel: "Whatever your hand finds to do, do it with all your might" (Eccl 9:10). For, as Paul says, "your labor is not in vain in the Lord" (1 Cor 15:58).

16

Making

IN THE BEGINNING GOD CREATED THE HEAVENS AND THE EARTH.
—GENESIS 1:1

God created man, male and female, in His own image, after His own likeness (Gen 1:26–27). What does that mean?

We get a clue from the following verse: "God said to them, 'Be fruitful and multiply, and fill the earth, and subdue it; and rule over the fish of the sea and over the birds of the heavens and over every living thing that swarms on the earth' " (Gen 1:28). God rules the world He created. Men and women image the Ruler by ruling His world.

We gather more clues in the preceding verses. By the time we get to Genesis 1:26, we know a lot about God. An image of God is like God. To figure out what it means to be made in the likeness of God, we should ask, "What is God like?"

First and foremost, God "creates" (Heb. *bara'*). That Hebrew verb is used seven times in the first two chapters of Genesis. God creates "the heavens and the earth" (Gen 1:1). He creates great sea monsters (Gen 1:21), and He creates—creates—creates man (Gen 1:27). On the Sabbath, God "rested from all the work which God had created and made" (Gen 2:3), and the next section of Genesis describes things generated by heaven and earth "when they were created" (Gen 2:4).

The Creator is a Maker. The verb "make" (Heb. *'asah*) is used ten times in Genesis 1, eight times with reference to things God makes—the firmament (Gen 1:7), the lights of the heavens (Gen 1:16), the beasts of the earth and cattle (Gen 1:25), man (Gen 1:26, 31). On the Sabbath, God rests from the "work which He had *made*," that is, "from all His work which He had *made*" (Gen 2:2). In case we don't get the point, the author adds, "He rested from all His work which God had created and *made*" (Gen 2:3).

As Athanasius observed, God's productivity and fruitfulness isn't accidental. He doesn't become productive when He creates. It's not as if God were eternally unfruitful and then became fruitful. The Father is eternally productive, eternally generating His Son who is His living Art and His Image. The Son is not created, but He is produced by the Breath and Power of the Spirit, the firstfruits of the Father's eternal creativity.

God is a Creator and Maker. If we're made in His likeness, we too are creators and makers. Made in His image, we're made to make.

MAN, THE MAKER

Christians sometimes minimize human creativity. "We don't make anything," they say. "We just rearrange what's already there." Maybe you've said it yourself.

Of course, there's a difference between God's making and ours. God says, "Light, please," and there's light where there's never been light before. He says, "Let the waters teem," and presto! they teem. He says, "Let us make man," and man is.

We can't do that. We can't create from nothing, simply by speaking. We always use pre-existing raw materials, which we receive as gifts from God. We break them down, mold them, and reassemble them. We don't make animals. We tame them, so they provide work and, eventually, food. We don't make trees. We plant them, cut them down, reshape the wood, and turn it into a shelter. We break and chisel God's stones to make blocks and bricks for temples and palaces. We shear God's sheep, spin their fleece into thread, and weave clothes. Or we wear God's plants—flax, linen, cotton.

God hid some of His most valuable treasures deep in the ground. We mine and smelt His metals to make tools; we dig up gold and polish precious stones to make jewelry. We plant and harvest wheat, grind it to flour, and mix it with other ingredients to make bread. We learn to cultivate grapes, crush them, and slowly ferment them into wine. Eventually, we turn sand into silicon chips and metal into cars and planes and oil into plastics. But we don't make wheat, grapes, sand, or oil. We simply transform them.

But we shouldn't over-stress the contrast between God's making and ours. After all, He doesn't make everything *ex nihilo*. He makes from pre-existing material too. God makes the formless void, He speaks light into existence, and He appears to make other things by pure *fiat*.

Overall, Genesis 1 shows God shaping and filling the dark, watery earth He creates in Genesis 1:1–2. He spends the first half of the week forming the formless void, giving it light and shape. He spends the second half of the week filling the spaces He forms. But He doesn't fill the world directly. Empowered by the creating Word, the world fills itself.

Trees and plants spring up because God speaks to earth: "Let the earth sprout vegetation" (Gen 1:11). Genesis doesn't say, "God said, 'Let there be vegetation,' and poof! there was vegetation." He speaks to earth, and earth produces grasses with grain and trees with fruit. God speaks to the seas, and the waters teem with living souls (Gen 1:20). The first living souls on earth aren't directly created by God's Word. Sea creatures swarm from Word-fertilized waters. Earth brings forth land animals (Gen 1:24). Human beings are the *least ex nihilo* of creatures. Yahweh forms Adam from the *'adamah* (earth), and He builds Eve, the *'ishshah*, from Adam, the *'ish* (Gen 2:7, 21–22).

In fact, once in Genesis 1, something other than God makes. On Day 3, God commands the earth to produce "fruit trees making fruit" (Gen 1:11–12). God makes trees, and trees can't bear fruit unless God speaks and gives them the power to do it. But don't miss the punch line: Empowered by the command of God, trees become Godlike. The Maker makes them, and then trees make fruit.

By the power of the Creator's Word, earth and sea produce all that is, and the things earth and sea produce continue to fill sea and earth, from God's first Word all the way to today. God doesn't make every single fruit tree or blade of grass that will ever exist during the creation week. He makes trees and grasses with *seed* (Gen 1:11), capable of reproducing themselves. He blesses sea creatures, birds, animals, and human beings with power to multiply, so as to fill the seas and the earth (Gen 1:22, 28). Filling is part of the creation process, and the world fills itself.

We can draw this rather astonishing conclusion: Creation participates in its own creation. God completes creation by giving creation power to complete itself. With infinite humility, the infinite God creates by giving creatures power to create.

Throughout Scripture, human beings are the most creative creatures, the most inventive makers. Adam and Eve make loin cloths to cover themselves (Gen 3:7). Noah makes an ark (Gen 6:14–22; *'asah* is used seven times). Abraham makes altars (Gen 13:4), and Sarah makes bread when visitors approach her tent (Gen 18:6–8). Yahweh's Spirit equips Bezalel and Oholiab to make the furnishings of the tabernacle (Exod 31:6, 11), and Solomon makes the temple (1 Kgs 7:51).

Human makings are complex. Cain builds a city and calls it by the name of his firstborn, Enoch (Gen 4:17). No doubt, Cain's city has walls to protect him from avengers (Gen 4:14). It has residents and residences. It has some sort of political order—a town meeting, government by selected rulers, a king. The residents speak the same language, so they can dicker in the market, teach their children, share the day's events of an evening. They adopt common customs of dress, food, work. To live together peaceably, they develop common habits of life and common moral standards. Like most ancient cities, it's likely organized around a civic religion, with a temple and its altar on the central agora.

Cain's descendants produce other new things. Lamech takes two wives, initiating a millennia-long experiment in alternative marriage. Jabal tames livestock, and his brother Jubal is "father of all those who play the lyre and pipe" (Gen 4:20–21). Another son of Lamech, Tubal-cain, invents metallurgy, becoming the first "forger of implements of bronze and iron" (Gen 4:22).

Each of these inventions replicates God's way of making. He lights and forms and fills. So do we. We make plans for a house, then frame, roof, and close it in; then we furnish it and, we hope, fill it with joy and life. A dark and unformed patch of the world takes visible shape. We plot out the yard, plow up a garden patch, then fill it with seeds that, we hope, will fill the patch with vegetables. We have a bright idea that leads to a business plan. Over time, we fill out the form by finding investors and partners, hiring employees, purchasing equipment, filling an office or a factory. Light, form, fill. Just like God.

To be the image of God is to be a working, making creature. To be the image of God is to be a cultural being, always engaged in forging a man-made world within the God-made creation. Enlivened by the Breath of God, commissioned by His Word, we are created to be creative.

I've been saying God uses pre-existing materials to create and make, just as we do. God forms and fills, and so do we. We can see a similarity from the opposite direction too. God makes new things. So do we. Of course, we first receive God's gifts, but when we've reassembled them, we've made new things, entirely new things, entirely new categories of things. A table isn't merely a rearrangement of wood. It's a table, the sort of human creation that doesn't exist in nature, a created thing God didn't create during the six days. When we've learned to spin metals into filaments, and to harness electricity, and to blow glass, we can make a new thing: an electric light.

Think about the humble art of spoon-making, as Nicholas of Cusa invited us to do long ago. There are no spoons in nature, and it's weird to think The Form of Spooniness is secretly hidden within chunks of wood or lumps of metal (along with the Forms of Chairness, Tableness, Coffeetableness). When a man carves a wooden spoon, he's not drawing out a "potential" spoon that's already there in the wood. He's perfecting the wood by bringing something entirely new to birth. He gives the wood a new form, so as to make it a new thing. Spoon-making is a Little Bang, a faint reverberation on God's original *fiat*.

We're creative because God is creative. More than we realize, we're creative in the same way God is creative.

ANIMALS AND ARTISTS

I hear an objection: Animals make things too. Beavers make dams. Birds and wasps build nests. Fire ants dig intricate tunnels, the better to attack our bare feet. All these animals create things that didn't come directly from God's hand. Beavers, birds, and wasps give new forms to created things.

Animals make tools too. Apes use twigs to hunt and collect honey, rocks to break nuts, leaves to collect water, sticks to ward off enemies. Chimps strip leaves from twigs to make them suitable for fishing, and other primates have been spotted making moss "sponges" to scrub down their mates. Some fish beat oysters against rocks to open them, and octopi have been known to settle in discarded coconut shells.

Those are impressive achievements and prove that animals share some of the creativity of the Creator. When all is said and done, though, human making is quite different. Think about the difference between human and animal tools. We need food, water, shelter, air, and we make things to help us meet those needs. Tools are conveniences. Strictly speaking, we don't need implements to plow, plant, harvest, winnow, and grind. We could dig with our hands, harvest by pulling up plants, grind wheat by stomping on it with heavy boots (but then the boots would be tools!). We could twist wool into thread with our fingers and weave the thread without a loom.

Maybe, but we've never done that. We've always been tool-making creatures, not because tools meet our needs directly but because tools make the work of meeting our needs so much more efficient. Tools extend our created powers. I can jump (barely), but if I want to get to Albania, I can't rely on my innate powers of propulsion. I can run (barely), but I can't run to visit my grandkids in Idaho, Washington, or coastal Georgia.

We make tools, but then tools recoil and make us. Use a tool for a time, and it stops feeling like an add-on. An experienced carpenter uses his hammer and saw as parts of his body. To a sedentary theologian like me, the keyboard is critical to my thinking process and sometimes feels more critical than my brain. If brain scientists are to be believed (I think they are), my brain changes as I use the keyboard. We're both tool-making and tool-made creatures. Our makings make us.

Besides, many things we make with tools aren't necessary for survival. Mill stones and ovens are necessary to bake bread, but we don't need bread to keep our biological machine sputtering along. We could, like Jesus' disciples, live on what we rub from ears of grain. We don't need the tools of wine-making because we don't need wine. Who needs to go to Albania, Idaho, or Georgia anyway? If we had to run everywhere, my grandkids wouldn't be living in Idaho and Georgia in the first place. My computer is the product of a vast and complex sequence of theories, experiments, designs, and manufacture. But who needs it? Give a real poet a soft clay tablet and a stylus, and he can cuneiform an epic. For that matter, who needs to write?

Our making has a uniquely Godlike character. God makes the world He doesn't need. He doesn't dwell in temples made by hands. He isn't served by human hands, as if He needed our help. He gives everything life and breath, for in Him we live and move and exist (Acts 17:24–28). God makes the world out of sheer delight in making, out of a sheer desire to share His life and glory with creatures. Creation is gratuitous all the way down and all the way in. At the inner core, everything God makes is a gift.

No animal makes like that. No animal has made even so simple a tool as a screwdriver, and all animal tools have a direct relation to the animal's basic need for food, water, and shelter. Animals don't adorn. Birds build nests for shelter and to store eggs, but there are no schools of ornithological architecture. Beavers don't put solariums on their dams, and no bear decorates his den with wall paintings commemorating his hunting exploits. No animal makes for the sake of making.

That is how human beings, made in the image of God, make. Perhaps especially in the modern age, we're surrounded by gratuity, a surfeit of unnecessary comforts and ornaments. Perfumes and potpourri suffuse the air. Colors and shapes catch our eyes. Composers organize tones and harmonies to tickle our ears. We surround ourselves with textured surfaces and mix spices to inflame our tongues. We make playfully, for the sheer delight of making. Our making is erotic, driven by desire for beauty, truth, goodness, and ultimately, by a desire to imitate the God whom we image.

Even when we make useful things, we're not content with mere utility. We don't just make chairs or tables, but well-crafted chairs and tables; not just shelters, but cozy or majestic shelters; not just clothing, but colored clothing with alluring patterns and pictures; not just machines of transport, but flying machines that thrill us and make us feel alive; not just walls and roofs, but painted walls, hung with more paintings, and ceilings; not just communication devices, but communication devices with smooth edges and elegant not-quite-buttons; not just food, but aesthetically pleasing food. For goodness' sake, these days we design boxes. Animals play, but no animal can invent cricket or basketball. Animals do wondrous things, but, as Samuel Johnson said, no beast is a cook.

We spend a lot of time and energy maintaining things we make. Once we build a bridge, we need to defend it from use and erosion. Ignored buildings crumble, old tools break, untended gardens are overrun with weeds, paint fades. Our makings aren't once-for-all. But neither are God's. He makes, and He providentially cares for the things He makes. He is Creator and Caretaker. Our maintenance work, like our creative work, is Godlike.

Human making verges toward art. Our work aims at glorifying, beautifying, and enhancing creation and human life.

Making *per se* isn't unique to the image of God. God-like making and gratuitous creativity: These are unique to the image of God. To be the image of God is to be an artist. Artifice isn't an add-on to human nature. It is our nature.

Art, in turn, makes the artist. That's true in a trivial sense: A painter is someone who paints, a composer someone who composes music, a poet someone who writes poems, a cook is someone who cooks. But art makes the artist in more profound ways. We dwell within our makings, and our cultural creations mold our experience of the world. When the public square is filled with ugly, brutal buildings, we're liable to be anxious, fearful, depressed. When our lived space is full of flowers and trees, we encounter the beauties and joys of creation. When our city is adorned with pillars and spires stretching toward the firmament, our spirits strain for heaven. A dark, formless, empty home will bear different fruit than one that's bright, ordered, and filled with things of beauty.

Man is created as priest to preside at a cosmic liturgy. All our makings are surrounded by praise and thanksgiving. We receive God's created gifts with thanks so that we can re-create them, giving them fresh forms, new uses, enhanced beauty. Then we present the products of our making with thanks and praise. Our making begins in Sabbath and moves toward Sabbath. It's the middle term between first thanks and final thanks, between the rest of the first day and the final rest of the new creation. One day, in union with the Last Adam, we shall deliver up all things to our Father in an eternal act of thanksgiving, an eternal Eucharist.

Empowered by the Word, earth becomes more fully itself by bringing forth plants. Seas become more fully seas by teeming with sea creatures. Trees are fulfilled as trees by producing fruit. We are earth and trees, and so our makings, gifted by the Spirit, are also self-makings. Made to make, we make ourselves by what we make.

TALKING ANIMAL

Anthropologists tell us that human beings begin as natural beings and evolve into culture. That's one source for the euphoria surrounding every small hint that animals use tools.

It proves the distance between human beings and other creatures isn't as great as we think. Chimps aren't inferior. They're just running a few million years behind and may catch up if human beings stall out.

Scripture tells us the opposite. God breathes life into Adam's nostrils to make him a living soul. He plants the garden, then whisks Adam into it (Gen 2:7–8). A garden is full of natural things, but it doesn't occur unless an intelligent someone organizes natural things into rows and circles and labyrinths. God plants the garden (Gen 2:8) with a gate to the east (Gen 3:24).

Paradise means a bounded enclosure. Solomon describes his beloved as a garden locked, a paradise of pomegranates (Song 4:13; cf. Eccl 2:5). Jesus promises the Ephesians they will eat the tree of life in the Paradise of God (Rev 2:7), a renewed Eden. Adam's first moments are spent watching God organize His park, and then he's placed in that park. Not for a moment is he in a state of nature. Not for a second is he a purely natural being. Culture comes naturally to man.

Before his first day is over, Adam is using language. He doesn't begin with Neanderthal grunts. He doesn't point and gesture. He uses words. This is another sign Adam is made in the image of God. God is Speaker as well as Maker. He makes by speaking. Ten times, Genesis 1 repeats, "And God said." God speaks light into existence, and a firmament, and a division of waters (Gen 1:3, 6, 9). He calls on the land to produce plants (Gen 1:11) and speaks lights into the heavens (Gen 1:14). He deliberates with Himself before making man, male and female, according to His image and likeness (Gen 1:26–27). Over the course of history, God's crowning work will be to bring man to his full realization as His image and likeness. After He speaks light, He calls it light (Gen 1:5). After He examines ("sees") what He makes, He judges it good—not an explicitly verbal act but an act of evaluation. Beginning on Day 5, He blesses creatures of the sea (Gen 1:21), then man (Gen 1:28), then the Sabbath day (Gen 2:3).

The New Testament reveals the fuller truth: God doesn't just speak, but is Word (John 1:1–3). The speaking God makes man in His own image and likeness, a speaking creature who can talk back to Him in prayer, praise, conversation, argument. The God who is Word makes human beings by His Word in the image of His Word, so we're equipped to make words and sentences and dramas and epic poems as well as things. I hear that objection again: Animals communicate. Birds and monkeys signal with sounds. Scouting bees dance their buzzy dance to pass information to the drones. Your watchdog barks when he sniffs an intruder. But human language is of a different order altogether. No animal talks or writes. Animals can come to know their names. No animal assigns names.

Adam uses language to take hold of the world and make it his own. His first act of rule is to name the animals (Gen 2:19). It is a Godlike act of calling things by name (cf. Gen 1:5, 8, 10). Adam fulfills the creation pattern in miniature, as observer and participant. God lights, forms, fills, names. So do we. We shape and fill the world and then give names to our creations. In His infinite humility, God receives our naming as His own. God names only a handful of things. The rest He leaves to Adam. Whatever Adam calls something, it bears that name, both for Adam and for God (Gen 2:19; cf. Gen 2:23 with 3:15). What does God call a laptop? There's no mystery. He calls it a laptop. What does God call me? He honors my parents by calling me "Peter." What does God call you?

By naming, Adam both classifies and discovers, for he learns there is no animal helper suitable to him. It's likely Adam verbalizes created features of animals. There's something elephanty about the elephant; the mammoth is truly mammoth, and what else would you call a creature so strange as a platypus? At base, though, Adam creates names the same way he creates everything else: He makes them up, *ex nihilo*, as it were. His words don't just mirror the world. God's speech is creative. Adam's names make the world into a human world, made meaningful by human speech. Without Adam's names, the world remains un-verbalized, still formless and void.

Have you ever traveled in a foreign country, where all the signs and voices speak an unknown tongue? Disoriented, were you? Think of being plopped into the middle of a completely different world, surrounded by gadgets and gizmos you don't recognize. Are you fearful? Anxious? Giving names makes the world familiar and friendly, a human world submissive to the dominion of Adam and Eve. We inhabit a human world when we inhabit a named world.

To repeat my theme yet again: Creatures share in fulfilling creation. The human mission is to co-create creation. The world is meaningful because it's the product of the Word. But we don't merely discover meaning in creation. Meaning is always meaning-for-someone. The world has meaning-for-us when we're able to name it. In the image of the divine Word, we make creation meaningful.

Human beings are created to be priests who preside at a cosmic Eucharist. We receive the world from God, glorify, name, and fill it with meaning so we can offer it back to God. Our naming is the middle term between first and final thanks. Like our making, our naming begins in worship and is directed toward worship, the alpha and omega of human culture. The world we form by our hands and tongues is fulfilled in the liturgy.

Adam speaks again after Yahweh builds Eve. He names her (Gen 2:23; cf. 3:20), but the initial naming occurs in a burst of ecstatic poetry. With a flourish, he calls the woman "bone from my bones, flesh from my flesh." In the Bible, bone and flesh means kinship (cf. 2 Sam 5:1; 19:12–13). Here, finally, Adam says, is a helper who shares my bones and flesh. Though the grammar is different, the phrase resembles superlatives like holy of holies, which means most holy place, or song of songs, which means best song ever. Adam calls Eve bone of my bone and flesh of my flesh because he recognizes her as a glorified version of his flesh and bones. Adam glimpses what Paul explicitly declares: The "woman is the glory of man" (1 Cor 11:7).

Adam ends his poem with a play on words, which works as well in English as in Hebrew: She shall be called "woman" (*'ishshah*) because she was taken from "man" (*'ish*). Adam is only a few hours old, and he's already making puns (a sign, perhaps, that humanity is doomed from the outset). Adam speaks as God speaks: freely, gratuitously, not because he needs to speak but to say something lovely and good and true. Only human beings do this because only we are made in the image of God. Only we adorn our communication with metaphors and similes, with rhymes and rhythms, with music and dance. Animals communicate, but no beast is a poet. Animals make sounds, but there's no animal orchestra.

Before the beginning, God the Father generates His image, the Son (Col 1:15). In the beginning, He makes Adam and Eve as His image. Made in the image of God's image, we're image-makers, symbolic creatures. We grasp the world through linguistic symbols. When it dawns on Helen Keller that the cool liquid she touches is water, she doesn't just get a name. She gets the thing. The Word delivers the world. Linguistic symbols form a shared world. When I tell you, "That is water," the substance becomes water for both of us.

Symbols make human society possible. We commune with one another by communing together in symbols. We say "we" because we are creatures of symbols. Every society, Augustine says, is knit together by shared signs and sacraments. Because we make and share symbols, we can be more than a pack or a herd. Speaking together, we form one thing, a body. Symbols enable us to share ideas. As symbol-makers, we can con-celebrate the cosmic Eucharist. Sharing common symbols, we mimic the divine society of Father, Son, and Spirit.

Over time, word and thing become inseparable. I don't think of the word water as a label pasted on an anonymous liquid. The liquid is water, and we experience it as actually, naturally watery. The symbol contains the thing, and the thing seems to embody the symbol—a mutual indwelling that echoes the mutual indwelling of the Father and His Image, the Speaker and the Word He breathes. We inhabit the world we symbolize as our symbols inhabit us. We make ourselves in making our symbols.

MIS-MAKING

Almost at once, it all goes wrong. Adam speaks the first human words, but the next voice we hear isn't Eve's. It's the serpent's. Instead of using language to praise God and name His creatures, the serpent exploits language's capacity for duplicity and deception. He exaggerates God's prohibition, making God out to be a cheap Creator who won't share good things with His creatures: "Has God said, 'You shall not eat from any tree of the garden?'" (Gen 3:1). He contradicts God: "You surely shall not die" (Gen 3:4; cf. 2:17). He tells partial truths (Gen 3:5)—Adam's and Eve's eyes are opened, and they become as gods (Gen 3:7, 22)—but he uses truth to tempt.

Eve corrects the serpent's initial misrepresentation (Gen 2:2–3), but after she inspects the fruit, she concludes it's "desirable to make one wise" (Gen 3:6). Satan's temptation works. The woman is deceived (1 Tim 2:14). She gives the fruit to Adam, who is with her the whole time, and he eats (Gen 3:6).

Immediately, they begin to mis-make. They see they're naked, vulnerable to God's scrutiny, so they sew fig leaves to make aprons (Gen 3:7; Heb. *'asah*). It's the first human artifact, a potent symbol of our distorted, fallen creativity. Instead of re-creating creation as an offering to God, we remake creation to shield us from God's presence. We design and build elaborate cultural, political, social, economic systems to keep God at a distance so He'll leave us to ourselves. We'll do nearly anything to keep ourselves from standing naked before God, anything to save us from that shame. Much of our cultural production are no more than sophisticated, ingenious, but ultimately useless fig-leaf aprons.

Adam and Eve mis-make because their hearts are damaged. They sin and are alienated from God. They don't make according to God's Word but in response to Satan's lies. Since the fall, our makings express our rebellion. It works in the other direction too. The things we make and the words we speak further entrench us in rebellion. Misshapen works come from deformed workers; misshapen works further deform the shaper. We are mis-made by our mis-makings.

When Yahweh arrives in the garden, Adam and Eve talk to Him for the first time. It's not pretty. In answer to Yahweh's question, Adam says he's afraid and hides (Gen 3:9–10), a truthful but tragic response. When Yahweh asks if he ate from the tree, Adam turns accuser and points the finger at Eve (Gen 3:12). Designed as an instrument of praise and dominion, designed to grasp, beautify, and give meaning to creation, language becomes another set of protective fig leaves. The tongue becomes a sword. Adam uses words satanically, to undo communion. Instead of joining Adam and Eve in con-celebration, distorted symbols tear them asunder.

Adam comes from earth and works the ground, but Yahweh will make his work more difficult: "Cursed is the ground in relation to you. ... Both thorns and thistles it shall grow for you. ... By the sweat of your nose you shall eat bread" (Gen 3:17–19; my translation). Adam will still work in the world, but the world won't cooperate. Alongside grass yielding seed and trees making fruit, earth will bristle with hurtful weeds. Instead of sending down the heavenly rain, the sky will become an iron dome over a bronzed earth (Lev 26:19). Men seek to domesticate animals, but animals kick against the goads. Men build cities only to see them collapse before earthquakes, tsunamis, hurricanes. Men create worlds designed to push God out, but the world is on God's side and rips our flimsy barriers to shreds. We still work toward Sabbath, but now Sabbath becomes a blessed respite from the rat race.

Yahweh's curse isn't just about natural obstacles and disasters. Plants symbolize human beings. Tall, sturdy, fruitful trees portray righteous men (Ps 1:3). Fruitful vines are fruitful women (Ps 128:3). Grains produce chaff, scattered like the wicked (Ps 1:4). Thorns and thistles are dangerous and unproductive human beings, the kind of men who aspire to kingship (Judg 9:7–15), who provide kindling for wildfires (Exod 22:6; cf. Jas 3:5–6), who pierce the heels of the righteous (Isa 27:4; cf. Gen 3:15).

Other people are the primary obstacles to creative making. Lies, slander, and gossip form us into monstrous bodies, a war of organs, all against all. Jezebel pays false witnesses to sway a court against Naboth so Ahab can seize Naboth's vineyard (1 Kgs 21). The wealthy bribe judges to get favorable treatment in disputes over land and rights. Landowners add house to house, squeezing out their neighbors (Isa 5:8–10). Powerful companies lobby and bully to drive small craftsmen out of business. Brutal shepherd-kings devour the flocks they're supposed to guard. Humanity's cultural mission is un-made by social disorder and by political and economic injustice. If our making is going to be remade, people need to be remade according to the Word.

Eve is cursed in regard to childbirth ("I will greatly multiply your pain in childbirth") and in her relationship with her husband (Gen 3:16). These strike at the heart of Eve's role in the human mission. Among other things, women are called to join with men to fill the earth, but barrenness, miscarriages, and the trauma of labor make that mission more difficult. Eve is created to be a harmonious helper to Adam, but their relationship becomes dissonant. Men follow Adam in failing to guard and then blaming women; women seek to manipulate the men around them.

Grim mis-making continues throughout Scripture. Cain kills his brother and then proceeds, like Romulus, to build a city (Gen 4:1–17). We aren't told anything about life in the city of Cain, but we can surmise it wasn't full of justice and peace. No city founded on the blood of victims can be stable. Cain's descendants show supreme creativity, inventing herding, music, metallurgy, tool-making, as well as politics. But their making is destructive. Jubal doesn't play his lyre and pipe to praise the Creator, Jabal doesn't raise sacrificial animals to offer to Yahweh, and Tubal-cain makes deadly weapons as well as tools to cultivate the earth.

God destroys the world in the flood, but within a few generations after the flood, human beings are right back to mis-making. The men of Babel build a city and a tower to connect heaven and earth. Most of all, they want to make a name (Gen 11:4), which they do, though not the name they hope for (Gen 11:9). That construction project ends when God confuses their language and worship and scatters them over the face of the earth. Babel intensifies the abuses of language that began in Eden.

As speaking and making are perverted, society becomes oppressive and wicked. The major city in Abraham's time is Sodom, a city of sexual perversion, an inhospitable city that welcomes strangers by gang-raping them (Gen 19). In Egypt, Assyria, Aram, Babylon, and Persia, human beings use their Godlike creativity to make cities of death. We devote our human creativity to an inhuman mission of de-creation.

Still today, we devote our ingenuity to making idols. We use linguistic symbols to deceive and sow hatred, to slander and to blame. We fly flags and manipulate national symbols to justify killing and stealing. Human beings invent a magical entity called money, then use it to control, exploit, cover crime, purchase injustice. Our music and art don't enhance the beauty and truth of things but seduce or attempt to convince us of the world's fundamental ugliness. We create under the sign of Abaddon and Apollyon (Rev 9:11). Our mis-made makings unmake the world, and, in unmaking the world, we unmake ourselves.

THE CARPENTER

We don't know how long Cain or any of his descendants lived. But we know the ages of all of Adam's descendants through Seth (Gen 5:1–32), including Methuselah, the oldest man on record (Gen 5:25–26). We can't construct a chronology from Cain's genealogy, but we can from Seth's. Cain's descendants make all the discoveries, but time is on Seth's side.

When the descendants of Seth (the "sons of God") intermarry with the descendants of Cain (the "daughters of men"), things go from bad to worse (Gen 6:1–4). The godly influence of Seth's line wanes, and the world becomes utterly Cainite. Strong men dominate (Gen 6:4). Wickedness becomes great (Gen 6:5). Imagination, so crucial for human creativity, is only evil continually (Gen 6:5; KJV). God regrets making man and destroys the world.

The world is saved by a carpenter. Noah is the first rightmaker in human history, a true heir of Adam. He makes according to the Word of Yahweh (Gen 6:13–16): "Noah made (*'asah*); according to all God commanded him, thus he made (*'asah*)" (Gen 6:22; my translation). Instead of making aprons of figs to screen himself from God, he makes an ark of wood in obedience to God. God's Word is the inner essence of Noah's makings. Noah is another Abel, a godly Jabal, who gathers animals and cares for them within the ark (Gen 6:27–21). The ark is a saving vessel, a miniature world, a rescue pod filled with the seeds of a new world. Through this saving vessel, Noah not only escapes the flood but reaches a higher plane of human maturity. He renews humanity's priestly task as he offers the firstfruits of the new creation to Yahweh as an ascension offering. But Noah isn't just Adam redux. He's a new and better Adam, a royal Adam, enjoying Sabbath wine.

Noah the carpenter saves the world, but soon enough, men begin mis-making again. Yet Noah is a sign of hope, a type of another and greater Carpenter (cf. Matt 13:55; Mark 6:3), who makes another saving vessel according to the pattern of the Word—a saving vessel made of people who will serve as a nursery of a renewed creation.

17

Carpenter

IS THIS NOT THE CARPENTER'S SON?
—MATTHEW 13:55

Jesus is the new and greater Noah. He comes at the fullness of time, when storm clouds are ready to burst. A flood is coming (Matt 24:48–49), one that will destroy the ancient world. Roman armies will soon dismantle the temple and burn Jerusalem, and Rome herself will be shaken to her foundations.

The Carpenter of Nazareth (Matt 13:55; Mark 6:3) builds a vessel of salvation to carry the world through the end of the age into a new age. To remake creation, Jesus has to remake us. He doesn't build an ark of wood, but harvests from the forest of humanity. He planes, shapes, and assembles a human ark. He remakes us as God created the world, as Noah made the ark: He makes according to the Word of His Father.

Jesus makes a saving vessel because He is Himself a saving vessel. His cross is a new ark, sheltering humanity from storm and fire and offering safe passage to a newer world. Joined to the cross, built according to the pattern of the eternal Word, the church becomes the saving ark for all nations and for creation itself.

SCRIPTED MISSION

Jesus is the Word of His Father, Himself the blueprint of His own construction project. He's the "heavenly man" (1 Cor 15:48–49), the Word made flesh (John 1:14). Moses goes to the mountain to see the pattern for the tabernacle (Exod 25:9, 40). Yahweh reveals the temple pattern to David (1 Chr 28:19). Jesus is the heavenly pattern, now descended from the mountain into full view of all. He builds a people-ark by impressing the pattern of His own character, His own life, death, and resurrection, on the lives of His disciples. He makes His ark from small-c "christs."

For Jesus and the apostles, Jesus the living Word is the key to and content of the written Word. After His resurrection, Jesus teaches His disciples everything concerning Himself in all the Scriptures. The main story of the Bible, He says, is this: The Christ will suffer and rise from the dead on the third day so that forgiveness and repentance can be preached to the gentiles (Luke 24:25–27, 44–49). His life, death, and new life are scripted by Scripture. He remakes us by orchestrating our lives to repeat His, by scripting our lives the way His life was scripted. He scripts our lives by Scripture, even as He is scripted.

Jesus accomplishes this through the Spirit. Throughout the Old Testament, the Spirit equips leaders to carry out their mission. The Spirit clothes judges so they can deliver Israel from her enemies (Judg 6:34; 11:29; 14:6, 19). The Spirit rushes on Saul so he can fight and defeat the Ammonites at Jabesh-gilead (1 Sam 10:10; 11:6). The Spirit comes on David to battle the evil spirit that plagues Saul, to fight Goliath, to give him patient hope as he waits for Yahweh to give him the kingdom (1 Sam 16:13–16). The Spirit takes hold of prophets so they can write the Word of the Lord (Ezek 2:2; 3:12–14).

The Spirit does the same in the new covenant. He writes the law on our hearts (2 Cor 3:3), encourages us (Acts 9:31), intercedes for us as we cry "Abba, Father" (Rom 8:26–28). The Spirit also clothes and equips us for mission. The apostles receive the Spirit of Jesus so they can continue to do what Jesus did. They receive the Spirit so they might become the body of Jesus,

Jesus' presence and action in the world. By the same Spirit, the Greater Noah shapes us into a new humanity.

From the day of Pentecost on, the Spirit of the risen Jesus is the Spirit of resurrection and new creation. The Spirit rushes on the disciples like a mighty wind (Acts 2:2), like the wind of the Spirit who hovers over formless depth at the beginning (Gen 1:1–2). The Spirit comes like Yahweh entering the garden in the "Spirit of the day" (Gen 3:8; my translation), not to curse but to bless. The Spirit begins remaking His world by remaking the makers who are His image.

Speaking by the breath of the Spirit, the disciples speak other languages. Luke writes a little table of nations (Acts 2:9–11), an echo of the table of nations in Genesis 10. The Spirit performs a miracle of tongues, like the miracle of tongues at Babel (Gen 11). Instead of confusing languages, the Spirit makes it possible for people with different languages to understand one another. Instead of scattering, the Spirit gathers people from all tribes and tongues into one body. Yahweh promises Abraham his seed will bless the gentiles, and the Spirit of Pentecost is the promised blessing. Since Eden, human beings have misused linguistic symbols. Through the Pentecostal Spirit, language is restored to its original purpose, to facilitate communion rather than to spread chaos and conflict. Pentecost replicates Babel in order to undo Babel.

As Acts unfolds, the Spirit molds the apostles' lives to the scripted life of the heavenly Man. Jesus receives the Spirit at His baptism; the apostles receive the Spirit at Pentecost. Filled with the Spirit, Jesus preaches and performs signs; filled with the Spirit, the apostles preach and perform wonders in Jerusalem. The scribes, Pharisees, and priests oppose Jesus; the same Jewish elites oppose the apostles. Jesus is arrested and crucified, but rises again. Peter and John are tossed into prison, but are miraculously released to return to their mission, an echo of death-and-resurrection (Acts 5:17–21). By the Spirit, Jesus scripts our lives according to the Scriptures, the Scriptures that reveal Him.

Luke sees the apostolic age as a replay of Joshua's conquest. At the beginning of the book of Joshua, Moses has departed (Josh 1:1–2); at the beginning of Acts, Jesus leaves His disciples. Joshua leads Israel and performs the same signs as Moses (e.g., splitting waters, Josh 3:5–17); Jesus' disciples receive His Spirit and perform the same signs as their Master. Joshua surrounds and destroys the leading city of the land, Jericho (Josh 6); the apostles conquer Jerusalem, Judea, Samaria, and the uttermost parts of the earth. At the battle of Ai, Achan grabs and hides plunder (Josh 7); Ananias and Sapphira lie to the Holy Spirit about their donation (Acts 5:1–16). Joshua is deceived into letting the gentile Gibeonites join Israel (Josh 9); gentiles join the Jewish apostles without deception. Joshua conquers the land and then distributes it to Israel as an inheritance. The apostles extend the kingship of Jesus all the way to Rome, claiming the inheritance of Abraham, heir of the world (Rom 4:13).

The Spirit directs the mission of the church by nudging them from place to place. By the Spirit, Peter unmasks the deception of Ananias and Sapphira (Acts 5:3, 9). The Spirit tells Philip to run up to the Ethiopian eunuch's chariot (Acts 8:29), then snatches him away to another place (Acts 8:39). The Spirit doesn't just accompany the apostles, but goes before them, breaking new ground, producing new fruit. When the Spirit falls on the household of Cornelius (Acts 10–11), Peter and other Jews are astonished. They recognize the Spirit has been poured out on gentiles as well as Jews, and they respond by baptizing Cornelius and his house. It's a lesson for us too: If we keep in step with the Spirit, we'll find ourselves breathless, rushing to catch up to the Spirit who is always ahead, always surprising.

Wherever the apostles go, they do signs and wonders. Peter and John are wonder-workers (Acts 4:30; 5:12). So are Stephen (Acts 6:8) and Philip (Acts 8:13) and Paul (Acts 14:3; 15:12; 19:11). They aren't just imitating Jesus. Moses was the first to do "signs and wonders" in the land of Egypt (Exod 7:3; 11:9–10; Deut 4:34; 6:22; 7:19), which warned Pharaoh of his approaching doom. The apostles learn from Jesus that the end of the age is coming soon (Matt 24), and their signs and wonders point to that fast-approaching end.

Jesus tells His disciples they will do greater things than He did because Jesus goes to the Father and sends the Spirit (John 14:12). Jesus keeps His promise. Filled by the Spirit with the resurrection power of Jesus, they heal the lame (Acts 3:1–8), raise the dead (Acts 9:36–43), give sight (Acts 9:17) and blind (Acts 13:8–11), cast out spirits (Acts 16:16–18). Jesus does all those things, but Jesus never converts three thousand on one day (Acts 2:41–42), never heals the sick with His passing shadow as Peter does (Acts 5:14–16), never heals or expels demons with a handkerchief as Paul does (Acts 19:10–12).

Over and over, early Christian leaders relive the life of Jesus, differently. Stephen performs wonders and bests his opponents in debate (Acts 6:8–10). Mad with jealousy, the elders and scribes stir up the people against him and find false witnesses to accuse him of speaking against Moses and the temple (Acts 6:11–14). After Stephen accuses them of being prophet-killers, they prove him right by stoning him (Acts 7:51–58). Sound familiar? If not, the climax of the story will: As Stephen dies, he echoes the words of Jesus from the cross: "Lord Jesus, receive my spirit," and "Lord, do not hold this sin against them!" (Acts 7:59–60; cf. Luke 23:34, 46).

Peter's final apostolic adventure follows Jesus step-by-step (Acts 12:1–17). Herod seizes Peter and throws him into prison. That night, an angel appears and opens the prison. When Peter arrives at the house where the disciples are praying for him, a woman comes to the door. She reports Peter is free, but no one believes her. Finally, they let Peter in, and he tells them what happened and leaves. Imprisonment, miraculous release, appearance to a woman, report to the disciples, departure: Readers of Luke's gospel have seen it all before. It's a variation on the theme of Jesus' death, resurrection, appearances, and departure to His Father. Jesus the Carpenter makes Peter according to the blueprint of the Word, which is the pattern of Jesus. Like Jesus, Peter is scripted by Scripture.

Paul's life also repeats the life of Jesus. Like Jesus, Paul is a divine warrior, carrying out the new covenant war of utter destruction, eager to cast down every idol. Paul could slip in and out of cities without anyone noticing. He doesn't. When he arrives in a city, he heads straight for the synagogue, knowing that he'll soon be embroiled in battle. In Athens, he debates on Mars Hill (Acts 17:16–34), the most public place in the city, and in other cities he's notorious enough to spark riots. The Spirit of Gideon and Samson emboldens Paul for warfare in public places, in synagogues and town squares. Again, it's a lesson for us: The Spirit drives us into the fray. If you're keeping in step with the Spirit, get ready to fight with the Spirit's weapons. If you're walking in the Spirit, you'll be driven into public places to preach the public truth of the gospel.

As Paul travels through Philippi, Thessalonica, Corinth, and Ephesus (Acts 16–19), he's accused of stirring up trouble, undermining local customs, challenging the authority of Caesar. gentiles and Jews, Jews and gentiles: The whole world accuses Paul, as it accuses Jesus.

Acts 16–19 lay out the charges, but Paul doesn't get a chance to defend himself. Once he gets an opening, he doesn't stop talking. He defends himself to a Jewish mob in Jerusalem (Acts 22), to the Sanhedrin (Acts 23), to two Roman governors—Felix and Festus—(Acts 24–25), and finally to Herod Agrippa (Acts 26). When all's said and done, Paul has been tried by the same courts that tried Jesus—the Sanhedrin, a court of Herod, and the court of the Roman governor. Acts 16—26 form a stretched-out trial scene: first the indictment, then the defense. Paul is another Jesus. Like Jesus, his life is scripted by Scripture, made according to the pattern of the Word.

The Carpenter of Nazareth makes the lives of the apostles like His own. But the apostles also consciously and deliberately live by the blueprint of Scripture. They don't think the fulfillment of the Scriptures ended with Jesus' resurrection. They don't think that God's story wrapped up when Jesus ascended. They decide to fulfill Scripture in their own ministries. They know the drama of Scripture is being played out, with the church in the central role.

The eleven justify the selection of a replacement for Judas by citing Psalms 69 and 109 (Acts 1:20). At Pentecost, Peter tells the crowds that Jesus fulfills David's prophecy about rescue from Sheol (Acts 2:25–28; Ps 16:8–11) and also claims the Spirit's coming fulfills a prophecy from Joel (Acts 2:16–21; Joel 2:28–32). When the Jewish leaders oppose the church, the apostles understand their experience through the lens of Psalm 2 (Acts 4:24–30). At the Council of Jerusalem, James cites Amos 9 as Scriptural support for reception of gentiles (Acts 15:15–18).

In his defense before Agrippa, Paul describes himself by referring to biblical models. Jesus' appearance on the Damascus Road (Acts 26) is like the vision of Ezekiel (Ezek 1—3). Like Jeremiah, Paul is promised protection from enemies (Acts 26:17; Jer 1:19). Most strikingly of all, Paul describes himself as the servant of Yahweh, who leads Israel in a second exodus. Like the servant, Paul opens the eyes of the blind, shines light into the darkness, delivers slaves from the realm of death and Satan into the light of God (Acts 26:18; Isa 42:6–7; 49:6). Jesus is the Servant. As a servant of the Servant, Paul too carries out the Servant's mission.

It's not just what the apostles say and do. It's how they say and do it. What Jesus whispered in secret, the apostles proclaim in the public squares. Peter speaks boldly and unreservedly (*meta parrēsias*) at Pentecost, before an international crowd of thousands (Acts 2:29). In the Spirit, Peter speaks before the Sanhedrin (Acts 4:8) and so passes on the fullness of the Spirit to the other disciples, who speak the Word of God openly, with boldness (Acts 4:31; *meta parrēsias*). At the close of Acts, Paul is in Rome, but he too preaches "with all openness, without hindrance" (Acts 28:31; *meta pasēs parrēsias, akōllutōs*). It's the last word of Acts and sets the trajectory for the continuing mission of the church. We speak what Jesus spoke. We speak *as* Jesus spoke, with no hedging or holding back, just straightforward truth.

Scripture gives the apostles their boldness in preaching and witness. It gives them their sense of destiny because what they do is as necessary as what Jesus did (Luke 24:26, 44; Acts 1:16; 17:3). Paul must go to Rome (Acts 19:21; 27:24), just as it was necessary for Jesus to die in Jerusalem (Luke 9:22; 13:33). The apostles' confidence in their mission comes from their conviction that what they do is what Jesus continues to do (Acts 1:1). They have a sense of destiny because they see their lives as a repetition of the destined life of Jesus.

For Luke and the apostles he writes about, the fulfillment of Moses and the prophets extends to the history of the church. And the fulfillment continues down through the centuries, all the way to you and me. Incorporated into Christ, we're incorporated into His life of suffering and glory as we repeatedly live out Jesus' dying and rising. Our lives, as much as the life of Jesus, are scripted by Scripture, destined to conform to the blueprint. Still today, the Carpenter of Nazareth is remaking the crooked timber of humanity according to the pattern of the Word.

For many Christians, the Old Testament is a closed book. Today, typological interpretation of the Old Testament is seen as quaint, something that childish Christians used to do, until we grew up and learned how to do hard-headed historical research. That's not the apostolic view. As the story of Jesus, the Old Testament is the stuff of their mission. Today's church can do no less. We will not fulfill our mission, which is the mission of the Father through Jesus and His Spirit, unless we follow Jesus' example in our reading and teaching of Scripture. We cannot grow into the ark of salvation unless we recognize Jesus as the One made according to the pattern of the Word, unless we recognize that we are also scripted by Scripture.

NEITHER JEW NOR GREEK

Since Adam's sin, men and women have been mis-making the world and themselves. At Babel, rebellious men try to construct a city and tower in defiance of God. Instead of uniting humanity in a grand project, they scatter and divide. In constructing His own saving vessel, His city and tower, the Carpenter of Nazareth makes a single ship from all sorts and conditions of men, all species of human trees.

Unifying the human race is integral to the apostolic gospel. In ages past, gentiles walked in futility and darkness, excluded from the life of God. They were separated from Christ, excluded from Israel, strangers to the covenant promise, without God and without hope (Eph 2:12; 4:17–19). God doesn't leave them in that condition. Jesus brings near those who are far off. He dies to break down the dividing wall, the wall of Torah that separated Jews and gentiles (Eph 2:14–15). Jesus' death doesn't just reconcile sinners to God. It reconciles Jews with gentiles and forms a new, reconciled humanity among Babelic nations. Gentiles are no longer strangers and aliens but fellow citizens with Israel and the holy ones, the saints (Eph 2:14–19).

Acts narrates this apostolic mission of unity. Peter preaches to people of many nations, languages, and cultures at Pentecost. Some are Jews, some proselytes, some entile God-fearers (Acts 2:9–11). When Peter is finished, three thousand are baptized (Acts 2:41), and immediately they adopt the customs of the apostles (Acts 2:42–47; 4:32–37).

After persecution breaks out in Jerusalem, many disciples flee (Acts 8:1–2). Philip makes his way to Samaria and begins preaching Jesus as the Christ, the anointed King (Acts 8:4–8). The despised Samaritans rejoice in the good news, receive the Word, and are baptized (Acts 8:5–8, 16). Later, Peter and John go to Samaria to lay hands on the new believers so they too can receive the Spirit (Acts 8:14–17). Like Jerusalem, Samaria experiences Pentecost, and the Samaritans join the Jews of Jerusalem in the one body of the Christ, the one vessel of salvation.

An angel directs Philip south to the road that connects Jerusalem to Gaza, and there he meets an Ethiopian eunuch returning from a feast in Jerusalem, a high official in the court of Queen Candace (Acts 8:25–40). We're not told whether the eunuch is a Jew or a God-fearing gentile, but he's from a foreign country, an outcast from Israel because of his physical condition (cf. Deut 23:1). He too receives the word and is baptized.

On his way to Damascus to torture, imprison, and kill Christians, Saul encounters Jesus (Acts 9:1–9). Blinded by the bright light, Saul continues on to Damascus, where a believer named Ananias has also received a message from Jesus, telling him to welcome Saul (Acts 9:10–16). Saul's conversion is a turning point in human history, but it won't take unless Ananias is converted too. Like Saul, Ananias needs to see with new eyes. He needs to trust Jesus can turn a violent opponent into an apostle. At the climax, Saul receives the Spirit, his eyes are opened, and he breaks his fast as he's baptized into a table fellowship. At that same moment, the story of Ananias also comes to a climax as he lays hands on Saul and embraces him as "Brother Saul" (9:17). Saul isn't just brought into fellowship with Jesus by the Spirit. He's brought into a new family as a brother to those whom he formerly tried to kill.

Jews, Samaritans, a eunuch from Africa, and a vicious persecutor are joined as brothers. These are the surprising raw materials that become planks in the human ark of the Greater Noah.

Jesus isn't finished. In Caesarea, an angel visits the Roman centurion Cornelius, a God-fearing gentile, and tells him to seek out Simon Peter at Joppa (Acts 10:1–9). Cornelius quickly sends servants to fulfill the angel's instructions. While they're on their way, Peter sees a vision of a sheet lowered from heaven, full of animals and creeping things of all kinds, and is told to eat them. When he objects, a voice tells him, "What God has cleansed, no more consider profane" (Acts 10:15). When Cornelius's servants arrive, Peter realizes the vision is about them and receives them into Simon's home (Acts 10:23). Formerly separated, gentiles and Jews share a house for the night.

The next day, Peter and Cornelius's servants go on the return journey, from Joppa to Caesarea, to Cornelius's house, where he's gathered friends and relatives. Peter and Cornelius recount their dreams. As Peter preaches the gospel to the assembled gentiles, "the Holy Spirit [falls] upon all those who [are] listening." The Jews with Peter are surprised that "the gift of the Holy Spirit [has] been poured out upon the Gentiles also" (Acts 10:44–45). If God accepts gentiles as well as Jews, gentiles must be worthy of baptism (Acts 10:47). Through the waters of baptism, Jews and gentiles are made one. Newly baptized, Cornelius returns Peter's hospitality and allows him and his Jewish friends to stay with him (Acts 10:48).

Soon, the Christians who flee Jerusalem because of persecution end up in Antioch, where they preach the Lord Jesus to gentiles (Acts 11:20). Antioch becomes the base of the mission to the gentiles, sending out Paul and Barnabas (Acts 13:1–3), then Paul and Silas (Acts 15:35–41). The gentile mission isn't just a mission of evangelism. It's a mission of unification. It forms a body of people founded on the truth that God made all men "of one blood" (Acts 17:26; KJV). Through preaching and baptism, the Spirit forms a body united by the blood of Jesus.

Bringing gentiles into the church proves controversial. When Peter returns to Jerusalem after visiting Cornelius, some go on the attack: "You went to uncircumcised men and ate with them" (Acts 11:3). It's true, but Peter explains he is following cues from God, who "gave to them the same gift as He gave to us." God is doing a new thing. How can he stand in God's way (Acts 11:12–18)?

Other Jewish believers, especially Pharisees, demand that the gentiles be circumcised before they can participate fully in the life of the church (Acts 15:1–5). At the Council of Jerusalem, Peter reminds the elders and apostles that God "made no distinction between us and them, cleansing their hearts by faith" (Acts 15:8–9). Paul and Barnabas testify to the fruitfulness of the mission among gentiles (Acts 15:12), and then James offers Scriptural proof from Amos 9: God promises to rebuild the fallen tent of David so that all men can seek the Lord (Acts 15:15–18). The Council of Jerusalem imposes essential restrictions on the gentiles but refuses to trouble them (Acts 15:19–21). Gentiles and Jews worship together in the tent of David, the ark of the Greater Noah.

The new thing isn't that gentiles are saved. Gentiles have been saved as long as there have been gentiles. Abraham, the first circumcised Hebrew, meets Melchizedek, priest of the Most High God (Gen 14:17–20). Moses takes his wife from the daughters of Jethro, a Midianite who is a priest of the living God (Exod 2:16–22). When Jews are sown into exile throughout the Mediterranean, they produce an abundant harvest. By the time of Jesus and Paul, there are communities of Jews and God-fearing gentiles all over the Roman world.

Gentiles being saved is old news. The new news is that gentiles are no longer separate from Jews. In the church, gentiles are no longer second-class members. Both Jews and gentiles receive the Spirit. Both Jews and gentiles are baptized. Jews and gentiles eat together at a common table and share common prayers. Jews and gentiles don't become identical. Jews don't give up their ancestral customs, and gentiles don't have to be circumcised. But Jews and gentiles become fully equal within the church. Together, they're remade to be makers who fulfill the original human mission. Together, they form the ark where the world will find shelter from the coming storm.

God separates Jews and gentiles when He calls Abram. Circumcision is the wound in the flesh of humanity, a sign of the separation of Israel from the nations. But God the Creator always separates to reunite. He divides light and darkness in order to harmonize them into the dance of evening and morning. He separates Eve from Adam so the two can become one flesh. He separates Jews and gentiles so they can be reunited in Jesus. Jesus is circumcised on the cross to heal the wound in humanity, and the church's mission has always been, and must always be, to welcome every tribe, tongue, nation, and people.

In the Spirit, the early Christians pursue unity of mind, purpose, and love (Phil 2:1–2), as we share in a common mission (Phil 1:5). Even before the Spirit falls at Pentecost, the people of the church are of "one mind" (*homothumadon*), devoting themselves to common prayer (Acts 1:14). After the Spirit falls, they continue daily in one mind (Acts 2:46). Persecution doesn't divide them, but they respond with common prayer, in one mind (Acts 4:24). Living together with one heart and soul, they sell their property to share the proceeds with those who have need (Acts 4:32). The crowds who hear Philip preach in Samaria come to a united mind (Acts 8:6).

The church even unites her enemies. Because of Jesus, Pilate and Herod become friends (Luke 23:12). In response to Stephen, the Jews of Jerusalem rush at him with one mind (Acts 7:57). In Thessalonica, the Jews unite to bring Paul's hosts before the Roman proconsul, Gallio (Acts 18:12), and the Ephesians are gripped with a single mob-mind when they grab Paul's companions and drag them into the agora (Acts 19:29).

Few features of the church are more crucial to her mission than unity. From the time of Abraham, Yahweh's plan was to reunite the nations under the blessing of God, to undo the fracturing of the nations at Babel. The church is and is called to be that united people. Unity is essential to our witness, a witness against divisive principalities and powers, a witness against national arrogance, a witness against ethnic hatreds.

During the age of Christendom, baptism harmonized people from different clans and nations. Teachers from Lombardy, Germany, and Italy gathered at the University of Paris. Spanish monks led monasteries in Scotland and served in the imperial court in Vienna. Regions and peoples of the medieval West retained their local flavor. But each ethnic group locale, with its own customs, was united in the larger whole of Christ's domain.

Over the past century, Christianity has exploded in the southern hemisphere and parts of the far east. As Philip Jenkins has pointed out for years, the statistically average Christian today is a black woman, not a white European male. The church truly is an international people gathered from hundreds of tribes, tongues, and nations, united by a million bonds of prayer, sharing, fellowship, and friendship. With the apostolic history as guide, we can anticipate conflicts over receiving these new peoples. The issue won't be whether Nigerians and Malaysians and Uzbeks can be saved. As in Acts, the conflict will be over their equality in the church. Western Christians have been dominant in the global church for several centuries. That's changing, and we white northern believers need to be prepared to take a subordinate role as deck hands on an ark captained by strangers who have become brothers.

In recent centuries, the churches of Europe and North America haven't had a great track record of unity. Tragically, since the Reformation, the church has fractured. Church splits aren't always bad. Sometimes the church must fracture. Sometimes faithful Christians must separate from false brothers and churches that have become synagogues of Satan. The Reformation was one of those times. Yet for centuries, Catholics and Orthodox, Protestants and Catholics, have refused to seek the kind of one-mind unity that is supposed to characterize the church of Jesus Christ. Our mission is to be a people in communion with Jesus by His Spirit so that we can be a people in communion with one another. God never breaks the church in pieces without intending to join it together again in one Spirit and one flesh. He doesn't dismantle the church except to restore it in a glorified form.

We've grieved the Spirit with our divisions, and we must get back in step with the one Spirit who forms and animates *one* body. We need a massive mission-correction. Jesus is making *one* ark, not a flotilla. Unity is His mission. It must be ours.

CONCLUSION

As the body of Christ, the church carries on Jesus' mission. Through our work, Jesus saves individual souls, plants churches, and establishes true worship throughout the world. From the beginning, the church does all that. Despite opposition, the Word spreads (Acts 6:7; 13:49). Thousands believe (Acts 2:41; 4:4; 21:20). Wherever the apostles go, they leave Spirit-filled churches behind (Acts 11:26; 13:1; 14:23; 15:41), each doing what the early Christians in Jerusalem did—devoting themselves to the apostles' teaching, to *koinonia*, to the breaking of bread, to the prayers.

But Jesus' mission is bigger than that. Noah is the first righteous king in Scripture. He builds, commands his family, and rules over birds, animals, and creeping things (Gen 6:13–22). After the flood, he offers an ascension offering, is authorized to carry out capital punishment, plants a vineyard and enjoys wine, the royal drink (Gen 8:20—9:7, 20–21). He pronounces curses against Canaan and blessings to Shem and Japheth (Gen 9:25–27). Noah is an Adam elevated to royalty.

The Carpenter of Nazareth is also a royal figure. He comes in the fullness of time to proclaim the kingdom. Through Jesus and His Spirit, God takes charge of His wayward world. God becomes king when Jesus the Son goes to the cross, rises again by the power of the Spirit, and ascends to take His throne at the right hand of the Father. As Paul says, the gospel heralds the coronation of Jesus the Son of David, declared Son of God with power by His resurrection (Rom 1:1–4). "Son of God" is a royal title in the Bible (2 Sam 7:14; Ps 2:4–7). This is the good news: Jesus is king. Not brutal Caesar, not bloodthirsty Herod, not the cunning high priest. Jesus, Last Adam and Greater Noah.

If Jesus is king, His body the church is a royal body. Jesus doesn't do anything by or for Himself. We're His body, and His body goes with Him everywhere He goes. We share His sufferings. We receive resurrection life. We're enthroned with Him. Jesus makes His ark-people according to the pattern of His own royal life and so makes us a kingdom and priests (Rev 1:6; 5:10). All who follow Jesus are kings and queens. He comes to perfect us, to bring many sons to glory (Heb 2:10). Jesus is exalted as King and will reign until His enemies are placed beneath His feet. He comes to restore and perfect creation so that it becomes all God intended it to be.

The church's mission is bigger than individual evangelism and church planting. As the body of the Last Adam, the church aims to turn the mis-made world upside down (Acts 17:6), which means right-side up. And it does! By making us kings, Jesus renews our hands for making and our tongues for speaking truth. By making us priests, He restores us to our position in a cosmic Eucharist as we receive all with thanks and offer the works of our hands and the words of our mouths in praise. The Greater Noah's first work of making is to remake humanity so we can become makers, fulfilled as the creative creatures we're created to be. Jesus remakes us according to the pattern, the pattern that He is. His mission is to remake the makers so we can resume Adam's original mission of glorifying the world.

18

Edification

THE WHOLE BODY, BEING FITTED AND HELD TOGETHER
BY WHAT EVERY JOINT SUPPLIES ...
CAUSES THE GROWTH OF THE BODY
FOR THE BUILDING UP OF ITSELF IN LOVE.
—EPHESIANS 4:16

God creates by forming and filling. He forms by His Word, and He fills by empowering creation to fill itself. God creates by giving creatures power to create so that, empowered by His Word and Spirit, creation completes itself. This is especially true of human beings, made in the image of the creating and making God. Obeying God's Word and keeping in step with His creative Spirit, we perfect God's glorious world by the things we make and do. In so doing, we perfect ourselves.

Jesus is sent to remake humanity and the world. As the Greater Noah, His first task is to build the ark of the church by choosing and assembling timber from every tribe, tongue, people, and nation. In the ark, He nurtures a new creation. But the principle of creation applies to redemption too: Empowered by Jesus the Word and His living Spirit, human beings complete our own re-creation. By the power of the Carpenter of Nazareth, the living ark builds itself.

Does that sound blasphemous? It's not. It's the straightforward teaching of the New Testament. When Jesus ascends, He gives gifts—apostles, prophets, evangelists, pastors, and teachers. Jesus gives gifted men and women "for the equipping of the saints ... to the building up (*oikodome*) of the body of Christ" (Eph 4:10–13). Who's doing the building—the apostles and prophets and teachers, or the saints? We don't have to decide to get the point. Either way, Jesus equips *human beings* to build His own body.

This isn't a side theme in Paul. When he talks about the church, he talks about the members edifying the body; that is, we build the edifice of His body. Paul imagines himself as a craftsman like Bezalel or Oholiab, working to complete God's temple (1 Cor 3:10–17). Even when Paul has to speak severely, he does it to build and not to tear down (2 Cor 13:10). Prophets speak to build others (1 Cor 14:3, 5, 12), and tongues edify when they're interpreted (1 Cor 14:4). Whenever anyone speaks in the church, it should be for edification (Eph 4:29; 1 Thess 5:11). All is lawful, Paul says; but we're called to use our freedom for edification (1 Cor 10:23). We live in love because love edifies (1 Cor 8:1). We're called to use the gifts we receive from the Spirit for the common good of the body so the body will be built up into the fullness of itself, which is the fullness of Christ. The principle of ministry in the church is simple: "Let all things be done for edification" (1 Cor 14:26). This is the rule: Do everything you do to complete Christ's body.

We build one another and the body until we attain unity, maturity, the full stature of Christ (Eph 4:13). As we speak the truth in love, we the body grow up into the Head, Christ. Paul's convoluted syntax captures the complex reality: The power to cause the growth of the body comes from Christ the Head. But Christ the Head "causes the growth of the body for the building up of itself (*eis oikodomen heoutou*) in love" (Eph 4:16). As we receive life from the Head, we the body grow *ourselves* into the Head.

The body builds itself. Let that sink in for a moment. Jesus is the Christ, both head and body (1 Cor 12:12). He's what

Augustine called the *totus Christus*, the whole Christ. He doesn't perfect His own body—His own whole self—directly. We're the hands and tools by which He builds His body. We fill up the fullness of Christ. Christ leaves His own completion in our hands. Jesus is the ark of salvation. As body, the church is the ark of salvation. Jesus makes the ark; in Him, we make the ark that we are.

Change the filter, and we reach the same conclusion. In Eden, Yahweh builds (Heb. *banah*) Eve from the rib of Adam (Gen 2:22). She becomes one-flesh, one-body with the first Adam. The Last Adam also has a Bride, born from the water and blood that flow from His crucified body. But God doesn't finish building the bridal body for His Son. Not even the Last Adam completes the Bride for Himself. We the Bride build ourselves as the new Eve, Queen to the Last Adam, helper to the Greater Noah.

TOOLS

We build ourselves as body and Bride because the Carpenter of Nazareth pours out the Spirit of wisdom and craftmanship onto and into us. We build ourselves up as body and Bride through the tools Jesus gives, the tools Jesus energizes by His Spirit. These tools of edification are the customs of the church.

As the Word spreads through Jerusalem and Judea, and then out into gentile territories, everyone recognizes the church as a people with her own customs. They see that Christians want to persuade others to adopt their customs. Jews complain that Christians threaten their customs, derived from Moses and the Prophets (Acts 6:14; 21:21). Some Jewish Christians, especially those who were Pharisees, want the church to conform to the customs of Moses and circumcise gentile converts (Acts 15:1). Gentiles accuse Christians of teaching customs contrary to the Roman way of life (Acts 16:21).

Jews and gentiles each have their customs and ways of living. The church appears on the scene as a third race, with customs of her own. Luke tells us early in Acts what these customs are. After the Spirit falls at Pentecost, three thousand new believers join the one hundred and twenty who have been meeting in Jerusalem (Acts 1:15; 2:41). The Spirit gathers them into a separate network of local communities, each following distinctive Christian practices. The Spirit builds the ark through the church's concrete forms of life, habits, ways of speaking, rituals, events, and forms of prayer:

I. Baptism (Acts 2:41).

II. Continuous devotion to apostles' teaching (Acts 2:42a).

III. Continuous devotion to communion (*koinonia*), including communion of goods and property (Acts 2:42b, 44–45).

IV. Continuous devotion to the breaking of bread and common meals (Acts 2:42c, 46).

V. Continuous devotion to the prayers (Acts 2:42d).

VI. Signs and wonders performed by the apostles (Acts 2:43b).

These customs form the distinctive ethos of the community of Christians. Believers who practice these things experience ongoing joy and gladness (Acts 2:46c) and maintain unity of mind (Acts 2:46a). They're built and build themselves into a unified ark and temple, full of the joy of festivity.

These don't look like the kind of tools we need to make a new humanity as an ark for the world. They don't look like customs that will overturn the world, transform the mis-makings of human culture, and move the devastated world toward justice and peace. But if we despise these customs, we're seeing with eyes of flesh. For these are Spiritual weapons and tools, designed to turn the world upside down (Acts 17:6).

BAPTISM INTO THE NAME

Peter compares the flood to baptism (1 Pet 3:18–22) because baptism, like the flood, rescues the early Christians from their perverse generation (Acts 2:40). Jesus condemns the adulterous generation during His own ministry (Matt 12:39, 41–45; 16:4; 17:17) and warns that a flood-like judgment looms over "this generation" (Matt 23:36; 24:34, 37–38; Luke 17:26–27; cf.

Matt 7:26–27; Luke 6:47–49). God is preparing one final deluge to wash away the ancient order of Israel-and-empire. When it comes, those who cling to the true Bridegroom, Jesus, will be saved.

Baptism assembles the material and crew for Jesus' ark. As we've seen, each new group is incorporated into the church by baptism. Philip baptizes Samaritans (Acts 8:12–13), then the Spirit sweeps him away to meet an Ethiopian eunuch, whom he baptizes at an oasis in the desert (Acts 8:36–38). When the Spirit falls on the household of the gentile God-fearer, Cornelius, Peter determines they should be baptized (Acts 10:48). At Philippi, Paul and Silas baptize the jailer and his household (Acts 16:33), and many in Corinth are baptized (Acts 18:8). Through baptism, Jesus makes His one people. As the church baptizes, she makes herself the one new man.

Noah's ark is a sacred space. Like other sanctuaries in the Bible, it's measured and constructed according to a revealed blueprint (Gen 6:15; Exod 25:9, 40). It has three decks (Gen 6:16), as the tabernacle and temple have three zones: the court, the Holy Place, and the Most Holy Place. Like later sanctuaries, it's filled with animals (Gen 6:19–20). During the flood, the ark ascends closer and closer to the firmament, above the highest mountains. It becomes a link between heaven and earth, the very gate of God. After the flood, it comes to rest on an Eden-like mountain (Gen 8:4), and Noah offers clean animals as ascension offerings on an altar built in front of the ark (Gen 8:20–21). Noah's ark is a floating ziggurat, a nautical holy mountain.[1]

The ark of the Carpenter of Nazareth is likewise a holy place, a temple of the Spirit. The baptized are living stones and planks in God's house, prepared to offer Spiritual sacrifices of praise (1 Pet 2:5). The baptized are safe in the sanctuary of the ark. The baptized are also called to serve as priests in the Spirit's ark-temple.

[1] For more on biblical sanctuaries, see chapter 11.

In the church, priestly service means practicing Christian customs—the apostles' teaching, the breaking of bread, the prayers. By the Spirit, baptism equips us to be wise craftsmen in building His church. In baptism, the Carpenter of Nazareth fills our hands with tools to edify His body. Luke uses verb forms that emphasize the continuous nature of these customs. They are continually devoted to the practices of the church. Luke alludes to the Hebrew word *tamid*, which describes the continuous liturgical practices carried out in the temple in Jerusalem (Exod 27:20; 28:29–30, 42; Lev 6:13; 24:2). Priests in the old order continually carry out the liturgy of temple worship. The baptized are priests of the new temple and continually carry out the liturgy of life that makes up the life of the church. Baptism restores us to our priestly calling so that our making is embedded in a cycle of thanks and praise.

Cleansed and sanctified to labor in the holy house of the Spirit, the baptized are also enlisted to carry out public service in the world. We present our clean bodies as living and holy sacrifices, performing the good and acceptable liturgy of common life (Rom 12:1–2). We devote the members of our body to the justice of God's kingdom (Rom 6:1–14). The baptized follow Jesus by practicing hospitality, blessing persecutors, refusing vengeance, overcoming evil with good (Rom 12:13–14, 19–21).

The church fathers describe baptism as a seal and often compare it to the brand on an animal, the owner's mark on a slave, or the regimental tattoo on a Roman soldier. Baptized into the name of Jesus, disciples of Jesus wear His name. We're called not only to maintain the Lord's house, the church, but to battle giants in the land, taking down principalities and powers and everything that stands against Jesus.

PATTERN OF TEACHING

Jesus teaches His disciples "everything concerning Himself in all the Scriptures." The apostles learn the lesson well. Whenever they teach, they teach from the Scriptures, showing that Jesus is the message of Moses and the prophets.

At Pentecost, Peter quotes a section of Psalm 16 and concludes that Jesus, not David, is the One saved from Sheol (Acts 2:25–29). In the next breath, he cites Psalm 132, a promise that David's Seed will sit on his throne. He applies it to Jesus (Acts 2:30). Preaching at the portico of Solomon after healing a lame man, Peter quotes Deuteronomy 18 to show that Jesus is the new Moses-like Prophet (Acts 3:22).

According to Peter, Jesus is the "stone which was rejected" (Acts 4:11; Ps 118:22), and Philip teaches the Ethiopian eunuch that Jesus is the suffering Servant of Isaiah 53 (Acts 8:26–35). Paul says Psalm 2's declaration about Yahweh's Son is fulfilled in the resurrection of Jesus (Acts 13:32–33). At Thessalonica, Paul teaches from the Scriptures that "the Christ had to suffer and rise again from the dead," a virtual quotation from Jesus' own teaching (Acts 17:2–3). Later, Paul assures Herod Agrippa he believes Moses and the prophets, who teach "that the Christ was to suffer and that by reason of resurrection from the dead He should be the first to proclaim light both to the people and to the Gentiles" (Acts 26:22–23).

The apostles don't cherry-pick quotations from the Old Testament. They retell the story of the Old Testament as a story that climaxes in Jesus. When Peter and John are brought before the Sanhedrin, they remind the Jewish leaders of God's promise to Abraham: "in your seed all the families of the earth shall be blessed" (Acts 3:25; Gen 22:18). The God of Abraham, Isaac, and Jacob sends Jesus to fulfill this promise and has "glorified His servant Jesus" by raising Him from the dead and by elevating Him to heaven (Acts 3:13–21).

Stephen preaches about Abraham's call to leave his country for the land of promise (Acts 7:2–8), tells the life of Joseph (Acts 7:9–16), and recounts the exodus, focusing on Moses' two visitations to deliver Israel (Acts 7:17–41). Instead of listening to Moses, Israel rejects him and goes after other gods, both in the wilderness and in the land (Acts 7:42–43). Stephen charges his hearers with repeating the sin of their fathers. Israel has always persecuted prophets and killed those sent to them (Acts 7:51–52).

They rejected Jesus just as they rejected Moses. Now they reject Stephen himself.

At Pisidian Antioch, Paul reminds the Jews they're chosen and redeemed from Egypt to receive the inheritance of the land (Acts 13:16–19). After Saul, Yahweh raises up David and promises David's seed will sit on His throne forever (Acts 13:21–22). Jesus is the fulfillment of this promise, but the Jews put Him to death. But God raises and enthrones Him (Acts 13:30–33), so the promise made to the fathers can be fulfilled, forgiveness can be preached, and Jews can be freed from everything the law was powerless to achieve (Acts 13:32, 38–39). Paul's sermon is about Israel's story, which culminates in the sufferings and glory of Jesus the Christ.

Paul preaches to gentile audiences too, and the emphasis is different. He tells gentiles about the God who creates all things, shows Himself even to ignorant gentiles, and now holds all men to account (Acts 14:15–17; 17:16–31). These sermons also hinge on the coming of Jesus. Because of Jesus, God no longer allows nations to go their own way (Acts 14:16). Because of Jesus, the times of ignorance have come to an end, and God is calling all men to repent. Athenians aren't permitted to worship the "unknown god" anymore, since Paul has made Him known. For the gentile world, the sign of the new age is the appointment of Jesus, the resurrected Jesus, as Judge of the world (Acts 17:30–31). According to Paul, Jesus is King and Judge of gentiles as well as Jews. Jesus isn't just the center of Israel's history. He's the center of human history.

By the Spirit, this pattern of teaching—which is the pattern of Jesus' own life—is imprinted on the church. Through such teaching, the church builds herself up as body, Bride, and ark because through such teaching, the church is conformed to the pattern from heaven. When the church strays, the Spirit speaks in Scripture to call her back to Jesus. Through apostolic teaching, we the members of the church learn how to build, to follow the Carpenter of Nazareth in making rightly. Apostolic teaching unveils the pattern of Christ, which is the blueprint for our lives, for the church, for the world.

COMMUNION IN THE SPIRIT

Baptized into the Spirit-filled body of disciples, the converts on Pentecost begin to live a Pentecostal body life. Luke sums it up in one word: *koinonia*, fellowship (Acts 2:42). For many Christians, fellowship involves potlucks and post-worship conversations about football or politics. Luke has something thicker and more challenging in mind. For ancient Greeks, *koinonia* is a political term. Derived from the Greek word *koinon*, common, it refers to the things all citizens of a city share. A collection of individuals becomes a civic community because each citizen has some share of the tangible and intangible goods of the city. The city's wealth and prosperity, its safety and public order, its institutions and education, its architecture, music halls, and museums are all *koinon* goods.

Just as importantly, all citizens share in the common project of advancing the good of the city. Sailors, soldiers, and craftsmen each have their own specialized communities, which aim at limited goods. Sailors pursue the good of sailing together. Soldiers join together to better themselves as soldiers. Craftsmen form guilds to improve their craft. The city embraces and encompasses all these smaller communities. In the civic *koinonia*, each citizen and each smaller *koinonia* aims for the good of the whole city. Sailors pursue the good of sailing for the sake of finding new trade routes to enrich the city. Soldiers improve their fighting skills to defend the city. Craftsmen hone their skills for the sake of beautifying civic life.

When the New Testament writers use *koinonia*, they're pointing to the civic character of the church. The church is the city of God among the cities of men. Each member and congregation shares the common goods of the church, and each member and congregation contributes to the common good of the whole.

The city of man cannot realize this aspiration. No matter how rich a city is, its resources are limited. No matter how widely or equally shared its goods, some are excluded. In ancient cities, most of the residents of the city don't share in the *koinonia* of the city. Slaves, women, foreigners, and people of low birth aren't citizens. They contribute to the city but don't share in the common goods of the city. No city of man fully practices the customs of *koinonia*.

The church is able to achieve what the ancient city could not achieve because her common things are genuinely common. What holds the church together is a common share in God Himself. The church is deeply unified because her members have the Spirit in common. The union of Jew and gentile, of nation and tribe, isn't social, but spiritual (1 Cor 1:9; 2 Cor 13:14). Every member receives the Spirit according to the measure of Christ's gift (Eph 4:7).

The goods of the church are inexhaustible. The Spirit is a river of life who never runs dry. Filled with the Spirit He receives from his Father, Jesus has an infinite supply of gifts. He'll never run out of gifted people to give to the church. The Father is the Giver of every good and perfect gift. The living God needs nothing from us. Precisely because He has no needs, He gives to us life and breath and all things (Acts 17:25). He's the only possible source of *koinonia* because He's the only possible source of unbounded generosity.

And the goods of the church are available to all. *All* members of the body share the work of building the body. The word for "common good" in 1 Corinthians 12:7 is *symphero*, carrying together. In the church, *koinonia* isn't merely a sharing-together but a bearing-together, as each member uses the gifts he receives from the Spirit to edify the communion of believers, the body, Bride, and ark of Jesus (1 Cor 12:14–21). There are "master builders," and there are drones, but all edify the self-constructing ark of Jesus' body.

Eyes exist to serve all the sightless organs. Ears serve deaf eyes and mouth and hands and feet. Hands lend their manual power to the whole body. Eyes serve hands by directing the hands to things to touch and hold and avoid; hands serve eyes by shooing away bugs or putting on spectacles. It would be absurd for the eyes to become envious of the ears' power of hearing, or for the stomach to long to have his own feet. The body's feet are the stomach's feet; the body's ears are the ears of the eyes, as well as the ears of the nose, the tongue, the lungs, the muscles, the bones, the spleen. Each member of the body does his unique work for all the other members of the body. Each builds up the whole. Each serves each for the edification of the whole.

In Christ's body, no organ is vestigial. The parts that seem less honorable receive more abundant honor. Unpresentable members are adorned to become presentable. Despised, lowly, and weak members have their own special work to do in building up the body (1 Cor 12:22–26). Jesus gives capacities or abilities through His Spirit. Jesus gives people with Spiritual abilities or gifts: apostles, prophets, pastors, teachers, administrators, helpers, healers, secretaries, servants. In the church, there are no small gifts or small people. Everyone has the dignity of serving God in serving His house. All of us share in the work of building the ark of Jesus. Administration (1 Cor 12:28) doesn't seem as sexy as prophecy or tongues or gifts of healing, but it's no less necessary to the body. If you don't believe me, try running a church without a secretary.

Devotion to *koinonia* (Acts 2:42) includes holding all property in *koinon* (Acts 2:44; 4:34–37). Filled with the Spirit, the early Christians in Jerusalem sell their goods to help impoverished brothers and sisters. Material goods are like Spiritual goods. We receive everything we receive to edify the body and Bride, to build the ark of Jesus. And we receive everything. We possess our material property as we possess our Spiritual capacities, as gifts to be shared.

The church in Jerusalem has unique needs. Thousands join the church on a single day, and some need support. Besides, Jesus predicts Jerusalem will be destroyed. Christians don't have much incentive to invest in real estate within the holy city. With a flood coming to overwhelm Jerusalem, there's little reason to retain a portfolio of properties. Sale of land and houses is voluntary. When Ananias and Sapphira lie about their gift to the church, Peter reminds them they could have kept their property if they had chosen (Acts 5:4).

But the custom of sharing goods isn't confined to Jerusalem. Jerusalem is the standard for all churches in all times and places.

After all, the Jerusalem church isn't the only New Testament church where believers sacrifice their own wealth to build the body. Many of the New Testament's uses of *koinonia* refer to sharing material goods (Rom 15:26; 2 Cor 8:4; Heb 13:16). Because of the church's *koinonia* in material goods, the church fulfills the hopes of Israel (Deut 15:4): "there was not a needy person among them" (Acts 4:34).

Wealth might be used to build a business to employ others. A wealthy person might create a foundation to fund cultural or political projects. Wealth can be given away as charity. Whatever form it takes, wealth, like Spiritual gifts, is given for the sake of the body. Christian *koinonia* demands that each distributes to each as any has need (Acts 4:35). This is the custom of the church that builds the body.

Material *koinonia* serves Spiritual *koinonia*. Jews and gentiles are united by the Spirit in Christ, but for Paul this union is realized by the sharing of goods—the Jews sharing their Spiritual goods with gentiles, and gentiles responding with funds for famine relief in Jerusalem (Rom 15:27). Macedonians make a *koinonia* contribution to poor saints in Jerusalem (Rom 15:26). As Paul sees it, they don't throw money at a problem from a distance. Rather, their generous gifts overcome distance, joining Macedonian gentiles and Jerusalem Jews in one fellowship of the Spirit. Material gifts have a quasi-sacramental power to join the members of the church into one body. Charity is a tool for erecting the ark of the Carpenter of Nazareth.

In Acts 2, Luke uses a definite article: *the koinonia*. He refers to an event of communion, not merely a quality or general practice of communion. The liturgy is that event of communion. In it, we gather to share together in Jesus and His Spirit. In the liturgy, we receive the teaching of the apostles, and we devote a portion of our goods to God and to one another. The Eucharist is a ritual expression of the *koinonia* of the church, which is also a means to realize that unity (1 Cor 10:16). In the liturgy, we share together in the prayers (Acts 2:42). Liturgy is at the center of the common life in Jesus' holy ark.

Gathered or dispersed, the church is always and everywhere a communion. But it manifests its *koinonia* to the world's powers particularly in its weekly gatherings on the Lord's Day. Then we join with the joyful assembly on the heavenly Zion, as the Spirit joins heaven and earth (Heb 12:22–24) so that we on earth can share the good things of the age to come.

BREAKING BREAD

Through baptism, Jesus gathers the lumber and workmen to build His people-ark and equips them with skill to make well. Through practices of communion, Jesus builds up His body. Through baptism and *koinonia*, *we* build the body and Bride of Christ. As we raise the edifice, we enjoy the abundant life of the kingdom at the Lord's table. Like Paul *en route* to Rome (Acts 27:33–36), Jesus gives thanks, breaks bread, and feeds the crew aboard His ark. Feasting is the work of the church.

Hosting a feast is hardly new for the Christ who comes eating and drinking (Luke 7:34). Luke records at least ten meals (Luke 5:27–39; 7:36–50; 9:10–17; 10:38–42; 11:37–54; 14:1–24; 19:1–10; 27:7–38; 24:13–35; 24:36–53), which symbolize Jesus' mission to preach good news to the poor and announce the favorable year of the Lord (Luke 4:16–30). In meals with Jesus, the poor and hungry are restored to the fat of the land.

Jesus forms a new Israel at His table. The people He eats with, often outcasts, are the first members of a new people of God. Jesus cleanses the unclean. He purifies lepers, stops the flow of blood, raises the dead. He defeats the powers of death and impurity so He can welcome every penitent to His table. The meal is both a sign of the presence of the kingdom and a visible realization of that kingdom. Asked to point to the kingdom of God on earth, we should point to Jesus eating a meal with sinners.

For Jesus, table manners provide patterns for life. The virtues cultivated at the table are the virtues of the disciples. Jesus observes the competition among guests for important seats at the table (Luke 14:7). He rejects the honor game and commands

His disciples to seek honor from God rather than from men. Jesus turns to the guest list (Luke 14:12) and warns against calculating hospitality (cf. Luke 6:30–35). We should imitate the hospitality of God, who gives generously even though we can never repay Him. Jesus doesn't consider repayment evil. Those who seek an invitation in payment for an invitation want too little, not too much (Luke 6:35). They seek a paltry reward in this age rather than the wealth of the age to come.

After the Spirit falls, the church continues on Jesus' table mission. Alongside *koinonia* in the Spirit and in goods, Jesus' disciples commune in bread (Acts 2:42). They break bread in the various house gatherings that spring up after Pentecost (Acts 2:46). At Ephesus, Paul gathers with the church on the first day of the week to break bread (Acts 20:7, 11). Paul teaches, but the purpose of the Sunday gathering isn't to hear a sermon.The believers pray, but the purpose isn't to pray together. The goal of gathering is to break bread, to have a meal together. As Paul puts it elsewhere, Christians come together to eat (1 Cor 11:33).

Luke emphasizes bread, specifically breaking bread. You break a loaf to share it. But Jesus highlights another aspect of breaking. At the Last Supper, Jesus calls the bread His body, given for the disciples (Luke 22:19). Jesus is the bread broken in His trial and death. After Pentecost, the church sees herself in the broken bread. Filled with the leaven of the Spirit, baked in fiery trials, the church is the bread of life, broken for the life of the world.

Throughout Acts, shared meals are evangelistic and edifying. They bring new members and groups into the *koinonia* of the church and continue the building project. Saul breathes out (*empneuo*) threats and murder against the church (Acts 9:1) until Jesus confronts him and turns him from a persecutor into a persecuted apostle. In Damascus, he's baptized and filled with the Spirit (*pneuma*, Acts 9:17) and shares a meal with his former enemy (Acts 9:19). Saul becomes a table companion to those he once tried to destroy.

When Cornelius's servants arrive at Simon's house, Peter and Simon welcome them and show hospitality, feeding the strangers and spending the night under the same roof (Acts 10:23). When Peter returns with them to Caesarea, he remains a few days (Acts 10:48), sharing a house and a table. This is the aim of the gospel: to overcome distance, to break down the dividing wall between Jew and gentile, slave and free, male and female, to clothe all with Christ so all can share the table of Jesus.

Common meals aren't mere symbols of *koinonia*. They're acts of *koinonia* that encompass acts of charity. The first internal conflict of the early church has to do with inequitable distribution of food. Hellenistic Jewish widows complain that the Hebrew widows are being favored in the daily serving of food (Acts 6:1). The apostles instruct the church to select six men to oversee the serving of tables (Acts 6:2). Within weeks of Pentecost, the church has its own rudimentary charity system where food is distributed to those without means to support themselves. Later, when famine threatens Judea, the common table expands beyond Jerusalem to encompass the empire. Each gives according to his means to relieve the saints in famine-ridden Jerusalem (Acts 11:27–30). Scattered as they are throughout the empire, the church feasts at a single table.

The shared meal is the biblical paradigm of Christian charity. At the table, those with goods share them with those who have none. Rich and poor share bread together and so also share time, conversation, burdens, laughter, tears, life. Whatever charity work the church engages in, it should take the common table as a paradigm.

A church isn't carrying out the mission of Jesus if it doesn't gather on the Lord's Day at a common table. A weekly Eucharist is a minimum. A church isn't carrying out the mission of Jesus if it doesn't hospitably welcome former enemies to break bread. A church isn't carrying out the mission of Jesus if it shuns outsiders, treats them as unclean, and refuses to eat together. A church isn't carrying out the mission of Jesus if it doesn't excommunicate impenitent sinners. A church isn't carrying out the mission of Jesus unless it serves tables, cares for its own widows and orphans, contributes to relieve the needs of brothers and sisters on the other side of the world.

Jesus ministers at tables. His church carries on His mission to the world by continuing His table work. Within His ark-temple, His disciples enjoy a continuous feast.

THE PRAYERS

Ancient Greek cities boasted of their democratic politics. Each citizen had a voice in public assembly. But many weren't citizens and so were voteless and voiceless.In the church, everyone has a voice. Every member is in Christ, and so all share the same status before the Father. All are filled with the one Spirit who intercedes for us. No voices are drowned out. The least and lowest has as much right to be heard as the high and honored. At prayer, the church is, as Robert Jenson put it, a perfect participatory democracy.

The church's mission is saturated with prayer. Before the Spirit falls at Pentecost, the disciples are continuously devoted to prayer (Acts 1:14). Throughout Acts, the apostles and churches pray before they set apart leaders of the church (Acts 1:24). Through prayer and the laying on of hands, the apostles commission six men to carry on table service to the widows of Jerusalem (Acts 6:6). By prayer and fasting, the church at Antioch sets apart Paul and Barnabas for their mission to the gentiles (Acts 13:3). When Paul visits established churches, he prays and appoints elders to carry on the work he started (Acts 14:23).

Prayer is one of the church's weapons for combatting death and disease. Peter prays to raise Tabitha from the dead (Acts 9:40), and Saul prays in Damascus after his life-altering encounter with Jesus (Acts 9:11). Paul prays and lays hands on the father of Publius to heal him (Acts 28:8).

Prayer is also a shield and a city wall. When the apostles come under attack, their first response is to pray. When the Jewish establishment in Jerusalem arrests and tries Peter and John, the church offers a remarkable prayer (Acts 4:24–29). They appeal to the Creator using words from Psalm 146 (cf. Acts 14:15) and then quote the opening verses of Psalm 2. The Jews of Jerusalem have become raging gentiles who gather against the Lord and His Christ. They've done it before, when they joined with Pilate and the gentiles in opposing Jesus. Now they're doing it again, attacking the body of Christ.

The whole prayer is premised on the instruction Jesus gave the Eleven during the forty days after the resurrection: They've learned to see the Scriptures as the story of Jesus, and they've learned to see their own lives embedded within the story of Jesus. They ask God to take note of their threats, to silence their accusers. They ask the Davidic King who reigns from Zion with an iron rod to dash His enemies like pottery. In the face of threats, the church doesn't pray for rescue or relief. They pray for boldness in speech and receive a renewed filling of the Spirit, who loosens their tongues for witness (Acts 4:31). Their prayers literally shake the land.

Paul and Silas's prayers and songs shake Philippi and open the prison doors (Acts 16:25). The incident is so impressive that the jailer asks how he can be saved, and their prayers humble the magistrates who put them in prison in the first place. When Peter is sent to prison, prayers spring him out too (Acts 12:5). Against the prayers of the church, no enemy can stand. No jail can hold a praying and singing church. If the prison doors stay closed, the prison itself becomes a temple filled with prayer and praise. Jesus keeps building His human ark even when His crew is in custody.

Paul's and Silas's song in the Philippian jail is the only reference to Psalm-singing in the book of Acts. Yet the frequent quotations show that the early church was deeply familiar with the Psalter (Acts 1:20; 2:25–28, 34–35; 4:25–28; 7:46; 13:33, 35; 14:15). Paul makes clear that singing is a gift of the Spirit. Don't be drunk with wine, Paul writes, but be filled with the Spirit, who inspires psalms, hymns, Spiritual songs, and melodies in the heart (Eph 5:18–19). In song and prayer, the church shakes the world and brings down principalities and powers.

Many prayers in Acts are occasional, tied to specific needs and occasions. But Acts 2:42 suggests something more. The baptized were devoted to the apostles' teaching, to the *koinonia*, to the breaking of bread, and to the prayers. The noun is plural, and it's preceded by the definite article, "the." These prayers are occasional or spontaneous. The early disciples follow a form of prayer, a liturgical order of prayer that guides collective prayers during the church's gatherings. It's not surprising that the apostles continue to observe the hours of temple prayer and sometimes pray in the temple (Acts 2:46; 3:1; 10:9, 30). In Philippi, Lydia initially joins a group of Jews and God-fearers praying outside the walls of the city (Acts 16:13, 16). After Paul and Silas leave the city, Lydia's house within the city walls becomes the center of prayer. Every church Paul starts is a prayer meeting. The church's communion in prayer is liturgical communion in prayer.

CONCLUSION

The Carpenter of Nazareth comes to remake creation, but His first task is to construct an ark made of people, which He makes through the people. We're a self-forming body, a self-edifying ark, both material and builders. We're God's workmanship (*poiema*, a made-thing), but He completes His *poiema* through us (Eph 2:10) as we keep the customs of the apostles. The church is the greatest artifact of man the maker, the greatest artwork of the Last Adam and His body. It's breathtaking to realize we share in this project. But it's just what we expect from a Creator who creates by giving creatures power to create, a Maker who makes man a maker.

This task is foundational, but it's not the final task. The ultimate task is to bring the world into the ark, to remake the cities of men to resemble the city of God.

19

Pilot

WE MUST RUN AGROUND ON A CERTAIN ISLAND.
—ACTS 27:26

Luke's account of Paul's life and ministry can seem like a geography lesson, and a confusing one. After his breach with Barnabas, he travels through Syria and Cilicia, then to Derbe and Lystra, Phrygia and the Galatian region, and finally to Troas, where he receives a vision instructing him to move on to Macedonia (Acts 15:41–16:2, 6–10). Sprung from a Philippian jail, he journeys through Amphipolis and Apollonia to Thessalonica (Acts 17:1). As Paul makes his way to Jerusalem, he takes a farewell tour of the churches, from Ephesus through Macedonia to Philippi to Troas, then to Assos and Mitylene and, having crossed to Samos, to Miletus (Acts 20:1–6, 13–15).

Got it?

Luke is recording history, but he's doing more. He's showing the Scriptures fulfilled in the suffering and glory of Christ and in the suffering and glory of the apostles. Paul resembles the original traveler, the peripatetic Abraham, who leaves Ur for Haran (Gen 11:27–32) and then, commanded by Yahweh, moves from Haran to the land of Canaan (Gen 12:1–5). He doesn't settle for long. At Shechem, Yahweh appears to him, and Abraham builds a commemorative altar (Gen 12:6–7). Then he moves east of Bethel to build another altar (Gen 12:8), before moving south to the Negev (Gen 12:9), then to Egypt to escape a famine (Gen 12:10–20). When he returns, he still doesn't stay put. Yahweh appears to him at the oaks of Moreh near Shechem (Gen 12:6–7), and he later moves on to a site between Kadesh and Shur, becoming a resident alien in Gerar (Gen 20:1–20).

Genesis isn't a mere travelogue any more than Acts. Abraham is heir of the land, and his travels are a walk-through of his descendants' inheritance. As Yahweh tells Joshua, "Every place on which the sole of your foot treads, I have given it to you" (Josh 1:3; cf. Deut 11:24). Joshua conquers and takes possession of the land because Abraham has pre-conquered it by erecting altars to Yahweh throughout Canaan. Joshua wins battles at places where Abraham built altars. First worship, then conquest.

The other great travelogue in the Old Testament is Israel's itinerary through the wilderness. Israel leaves Egypt on the way to the land of promise, camping along the way. When they get to Mount Hor, Aaron dies (Num 20:22–29; cf. Num 33:38), and Israel immediately begins the conquest, defeating the king of Arad (Num 21:1–3), Sihon (Num 21:21–25), and Og (Num 21:33–35; cf. Ps 135:11; 136:20). Numbers 33 plots the journey in great detail.

Paul is an apostle of the God of Abraham, who is, Paul says, "heir of the world" (Rom 4:13). He's an ambassador of the High King of heaven and earth, a member of Christ's body. Wherever he goes, Christ goes. Wherever he proclaims, Christ claims. Paul builds living temples throughout the Eastern Mediterranean, filled with living images of the living God. His foot treads around Syria, Asia Minor, Greece, and eventually to Rome because King Jesus lays claim to these lands and peoples. Paul's travels are also a passage through the wilderness as he approaches the "promised land" of Jerusalem, capital of Judaism, and then Rome, capital of the gentile world. Both are Jerichoes, whose walls will fall before a greater Joshua. The promise to Joshua applies to Paul: Every place his foot treads is given to him.

Halfway through Acts, Paul becomes a sailor, and we get another travelogue. He sails from Troas to Macedonia, from Macedonia to Miletus, from Miletus to Caesarea and Jerusalem. From Jerusalem, he returns to Caesarea, where he begins his long, turbulent voyage to Rome. Abraham and Joshua were landlubbers, tracing the contours of the land of promise. Like Jesus, Paul can stride the waves. He measures out the gentile sea, claiming it as the holy dwelling place of the God of earth and ocean, claiming the world for the Greater Noah.

Acts ends with a long sea yarn. Paul's voyage to Rome is an allegory of the aims and trajectory of Christian mission (Acts 27:1–28:16). His journey is a new exodus as he crosses water from Jerusalem, the new Egypt, toward Rome, the great city of the empire. He moves from the land of Israel through the gentile sea. The ship is a fairly obvious symbol of the Roman ship of state. Paul sets sail in a Roman ship as a Roman prisoner, under custody to a centurion named Julius, who is from the Augustan battalion (Julius! Augustan!), who treats him with consideration (Acts 27:3).

Against Paul's advice, Julius sets out from Fair Havens and immediately runs into a turbulent storm. The sky turns apocalyptic; darkness blots out sun and stars (Acts 27:20). It's another Deluge. A world is coming to an end, and the Roman ship of state is sure to be wrecked. During the storm, Paul effectively becomes the ship's captain. He assures the crew that no one will be lost (Acts 27:21–26) and orders the sailors to stay on the ship (Acts 27:30–32), while Julius prevents the soldiers from killing the prisoners because of his determination to bring Paul to Rome (Acts 27:42–43).

On the morning of the fourteenth day after Yom Kippur (Acts 27:9, 27, 33), Paul encourages the crew to eat. He takes bread, gives thanks, breaks it, and passes it out to the 276 on board (Acts 27:35–37). He turns the Roman ship into a church, the site of Eucharist. He's another Jonah who leads a ship's crew to worship the living God while traveling to preach in a city threatened with destruction.

A skilled workman in the company of the Carpenter of Nazareth, Paul measures not only the church but the world, in anticipation that both the land of Israel and the sea of Rome will be brought into the ark of Christendom, dry and safe. This is what Paul is after from the outset. He doesn't intend merely to rescue a few from the shipwreck. He and the other apostles aim to save *everyone* and to pilot the Roman ship safely through the storms of coming judgment. He intends to overthrow the powers and replace the sacrifices to demons with the Eucharistic sacrifice. As an apostle of the Greater Noah, he pilots a new ark that will bring the voyagers to a new world.

Acts is an incomplete story. The final chapters anticipate Paul's trial in Rome, as the gospels anticipate Jesus' trial in Jerusalem. But when Acts ends, Paul is still under house arrest, preaching the gospel and awaiting his hearing before Caesar. Luke's open non-ending is deliberate. Acts is unfinished because the history Luke records is unfinished. Paul completes his inspection of the Roman world. He has finished his walk-through. Rome is ripe for Jesus' conquest. But there are worlds elsewhere.

Over the centuries, others pick up where Paul ends, walking through other lands of Abraham's inheritance—through Armenia and India, China and Japan, the Near East and the Far East, the Americas and Oceania and the islands of the sea. We're still walking. Every land where the feet of Christ's body tread belongs to the Seed of Abraham, heir of the world. We claim every sea we traverse as His realm. Wherever Jesus builds temples, everywhere we build temples, Jesus lays His claim. Wherever we sail, Jesus builds His saving vessel. Jesus sends us to take charge of the world and to pilot the nations toward fair havens.

PROCLAMATION TO POWERS

When the flood destroyed all flesh, Noah's ark saved eight persons. In the first century, a flood threatens to sweep away the world as ancients know it. The Carpenter of Nazareth makes an ark big enough to carry the world over the waves onto dry land, where the world can be born again. The church's mission is never simply a rescue operation, snatching a few sinners from Satan's claws or from the fires of hell. The church's mission is a conquest. She aims to disciple the nations so they become the inheritance of the Christ and His Bride.

We accomplish this by proclaiming and enacting the mystery. God unveils His manifold wisdom to rulers and authorities in heavenly places through the church (Eph 3:9–10). A mystery is something hidden in God for ages past and now revealed in Christ. In Ephesians, the mystery is the union of Jews and gentiles in the one body of Jesus, the good news that gentiles are "fellow heirs and fellow members of the body, and fellow partakers of the promise" (Eph 3:4–6). A unified humanity: This is the truth we proclaim to the powers.

Principalities are Babelic. They obliterate differences and force unity. Or, they exploit division by deepening the chasm between masters and slaves, by turning the fruitful created difference of male and female into a structure of oppression or envy, by protecting the unjust wealth of the wicked wealthy and justifying indifference to the poor, by twisting the healthy diversity of languages and cultures into mutual hatred.

As the one body, the church demonstrates that fleshly markers of division have been overcome in the resurrection of Jesus. Masters and slaves continue to exist, but masters treat slaves as brothers and slaves live as freemen in Christ. Men and women are reconciled in one flesh by the Spirit. The wealthy open their hands so that the poor have enough to share. People from every tribe, tongue, and nation are bound by mutual exchanges of Spiritual and material goods.

The mystery isn't perfectly realized in the church. Christian masters are cruel, Christian husbands and wives abuse one another, rich Christians hoard wealth, and poor Christians become envious and resentful. National hatreds divide the church. Yet the mystery does become visible, and when it doesn't, the Word, Spirit, and Sacraments continually call the church to repentance, to exhibit the mystery more fully.

For all the church's blemishes, her sheer existence exposes the lie of rulers and authorities, the lie that social order requires division and domination. The church proclaims this: There's another game in town, another civic order within the city of man. There is an alternative. Every time the church celebrates Eucharist, or gathers donations for victims of a natural catastrophe on the other side of the world, or reconciles warring tribes, it brings the mystery to light. It makes known the wisdom of God to the rulers and authorities. Every time the church exhibits *koinonia*, she demonstrates the rulers and authorities are powerless. Every faithful act of the church shakes the foundations of the world and brings some plot of earth into the ark of Jesus.

DEFEATING THE DEVIL

Jesus is Prince of Peace. He will reconcile heaven and earth and bring peace to earth. The road to peace is, inevitably, a road of conflict and suffering. The road to new life for the world runs past Golgotha.

The church continues Jesus' warfare against Satan and his demons. Jesus' ministry begins with His baptism, quickly followed by forty days of temptation in the wilderness (Matt 3:13–4:11; Mark 1:12–13; Luke 3:21–4:12). The devil tempts Jesus to prove Himself Son of God by turning stones to bread, by throwing Himself from the temple tower, by bowing to Satan. In each case, Jesus responds with Scripture: "Man doesn't live by bread alone," and "You shall worship the Lord your God and serve Him only," and "You shall not put the Lord your God to the test." Jesus is the true Israel, resisting temptations in the wilderness. He's the Last Adam, driven into the cursed desert to do battle with the serpent.

Jesus conquers the devil in the wilderness, then embarks on the mission of overthrowing Satan's kingdom. He exorcizes a demon from a man who confronts Him in a synagogue (Mark 1:21–28). In the country of the Gerasenes lives a man possessed by a Legion of demons. He's too strong for anyone to bind, a zombie living among the tombs. Jesus casts the Legion into a herd of pigs, which charge into the water and drown (Mark 5:1–20). He delivers the daughter of a Syrophoenician woman (Matt 15:21–28; Mark 7:24–30), a blind and mute man (Matt 12:22–32; Mark 3:20–30; Luke 11:14–23), and a boy whose demon throws him into water and fire (Matt 17:14–21; Mark 9:14–29; Luke 9:37–49). He establishes a house of healing, where He heals diseases and casts out demons (Matt 8:16–17; Mark 1:32–34; Luke 4:40–41).

Jesus is the Stronger Man who binds Satan, the strong man, and plunders his house (Matt 12:29; Mark 3:27; Luke 11:21). Even if Jesus' enemies are right and He casts out demons by the power of Satan, His exorcisms are still a sign of Satan's impending defeat. Once Satan starts casting out Satan, his kingdom is divided and about to fall (Matt 12:24–26).

Jesus' exorcisms dramatize the arrival of the kingdom. If He casts out demons by the finger-Spirit of God, the kingdom of God has come upon Israel (Matt 12:28; Luke 11:20). Pharaoh's magicians recognized Yahweh's Finger in the plagues (Exod 8:19), but the blinded Jews can't see the divine Finger when it pokes them in the eye. Jesus has Satan on the run. Especially in His death, He drives the ruler of this world from the field (cf. John 12:31–32). This is what the coming of the kingdom means: God overthrows His enemies and wrests back control of His world.

That is what Jesus began to do and teach (Acts 1:1). After the apostles receive the Spirit-finger at Pentecost, Jesus continues His warfare through them. They preach and heal and drive out demons. Paul exorcises a spirit of divination from a slave girl in Philippi (Acts 16:16–18). More typically, the apostles don't encounter Satan or demons directly. They battle Satanically inspired people. Peter says Satan drove Ananias to lie to the Holy Spirit (Acts 5:3), and Paul denounces Bar-Jesus or Elymas as a "son of the devil" (Acts 13:10). Paul's entire mission is a deliverance, calling Jews and gentiles from darkness to light and from the dominion of Satan to God (Acts 26:18).

The entire church is enlisted into the host that battles Satan. Our battle is against principalities and powers and Spiritual forces in heavenly places (Eph 6:12). Peter warns that the devil prowls like a lion seeking prey (1 Pet 5:8), and James says hell-fire can inspire our speech (Jas 3:6). Once Paul establishes churches, he feels responsible to preserve them from Satanic seduction. He compares the Corinthians to Eve and himself to a servant of the Last Adam, who guards the Bride from the serpent (2 Cor 11:3).

When Jesus pulls back the veil, John sees the demonic powers behind the church's human enemies. Jews who oppose the Messiah become synagogues of Satan (Rev 2:9; 3:9), false teachers in Thyatira urge believers to penetrate the "deep things of Satan" (Rev 2:24), and Pergamum is the place "where Satan's throne is" (Rev 2:13). Once the dragon is tossed from heaven (Rev 12:1–12), he pursues the Bride and her children (Rev 12:13–17) and then calls up monsters from the sea and land to overcome the saints (Rev 13:1–18). Inspired by the dragon, Romans and Jews ally together against the church.

In Revelation, Babylon represents Jerusalem, the city that drinks the blood of the prophets and saints (Rev 18:24; cf. Matt 23:35). She's a harlot and a sorceress (Rev 18:23), and she's not the only one. In Samaria, Philip encounters Simon Magus, a prophet and magician who is baptized and joins the church. When he sees Peter and John confer the Spirit, he offers to pay to learn the trick. Peter rebukes him severely (Acts 8:9–24). Paul's impact on Ephesus is even more dramatic. Ephesus is the climax of Paul's gentile mission. He stays three years, until "all who lived in Asia heard the word of the Lord" (Acts 19:10). His success provokes opposition. Demetrius the silversmith objects that "not only in Ephesus but in almost all of Asia, this Paul has persuaded and turned a considerable number of people" from idols (Acts 19:26).

Paul's exorcisms are so successful that unbelieving Jews start imitating him. Seven sons of the Jewish priest Sceva attempt to exorcise a demon-possessed man with the words, "I adjure you by Jesus whom Paul preaches" (Acts 19:13). The demon knows Jesus and Paul but doesn't recognize these exorcists. The man is as powerful as the Gadarene demoniac, pouncing on the Scevans and driving them away wounded and naked (Acts 19:13–16). When the news spreads through Ephesus, many acknowledge the power of Jesus, before whom even the demons bow. He's Lord of demons, who takes away the potency of magical practices. Like one of the cities of Canaan under the ban, Ephesus becomes the site of a conflagration as the residents burn fifty thousand silver pieces' worth of magical books (Acts 19:19). Paul's signs and wonders surpass magic. The Word of the Lord is more powerful than any incantation. Jesus has overcome the prince of this world, and the world ruled by that fallen prince won't survive for long.

WAR ON MAMMON

Mammon is one of the chief powers of the world, one of the primary idols against which Jesus and the church wage war. Jesus preaches an economically-charged gospel. In the synagogue of Nazareth, Jesus introduces Himself as the Servant of Yahweh prophesied by Isaiah. Filled with the Spirit, the Servant preaches good news to the poor, release to captives, sight to the blind, and rescue for the downtrodden (Luke 4:16–21;cf. Isa 61:1–2). Jesus announces a great Jubilee, which brings release to slaves and a restoration of Israel to the land (cf. Lev 25).

Throughout His public life, Jesus confronts the powerful wealthy with a call to sacrificial generosity. "Woe to you who are rich," He says, and "woe to you who are well-fed." The time is coming when the rich will no longer be comforted, when the well-fed will be left hungry (Luke 6:24–25). Jesus targets the Jerusalem elites, who combine wealth with political clout. The parable of the good Samaritan contrasts priests and Levites, finicky about purity, with the Samaritan who proves himself a good neighbor to the man who was robbed (Luke 10:25–37). The rich man in the parable of Lazarus is dressed like a priest, in purple and fine linen, and lives in splendor and festivity (Luke 16:19–31). Jesus doesn't condemn wealth, but He eviscerates ungenerous temple elites, who devour widows' houses and ignore the ulcerated beggars sitting at the gates of the temple. Nothing raises His ire like abuse of the weak.

The parable of the unjust steward ends with Jesus' observation that possessions ("mammon") should be used to make friends so that one can be received into eternal dwellings (Luke 16:1–13). The steward, wicked as he is (Luke 16:8), knows what money is for: Money is not to be worshiped or hoarded. It's not a lord or god (Luke 16:13). Money is for making friends. The only question is what friends we're trying to make. Do we make friends with powerful elites, or do we make friends with God by making friends with the poor?

As soon as the Spirit falls on the disciples, they continue the Servant's mission, including His war on Mammon. Like Jesus, they preach the gospel to the poor, release to prisoners, liberty to the oppressed. The three thousand disciples begin to sell their possessions to provide for needy brothers. In Acts 6, the church sets up a system of charity to care for widows. They faithfully break bread together and—as Jew and gentile, Parthian and Mede and Elamite, Cretan and Arab—sit at a common table. By their *koinonia* in material goods, Christians proclaim the mystery. By their generosity, they announce Jesus' victory over Mammon.

Mammon's worshipers don't want to hear the news. Ananias and Sapphira keep back part of the proceeds of the sale of their property. They give the illusion of generosity without suffering any loss; they're greedy both for money and for a reputation for giving away their money (Acts 5:1–11). In Philippi, Paul's accusers are riled when Paul drives a spirit of divination from a slave girl. As soon as the demon comes out, they see their hope of profit coming out (Acts 16:18–19). In Ephesus, Demetrius whips the silversmiths into a riotous froth by reminding them how much they're liable to lose if Paul's message about idols takes hold (Acts 19:23–27). Greed infects the rulers who judge Paul. Felix keeps Paul in prison in Caesarea because he wants a bribe (Acts 24:26). The enemies of Jesus and Paul are all lovers of money (cf. Luke 16:14), and so are ours. Throughout the ages, the church suffers persecution when she dares to confront the powerful who get fat by devouring the poor.

Demetrius and the owners of the slave girl are entrepreneurs of religion, using religion as a cover for greed. When their wealth is threatened, they respond violently, but deceptively, with a show of public-spirited concern for the common good. "These men are throwing our city into confusion," say the Philippian slave-owners (Acts 16:20). Artemis is being "dethroned from her magnificence," says Demetrius (Acts 19:27). In a sense, they're right. Philippi and Ephesus are ordered by worship of Mammon, and Paul challenges the foundations of society when he takes away their idols. The apostles wouldn't be the least surprised by today's surfeit of religious kitsch, our multi-millionaire preachers, or the contemporary uses of God-speak to conceal envy and covetousness. Money continues to corrupt the faith, and it's the church's mission to obliterate Mammon's reign in the church as much as in the world.

Paul's own practices stand in sharp contrast. When he stays for a long time in Corinth, he finds work as a tent-maker (Acts 18:1–3). At Ephesus, he works with his hands to meet his own needs (Acts 20:34). He can say without pretense, "I have coveted no one's silver or gold or clothes" (Acts 20:33) because he has followed Jesus' instruction: "It is more blessed to give than to receive" (Acts 20:35). Paul learns the lesson of the parable of the steward: He uses Mammon to make friends with the poor and hence with God.

Money forges a friendship between Jews and gentiles. As he travels from gentile church to gentile church, Paul raises funds to carry back to Jerusalem as famine relief. Gentiles have become partakers (*koinoneo*) of the Jews' Spiritual goods and should respond by sharing material goods (Rom 15:27). Like the table fellowship where Jew and gentile share bread (see Gal 2:11–14), money breaks down the dividing wall and forms one new humanity. Money forms a communion in mission. As an apostle, Paul sows Spiritual goods among the churches (1 Cor 9:11), and he expects to reap a harvest when the Corinthians help him with donations. Out of this sowing and reaping, Paul's communion with the churches deepens. The Philippians share (*sugkoinoneo*) both Paul's affliction and his work as they commune (*koinoneo*) with him in giving and receiving (Phil 4:15).

In the market, money causes a break of fellowship. We pay the clerk or waiter, and we don't have to have any further dealings with him. We don't want to buy friendship, only goods and services. The gospel radically transforms our notion of money and its uses. Not only in the church but also in the marketplace, money is a sign and seal of personal communion. The hippies were right: Money is bread, like the Eucharistic bread that serves as an effective sign of the communion of giver and receiver in the mission of Jesus and in His Spirit. The economy of the church is a Eucharistic economy, and the church is called to pilot the world economy away from the shoals of Mammon into the safe haven of *koinonia*.

THE POWERS STRIKE BACK

Everywhere Jesus goes, He provokes opposition. So do His disciples. Peter and John heal a man who has been lame from birth (Acts 3:1–10). While Peter preaches to the amazed crowd, the captain of the temple guard seizes them and takes them to prison (Acts 4:1–4). Later, they perform signs and wonders in Solomon's portico, and the high priest again arrests and imprisons them (Acts 5:12–18). When an angel leads them from the prison, they don't take a break or skip town. They head straight back to the temple to start preaching again (Acts 5:21–22). This time, the Sanhedrin flogs them and orders them to stop talking about Jesus (Acts 5:40–41).

Opposition escalates. After Stephen's death, the Jews begin a systematic, officially sponsored persecution. Saul pursues Christians from house to house, arresting and imprisoning both men and women (Acts 8:1–3). He tortures them to blaspheme Jesus, and he casts his vote to put them to death (Acts 26:10–11). Herod puts James to death and imprisons Peter (Acts 12).

Arrest and warning. Arrest and imprisonment. Then arrest and beating. Then a mob execution. Then systematic persecution. The conflict escalates and doesn't stop when Paul converts. On the contrary, the chief persecutor becomes the persecuted.

While Paul is still in Damascus, Jews plot to kill him. The disciples help him escape through a window in the city wall

(Acts 9:23–25), like the spies from Rahab's house (Josh 2:15–21) or a new David (1 Sam 19:11–17). When Jews at Pisidian Antioch become jealous of Paul's success, they contradict him and blaspheme Jesus (Acts 13:44–46). At Iconium, the Jews again oppose Paul and attempt to stone him to death (Acts 14:4–6).

Like Paul himself in his earlier life, the Jews move from city to city, carrying on an anti-mission. Jews from Antioch and Iconium stone Paul and drag him out of Lystra, leaving him for dead (Acts 14:19–20). Everywhere, Paul is accused, beaten, arrested, and imprisoned. No wonder Paul speaks like a madman (2 Cor 11:23) and boasts of his sufferings: beatings, stonings, shipwrecks, journeys, dangers from rivers, robbers, Jews, gentiles, threats in the city and in the wilderness and among false brothers (2 Cor 11:23–27).

Conflict is no accident, nor is it avoidable. Suffering is the only path into the kingdom, an inevitable part of mission. If you want a painless and comfortable life, it's best not to board the ark of a crucified Savior. Peter and John rejoice they are worthy to suffer for Jesus (Acts 5:41). Paul boasts of his brandmarks because his scars are physical evidence that he shares in Christ's sufferings for the sake of the church (Col 1:24). There's no mission without the cross. The church must be as crucifiable as her Lord. Jesus' self-building ark is constructed from the wood of a cross.

ADVISOR TO THE KING

The apostolic mission is Spiritual war. It's also, at the same time, political combat. The apostles don't carry out their mission in the catacombs or retreat into secret intentional communities. They preach and act in public, in synagogues and town squares. Naturally, they end up in public squabbles with Jews and gentiles who don't want Jesus to take over public life.

The Spirit and political battlefields overlap so much that they become indistinguishable. In Philippi, Paul expels a spirit of divination from a slave girl. Deprived of their livelihood, the girl's owners drag Paul and Silas to the magistrates, charging them with attacking the customs of the proudly Roman colony of Philippi. The mob and the magistrates strip the missionaries and beat them with rods, and the city leaders throw them into prison (Acts 16:16–24).

Overnight, an earthquake shakes the prison open, which leads to the conversion of the jailer and his household. The next morning, the humbled magistrates offer to let Paul and Silas leave town quietly, but Paul refuses. He suddenly reveals he's a Roman citizen and reminds the magistrates that they've permitted him to be beaten and imprisoned without trial. Paul wants the magistrates to admit their error in person (Acts 16:35–39). Paul demands a vindication as public as the violation.

Paul's demand has long-term effects. If the magistrates of Philippi allow Paul and Silas to preach, they'll also tolerate the group of believers gathered at Lydia's house (Acts 16:40). Paul wins a legal and political skirmish, but he achieves far more. He leaves behind a new Philippi, which now tolerates a church that teaches a subversive Way that, by the Philippians' own admission, "it is not lawful for us to accept or to observe, being Romans" (Acts 16:21). The mere existence of a Christian community in Philippi forces the city to alter public norms. Jesus builds His ark in Philippi, and the city begins to clamor aboard.

The apostles' triumphs over false prophets, magicians, and idolaters are also political victories. In Samaria, Peter and John lay hands on believers to confer the Spirit. Simon, a magician who "claimed to be someone great" and is known as "the Great Power of God," offers to pay the apostles to teach him the trick. Peter severely rebukes Simon for his bondage to iniquity and the "gall of bitterness" (Acts 8:9–24). Simon, recognizing a power greater than his own, pleads with the apostles for forgiveness. You can bet Simon lost some prestige among the Samaritans after that incident. You can bet the apostles gained status. Exotic messengers from Judea who win power battles with magicians and prophets are a political force to be reckoned with.

Paul's confrontation with Bar-Jesus at Salamis is of particular note. At the beginning, Bar-Jesus is "with the proconsul, Sergius Paulus" (Acts 13:6–7), a court magician and prophet, like the magicians of Pharaoh or the prophets of Ahab. When Paul rebukes Bar-Jesus as a "son of the devil," Sergius Paulus is impressed: "the proconsul believed ... being amazed at the teaching of the Lord" (Acts 13:12). A Roman proconsul named Paulus stops taking advice from one Jew in order to listen to his namesake.

In Luke's Gospel, Jesus' first sermon at Nazareth anticipates His entire mission as Isaiah's Spirit-anointed Servant of Yahweh (Luke 4:14–30). Set at the beginning of Paul's first missionary journey, the story of Bar-Jesus and Sergius Paulus previews his whole mission. The apostle to the gentiles prevails over false teachers so Roman officials will submit to the teaching of the Lord. Paul takes over as advisor to the king. From the beginning of his mission, Paul is on his way to becoming the pilot of the Roman ship.

It's nothing new. When Israel is sown into Babylonian exile, Jeremiah instructs them to seek the peace of the city where they're sent (Jer 29). Jeremiah's instruction continues to apply after Persia defeats Babylon, after Alexander the Great defeats Persia, and after Rome conquers the Mediterranean world. As the Jews pursue the peace and good of the city of man, the Lord places some in high office. At the beginning of Israel's history, the Lord sends Joseph into Egypt ahead of Jacob and his sons. Pharaoh sets Joseph over the land of Egypt (Gen 41:41) to oversee the famine relief program. By the time Joseph's brothers arrive, Yahweh has prepared a place for them.

Yahweh does the same when Nebuchadnezzar threatens Judah. Daniel and his friends are taken to Babylon in the first deportation. By the time Nebuchadnezzar destroys the temple and the city, Daniel is already ruler of the province of Babylon and chief of the company of wise men (Dan 2:46–49). No wonder Jeremiah feels confident enough to urge the kings of Judah to surrender to Nebuchadnezzar. They have a friend in the highest place. When Persia overthrows Babylon, Daniel again rises to a high position, as one of the three commissioners over the 120 satraps of the Persian empire (Dan 6:1–2). Other Jews are highly placed in Persia too. Nehemiah is cupbearer to the king (Neh 1:11), Ezra is well-known as a scribe (Ezra 7:1–26), Esther becomes queen, and Mordecai ends up as the second to King Ahasuerus (Est 10:1–3).

These elite Jews are effective witnesses. Yahweh sends bad dreams to Pharaoh, sparking a series of events that elevates Joseph. Nebuchadnezzar too has a perplexing dream, which Daniel, a new Joseph, interprets (Dan 2). The Lord sends another dream in which a tree representing Nebuchadnezzar is cut down. Nebuchadnezzar is humbled and lives as a wild beast for a time before his human sanity is restored (Dan 4). In each case, the dreaming ruler ends up confessing the power of the God of Israel. Pharaoh recognizes a spirit of God in Joseph, which allows him to foresee the future (Gen 41:38–39). Nebuchadnezzar's confessions are among the most remarkable in Scripture:

> Surely your God is a God of gods and a Lord of kings and a revealer of mysteries, since you have been able to reveal this mystery. (Dan 2:47)
>
> I blessed the Most High and praised and honored Him who lives forever; for His dominion is an everlasting dominion, and His kingdom endures from generation to generation. And all the inhabitants of the earth are accounted as nothing, but He does according to His will in the host of heaven and among the inhabitants of earth; and no one can ward off His hand or say to Him, "What hast Thou done?" (Dan 4:34–35)

When interpreting Nebuchadnezzar's dream of the tree, Daniel rebukes the king not only about his pride, but also about the injustice of his reign: "break away now from your sins by doing righteousness, and from your iniquities by showing mercy to the poor, in case there may be a prolonging of your prosperity" (Dan 4:27). We aren't told what changes Nebuchadnezzar makes when he recovers, but we can guess he takes Daniel's warning seriously. He acknowledges Yahweh's dominion and kingdom. We can surmise that the chastened emperor seeks to conform his own kingdom to Yahweh's justice.

The effect in the Persian empire is even more dramatic. As Isaiah prophesies, the Persian rulers take on the role of the anointed kings of the Davidic dynasty. They become Yahweh's servants and shepherds, who build Jerusalem, protect the Jews from their enemies, and restore the ruined temple (Isa 44:24–45:7). When Israel returns to the land in a second exodus, there are no plagues, no repeat of Passover, no deadly Red-Sea baptism. There doesn't need to be. Instead of resisting Yahweh's demands, the Persians set Israel free. Cyrus is the Moses of the new Exodus. Israel doesn't need to plunder Persia because the Persians supply them with all the materials they need to rebuild the temple (Ezra 1:5–11).

The church takes over this Jewish mission. Christians are model citizens, seeking the peace of the city. As the church's mission goes forward, high-placed Jews are converted or replaced by believing Jews or converted gentiles. Over the following centuries, Christian communities become the moral center in Roman city after Roman city, and Christian charity becomes the welfare system of the empire. As the Philippians fear, the customs of the church displace the customs of Romans.

CONCLUSION

Acts doesn't tell of any converted kings. No Constantine appears, no Charlemagne or Vladimir or Tiridates. Yet the story of Acts presses toward Christendom. Through Spiritual and political battles, through suffering and service, Christians rise to positions of authority as advisors to kings. Eventually, kings will submit to the King of kings and, like Nebuchadnezzar, confess their allegiance to the kingdom of God. The church builds herself as a saving vessel within the Roman world. Eventually, the whole Roman world finds its home in Jesus' ark. Eventually it's official: The heirs of the apostles pilot the Roman ship of state.

20

Vessels of Salvation

THE ARK, IN WHICH A FEW, THAT IS, EIGHT PERSONS, WERE BROUGHT SAFELY THROUGH THE WATER.
—1 PETER 3:20

After Yahweh forms Adam, He plants an enclosed garden and causes every tree to grow there (Gen 2:7–8). Noah turns trees into gopher wood lumber to build a nautical garden (Gen 6:14). Noah's ark is a sanctuary, measured and divided—like the tabernacle and temple—into three zones. The ark is a new Eden, the first manmade sanctuary on earth.

Every sanctuary is made after the pattern of the heavenly sanctuary (Exod 25:9, 40). As heaven-on-earth, the sanctuary sets the pattern for the world. The liturgical work of the sanctuary is a model for the political work of kings in the land. Liturgical culture models and renews world culture. The beauty and glory of the sanctuary is to be replicated in the beauty and glory outside. Like the sanctuary, the land is to be a place of food and festivity, joy and communion. During the ideal reign of Solomon, every Israelite lived in joy under his own vine and fig tree (1 Kgs 4:25). Every house and town is remade according to the pattern of the temple. "Thy will be done on earth as it is in heaven" can be translated as

"Thy will be done in the land as in the temple, in the world as in the church."

Noah's ark is a microcosm *because* it's a sanctuary. The ark's three decks correspond to the three stories of Yahweh's cosmic house—heaven, earth, and sea. Like the firmament, the ark has a window (Gen 6:16; cf. Mal 3:10). It floats over the formless void of the deep (cf. Gen 1:2), a miniature of land + firmament. Like creation itself, the ark contains all living things. Eight men and women enter the ark, and Noah is a new Adam, herding a pair of every kind of bird, beast, and creeping thing (cf. Gen 1:20, 26), seven of every clean animal, into the ark (Gen 6:19–20; 7:2). Noah stores the ark with plants for food (Gen 6:21), and the ark itself is made from plants.

In fact, the account of the ark follows the order of creation. Yahweh forms a three-story universe (Gen 1:1–10), and Noah builds a three-story ark (Gen 6:16). Yahweh places Adam and Eve in the garden (Gen 2:8, 21–22) and brings Noah and his family into the ark (Gen 6:18). Yahweh gathers cattle, beasts, and birds to Adam to be named (Gen 2:19–20), and Noah gathers birds, beasts, and creeping things into the ark (Gen 6:19–20). At the climax of Genesis 1, Yahweh offers the world to man as food (Gen 1:29–31). At the climax of His instructions to Noah, He commands Noah to take food into the ark (Gen 6:21).

The remarkable difference, of course, is the maker. Yahweh makes the original cosmic house and the original sanctuary. Yahweh designs the ark, but Noah makes it. As I've said, Noah is the first human to make rightly. He follows Yahweh's instructions and becomes a Godlike creator, capable of creating a cosmos. His manmade microcosm saves the Creator's macrocosm. After the flood, Noah and his family and all the animals emerge from the ark to start the world over again. Noah preserves seeds of the old world so he can plant them in a new creation. His ark is a saving vessel, not for a few scattered souls but for the world.

Today, the Carpenter of Nazareth, true man, is still at work building a microcosmic sanctuary, the church. As we've seen, we build His body alongside Him. The church is the artwork of the Son and Spirit; it's also the work of master artisans like Paul (1 Cor 3:10) and the millions of Spirit-filled believers who share the work of edifying the church. We're all Bezalels and Oholiabs (Exod 31:1–11) since we all receive Jesus' Spirit of skill (Acts 2:17; 1 Cor 12:13; cf. Isa 11:1–2). Together, we build ourselves into the ark that is also the body, Bride, and church of Jesus.

Like the ark, the church receives and preserves the treasures of the world (Rev 21:24) so they can be purged, transfigured, and brought out again to adorn creation. As worlds collapse, the world's riches are kept safe in the ark of the church. All things are gathered into the church so that all things can disembark into a new creation. Noah performs this magic only once, but Jesus does it continuously. Treasures flow continuously into the ark of Christendom. The church has received the treasures of Greek and Roman art, philosophy, and politics, to purify them and bring them to fulfillment. It will plunder the gold of China, Japan, and India, of the Masai and Zulu, of Arabia and Iraq and Afghanistan. Treasures from the city of man enter the city of God so they can return to the city of man, renewed. The city of man enters the ark of God so it can become more perfectly what it's supposed to be, more perfectly an image of heavenly Jerusalem.

The church pilots the world. What happens in the holy church guides what happens outside. If the church is unfaithful, leaves her first love, and turns to false teachers, Jesus will remove the lampstand and abandon the house (Rev 2–3). If the church keeps her lamps burning, continuously supplied by the oil of the Spirit, the world will be full of light. Sanctuaries are springs. They can flow with poison (Rev 10–11) or with life-giving waters (Ezek 47; Rev 22:1–5). The church is the new covenant sanctuary—a spring of life or a source of death.

This is imagery, but not *mere* imagery. It's the way the world works. It describes what the church has always been and done, what she will always be and do. Within the ark of the church, Jesus incubates new forms of social and economic life, new initiatives of work and creativity, new forms of charity, new modes of instruction, new artistic subjects and standards of beauty. The church is the nursery of the kingdom, the ark that preserves, purges, and transforms the treasures of the world. She's the place where the new heavens and earth first take form.

To return to chapter 16: Human beings are created in the image of a Creator. We're made for making. In Adam, we mis-make and mis-speak, but in the Last Adam we are re-made into godly speakers and makers. The church is the forge where our making and speaking is smelted and shaped. As the church's history is scripted by Scripture, as we practice the apostolic customs of *koinonia*, as we battle Spiritual and political enemies, we remake the social worlds around us.

REMAKING MAKERS

Jesus remakes our making by first re-making us as makers. He does this in the liturgy, where we are molded into the shape of Jesus. Worship is *leitourgia*, the work of the people. Our postures inscribe humility, attention, and rest on our bodies. In song, we tune our life's breath to the praise of God. In prayer, we cast our cares on the one who cares for us; in common prayer, each of us has voice before the King of all.

All this activity is grounded in a more fundamental passivity. Our giving arises from a more fundamental reception. Liturgy is the work of the people of God, but more fundamentally, it's the work of God on the people. It is the Lord's gracious service to us, gifts of God for the people of God. Every week, Jesus puts on the servant's apron to wash the feet of His disciples.

Jesus remakes us by restoring us to priesthood. Man's first vocation is priestly, and his first labor is the labor of the sanctuary (Gen 2:15). All making in the land and world reflects the pattern of priestly serving and guarding. All our making in the world is formed and re-formed by our participation in the priestly work of the sanctuary. As priests, we receive God's gifts with thanks; as priests, we offer our makings to God in praise. Our priestly work is itself a gift of God. By the Spirit, we edify one another and are built up together as the body of Christ. As we carry out the liturgy in step with the Spirit, we are the self-constructing ark that is a microcosm and model for the world.

We often focus on the liturgy's power to renew minds and souls, but Jesus renews bodies too. He's a healer, the divine Physician. He gives sight to the blind and hearing to the deaf, loosens the tongues of the dumb, straightens limbs and cleanses lepers, casts out demons that slash and beat the bodies they possess. Ancient pagans have their Asclepius. But no ancient myth tells of a High God who comes near to mingle and mix with the diseased and demon-possessed. In no mythology or philosophy does the High God show pity for His creatures.

When the apostles receive the Spirit, the apostles continue Jesus' ministry, healing the lame and expelling demons (Acts 3:1–5; 5:12–16; 20:7–12). The church is and has always been a place of healing, and that healing takes form in the quasi-sacrament of anointing (Jas 5:13–18). The sick call for the elders of the church, who anoint with oil and pray over the sick, while the sick confess their sins. Healing is embedded in the liturgical life of the church.

From those seeds—the seeds of a gospel of healing and a rite of anointing—grow the unprecedented Christian attention to health care. Pagans have their medical philosophers like Galen, just as they have their gods of healing. But the Christian mission of healing is qualitatively different. Like Jesus, Christians are incarnated among the sick. When plagues and pandemics hit Roman cities, pagans fled, including Galen. Christians stayed to nurse the sick to health. Over time, they developed institutions like the hospital and techniques of healing that were unknown in the ancient world. In the sanctuary-ark of the church, Jesus nourishes new forms of compassion, which, over the centuries, have transformed the world.

LOOSENING TONGUES

We gather in the Lord's presence on the Lord's Day to receive the Word of the Lord at the Lord's table. We are brought into the Triune conversation, united to the Son by the breath of His Spirit. In worship, we hear the Word read, taught, and preached. We sing the Word and pray the Word. We respond to the Word with the Word. Christian worship should be drenched, saturated, flooded with the Word.

When it is, the liturgy produces new forms of speaking and writing outside the sanctuary. To prepare sermons, preachers study biblical texts. They learn biblical languages and refine techniques for historical research and literary interpretation. Nothing like the medieval fourfold method of interpretation existed in the pre-Christian world. Over centuries, that method developed into a complex method of reading that preserves history and fact, while discerning also the blossoms of Spiritual meaning that unfold within events. The fourfold is more than a method of reading. It's a biblical theology of history, society, and politics.

As Augustine says, every form of study serves biblical interpretation and teaching. To know what Jesus means when He says, "Be wise as serpents," you need to know something about the cunning habits of serpents. To know what happens to the Jews between the end of the Old Testament and the beginning of the New, you need to study the books of the Maccabees and Ben Sirach, the visions of Enoch, the historical work of Philo and Josephus. To grasp the long passages of symbolic architecture in Exodus, Kings, and Ezekiel, you need to know something about architecture. You need to know something about political theory to grasp the historical books of the Bible, and those books also serve as a primer of biblical politics.

A full curriculum for Bible readers quickly becomes a curriculum about everything under the sun and many things beyond the sun. Bible teaching incorporates all knowledge outside the Bible. The Bible also serves as a foundry where all knowledge is purged and re-shaped. The liturgy thus inspires a transformation of education. The liberal arts have roots in the classical world, but in the church, they're refreshed by Scripture. The Reformers insisted everyone needed to learn to read so that all could read Scripture. Within the ark of the church, education is oriented to the liturgy. When it emerges from the liturgy, it's something quite different. The apostles' teaching spills out of the ark of the church in new forms of literary culture.

The liturgy is more than teaching. It's formation. It not only fills the heads of worshipers with biblical truth. The Word forms the hearts of worshipers with the beauty and glory of God. The liturgy inscribes honor for God on our bodies. It trains our tongues to speak His Word. It's not merely teaching, but *paideia*, the training of whole persons in the ways of the Lord.

In this way too, the liturgy renews culture. Education is culture, and culture is education. A culture isn't a culture if it lasts only a generation. A way of life must pass as a tradition from generation to generation. *Paedeia*, the Greeks know, is the very essence of culture. By generating new forms of study and education, the Christian church forms a new culture, new habits of speaking and making.

STRENGTHENING HANDS

Miraculous as it is, the Eucharist isn't a strange anomaly within an impersonal, insignificant, mechanistic universe. It discloses the reality deep down things. It shows us that creation is personal and meaningful from top to bottom. Everything we see, touch, taste, and handle is a sign-gift of the Creator's love. In the Eucharist, we receive the world—this world, the everyday world of bread and wine, of eating and drinking—as it was meant to be: a joyous communion with the Triune God. The table shows that every encounter with reality is an encounter with God.

The Eucharist makes us attentive to creation. Every bird, every blade of grass, every delicate winter rose, every passing cloud, every scurrying squirrel, every flake of sparkling rime is a loving gift from our heavenly Father, to be received with ecstatic thanks. Christians should devote ourselves as closely to the details of our craft or profession as anyone else. Indeed, we have more cause to do so since for us there are no dispensable facts, any more than there are dispensable people. All the scientist's data, every slab of granite, every drop of paint, every block of wood comes from a Creator who spoke them lovingly into being. If God loves them enough to make them, we must love them too, with all their fascinating intricacies and eccentricities, with all their knotted riddles.

At the table, Jesus remakes our making. The Eucharist is a glimpse of the end of all things. The church gathers at the Lord's table to receive the gifts of God with thanksgiving in the presence of God. All things are moving toward this final destiny, toward translation into the feast of the kingdom. The human race will come to fullness at the marriage supper of the Lamb and His Bride, and all our makings will be transformed by Spirit-guided human labor into adornments of that feast. The table orients our making toward this final destiny. It assures us our labor won't perish but will have a place in an eternal Eucharist.

The table also points to the temporal destinations of our makings. At the Lord's table, we share bread—in some liturgies, bread is passed from hand to hand—an effective emblem of the gift-exchange that makes up the Christian community. We're the one-and-many body because we who are many partake of the one loaf (1 Cor 10:16–17). Bread and wine are paradigms of human products. We do with all our making what we do with the Eucharistic food and drink. We offer everything to God in worship and share all we produce for the edification of the body. Our making isn't simply utilitarian, and yet our makings, even the most needless, are designed to meet needs.

Thanksgiving sanctifies everything (1 Tim 4:4–5). If that's the case, we know the destination of our holy products: Holy things go to holy people. We offer our works to God by distributing them to the people of God as gifts for their edification. Christians are kings who bring our treasures as offerings to adorn the civic most holy place that is the Christian church.

All making involves give-and-take with creation. I take in some bit of the world, work on it, and it becomes part of me. I grow as I take and make; I become more fully who I am created to be. The table I build is my table, the book I write, my book. At the same time, I give myself to the world, pouring myself into the world to put my stamp on these materials. By making, men and women humanize the world, stamping it with the stamp of the image of God. In that exchange, we commune with the world as labor links the maker, who matures by his making, with the made-thing, which bears the imprint of its creator.

The Eucharist portrays the way making ought to be. At the Lord's table, we commune with the world. Eating becomes the paradigm of our relationship to creation. But the Eucharist also embeds our communion with the world within our communion with God. In holy communion, we commune with God through our makings. The Eucharist renews our relationship with the products of our labor. The minister goes through a series of actions (takes bread, gives thanks, breaks, distributes, eats; takes cup, gives thanks, distributes, drinks) involving things (bread and wine). Through these actions on these things, we encounter a person, the Lord Jesus, through His Spirit. That is the reality of all our making and labor. The Eucharist places all our communion with the creation within our communion with the Creator.

As God remakes us at the table, He corrects our egotism and our deep belief that our things are ours. The Supper infuses all our making with gratitude. We receive the materials and tools of our labor with thanks. We sift, mix, chisel, shape, and reshape the materials with thanks. When we have produced a work, we acknowledge with thanks that, though our work is ours, it is, like bread and wine, a gift from God. When we give thanks, we acknowledge our dependence on the Giver. Like everything we possess, our making is modified by a double possessive. Everything we make is both ours and God's.

The Eucharistic liturgy establishes a pattern of Eucharistic living, a life of thanksgiving in all circumstances for everything. All things are consecrated by thanksgiving and prayer (1 Tim 4:4–5). Every human endeavor moves from thanks to thanks. Even things we make—bread and wine, the work of human hands—are gifts from God. At the table, we're remade to make as priests of a cosmic Eucharist.

We give thanks not only for the materials we receive, but for God's kind providence that guides our making. Beginners believe every discovery is the product of rigorous, thorough, exhaustive engagement, research, experiment, and labor. The historian discovers the decisive, field-changing text because he has spent decades in the dusty archive. The scientist uncovers a secret of the universe because of the comprehensiveness of his controlled experiments. The poet hits upon the right pattern of words after deep reflection. The plumber knows how to design the plumbing because of his deep experience with pipes and couplings.

Any self-aware maker is painfully aware of his limitations and also joyfully aware that insight can come from anywhere. Fresh creativity might come from a chance conversation with a colleague, or a student, or a child, or a grandmother in the early stages of dementia. A researcher spies a forgotten monograph while browsing the stacks or stumbles on an article while surfing the web to check the football scores. A poet overhears a snatch of conversation on the Tube that breaks through his writer's block. A builder figures out how to handle a complicated construction problem while tussling with his toddlers after dinner.

Breakthroughs come at us as unbidden, unbiddable possibilities, and the best makers know how to spin detritus into gold. The Eucharist trains us to take hold of the world expecting our Father to provide what we need to complete our work, to polish surfaces of the made-thing we produce. We expect our Father to leave fresh gifts around every corner of the twisting path.

The Eucharist doesn't merely teach us we ought to be Eucharistic. Sharing the Eucharist, we are caught up in Eucharist and become Eucharist. By the Spirit of the Crucified, we become living sacrifices, offering ourselves and the works of our hands in worship (Rom 12:1–2). This happens only when we commune with Christ and His body in the meal of bread and wine. Once again: Through the table, all our making is folded into His priestly service, which is also our priestly service.

At the table, we're called and called again from idols to communion with the living God. Every time we eat and drink, the Lord issues the double command of the Son of Man: "Worship God," and its corollary, "Flee idols" (1 John 5:21; Rev 22:9). We pulverize idols by bearing witness, and we become witnesses as we ingest Jesus, true and faithful *martus* (Rev 3:14). Consuming Him, we're made like Him. By sharing the sacrificial meal, we commit ourselves to self-sacrificing witness. It's more than a commitment: By the Spirit, the feast conforms us to the self-sacrificing witness we consume. It's physically possible to partake of the Lord's table and the table of demons, but it's Spiritually perilous. Having feasted at the marriage supper of the Lamb, we provoke Him to jealousy if we scramble for a seat at the table of demons (1 Cor 10:14–22).

The Lord's table liberates us from the cultural trends, fads, and fashions that grip the mob. Conformed to Christ's death, we rejoice to be outcasts from inner rings. Fashions and fads are often idolatrous at root, and our task is not to worship idols but to expose and expel them. Exposing idols is bound to make us unpopular, as the apostles found. You embarrass an opponent if you call attention to his ignorance or sloppiness. You enrage him if you defile the object of his worship. At the least, we'll be ridiculed as we're faithful. But things can get worse. The fashion mob can become a lynch mob. By giving us a share in the cross of Jesus, the Supper prepares us to take up our own cross.

We transform culture by bearing witness, which is always risky. If we're not prepared to suffer professional or vocational death because of our witness to Jesus, if we're not prepared to accept a lower place in the rankings, we have no business putting on the regalia in the first place. If we're not prepared for vocational martyrdom, we despise the table of the Lord, and our makings are nothing worth.

SEEING EYES, HEARING EARS

Transformed by the Eucharist, our making is freed from pure utility and functionality. Utility is good. A woodworker makes tables for meals, weavers make cloth for clothing, metalworkers make wires for electricity and rebar to strengthen walls. All these forms of making have practical ends. But when we make in order to offer our fruit to God in praise, we transcend mere usefulness. The cobbler doesn't just cover bare feet; he cobbles for the glory of God. At the same time, the sanctuary frees us from the sterile circularity of making for its own sake, the effete snobbery of art for art's sake. Making Eucharistically, a craftsman makes for God. Art for art's sake is a sign of decadence. It's a symptom of the decay of liturgy.

Separation of art and life, or art and craft, is likewise a result of the destruction of the liturgy. Many believe art lies in the realm of the imaginary, over-against the mechanical givenness of the real world. The liturgy reveals every thing as a gateway to God, every moment a moment to praise. Because liturgy anticipates the justice of the new creation, it's a site of resistance to the violence and injustice of the present age. Only the liturgy holds together ethics and aesthetics, imagination and reality, art and life, beauty and the mundane, affirmation and resistance, already and still to come. Outside the ark of the church, all human making will be drowned in the flood. Cut off from its source in the Eucharist, human making withers. Within the ark of the church, art reaches its destined purpose in praise.

Israel's sanctuaries are the primary sources of Israel's arts. Bezalel and Oholiab are Israel's first named artisans, and they devote their Spirit-given talents to molding gold furniture for the sanctuary, weaving threads to make the tabernacle curtains and the priest's garments, shaping wood for the frame of the tent (Exod 31:1–11). Solomon shows his wisdom by constructing the temple. Skilled or wise craftsmen sculpt stone into blocks for the temple, cast a giant bronze sea and tall bronze pillars, carve oil-wood cherubim, and decorate the cedar walls with blossoms and gourds. Israel's music is liturgical music, sung and played by the Levitical choir and orchestra David establishes (1 Chr 25:1–31).

No doubt, there were furniture makers, weavers and tailors, stonemasons and metalworkers in the villages and towns of Israel. No doubt there were butchers other than the sacred butchers at the altar. But the Bible focuses our attention on sacred craftsmen because the sanctuary is the spring and source of artistic life, of the life of making, which is human life.

That biblical pattern is repeated in the history of Christendom. Ancient tragedy ceased to be performed in the early Christian era. Drama was reborn in the liturgy, in mystery and miracle plays that enacted biblical stories or taught moralistic lessons to the illiterate multitudes. Western music began in the chants and harmonies of Christian worship.

For a millennium and more, the great architectural styles of the West were church styles—Romanesque, Gothic, neo-classical. Aspects of these styles have classical roots, but they were transformed, sometimes explicitly for theological reasons. Abbot Suger invented the Gothic style, with its majestic arches and its stunning glasswork, because he believed light is a material manifestation of the Spirit. Eastern churches and cathedrals were designed to leave people wondering whether they're in heaven or on earth. From the church, new styles and techniques flowed out to change the way we build Parliament houses and palaces.

In Scripture and Christian history, visual arts, architecture, and music come to birth as liturgical arts. Human making is purged and renewed in the sanctuary as the sanctuary, patterned by heaven, becomes the pattern for the world. Arts and artistic skills are born or reborn within the bosom of mother church.

GODLY RULE

The church produces new forms of political life, especially in the relations between church and state, religion and power. Like literary culture, like bread-making and wine-making, like architecture, art, and music, political power is transformed from the sanctuary. It begins with the restoration of Adam's priestly vocation. Earthly rule resembles heavenly rule when it passes through the liturgy.

We can see this in the history of Israel's regime of "church and state." Prior to Sinai, Israel has no sanctuary, no priestly class, and a much simpler and less explicit sacrificial and purity system. Once Israel arrives at the mountain, though, Aaron and his sons are ordained as priests (Exod 19; Lev 8–9), with exclusive access to the altar and the tabernacle (cf. Exod 29:37). Priests participate in every sacrificial rite at the tabernacle: the daily ascension offerings, the offerings brought by individual Israelite worshipers, and the massive sacrifices on feast days.

No lay Israelites, including elders, are permitted to perform these rites. In fact, every lay Israelite is excluded from the tent; the stranger who attempts to enter is executed (Num 1:51; 3:10, 38). Once Yahweh consecrates the tabernacle with His glory, not even Moses is allowed to enter (Exod 40:34–38). The church of the sanctuary is governed and run by priests, not by civil rulers.

On the other hand, priests have responsibilities for maintaining the holiness and purity of the land. Difficult criminal cases are brought to a priest (Deut 17:8–13), who inquires of Yahweh, perhaps using the Urim and Thummim. Whatever the priest decides is carried out: "According to the mouth of the law which they teach you, and according to the verdict which they tell you, you shall do" (Deut 17:11). Whoever refuses a priest's verdict is put to death (Deut 17:12). Before Israel goes to war, the (high?) priest warns them not to fear or panic because Yahweh gives victory (Deut 20:2–4), and priests lead the army at Jericho (Josh 6). Moses generalizes, "Every dispute and every stroke shall be according to [the priests'] mouth" (Deut 21:5).

Under the monarchy, power is centralized in the capital, first Hebron and then Jerusalem. David has a small court, consisting of military leaders, a bodyguard, secretaries, and priests (2 Sam 8:15–18; 20:23–26), as well as overseers of his lands and storehouses (1 Chr 27:25–31). Hushai, Ahitophel, and others serve as counselors to the king (1 Chr 27:32–34). To these, Solomon adds tribal administrators over the forced labor that builds the temple and Solomon's palace complex (1 Kgs 4:6; 11:28; 12:1–4). He organizes the land into twelve districts, each led by a deputy who gathers produce to supply the palace one month a year (1 Kgs 4:7–19). The abundance and elegant choreography of Solomon's court is enough to take the breath away from a monarch like Queen Sheba (1 Kgs 10:4–5).

David reorganizes the priests, and Solomon builds the temple, yet the priests retain their monopoly of the sanctuary. When King Uzziah attempts to offer incense at the golden altar inside the temple, Ahaziah the high priest warns him to leave: "It is not for you, Uzziah, to burn incense to Yahweh, but for the priests, the sons of Aaron who are consecrated to burn incense" (2 Chr 26:18). As Uzziah rages at the priests, the Lord strikes his forehead with leprosy, and he remains in isolation for the remainder of his life (2 Chr 26:20–21). Israel's kings aren't gods or priests. They don't run everything. The sanctuary is outside their jurisdiction. The very existence of a separate priesthood limits the scope of royal power. The church blocks the expansion of the state.

Kings can't do priestly things, but priests have significant political authority in the Davidic kingdom. Deuteronomy 17 anticipates a future monarchy, but it's a monarchy under priestly oversight. The king writes out his own copy of Torah in the presence of the priests and is required to study it throughout his life (Deut 17:18–20). Priests are the teachers of Israel (Mal 2:7), including teachers of elders and kings. It's not surprising that priests are included in listings of royal officials (e.g., 2 Sam 8:15–18).

Prophets begin to appear during the monarchy, and they have a prominent role in the governance of the land. Samuel anoints Saul and David, confronts Saul for his various sins, and guides David as he makes his way to the throne. Nathan, David's court prophet, condemns him for seizing Bathsheba and killing her husband, Uriah (2 Sam 12:1–15). Ahab has his own court prophets, who advise him about his planned military excursion to Ramoth-gilead (1 Kgs 22:1–6).

Though Elijah and Elisha are at odds with Ahab and his descendants, they engage frequently and directly with wicked kings. Elijah organizes a power contest with Ahab's prophets at Mount Carmel (1 Kgs 18:16–46) and confronts him about his murder of Naboth (1 Kgs 21:17–29). Despite antagonism with the dynasty of Ahab, Elisha is in the entourage of Jehoram as the king goes to suppress a Moabite rebellion (2 Kgs 3:4–20). Elisha gives a favorable prophecy about the deliverance of Samaria from an Aramean siege (2 Kgs 7:1), and his servant Gehazi has access to the king's court (2 Kgs 8:1–6).

In Samuel and Kings, prophets confront kings mainly for their personal sins and failings. Samuel rebukes Saul for not waiting to sacrifice and for failing to carry out the ban against the Amalekites (1 Sam 13, 15), and Nathan confronts David about adultery and murder (2 Sam 12:1–15). The writing prophets engage in prophetic punditry, judging kings, lesser rulers, and the entire nation for policy failures and their rebellion against the Lord's justice. Isaiah condemns Judah's rulers for failure to protect orphans and widows from exploitation (Isa 1:16–17) and for bribery (Isa 1:21–23), and he delivers "Woes" against those who gobble up land (Isa 5:8–10), who confuse standards of good and evil (Isa 5:20), and who enact evil statutes (Isa 10:1–4).

Jeremiah counsels King Zedekiah to submit to Nebuchadnezzar and warns that the nation will face sword, famine, and pestilence if he resists (Jer 27:1–15). Ezekiel prophesies against the "shepherds of Israel" (Ezek 34:2), a royal rather than a priestly metaphor. Israel's shepherds fatten themselves on the flock, fail to care for the sick, diseased, and broken; the flock of Israel is scattered for lack of shepherding (Ezek 34:3–6). Amos rebukes Israel for rejecting the laws of Yahweh and for abuse of the poor, sexual promiscuity, and cruel treatment of wage laborers (Amos 2:4–8), and Micah condemns prophets, seers, and priests as well as the cannibal kings who rip their subjects in pieces and cook their flesh (Mic 3:1–12). The sanctuary and priests set institutional limits to the state. Prophets remind kings they're responsible to God and subject to His judgment. Priests and prophets lay out the pattern of godly rule and call rulers to conform to it.

During the exile, Israel has no temple or king. Jewish communities are independent of the gentile state. Though embedded in the empire, they form separate communities. Yet Israel continues to carry out her priestly and prophetic vocation, including her political role. When emperors command faithful Jews to worship idols, the Jews defy them (Dan 2, 6). Yet Jews advise gentile rulers, both to protect the Jewish people and to pursue justice. Thick boundaries protect the Israelite church, but the church speaks Yahweh's Word even to non-Jewish states.

The church emerges from Judaism, both in Judea and in the diaspora. Like the exilic Jewish communities, the church is a self-governing community with its own customs of worship, teaching, and prayer. The church relates to the Roman empire as exilic Jewish communities did. Jeremiah instructs the exiles to seek the peace of Babylon, and the apostles regularly issue similar instructions to the early Christians. Echoing Jeremiah, Paul tells the Romans to submit to the powers, which are established for their good (Rom 13:1–7). Paul urges prayer for kings and authorities so Christians can lead quiet and peaceable lives (1 Tim 2:1–2). Peter echoes Paul: "Submit yourselves for the Lord's sake to every human institution," to kings and governors. By doing right, Christians will "silence the ignorance of foolish men" (1 Pet 2:13–17).

But the new covenant also gives birth to a new political reality. The primary innovation is the character of the church. In a sense, the church makes exile permanent. The church will never be settled in a land with a temple and a king. She will always be scattered among many states and societies that are more or less responsive to the gospel. By welcoming gentiles on equal terms with Jews, the church becomes a cosmopolitan communion, a geographically catholic church without any necessary links to any land, race, or political order.

Churches are outposts of a heavenly kingdom, akin to foreign embassies among the nations, governed always by the high King, Jesus. As such, the church is outside the jurisdiction of kings, governors, presidents, and prime ministers. As in Israel, the existence of the church sets institutional limits to the scope of the state. States can break down the barrier and take over the church. But if the church is faithful, there will be opposition. Any ruler who tries to intrude on the sanctuary should remember Uzziah. He should remember Jesus, who reigns from Zion with a rod of iron.

The church is independent of the state, yet the church takes over Israel's priestly-prophetic role of teaching and correcting rulers. Pastors and bishops call kings to submit to the Lord Jesus, for they are His servants, and they submit by listening to the voice of Jesus in the church and by honoring His Bride.

Meanwhile, the church nurtures virtuous leaders, who care for their people with pastoral love and concern. The church disciplines leaders and lays out standards of godly rule. Within the church, a new kind of prince comes into being—a saintly prince, whose public life is full of the fruits of the Spirit, who rules with love, joy, peace, patience, gentleness, and self-control (Gal 5:22). When kings enter the ark of Christendom, they're taught to govern with justice, to seek peace. They become rain on the mown grass, enabling their peoples to flourish (Ps 72).

CONCLUSION

The church is a self-constructing ark, built around pulpit and table, song, prayer, and communion. Each of these liturgical forms generates fresh political and cultural realities. The pulpit begets literary culture, renewing language and education. The Eucharist transforms human labor, transfiguring and sanctifying all human making. Rites of anointing blossom in charitable health care, while liturgical art, music, and architecture generate new forms of artistic expression in the city of man. By protecting her independence from the state, the church is the impetus for a new political order of justice, accountability, and freedom. By teaching the Word to kings, the church fosters godly rule.

To transform the city of man, the church only needs to do what she does, to be what she is. She needs only to teach, preach, sing, pray, break bread. Within the ark of Christendom, she need only keep the customs of the apostles, and all will be changed.

Conclusion: On Mission

I've been writing about permanent demands and patterns of Christian mission, demands and patterns that hold in all times and places. Always and everywhere, the church is the ark of the Greater Noah, building itself as a microcosm that preserves and renews the cosmos. Always and everywhere, the church is the presence of Jesus by the Spirit—baptizing, teaching, breaking bread, continuing in prayer. Always and everywhere, the lives of Christians are conformed to the suffering and glory of the Christ.

But the patterns I've described apply with particular force to the first readers of this book, in the early decades of the twenty-first century. A flood is coming, and while the storm clouds gather, we need to get busy building the ark of Jesus.

Noah builds his ark because Yahweh tells him, "Behold, I, even I, am bringing the flood of water upon the earth to destroy all flesh in which is the breath of life, from under heaven; everything that is on earth shall perish. But I will establish my covenant with you" (Gen 6:17–18). Noah's world is about to be swept away. He preserves the world by gathering a little world into the ark and riding out the storm until Yahweh opens the door on a new creation.

Jesus is the Greater Noah because He enters the world at a similar moment in history. As John the Baptist warns, the axe is already at the root, and the Lord is kindling a fire to burn fruitless trees (Matt 3:7–10). Jesus urges repentance for the same reason: The arrival of the kingdom is the arrival of judgment. That judgment will fall before His disciples die. It will be like the days of Noah (Matt 24:37–38; Luke 17:26–27). All the apostles say the same thing: The Lord is at hand. It is the last hour. Jesus is coming quickly.

Remember the historical context. From the exile to Jesus, Israel is nestled within a succession of ancient empires. In the time of Jesus and His apostles, the world is bipolar, its foci in Jerusalem and Rome, the capital of Jews and the capital of gentiles. *That* world is about to be washed away. Before the generation of the apostles ends, Jerusalem will be in ruins, the temple will be demolished, and the Roman world will be shaken to its foundations. The sun will go dark, the moon will turn bloody, and stars will fall. The clock is running out. The universe of Jerusalem-and-Rome is about to fall, and great will be its fall (Matt 24:29–31, 34).

As Jesus' ark, the church fills the same role as Noah's ark. As the world is shattered, the apostles call and baptize men and women and children into the body of Christ. There they attend to the apostles' teaching, break bread together, practice *koinonia*, devote themselves to continual prayer, thanksgiving, and praise. In the liturgy and the liturgy of Christian life, they form seedpods of new creation. Once the clouds clear, the seeds germinate and grow.

It takes a few centuries to see the full fruition of these events. When the Roman empire finally collapses for good, a new civilization is born from the womb of Christ's Bride. Monks preserve Greek and Roman learning and found monasteries as centers of prayer and worship and sources of technical innovation. Bishops care for the poor and sick in the cities, build churches and cathedrals, commission painters and sculptors and composers. Christendom produces new forms of political organization, guaranteeing many of the basic liberties we still enjoy in modern republics and democracies. Individual rights, personal liberty, constitutional government, the rule of law, limits to state power, the equal dignity of all: All of these are gifts of the church as it purged and transformed the political inheritance of Greece and Rome. They're gifts of Christ's reign.

Since the sixteenth and seventeenth centuries, Western civilization, the heir of Christendom, has become the foundation of global civilization. Even the values and politics of the secular Enlightenment and contemporary radicalism depend on treasures inherited from Christianity. For hundreds of years, the civilization that emerged from the ark of the church has molded the entire world.

At the beginning of the twenty-first century, we're entering a new epoch of world history. Non-Western nations and continents are on the rise. China dominates east Asia and is extending its economic power into the Middle East up to the edge of Europe and deep into Africa. India has become a global player. By the middle of this century, Africa will have over 2 billion people, and by 2100, one of every three human beings will be African. Africa is coming of age economically and will be the center of Christianity during this century. All of these up-and-coming regions depend on Western civilization's achievements and thus are the late fruit of Christendom. Yet, politically, economically, and religiously, the Western world is losing the dominant place it has occupied for half a millennium.

Meanwhile, Western civilization is disintegrating from within. Western intellectuals have lost confidence in our own civilization. Enlightenment values are under attack and in retreat. Western civilization has been severed from its Christian roots as churches decline in both numbers and influence. Ancient Israel is judged when they worship idols, commit sexual perversions, and murder the innocent. Western nations are guilty of all of these. We murder millions of unborn babies a year, and our militaries shed innocent blood in the far corners of the world. We now honor abominations like sodomy and turn a blind eye when surgeons reassemble girls into boys and boys into girls. The West has turned from Jesus to the false gods of Science, Reason, Power, Progress, Mammon, or to the equally false gods of Equality and Choice.

A flood is coming. It's already sweeping away the world as we know it. The world we know will be submerged as the Lord turns the world upside down and gives it a sharp shake (Hag 2:6–7).

It's not the end of everything. Creation will survive, and civilization will be reborn. Jesus will steer the ark of His church through the storm. As the clouds gather, as the thunder begins to roll, as the deluge crashes down, we're called to continue the often-imperceptible work of building the ark of Jesus. With our lives scripted by the Scriptures that reveal the Christ, we cling to the apostolic gospel, gather to break bread, share our material and Spiritual gifts, offer a continuous sacrifice of prayer and song. We preach the good news in false churches and public squares, endure the rage of the mob, suffer with Jesus so we may share His glory. We confront idols and demons and call all men from darkness to light, from Satan to the living God (Acts 26:18). In the Last Adam, we're made right-makers, grateful makers whose making is an act of worship. Some will slip, lizard-like, into palaces (Prov 30:28) and gain a hearing before prime ministers and presidents.

As we do these things, we preserve the treasures of the past and, by the alchemy of the Spirit, transfigure ancient treasures into new. When the storm is over and the flood waters recede, we'll have and be the seeds of a new creation. We'll flow like living water to fertilize the wasteland.

If you're a Christian, that's what you're doing. Your life may not look like a big deal. You're kind to your neighbors, serve your brothers and sisters in church, gather each week to receive God's Word and God's Bread. You train and teach your children as disciples; you love your husband or wife. You're an honest and productive employee, an attentive employer, an entrepreneur or bureaucrat in a well-established institution. You do and make, but no one notices.

Maybe you're a pastor or leader in a church. You preach and teach, lead worship, and preside at the Lord's table. You visit the hospital and the homebound seniors of the congregation, plan and execute evangelistic and service programs, baptize and catechize the children of the church. You're a big fish, but your pond is small and sometimes looks more like a puddle.

You feel invisible, but that's an optical illusion. You're participating in the biggest project imaginable. You're joining with millions of others to build the self-building ark of Jesus. Through your witness and labor, a new world is taking form. You're fighting the battle of the ages. You're constructing the city of God among the cities of men in order to transform the cities of men to become more like the city of God. Nothing is small in the kingdom of Jesus.

There's nothing to fear. We live in joy and expectant hope. Jesus is in the boat, and He calms the seas. The Carpenter of Nazareth will pilot His ark until it rests on a new Ararat, a new Eden, the garden-city where the river of life flows.

Theopolitan Theses

Theopolis comes from two Greek words, *theos* and *polis*, "God" and "city." The word refers to the final new Jerusalem that descends from heaven, and to the Christian church, which is the present form of God's city. The Fundamentals lay out a radical and comprehensive vision for the church's teaching, liturgy, and mission, a vision that enables the church to confront the myriad challenges of our time. The following theses summarize the Theopolitan vision.

I. THE THEOPOLITAN VISION is a *Trinitarian* vision. God *is* Father, Son, and Spirit, and that truth shapes everything we believe about God, man, and the character of creation.

II. THE THEOPOLITAN VISION is an *ecclesial* vision. The visible, historical church, made up of living men, women, and children, is the world's greatest mystery, a divine-human communion, a society of humans incorporated together into the fellowship of love that is the Triune God. The church is the family of the heavenly Father, the body and bride of Christ the Son, the temple of the Holy Spirit. The visible, historical church is the present form of the future new Jerusalem (Rev 21–22). Jesus calls us to overcome the church's unhappy divisions and to pray for and promote the unity of the church, so the church will be one as the Father is one with the Son.

III. THE THEOPOLITAN VISION is an *evangelical* vision. The gospel is inherently political. It announces God's intention to make the kingdoms of this earth the kingdom of the Lord and His Christ, to restore and transform the creation and human city into a new and better Eden. He accomplishes this transformation in history through the church's ministry of Word, Water, and Table, through which the church fulfills its being as the one, holy, catholic, and apostolic communion of saints.

IV. THE THEOPOLITAN VISION hopes for *world transformation*. As the church goes, so goes the world. Family, culture, and politics are downstream from the garden-temple (Gen 2:10–14; Ezek 47:1–12). What happens in worship is more critical to the world's future than what happens in the ballot box, the legislative chamber, the courtroom, the classroom, or the living room.

V. THE THEOPOLITAN VISION is a *biblical* vision, and a vision of how the Bible should be read. Scripture is about Jesus (Luke 24:44–49), the Last Adam, and His church, the Last Eve, who are foreshadowed by Old Testament types. Since Jesus is the Creator and the one in whom all things cohere (Col 1:15–18), typological reading of the Bible speaks about *everything*. Typology reveals the recurrent rhythms of God's actions in history.

VI. THE THEOPOLITAN VISION is a *liturgical* vision. Christian liturgy is the initial Christianization of the world. The liturgy of the word transforms an existing language by filling it with biblical content. The liturgy of the table unites people from every tribe, tongue, and nation into table companions. Church buildings Christianize space, the church calendar Christianizes time, the music and art of the liturgy Christianize high culture.

VII. THE THEOPOLITAN VISION is a *missional* vision. Made in the image of God, men and women create, speak, and make (Gen 1:26–28). Sin turns human speech to lies, slander, and Satanic education, and twists human creativity toward destruction and injustice. Jesus the Carpenter of Nazareth restores human beings to God's image, and builds them into the city of God, whose mission is to renew the cities of men.

VII. THE THEOPOLITAN VISION is a vision of *pastoral* ministry. The pastorate is the highest vocation imaginable. Through the Spirit, shepherds speak the Word of Christ to the body of Christ, announce the forgiveness of sins, baptize sinners into the family of God, gather the Lord's family at the Lord's table, equip the church to carry out the cosmic mission of Jesus.

EXPLAINING THE EIGHT THEOPOLITAN THESES

I. The Theopolitan vision is a *Trinitarian* vision. God *is* Father, Son, and Spirit, and that truth shapes everything we believe about God, man, and the character of creation.

The doctrine of the Trinity isn't about numbers: Is God three or one or both? It has to do with the very nature of God. The Triune God is a communion of infinite, eternal love, life, and faithful loyalty. His Triune character is inescapably imprinted on everything He has made. Human beings are made in and out of love, created for communion with God and one another. Creation is a radiance of God's eternal glory, a great symphony that echoes the eternal harmony that He is. To say the Triune God created the world is to say love is the depth dimension of all things.

II. The Theopolitan vision is an *ecclesial* vision. The visible, historical church, made up of living men, women, and children, is the world's greatest mystery, a divine-human communion, a society of humans incorporated together into the fellowship of love that is the Triune God. The church is the family of the heavenly Father, the body and bride of Christ the Son, the temple of the Holy Spirit. The visible, historical church is the present form of the future new Jerusalem (Rev 21–22).

In some Christian traditions, the church is treated as a help and support to individual salvation. Other traditions emphasize the invisible church in a way that undermines the significance of the visible church. But Jesus came to gather a people and a nation, not merely to rescue individual sinners. Because individuals are created in and for community, Jesus restores communities as well as individuals. The church is a city among the cities of men, with its own ethos, culture, and practices. According to the New Testament, the Spirit knits together real-life, mundane, flawed gatherings as He baptizes individuals into the body of Jesus. Every local church is an outpost of the city that will one day unite heaven and earth. When you see a local church, you see salvation achieved now, in social form.

III. The Theopolitan vision is an *evangelical* vision. The gospel is inherently political. It announces God's intention to make the kingdoms of this earth the kingdom of the Lord and His Christ, to restore and transform the creation and human city into a new and better Eden. He accomplishes this transformation in history through the church's ministry of Word, Water, and Table.

The gospel isn't a private message; it is public truth. Jesus came preaching the kingdom of heaven. Through Jesus' death and resurrection, God takes control of His rebellious world by setting the man Jesus on the throne at His right hand. Preaching the gospel means calling on all men everywhere, kings and judges included, to kiss the Son and submit to His reign and royal Word. The Father has given all nations to the Son as His inheritance, and Jesus will have all nations. Over millennia, Jesus restores, transfigures, and glorifies the creation as His church baptizes, teaches, and breaks bread. In the power of the Spirit, the city of God resurrects the dead cities of Adamic man.

IV. The Theopolitan vision envisions *world transformation*. As the church goes, so goes the world. Family, culture, and politics are downstream from the garden-temple (Gen 2:10–14; Ezek 47:1–12). What happens in worship is more critical to the world's future than what happens in the ballot box, the legislative chamber, the courtroom, the classroom, or the living room.

We're tempted to focus on political, social, and cultural pathologies. But these are symptoms. The church is a new Eden, a living temple, and as such is the source of life for the world. If the church becomes a poisoned spring, the world dies. If the church's light is quenched, the world plunges into darkness. The church is pre-eminently a liturgical assembly, and worship is the source of life not only for the church but the world. Reforming the church's worship is the wellspring of cultural and political transformation.

V. The Theopolitan vision is a *biblical* vision, and a vision of how the Bible should be read. Scripture is about Jesus (Luke 24:44–49), the Last Adam, and His church, the Last Eve, who are foreshadowed by Old Testament types. Since Jesus is the Creator and the one in whom all things cohere (Col 1:15–18), typological reading of the Bible speaks about *everything*. Typology reveals the recurrent rhythms of God's actions in history.

Scripture is God's infallible word in written form. Everything it claims to be true is true; everything it commands is good. Scripture is a book of books, unified around Jesus. Law, history, proverbs, psalms, prophecy all foreshadow Christ and His Bride, the church. Gospel, epistle, and apocalypse reveal the Christ concealed in the Old Testament shadows. There are many Adams—Adam, Abel, Noah, Abraham, Isaac, Jacob, Joseph, Samson, David, Solomon, Daniel, Ezekiel. Each refers back to earlier Adams and reveals a facet of the full beauty of Christ. There are many Eves—Eve, Sarah, Rebekah, Rachel, Miriam, Deborah, Jael, Hannah, Mary—each of which displays the loveliness of the church. Typology isn't an optional extra for Christian reading of Scripture; unless we read typologically, we don't read the Bible Christianly at all. Typology isn't an effete, artistic way of reading. Typology is fundamentally a theology of history, and reading Scripture typologically gives insight into the patterns and movements of history, equipping the church with wisdom to understand the times. Through Christ-centered preaching and teaching, the Spirit forms churches to carry out the mission of Jesus, the Last Adam.

VI. The Theopolitan vision is a *liturgical* vision. Christian liturgy is the initial Christianization of the world. The liturgy of the word transforms an existing language by filling it with biblical content. The liturgy of the table unites people from every tribe, tongue, and nation into table companions. Church buildings Christianize space, the church calendar Christianizes time, the music and art of the liturgy Christianize high culture.

The liturgy is a spring of living water, the light of the world, which flows into the wasteland and shines into the darkness. But the liturgy is also *in itself* a transfiguration of culture. Christian worship is saturated in the Word; worshipers hear, speak, sing, and eat the Word of God. As they do, they learn to speak their native language with new, biblical inflections. As we confess our sins, we learn to speak truth, even about ourselves. As we sing psalms, we learn God's vocabulary of exultation and lament, and learn to pray rightly. *All* biblical worship occurs at a table, first an altar (God's table, Ezek 44:16) then the Eucharistic table. The Eucharist makes the church. At the Lord's table, the Spirit breaks down national, ethnic, social, and sexual barriers to form one body of those who share bread and wine. In the liturgy, the church impresses the gospel on a culture's lived space and time, on its styles of poetry, music, and visual art. In the liturgy, creation and culture reach their final purpose, which is to bring praise to God.

VII. The Theopolitan vision is a *missional* vision. Made in the image of God, men and women create, speak, and make (Gen 1:26–28). Sin turns human speech to lies, slander, and Satanic education, and twists human creativity toward destruction and injustice. Jesus the Carpenter of Nazareth restores human beings to God's image, and builds them into the city of God, whose mission is to renew the cities of men.

The church's mission is as broad as creation, as extensive as the effects of sin. Jesus works through the church's teaching and liturgy to restore human beings to the image of God, retraining tongues to speak and hands to make. Through its ministry of Water, Word, and Table, the church confronts personal sin and public injustice, leading individual men and women to lives of repentant faithfulness and offering biblical guidance to every institution and sector of social, cultural, and political life. Building the city of God as the church, the church renovates the city of man.

VIII. The Theopolitan vision is a vision of *pastoral* ministry. The pastorate is the highest vocation imaginable. Through the Spirit, shepherds speak the Word of Christ to the body of Christ, announce the forgiveness of sins, baptize sinners into the family of God, gather the Lord's family at the Lord's table, equip the church to carry out the cosmic mission of Jesus.

Every member of the church shares in the mission of Jesus. The Spirit gives gifts to every member of the church, to be used for the edification of the body, for the building-up of God's city in the world. Pastors guard Christ's flock and lead them into the Father's presence. They are shepherd-kings who rule the people of God, lay down their lives for the sheep, and lead them in spiritual war. Pastors speak the prophetic word both inside the church and without. The church cannot be God's heavenly city, or carry out its mission to the cities of men, without capable, courageous, faithful pastors.

For Further Reading

THEOPOLITAN VISION

Jordan, James B. *The Sociology of the Church*. Eugene, OR: Wipf & Stock, 1999.

Leithart, Peter J. *Against Christianity*. Moscow, ID: Canon Press, 2003.

Leithart, Peter J. *The End of Protestantism*. Grand Rapids: Baker, 2016.

THEOPOLITAN READING

Jordan, James B. *Through New Eyes*. Eugene, OR: Wipf & Stock, 1999.

Jordan, James B. *Judges: God's War Against Humanism*. Eugene, OR: Wipf & Stock, 1999.

Jordan, James B. *Creation in Six Days*. Moscow, ID: Canon Press, 1999.

Jordan, James B. *Primeval Saints*. Moscow, ID: Canon Press, 2002.

Jordan, James B. *The Handwriting on the Wall*. Atlanta: American Vision, 2007.

Jordan, James B. *The Vindication of Jesus Christ*. Monroe, LA: Athanasius Press, 2009.

Jordan, James B. *From Bread to Wine*. Monroe, LA: Athanasius Press, 2020.

Jordan, James B. *Trees and Thorns: Studies in the First Four Chapters of Genesis*. Monroe, LA: Athanasius Press, 2020.

Leithart, Peter J. *A House For My Name*. Moscow, ID: Canon Press, 2000.

Leithart, Peter J. *A Son To Me*. Moscow, ID: Canon Press, 2003.

Leithart, Peter J. *The Promise of His Appearing*. Moscow, ID: Canon Press, 2004.

Leithart, Peter J. *1 & 2 Kings*. Grand Rapids: Brazos, 2006.

Leithart, Peter J. *From Behind the Veil*. Moscow, ID: Canon Press, 2009.

Leithart, Peter J. *Deep Exegesis*. Waco, TX: Baylor University Press, 2009.

Leithart, Peter J. *The Four: A Survey of the Gospels*. Moscow, ID: Canon Press, 2010.

Leithart, Peter J. *Revelation*. 2 volumes. London: T&T Clark, 2018.

Leithart, Peter J. *1 & 2 Chronicles*. Grand Rapids: Brazos Press, 2019.

Leithart, Peter J. *Matthew*. 2 volumes. Monroe, LA: Athanasius Press, 2018–2019.

Leithart, Peter J. *The Ten Commandments*. Bellingham, WA: Lexham Press, 2020.

Lusk, Rich and Uri Brito. *Under His Wings*. Monroe, LA: Athanasius Press, 2019.

Meyers, Jeffery J. *A Table in the Mist*. Monroe, LA: Athanasius Press, 2007.

Sumpter, Toby. *A Son for Glory*. Monroe, LA: Athanasius Press, 2014.

Wilson, Andrew and Alastair Roberts. *Echoes of Exodus: Tracing Themes of Redemption through Scripture*. Wheaton, IL: Crossway, 2018. Crossway, 2018.

THEOPOLITAN LITURGY

Jordan, James B. *Theses on Worship*. Niceville, FL: Transfiguration Press, 1998.

Jordan, James B. *The Liturgy Trap*. Niceville, FL: Transfiguration Press, 1998.

Leithart, Peter J. *Daddy, Why Was I Excommunicated?* Niceville, FL: Transfiguration Press, 1992.

Leithart, Peter J. *Blessed Are the Hungry*. Moscow, ID: Canon Press, 2000.

Leithart, Peter J. *The Priesthood of the Plebs*. Eugene, OR: Wipf & Stock, 2003.

Leithart, Peter J. *From Silence to Song*. Moscow, ID: Canon Press, 2003.

Leithart, Peter J. *The Baptized Body*. Moscow, ID: Canon Press, 2007.

Leithart, Peter J. *Baptism: A Guide to Life from Death.* Bellingham, WA: Lexham, 2021.

Meyers, Jeffery. *The Lord's Service.* Moscow, ID: Canon Press, 2003.

THEOPOLITAN MISSION

Jenkins, Philip. *The Next Christendom.* 3rd Edition. Oxford: Oxford University Press, 2011.

Jenson, Robert. "Eschatology" in *The Wiley Blackwell Companion to Political Theology*, edited by William T. Cavanaugh and Peter Manley Scott. 2nd edition. Hoboken, NJ: John Wiley & Sons, 2019.

Jordan, James B. *Christendom and the Nations.* Monroe, LA: Athanasius Press, 2019.

Leithart, Peter J. *Deep Comedy.* Moscow, ID: Canon Press, 2006.

Leithart, Peter J. *Solomon Among the Postmoderns.* Grand Rapids: Brazos, 2008.

Leithart, Peter J. *Defending Constantine.* Downers Grove, IL: InterVarsity Press, 2010.

Leithart, Peter J. *Between Babel and Beast.* Eugene, OR: Cascade, 2012.

Leithart, Peter J. *Delivered from the Elements of the World.* Downers Grove, IL: InterVarsity Press, 2016.

Middleton, J. Richard. "Creation Founded in Love: Breaking Rhetorical Expectations in Genesis 1:1–2:3," in *Sacred Text, Secular Times*, edited by Leonard Jay Greenspoon and Bryan F. LeBeau. Omaha, NE: Creighton University Press, 2000.

CHRISTIAN ESSENTIALS

The Christian Essentials series passes down tradition that matters. The ancient church was founded on basic biblical teachings and practices like the Ten Commandments, baptism, the Apostles' Creed, the Lord's Supper, the Lord's Prayer, and corporate worship. These basics of the Christian life have sustained and nurtured every generation of the faithful—from the apostles to today. The books in the Christian Essentials series open up the meaning of the foundations of our faith.

For more information, visit
LexhamPress.com/Christian-Essentials